Newcastle
City Council

Newcastle Libraries and Information Service

☎ **0845 002 0336**

Due for return	Due for return	Due for return
6. AUG '09		
30 NOV 09		

D1514531

Please return this item to any of Newcastle's Libraries by the last
date shown above. ff not requested by another customer the loan
can be renewed, you can do this by phone, post or in person.
Charges may be made for late returns.

FISH

TOM AIKENS

EBURY
PRESS

1 3 5 7 9 10 8 6 4 2

Published in 2008 by Ebury Press, an imprint of Ebury Publishing

A Random House Group Company

Text copyright © Tom Aikens 2008
Photography copyright © John Lawrence-Jones 2008, except pages
1, 2, 4–19, 29, 41, 74–77, 91–105, 153, 171, 201, 239, 251, 292, 352 © Ebury Press
2008; pages 307–344 © Tom Aikens 2008

Tom Aikens has asserted his right to be identified as the author of this
Work in accordance with the Copyright, Designs and Patents Act 1988

The Random House Group Limited Reg. No. 954009

Addresses for companies within the Random House Group can be
found at www.randomhouse.co.uk

A CIP catalogue record for this book is available from the British Library

The Random House Group Limited supports The Forest Stewardship
Council (FSC), the leading international forest certification organisation.
All our titles that are printed on Greenpeace approved FSC certified
paper carry the FSC logo. Our paper procurement policy can be found
at www.rbooks.co.uk/environment

To buy books by your favourite authors and register for offers visit
www.rbooks.co.uk

Printed and bound in Italy by Printer Trento

Design: Smith & Gilmour, London
Photography: John Lawrence-Jones and Cristian Barnett

ISBN 9780091924928

Every effort has been made to contact
copyright holders for permissions. Corrections
can be made in future printings. Please contact
the publishers with any queries.

CONTENTS

Introduction

We all have stories of when we first came into contact with fish: the smell of it, the peculiar shapes and sizes, the colours and varieties, even the first time we ate it. My earliest memory was when I must have been about five or six years old. I was playing in the sands of Salcombe beach and Noss Mayo in Devon and seeing for the first time all the bright sea anemones and little crabs in the many rock pools that were strewn along the beach. It was so exciting to potter around in the pools along the water line with a little net trying to catch anything that moved, waiting patiently for a shrimp or fish to jump out from the shelter of a loose rock. Together with my elder brother, Mark, and my twin, Robert, I used to catch fresh shrimps by the bucket load and these were then either put back into the sea or mum and dad would take them home and cook them up for tea.

There is one particular view that takes me right back to my childhood and it brings back memories of sandcastles and ice-cream – the traditional things. Newton Ferrers, on the estuary of the River Yealm, about 10 miles (16 km) from Plymouth, is a typical picturesque Devon village with thatched houses and a harbour known locally as the Pool. The road leading down to the estuary and the village is flanked by steep wooded banks, a largely unspoilt landscape where you can still see herons, kingfishers and egrets. At low tide you can walk across the causeway to Noss Mayo. You look right out to sea in one direction, but if you look back to the harbour you can see all the boats keeled over in the mud. It was, and still is, very beautiful; untouched almost.

Introduction

TOM AIKENS

Both my father and grandfather were fond of the sea and both were very keen sailors. My father had a 19-foot long, open sailing boat – a Drascombe lugger – called *Sea Lavender*, which he had bought second-hand. At weekends and during school holidays we often used to go to Blakeney on the north Norfolk coast and to Suffolk to go mackerel fishing from the back of the boat. These were great times. For my brothers and I it was our first taste of real freedom, the first time we experienced being alone with nature. There were some bad days when we caught nothing, but on the days we did, the mackerel either came home with us or were given to the neighbours.

I have always had a great fondness for the sea and although some of the reasons for that fondness have changed slightly, the feeling of what the sea is and what it holds is now even more important to me than ever. When I was a child, words such as sustainability, provenance and environment were rarely used, let alone thought about. The person who really brought them to my attention was my late father-in-law, Sir Nicholas Nuttall, who formed the conservation group Bahamas Reef Environment Educational Foundation (BREEF), (see page 349). If you look at the BREEF website you will understand his work and the amazing things he accomplished. I am very fortunate to have met someone who was truly dedicated to saving marine life and in writing this book my aim is that you too will start to think about some of the issues he raised with me. As you read and cook from it, my hope is that when you serve up your fantastic fish dishes you will have a better understanding of the story behind your meal – how it got from the sea to your plate – and why this is so important for the future of our waters, the fishing industry and the very existence of certain species of seafood.

A snapshot of fishing today

'Fishing industry on the verge of ruin' has been a headline we have seen many times, and may well continue to be one for years to come. What was once an easy pastime of just placing the net into the sea and hauling in a huge catch has now become an ever increasing mountain of bureaucracy for fishermen, governments and the EU. The industry has seen dramatic changes and enforced rules, regulations and policies have changed the course of fishing for ever. There have been bad times – with I'm sure more to come – but the words sustainability, provenance, air miles, environmental impact, traceability are becoming the words of today and will hopefully be the future.

Fishing in the UK
The seas belonging to the United Kingdom extend over 335,000 sq miles (867,000

Introduction

sq km), more than three times the nation's land area, and range in depth and climate from the warm temperate waters of the southwestern approaches to the deep sub-Arctic waters between the Faroes and Norway. In 2006, UK vessels landed 614,000 tonnes of sea fish, including shellfish, with a value of £610 million. There are fishing vessels all around the coast, with enormous diversity among all the different ports in terms of what they catch and the types of gear they use. The waters around the UK contain some of the most varied fishing grounds anywhere in the world. The most valuable species are sole, crab, langoustine, cod and lobster. Exports consist mostly of mackerel, herring and salmon. At present, the sea is very unbalanced. We are only really fishing for the top 6–8 species that make the most money: cod, salmon, haddock, plaice, sole, monkfish, turbot and halibut, with the result that we are putting stocks of these fish under huge pressure, and in some cases the stocks are now dangerously low. If we could all buy and eat the many other species of fish in the sea – such as dab, flounder, pouting, gurnard, pollock and coley, to name but a few – we could alleviate the pressure on the more heavily-fished species, and balance could be partly restored. One of the main problems at the moment is that because of the lack of demand, the fishermen aren't sure that if they land these fish they will be able to get a good price for them. A change in attitude is needed and this has to come from education. The government, chefs, supermarkets, restaurants and ultimately you, the public, need to embrace what we have and start changing the way we think about fish. It's all very well being told about fish stock demise but unless we all wholeheartedly support a change in buying practices, the situation isn't going to change. The fishermen need to know that you are going to support them by buying different varieties of fish. One of my main aims with this book is to encourage you to try something new and different. Fish is beautiful, very tasty and exceptionally good for you. It's simple to cook and to prepare, and trying out species other than the ones you're used to will bring many rewards.

FISHING METHODS

There are various methods of fishing, ranging from highly selective and sustainable ones such as handlining, which targets a specific fish, to extremely damaging bottom-trawling. In the North Sea, intensive fishing has transformed parts of this once abundant marine environment into a deserted wasteland. Some species have become locally extinct and large areas of the seabed that have been repeatedly trawled are now dominated by loose sediment and shingle, making the sea look like a muddy pool. The most common fishing methods are:

Beam trawling A large net (see page 10) attached to a heavy metal beam is dragged across the seabed behind a boat, digging into and ploughing up the ground. Environmental campaigners want a ban on beam trawling, which is a destructive way of 'strip-mining' the ocean floor. A single pass of a trawl removes up to 20 per cent of seafloor fauna and flora.

Bottom trawling Trawls that are designed to work near the sea bed.

Dredging A method used for harvesting bivalve molluscs such as oysters, clams and scallops from the seabed.

Drift nets Curtains or sheets of netting that hang vertically in the water. A drift net may be used close to the bottom, such as a shrimp drift net, or at the surface, such as a herring drift net, usually across the path of migrating fish schools. However, other aquatic animals also strike the net and become entangled in its meshes. Large surface drift nets are banned by a UN resolution.

Gill net Netting set out in a particular pattern so that fish are gilled, tangled or trapped. They may be set anywhere between surface and seabed, and either anchored or allowed to drift freely.

Handlining Also known as hook or line fishing. A highly selective method of fishing, that produces high-quality catch.

Line-caught A generic term used to describe pole (or rod) and line, handline or longline fisheries.

Longline fishing A method of fishing that comprises a main line to which are attached branch lines, each fitted with one or more baited hooks or lures.

Trawl A cone or funnel-shaped net that is towed through the water.

Otter trawl These take their name from the rectangular 'doors' or 'otterboards' that serve to keep the mouth of the net horizontally open while the net is being towed. The trawl is towed on the sea bed and is usually a much larger net than a beam trawl.

Pair trawl A trawl towed between two boats.

Purse seine A fishing method whereby entire shoals of fish are encircled by a sheet of netting, the bottom of which is then drawn together to form a bag or 'purse'.

Seine net A very long net usually set from a boat, which can be operated either from the shore, such as beach seines, or from the boat itself, such as Danish or Scottish seines.

Traps Structures into which fish are guided or enticed through funnels that encourage entry but limit escape.

AN INDUSTRY IN DECLINE

There has been significant decline in fishing activity everywhere in the UK over the past decade , but particularly in Fleetwood in northwest England, and in Hull, Grimsby and Lowestoft on the east coast of England. In 2006, the UK fishing fleet consisted of 6,372 vessels compared with 8,073 in 1996 – a reduction of 21 per cent. Of these, the majority are small; 77 per cent of boats are less than 10m, and fish mainly inshore with passive gear, 25 per cent are beam trawlers that fish in the North Sea or off the south coast of England. Along with a drop in the number of fishing vessels, there has been a 46 per cent drop in the number of full-time fishermen and a 65 per cent fall in part-timers since 1980.

The rewards from fishing are very small, and with fuel prices rocketing many

Introduction

fishermen are questioning if it's really viable to continue plying their trade. (Around 1,000 small boats have disappeared from UK ports in the past 12 years, with England bearing the brunt of this.) By the time the fishermen have paid their licence, quota, running costs, staff costs and landing taxes for the market, the final income they are taking home has shrunk hugely. The decisions that fishermen have had to make have not been easy and so many have been forced out of the industry. In one respect this has benefited the industry, as it has lessened the number of fishing vessels out fishing, and it has made some fishermen think about what can be done to improve their lives. Fishermen are incredibly tough, passionate, intelligent men and woman. The life they lead is incredibly hard. Not only are the hours and working conditions demanding, and the pay small, fishermen also take huge risks every time they put out to sea and loss of life is not uncommon. Of those that have decided to carry on, a small but increasing number are looking at ways of improving their standards through the gear type they use and, once they have caught their fish, ensuring they are being instantly iced and/or accurately labelled as line-caught. Slowly they are starting to see the benefits. I really believe that the next few years will prove to be very important and that we shall see a far more positive approach and outlook in the fishing industry.

The profitability of the industry varies by area and by the species caught. The fishing vessels that target pelagic fish (see page 16), such as mackerel and herring, are showing healthy profits, while the vessels trawling for langoustines or white fish, such as cod and haddock, are less profitable. The fishing boats with the highest fuel costs are the beam trawlers, which target flat fish such as sole, plaice and megrim. They are struggling just to break even. The continual rise in fuel prices is going to affect a lot of fishermen because fuel is the highest proportion of most of their costs. Over the last two or three years, the increases have been offset by steady increases in fish prices, due to more demand, improved enforcement (leading to a lower level of illegal landings), and fishermen marketing their fish more effectively. Fishermen are beginning to realise that the days of being able just to fish will soon be over and they need to be more business savvy. They are now looking at ways they can increase the bottom line, either through better quality landings or by fishing sustainably, which improves their own image and gets them an increased price for their fish.

Who manages our fishing?
COMMON FISHERIES POLICY (CFP)

The European Union policy for the management of fisheries and aquaculture imposes a regime of equal access for vessels from all member states into the EU's exclusive fishing zone. It was created with the aim of conserving fish stocks,

protecting the marine environment, ensuring the economic viability of the European fleets and providing good-quality food to consumers.

The CFP applies in all EU waters from the coastline out to the EU limit of 200 miles (320 km). Within 6 miles (10 km) of the shore, only the coastal Member State's vessels can fish, and this exclusion zone was set up to protect local fishing communities. Within 12 miles (19 km) of the coast, vessels of other Member States can fish, so long as their country has historic rights to those waters. Outside the 12 miles (19 km), all the Member States' vessels can fish.

There are also conservation measures in place under the CFP, which try to ensure that the fishing pressure in European waters is not at a level higher than the stocks can sustain. These comprise initiatives such as total allowable catches, rules relating to fishing gear and minimum landing sizes, and obligations to record and report catches and landings.

▶ **Total Allowable Catch (TAC)** The quantity of fish that can be taken from a stock each year. In Europe, the amount is agreed by the Fisheries Council of Ministers and EU Member States are allocated a fixed proportion of the TAC as their national quota. In recent years, some seriously depleted stocks have become the subject of emergency measures and TACs are a key part of the conservation of fish stocks. However, because fisheries within the EU are mixed, in practice this means that when the quota for one fish has been reached, fishing will still continue until the TAC that is held for any other fish stock has also been met. In this way the fish for which the quota has been reached will still be caught and either discarded or landed illegally, neither of which helps to conserve the stock. I see this happening so often. One of the fishermen that I use reached his quota of cod after only 2–3 months. With a quota of approximately 110 kilos of cod for the whole year, it's no wonder this was reached so early – the amount equates to less than one fish a day. If he catches any more cod than this throughout rest of the year he will have to throw it back, by which time it is usually dead.

▶ **Minimum Landing Sizes (MLS)** A measurement that defines the smallest size at which specific species of fish can be retained legally from a catch.

▶ **Maximum Sustainable Yield (MYS)** The largest yield or catch that can be taken from a species's stock over an indefinite period. The aim of MYS is to decrease the population density to the point of highest growth rate possible. This changes the number of the population, but the new number can, ideally, be maintained indefinitely.

▶ **Department for Environment, Food and Rural Affairs (Defra)**
The fisheries arm of this UK government department has long-term marine objectives, which include negotiations on the Marine Strategy Directive (MSD), improving the fisheries quota management, preparing for the next round of European Union (EU) fisheries negotiations, improving the Common Fisheries Policy (CFP) and making progress on the designation and implementation of Marine Protected Areas (MPAs).

► Environmental Justice Foundation (EJF)

The EJF has been set up to combat and conquer all aspects of pirate fishing, also called illegal, unreported and unregulated (IUU) fishing.

Pirate fishing is a huge problem, and as fish get scarcer it will increase, undermining any attempts at sustainable management. Pirates cause massive damage to the marine environment and jeopardise the food security and livelihoods of poor coastal communities in developing countries, particularly on the west coast of Africa. Huge unregulated trawlers, mainly from China, sail in under flags of convenience bought from very poor West African states. Not only do they flout laws and regulations, they also fish all year round and as a result are responsible for wiping out whole fishing communities.

The EJF wants to raise awareness of all the issues of piracy and sustainable fisheries management both here and abroad. By the time this book is out, I will have been to Sierra Leone and Guinea to make a film with EJF highlighting the illicit trade of fish and its impact. I hope this will really help to obtain more publicity for all the work that they are doing and show the human dimension of the problem on West African communities.

► Food and Agriculture Organization (FAO) of the United Nations

The FAO is one of the largest specialised agencies in the United Nations and its programme on fisheries aims to promote sustainable development through implementation of its Code of Conduct for Responsible Fisheries.

► International Council for the Exploration of the Seas (ICES)

ICES is the organisation that coordinates marine research in the North Atlantic Ocean and adjacent seas such as the Baltic and North Sea. Its advice is used by the 20 member countries to help manage these seas.

► Marine Conservation Society (MCS)

The MCS is a UK charity that campaigns for cleaner seas and beaches, sustainable fisheries and protection for all marine life. It provides advice primarily to the government, but also to the fishing industry, including supermarkets. It believes that consumers have an ever more important role to play and has developed a number of resources to help the public and retailers, including *The Good Fish Guide*, *Pocket Good Fish Guide* and fishonline.org. These provide information on the status of individual species and/or stocks with a rating based on their relative sustainability. Fishonline is the most comprehensive guide to sustainable seafood in the UK.

The MCS also operates a rating system to identify both species that are sustainably harvested and those that are not. A rating 1 is awarded to the most sustainably produced seafood, including fish from fisheries certified as environmentally responsible by organisations such as the Marine Stewardship Council. A rating 5 is awarded to fish that should be avoided, on the basis that the fisheries are poorly managed, unregulated, the fishing methods are damaging to the marine habitat or the stock is

Introduction

vulnerable to exploitation or overfished. Ratings from 2–4 indicate there may be some cause for concern.

► Marine Stewardship Council (MSC)

The MSC was launched in 1997 as a joint initiative by the World Wildlife Fund and Unilever. It is an is an independent organisation that promotes responsible fishing practices to find a solution to the problem of overfishing and seeks to harness consumer purchasing power to generate change and promote environmentally responsible stewardship. Its goal was to establish a standardised mechanism to certify the sustainability of wild fisheries against credible criteria, thereby creating a market-based incentive to maintain sustainable fish stocks. The MSC rewards environmentally responsible fisheries management and practices with a distinctive blue-tick label for fish. A fishery seeking MSC certification must submit to a rigorous third-party evaluation by an MSC-accredited certification body. Once the fishery is certified, it is entitled to use the MSC label; this means you can eat the fish with a clear conscience.

► WWF

A charity that's dependent upon its 5 million supporters worldwide, WWF-UK has campaigned for more than 8 years to secure proper legislation for UK seas.

Some other fishing terms to get to grips with...

Aquaculture The farming of fish, shellfish and aquatic plants under controlled conditions. For more information see pages 51, 60 and 70.

Bycatch This includes all marine creatures, except for the target species, which are caught while fishing, including discards (fish that are thrown overboard because they are deemed the wrong size) and any fish that get caught in the fishing gear. The FAO estimates that about a third of what is caught annually, approximately 25 million tonnes, goes over the side and is dumped. The amount of bycatch varies considerably among fisheries. Demersal finfish fisheries account for 36 per cent of global discards and shrimp trawl fisheries for 27 per cent, whilst together these fisheries only represent 22 per cent of total landings. In contrast, relatively low bycatch levels are associated with purse seines, handlines, jig, trap and pot fisheries.

Catch per unit of effort (CPUE) The quantity of a given species, or all species combined that is taken from the sea by a specific fishery.

Demersal fish Species that are normally caught on the sea bed, like cod, haddock and plaice.

Individual Transferable Quota (ITQ) An allocated privilege of landing a specified portion of the total annual fish catch in the form of quota shares. ITQs divide the total annual catch quota into smaller individual portions.

Mixed fishery A fishery comprising more than one species; for example, North European demersal fisheries typically include cod, haddock, whiting, pollack and saithe.

Nursery area An area providing a favourable environment for young fish.

Overfishing A stock is considered 'overfished' when it is exploited past the point at which its abundance is considered 'too low' to ensure safe reproduction.

Pelagic fish Fish that are normally caught on the sea surface.

Quota A share of the TAC allocated to a unit such as a country, a vessel, a company or an individual fisherman.

Spawning The release of ova (eggs) – fertilised or to be fertilised.

Stock A part of a fish population which occupies a well-defined range independent of other stocks of the same species. A stock will form the basis of a distinct fishery.

Subsidy A sum of money handed out by a government which allows a commercial business venture to go on trading or doing something beyond the point at which it would otherwise have gone bust or been forced into doing something else. According to the UN's Food and Agriculture Organization, many fishery managers feel that government subsidies undermine the sustainability of fisheries and aquaculture. The reason for this is that subsidies distort the conditions of trade in fish and fish products, favouring nations that provide subsidies over those that do not. Similarly, it is said that subsidies speed up the development of overcapacity and consequently threaten the continued wellbeing of wild fish stocks through overfishing. However, the relationship between subsidies and overfishing should not be taken for granted, the overfishing of stocks supported by subsidies can also result from poor management of the fisheries.

Sustainable fishing Fishing activities that do not cause undesirable changes to the biological diversity or ecosystem structure.

Target species The most highly sought component of the catch taken by fishermen.

Traps Structures into which fish are guided or enticed through funnels that encourage entry but limit escape. Also called pots, creels, fish traps.

Turtle exclusion device (TED) A modification to shrimp trawl nets that allows turtles to escape, while shrimp are retained.

Zoning Defining areas where fishing for certain species or the use of a certain type of fishing gear and/or other activities is either permitted or restricted.

Fishing facts and figures

▸ 75 per cent of the world's fish stocks are now overexploited or fully exploited.

▸ 90 per cent of stocks of large predatory fish have already gone, including species such as cod and swordfish.

▸ Between 1960 and 2002, the capture of wild fish for human consumption soared from 20 million tonnes to 84.5 million tonnes. A further 39.8 million tonnes came from fish farms.

Introduction
TOM AIKENS

▸ An estimated 27 million tonnes of living detritus, equal to 35 per cent of the total global fisheries catch, is thrown back into the waters every year as unwanted trash. And even this is a likely underestimate.

▸ It takes only 10–15 years to fish a buoyant healthy stock to within its death and to reduce it to a tenth of its original size.

▸ Sales of farmed species have grown by 11 per cent a year since 1984, making it the world's fastest-growing food sector. In 2001, some 29 per cent of all fish and shellfish eaten were farmed. The UN has predicted that aquaculture will have to grow sevenfold in the next 25 years just to maintain the world's consumption of fish.

EATING FISH

▸ About 950 million people worldwide rely on fish as their primary source of protein. In addition, ocean fisheries and fish-related industries sustain the livelihoods of some 200 million people.

▸ In the UK, fish consumption continues to grow at 9 per cent a year, while sales of 'exotic' fish grow at 20 per cent a year. Imports were highest for cod, haddock, tuna, shrimps and prawns.

▸ There were 1,300 fishmongers in the UK in 2005, although 85 per cent of fish sold was through supermarkets.

▸ Last year, only two of the major supermarkets – Marks &Spencer and Waitrose – were buying cod from sustainable sources.

FISH POLITICS

▸ Environmentalists have been saying that the total catch should be reduced by 30–40 per cent, but it has only been reduced by 3 per cent. In fact, quotas have remained so generous that fishermen have not been able to meet them for at least 10 years.

▸ ICES has warned for the fifth year running that a complete fishing ban is the only way to revive North Sea stocks.

▸ Without subsidies, the world's fishing industry would be bankrupt. In 1993, the UN reported that the operating costs of fisheries around the world exceeded commercial revenues by over $50 billion each year.

▸ Currently most countries, except the EEC, are reducing the level of all subsidies. The rumoured level of support has been put at $54 billion, which is 50 per cent of the annual industry income, with Japan handing out $19 billion, North America $8 billion, the EEC $14 billion and South America, $5 billion every year.

Choosing fish

When buying fish it is important to obtain as much information as you can about it – where it was caught, how far it has travelled, whether it is fresh, when was it was landed, what boat was it from, and whether you are paying the right price for it. These are all very valid questions. If you are one of the small proportion of the public that live by the coast and can get your hands on local day-boat-caught fish, you are extremely fortunate. One thing you will not have to consider is the cost of transport of the fish, which on occasion can outweigh the actual cost of the fish. If you always get your fish straight off the boat you have the satisfaction of knowing where the fish has come from, and probably how it was caught. The rest of us, who usually buy our fish from supermarkets, should not be too despondent, however, as they are now trying a lot harder and have really improved their general standards of quality, selection, sustainability and provenance. Hopefully, the days of mussels from New Zealand and farmed salmon and trout will soon be a thing of the past. Supermarkets are increasingly concerned with sourcing sustainably caught fish and shellfish, and are aware, too, that highlighting seasonally produced and traceable products gives them a great marketing pitch that can improve both their sales and their image. Supermarkets such as Marks & Spencer, Waitrose, Sainsbury's and Asda are all backing sustainability, as well as offering a better display of fish than was available a few years ago. Many of the supermarkets are also working with the MSC and MCS and using line-caught fish. You may be paying a few extra pennies, but you can at last be sure of where the fish has come from.

Choosing fish

TOM AIKENS

Increasing numbers of us are now turning to the internet for our weekly shop, and for some this has become the only way of ordering and getting food to the home. At the back of the book is a list of sites from which to get fresh fish, but don't forget that fish from the inter*net*, as opposed to straight from the fishing net, comes with horrendous amounts of packaging – polystyrene boxes, plastic sheets protecting the fish and ice packs – so the ready-to-eat chilled fish may not be as environmentally friendly as you think.

Choosing the best
RULES FOR FISH

One of the many problems with supermarket fish is the range of choice. Given the variety on offer, you may wonder how all of it stays fresh. Line-caught fish are usually killed, prepped and chilled individually, which helps the flesh remain in the best condition. Beam-trawled fish, on the other hand, is not iced instantly and is mashed together. Boats of 10 metres and under now place fish straight into slush ice as soon as it's caught, thus keeping it firm and fresh as a daisy. Fish will start to deteriorate as soon as it is landed. Unless it is cooled instantly, bacteria in the stomach will start to make the fish go off and it will begin to smell. If the fish is left out on the deck of the boat in the warmth and sun it will not last any time at all. Day boats are out at sea for no more than a few hours and will often be only between 2–10 hours at sea. Larger boats and trawlers, however, can be out for 2–5 days.

A lot of the fish from 10-metre boats will have their livers, heart and stomach removed out at sea, to keep them extra fresh, which the gulls love, of course, but the gills are left in as they are a great indicator as to the freshness of the fish. The pinker and redder they are, the fresher the fish. The edges of the gills should also be frilly and separate and the slime or mucus clear, though if there is any blood present that's fine as long as it's fresh looking, but if the gills are a brown colour then it means the fish is not as fresh as it should be, so my advice would be to avoid it. Don't be afraid to ask the fishmonger to allow you to check the fish that you are about to buy from him. I am sure he will be pleasantly surprised that you are knowledgeable about what a healthy fish should look like.

Fresh fish is also covered in a thin layer of moist slime that's clear in colour, uncongealed and smoothly 'spread' over the whole fish – but make sure that this slime is not going cloudy and has no fishy odour. Just because a fish does not have much slime does not mean that it's a bad fish – each fish has different levels of slime and they are not always covered in large amounts of it if they are spanking fresh. Being moved, put in boxes and having crushed ice on top of them will slowly take away quite a bit of the slime, as will handling. If you can, ask the fishermonger to bring the fish to you from out of the counter so you can sniff around the gills. It will smell a little fishy, but it should be a nice fresh fish

Choosing fish

smell, not an overpowering one. Some fish have a stronger smell than others, in particular ray, skate, John Dory and grey mullet, but it should be easy to detect a really off fish smell.

If you get to pick up or touch the fish, you should be able to do so without leaving any indents in the flesh. If you leave fingermarks, this means the flesh is soft and pasty and that the fish is fairly old. If the fish is very fresh it will still have rigor mortis – it will feel very firm and stiff – meaning that it has most likely just been out of the sea for just a few hours. Fish such as seabass, mullet, sardine, mackerel, herring, salmon and monkfish are all best eaten ultra fresh, but some flatfish are better eaten a couple of days old, which gives the flesh time to relax a little. Soles, particularly Dover and lemon sole, can be a little tough if they are too fresh.

Often, because of our strict health and hygiene regulations, you won't be able to touch the fish, so you will have to use your eyes to detect the level of freshness. For example, eyes that have sunk inwards towards the head of the fish are a dead giveaway that it is not fresh, just as a fish that is moist and wet looking, with a bright and shiny appearance, will undoubtedly be fresh. If the scales on the fish look dried out, its colour dull and its eyes clouded over, this is another indication that it is old. Look at the tail fin and main dorsal fin, if they are looking a little ropey and dried out then again the fish will not be fresh. If you can see the gills, make sure they are pinkish-red and not a dull brown. In other words, the fish that looks the brightest is the one that you should go for. Be adaptable – you don't always need to use the fish that is specified in the recipe, often there will be alternatives that you can use and, as you get more confident cooking fish, you'll get a sense of which ones will work so you can use your own judgement and experiment.

RULES FOR SHELLFISH

One of the easiest rules to remember when buying shellfish is that it is best to buy it if its moving and still alive. That goes for oysters, scallops, lobsters, crabs and mussels. Sadly, you are only likely to find this either at the seaside or in some of the fishing ports. I am very lucky: all my shellfish for the restaurant comes to me with a pulse. The shells of the hand-dived scallops that come down direct from Scotland on the overnight train are firmly shut when I get them in the kitchen the next day, but, once opened, they are still pulsating. If you cut through them once they have been prepared (see page 304) the whole surface of the scallop will wiggle. A lot of the great shellfish that you can get your hands on, such as crab and langoustine, will most likely have been precooked or dressed. Have a look at the sell-by date for the freshest fare, but also try ordering dived scallops, live lobsters and crabs – this should be possible in local fishmongers or over the internet. Supermarkets sell dredged scallops, but these are not really worth cooking as they are an inferior product. Once they have been dredged, taken out of the shell and cleaned, they are placed in plastic tubs that are filled with a salt water solution to keep them plump and fresh. The problem with this is that when they are placed in a hot frying pan all the water starts to ooze out and it is very difficult to get a good carmelisation on the outside.

All shellfish is different and there are various rules and simple things to look out for when buying shellfish. A few of the simplest rules to stick to are below.

▸ Lobsters, langoustines and crabs

As I said earlier, if you can get hold of live crabs or lobsters they are far better than those that are dead. If they have been dead a while, crab legs sometimes drop off naturally. With both types of shellfish it is best to pick those with the most rough looking shells – the ones covered in barnacles. The smoothest and cleanest shells aren't likely to be the original shells and will probably contain more water than meat. The same applies to spider crabs, although most of the meat is in the legs. Another tip is always to look for lobsters with long antennae, as they are more likely to be truly wild. When kept in a tank, the antennae tend to snap and rarely grow straight and long.

Langoustines are pretty much always dead when you see them on the ice at the fishmongers. Again, the ones that we get at the restaurant arrive alive, and they can give the nastiest nip if they get hold of your fingers, but in terms of spotting the freshest ones they should not be too limp in the hand and both the legs and antennae should still be intact. If they are missing or broken this could mean they are fairly old. Also look at their eyes, as they should be almost black in colour; if they are a milky colour or just don't look right I would not choose them – again, this suggests that they are old and the texture of the flesh will be like that of cotton wool.

▸ Squid and things

Squid and cuttlefish are almost translucent in appearance when they are just caught and are so beautiful when they are fresh out of the water. Squid can either be no bigger than your thumb nail or as big as your arm. Baby squid is about 10–15cm long and more fully grown squid will be anything between 25cm and 1 metre. You should always try to buy your squid whole with the tentacles intact and smaller squid should have a purple membrane covering the skin; this is very thin and can be ripped off very easily. Indications that your squid is less than fresh are a milky slime and, of course, the smell. In most supermarkets you will it cut into rings which, if I am honest, are not all that great, but if you cannot get whole squid then this will have to suffice. You may also find the really baby stuff in a brine. Larger cuttlefish are rarely found in local fishmongers as the fact that they are often covered in a load of black ink and are so messy to prepare means they are unpopular. If they have been looked after well and have not been chucked about the ink in the cuttlefish should remain intact and not be all over the place. Again, if they are not fresh, they will be covered in slime and will have an unpleasant fishy smell as well.

Choosing fish

▸ **Shellfish in shells (oysters, scallops and mussels)**

Detecting whether bivalves are fresh is one of the easiest things to do. The general rule of thumb is that if the shells are open and don't close when you try to press them shut, this means the meat inside is dead and you should not buy them. If they snap shut when pressed, this means they are as fresh as you could want them. Another indication that bivalves are fresh, particularly with scallops, is that there may be a little foam oozing out from the inside. This is produced as the scallop shuts and closes its shell. If they are extremely fresh, scallops will exert a serious amount of pressure when you try to open them, clamping the two shells firmly tight. And once you have managed to open and remove the scallop from the shell they can sometimes continue to pulsate, like a heartbeat.

All the shells must be in good shape, as once broken the bivalve's armour is useless against any predators or bacteria and they will soon die; so never choose something that has a broken shell. Once they are dead, the shell will not close and you will be able to tell if they are okay by whether they have a fresh or pongy fish smell. If you get your scallops out of the plastic tub with the orange roe removed and cleaned, it is a lot more difficult to tell if they are fresh, but it is more than likely they will be okay as supermarkets have very stringent quality control.

As with fish, always find out where your shellfish are from and whether they are farmed or caught, and in particular whether they are from clean water, away from pollution and sewage works or power stations. All mussels that are collected or grown on a rope go through rigorous controls, but, again, always make sure that they are firmly closed and press them shut to see if they stay closed. Another tip is to place mussels in a large bucket of cold water – if any of them float do not use them, as they will be bad. The meat inside has either been eaten away or the mussel is dead so it's full of air and they will naturally float.

The same rule about open shells closing when pressed together applies to oysters. Fresh oysters once they have been opened need to be consumed instantly if you want to get the best taste from them. Just look out for any shades of green on the oyster meat, as this means they have a bacterial infection and that you should not eat them. Never consume oysters when the weather turns warm. According to the old wives' tale you should only eat oysters when there is an R in the month – so not in May, June, July or August, when sea temperatures are higher and there is an increased risk of bacteria. If you ever get ill from eating an oyster it is very unlikely you will want to eat one again, as it's pretty much one of the harshest forms of food poisoning that you could get.

The best sustainable rules for buying fish

Now that you all know how to buy fish and to tell the good from the bad to the ugly, there are some simple steps to follow when trying to buy sustainable fish.

Listed below are the WWF's top tips for choosing sustainable seafood:

▸ **Buy MSC-certified fish** The MSC label guarantees that the product comes from a well-managed, sustainable fishery and has not contributed to the environmental problem of overfishing.

▸ **Buy a variety of fish** More than 50 species are regularly caught in British and Irish waters, many of which we export. So don't limit your choice, try new fish.

▸ **Buy locally caught fish** This supports the local economy and fishing industry, and also helps to ensure your fish is fresh.

▸ **Find out how it was caught** Methods such as line fishing, creeling, setting traps (such for lobster) and diver fishing have less environmental impact than less selective methods, such as trawling. These methods can target fully-grown fish and tend to be better at avoiding other species. Ask your fishmonger how the fish was caught.

▸ **Don't buy immature fish** Avoid 'baby' and 'fit to the plate' fish. Ask your fishmonger how big the fish is when fully grown.

▸ **Avoid deep sea species** We know little about the breeding patterns of fish such as orange roughy, blue ling and deepwater shark, and catches are plummeting. Avoid them until effective management plans are implemented.

MY TOP TEN FISH TO AVOID

Buying sustainable fish is dependent on so many factors – where you source it, how it's caught, whether it's from a sustainable fishery – which makes it quite difficult to offer you a concrete list of which fish are to be avoided. As stock levels are talked about in general terms rather than looking at different parts of the sea, there can be arguments and misunderstandings about whether a fish is sustainable or not. Ideally, when buying fish we need solely to consider the fishery from which it is sourced. Listed below are some of the most endangered and slow-growing fish species, but even some of these are caught sustainably in certain fisheries, so this is still quite a rough guide to which fish to avoid.

1 Whitebait (see page 345)
2 Cod (see page 307), unless MSC-certified
3 Tuna (see page 340)
4 Skates and rays (see page 336), unless Cuckoo, Starry or Spotted
5 Greenland halibut (see page 318)
6 Wild salmon (see page 331)
7 Freshwater eel (see page 314)
8 Swordfish (see page 340)
9 Sharks and dogfish/huss (see page 313)
10 Sea bass (see page 333), unless MSC-certified or line-caught

Choosing fish

MY TOP TEN FISHY FAVOURITES

Below is my list of some of the best fish to try and get your hands on, some of which may be new varieties that you may never have heard of or even contemplated trying; it's a list of fish that you can have a clear conscious about. They are not in any particular order, nor are some better than others, they are simply some of my preferred choices for cooking and eating. As well as using this list, make sure you look out for all the logos that you know will guarantee a sustainable choice – for example, the MSC blue-tick label and that of line-caught fish from the handline fishermens' association, www.linecaught.org.uk

Fish

1 Red/Grey gurnard
2 Cornish pollack
3 Loch Duart salmon
4 Dab
5 Flounder
6 Megrim sole
7 Grey mullet
8 Sardines
9 Mackerel
10 Coley

Shellfish

1 Cockles, particularly from the Burry Inlet
2 Mussels, particularly from the Isle of Shula
3 Brown crab
4 Spider crab
5 Dived scallops
6 Creel-caught langoustine
7 Razor clams
8 Hand-picked winkles
9 Falmouth oysters
10 Whelks

Potting a fish or making it into a pâté extends its shelf life – you'll be able to keep either for up to a week in the fridge. They are also great ways of using up scraps of fish. The additional ingredients in these recipes will showcase even more meagre cuts of fish to great effect.

Pâtés and Potted Fish

Salmon Rillettes

SERVES 4

500g good-quality farmed
  salmon fillet, such as Loch
  Duart, skinned and pin boned
  (see pages 296–7)
grated zest of 1 lemon
25ml lemon juice
1 tbsp chopped chives
1 tbsp chopped dill
200g unsalted butter, melted
  and cooled to room
  temperature, plus 80g cooled
  melted butter for the top
Maldon salt and freshly ground
  black pepper

For the court-bouillon:
2 celery sticks, sliced
1 onion, thinly sliced
1 leek, sliced
½ fennel bulb, sliced
1 large carrot, sliced
1 garlic clove, sliced
1 bay leaf
3 star anise
12 black peppercorns
16 pink peppercorns
4 sprigs of thyme
a few sprigs each of parsley,
  tarragon and chervil
grated zest of 1 lemon
juice of ½ lemon
2 tsp Maldon salt
150ml white wine
2 litres water

1 Place all the ingredients for the court-bouillon in a large pan, bring to a simmer and cook for 10 minutes. Season the salmon with salt and pepper, add to the pan and remove from the heat. Cover and leave to cool to room temperature.

2 Flake the cooled salmon into large pieces and place in a bowl. Mix in the lemon zest and juice, followed by the chives, dill and some salt and pepper. Carefully fold in the 200g of melted butter, then transfer the mixture to 4 ramekins and chill until set.

3 To finish the rillettes, pour the extra melted butter over the top of each ramekin to form a 5mm-thick layer. Chill until set. Serve with hot toast.

Where I'm from in Norfolk, brown shrimp are very much a speciality of the area, particularly along the north coast. I remember going to Blakeney where all the pubs in the area would be serving potted shrimp washed down with a local brew.

Potted Brown Shrimps or Devon Crab

SERVES 4
200g unsalted butter
1 tsp cayenne pepper
a pinch of ground mace
¼ tsp freshly grated nutmeg
a large pinch of grated
   lemon zest
400g cooked brown shrimps
   or Devon crab meat
¼ tsp Maldon salt
2 tbsp lemon juice

1 Melt three-quarters of the butter over a low heat, then stir in the cayenne pepper, mace, nutmeg and lemon zest and leave to one side.

2 Dry the shrimps well, then chop them roughly and place in a bowl (if using crab meat, just place in a bowl). Add the salt and lemon juice, mix well and leave for 20 minutes. Fold in the melted butter, then spoon the mixture into 4 ramekins and chill until set. Melt the rest of the butter and leave to cool. Pour over the shrimps in a thin layer, then chill for at least 6 hours. Serve with hot toast.

Potted Smoked Mackerel

SERVES 4
450g smoked mackerel fillets
4 tbsp Mayonnaise
   (see page 289)
grated zest of 1 lemon
25ml lemon juice
1 tbsp chopped chives
2 tbsp chopped shallots
1 tsp Maldon salt
a large pinch of freshly ground
   black pepper
55g softened unsalted butter,
   beaten until smooth

Flake the flesh from the mackerel fillets, discarding the skin and any bones. Mix the mackerel with the mayonnaise, lemon zest and juice, chives, shallots, salt and pepper. Finally, stir in the butter, being careful not to overmix or the mixture could separate. Divide between 4 ramekins and leave in the fridge to set for at least 2 hours. Serve with hot toast.

Pâtés and Potted Fish

Fresh Mackerel Pâté

4–5 mackerel, weighing
   300–350g each, cleaned
   (see page 293)
100ml olive oil
3 garlic cloves, cut in half and
   bashed with the flat of a knife
3 bay leaves, cut in half
2 sprigs of rosemary
1 tsp thyme leaves
250g unsalted butter, cut into
   1cm dice
½ tsp ground mace
2 pinches of cayenne pepper
2 pinches of smoked paprika
½ tsp Maldon salt
a large pinch of freshly ground
   black pepper
juice and grated zest of 1 lemon
freshly grated nutmeg
1 tsp chopped parsley

1 Place the fish in a roasting tray, pour over the olive oil and scatter the garlic, bay leaves, rosemary and thyme on top. Roast in an oven preheated to 180°C/Gas Mark 4 for 10–12 minutes, until the mackerel is just cooked through. Meanwhile, place the butter in a pan and melt over a gentle heat. The solids will go to the bottom of the pan. Pour the butter very slowly into a jug so that you have only the clear, clarified butter and the solids remain in the pan.

2 When the mackerel is done, remove from the oven and leave to cool for 5 minutes. Remove the bay leaves and rosemary and flake the flesh into a bowl with the garlic, being careful to discard all the bones. Add the mace, cayenne, paprika, salt, pepper, lemon juice and zest and grate in some nutmeg. Stir in two-thirds of the melted butter, then check the seasoning and add the parsley.

3 Divide the mixture between 4 ramekins, packing it down well. Pour the remaining melted butter over the top and leave in the fridge to set for 2–3 hours. Serve with toasted bread rolls and a little green salad.

Pâtés and Potted Fish

You can use ready-prepared salt cod in this recipe, but it can be difficult to find and the flavour can be too strong. It's not hard to make your own, and I think it will almost certainly taste better if you do.

Hot Salt Cod Brandade

SERVES 4

4 large red Desiree potatoes (you need them large enough to give 400g mashed potato)
Rock salt, to cover the cooking tray
300ml olive oil
8 garlic cloves, finely diced
200g shallots, finely diced
a large pinch of freshly ground black pepper
2 heaped tbsp chopped parsley

For the salt cod:
400g MSC-approved cod fillet, skin removed (see page 297)
100g coarse sea salt
400g salt cod, soaked for a day in cold water then dried

1 To make the salt cod, put the cod fillet into a metal bowl and add the salt. Turn gently so that the fish is well coated, then cover with clingfilm and put into the fridge for 24 hours. Turn the fish over and leave for another 24 hours, then rinse in cold water and dry thoroughly with kitchen paper. This is now ready to use straight away, or can be kept in the refrigerator for up to 2 weeks.

2 Wash the potatoes, prick them with a fork and put them on to a baking tray covered with rock salt. Bake in the oven at 200°C/Gas Mark 6 and cook for approx 1¾ hours. When they are cooked, remove them from the oven, cut them in half and scoop out the flesh into a bowl. Break up the potato with a fork until coarsely mashed.

3 Heat half the olive oil in a pan and when it is hot add the cod. Sauté until it is almost cooked, then add the garlic and shallots and continue to cook for 2–3 minutes, until soft. Add the pepper and transfer to a bowl. Add the mashed potato and the rest of the olive oil and beat together until well mixed. Check the seasoning, add the parsley, and serve.

You can serve this on buttered wholemeal or granary toast for a nice brunch dish.

Creamed Smoked Haddock
with Scrambled Eggs and Chives

SERVES 4
2 x 100g smoked haddock
 fillets

For poaching the haddock:
1 bay leaf
3 sprigs of thyme
2 garlic cloves
8 whole black peppercorns
a pinch of salt
150ml whipping cream
150ml milk

For the scrambled eggs:
50g unsalted butter
2 tbsp chopped shallots
8 large free range/organic
 eggs, beaten
3 tbsp chopped chives
2 tbsp crème fraîche
Maldon salt and freshly
 ground black pepper

1 Place all the poaching ingredients in a pan and slowly bring to a simmer. Add the smoked haddock fillets, then take the pan off the stove and leave to stand for 6 minutes.

2 Remove the fish from the poaching liquid and flake it into big pieces, removing any bones. Strain the liquid and set 2 tablespoons aside to cool to room temperature.

3 Heat a non-stick pan over a low heat and add the butter. When it has melted, add the shallots and cook for 2 minutes, then add the eggs, stirring every few seconds with a wooden spoon or spatula until you have smooth scrambled eggs. When the eggs are almost cooked, add the haddock and the reserved poaching liquid and cook for a further 30 seconds to warm through. Finally, add the chives, crème fraîche, salt and pepper, and serve.

Pâtés and Potted Fish

Salads, Raw & Marinated

Salads are one of the nicest ways of serving fish – fresh, healthy and quick. You only really need four main ingredients – your fish, some olive oil, lemon juice and a little salt. For extra flavour you could add fresh herbs and the zest of your lemon or an orange. In this chapter you'll find some simple salads for mid-week suppers, as well as some more elaborate ones, which are great for dinner parties or a fancy lunch with friends.

Salads, Raw & Marinated

Lentil Salad with Grilled Mackerel

SERVES 4

100ml olive oil
juice and grated zest of 1 lemon
1 tbsp thyme leaves
2 garlic cloves, finely chopped
8 x 60g mackerel fillets, skin slashed
1 x quantity Simple Vinaigrette (see page 290)

For the lentils:

250g green lentils, soaked overnight in cold water
400ml White Chicken Stock (see page 282)
1 shallot, cut in half
½ carrot, cut in half
1 stalk of celery, cut in three
2 bay leaves
8 sprigs of thyme
2 garlic cloves

To finish the lentils:

200ml olive oil
150g shallots, finely chopped
100g celery, cut into small dice
100g carrots, cut into small dice
2 garlic cloves, finely chopped
1 heaped tsp chopped thyme
1 bay leaf
100ml sherry vinegar
1 tbsp chopped parsley
2 tbsp chopped tarragon
2 tbsp chopped chives

1 Put the lentils into a saucepan with cold water and bring to a simmer. Drain, rinse, and add the chicken stock and enough water to cover the lentils. Add the vegetables, herbs and garlic and cook for about 14 minutes, until the lentils are tender. Drain the lentils, then boil the cooking liquid until it is reduced by half and set aside for later.

2 Mix the olive oil, lemon juice and zest, thyme leaves and garlic together and brush all over the mackerel fillets. Season each fillet with salt and pepper, then put the mackerel under the hot grill on a baking tray and cook for 4–6 minutes, leaving them slightly pink inside. Once the mackerel is cooked, drizzle a little vinaigrette on top of the fish and set aside to cool slightly.

3 To finish the lentils, put the olive oil into a pan over a medium heat and add the shallots, celery, carrots, garlic, thyme and bay leaf. Cook until the vegetables are soft, then add the vinegar and simmer until reduced by half. Add the reserved cooking liquid and simmer until reduced by half. Add the lentils and bring to a simmer. Cook for 5 minutes, then add the chopped parsley, tarragon, chives, salt, pepper and a little of the vinaigrette.

4 Serve the lentil salad with the grilled mackerel.

FISH OPTIONS: sardines, herring

Salads, Raw & Marinated

This is a variation of the classic salade niçoise using red mullet instead of the traditional tuna. Many stocks of the major commercial species of tuna are now fully or over-exploited which is why we should look at using sustainable alternatives, such as mullet.

Red Mullet Salade Niçoise

SERVES 4
4 free-range or organic eggs
12 medium-sized Charlotte
  or other salad potatoes
300g green beans, topped
  and tailed
80g shallots, finely chopped
40g pitted black olives, halved
40g pitted green olives, halved
80g capers, drained and rinsed
12 anchovy fillets, canned in oil
16 pieces of oven-dried
  tomatoes (see page 291)
60ml olive oil
1 garlic clove, finely chopped
juice and grated zest of 1 lemon
1 heaped tsp thyme leaves
4 x 110g red mullet fillets
Maldon salt and freshly ground
  black pepper

For the Dijon mustard and
  white wine vinaigrette:
80g Dijon mustard
60g honey
90ml white wine vinegar
30ml double cream
80g chopped shallots
1 garlic clove, finely chopped
30g sugar
a large pinch of Maldon salt
a pinch of freshly ground black
  pepper
180ml vegetable oil
80ml olive oil

1 Place a medium-sized pan of water on the stove and bring to the boil. Carefully, using a slotted spoon, place the eggs one by one into the water and cook for 9 minutes. Remove and place under cold running water. When they are cold, carefully peel away the shells. Cut the eggs in half or quarters, using a sharp thin-bladed knife, and dipping the knife in water or wiping it with a damp cloth to prevent the knife from sticking to the egg.
2 Wash the potatoes in cold water and place them in a pot with water to cover. Add some salt, bring to a simmer, and cook the potatoes for about 25 minutes until slightly soft. Drain and leave to cool. Cut the potatoes first in half lengthways and then in half again, and set aside for later.
3 Bring a good-sized pan of salted water to the boil and add the beans. Cook for 3 minutes, just to blanch them quickly so they retain their crispness, and place immediately into iced water to cool. Once they are cool, drain in a colander and dry on kitchen towel.
4 To make the Dijon mustard and white wine vinaigrette, whisk the mustard, honey, vinegar, double cream, shallots, garlic, sugar, salt and pepper together, then slowly whisk in the two oils until emulsified.
5 Put the potatoes, green beans, shallots, black and green olives and capers into a large bowl. Season with salt and pepper and dress with some of the vinaigrette. Toss together carefully and add the egg quarters, anchovy fillets and oven-dried tomatoes.
6 In a bowl, mix together the oil, garlic, lemon zest and juice and thyme leaves. Season with salt and pepper and brush over the tuna steaks. Put the fish skin-side down on a hot griddle and cook for 3–4 minutes, then flip it over and cook the other side for 1–2 minutes. Once the mullet is cooked, drizzle it with a little vinaigrette and leave to cool slightly. Serve with the salade niçoise, either leaving the fish whole or cutting it into slices.

Mackerel Salad with Watercress and Hard-boiled Egg

SERVES 4

4 free-range or organic eggs
8 x 60g mackerel fillets,
    skin slashed
100ml olive oil
juice and grated zest of 1 lemon
1 tsp thyme leaves
2 garlic cloves, finely chopped
1 x quantity Simple Vinaigrette
    (see page 290)
Maldon salt and freshly
    ground black pepper

For the watercress salad:

3 bunches of watercress,
    leaves picked
2 heads of red chicory, outer
    leaves removed
6 sprigs of tarragon, leaves
    picked
6 sprigs of chervil, leaves
    picked

1 Place a medium-sized pan of water on the stove and bring to the boil. Carefully, using a slotted spoon, place the eggs one by one into the water and cook for 9 minutes. Remove and place under cold running water. When they are cold, carefully peel away the shells. Cut the eggs in quarters, using a sharp thin-bladed knife, and dipping the knife in water or wiping it with a damp cloth to prevent the knife from sticking to the egg.

2 Wash and dry the salad leaves, making sure they are properly dry otherwise they will dilute the flavour of the vinaigrette.

3 Put the mackerel fillets on a baking tray. Mix the oil, lemon juice and zest, thyme and garlic in a bowl and brush over the mackerel. Season with salt and pepper, then put the tray under a hot grill and cook the mackerel for 4–6 minutes, keeping the fish slightly pink. Drizzle a little vinaigrette on top of the fish and leave to cool slightly.

4 Toss the salad leaves and herbs lightly in the remaining vinaigrette and place in a bowl. Either flake the mackerel and mix through the salad leaves or simply leave the fillets whole and serve on top of the salad, with the egg quarters around the edge.

FISH OPTIONS: sardines, herring

Salads, Raw & Marinated

Herring with Bacon, Sherry Vinegar and Spinach Salad

SERVES 4

4 x 120–150g herring, filleted
  (see page 294) and cut into
  5cm pieces
125ml olive oil
1 heaped tsp thyme leaves
1 tbsp Maldon salt
a large pinch of freshly ground
  black pepper
40ml sherry wine vinegar

For the bacon and spinach
  salad:

50ml vegetable oil
100g smoked bacon lardons
350g baby spinach leaves
4 spring onions, coarsely sliced
50g walnuts, roughly chopped

For the bacon and sherry
  vinaigrette:

110g smoked bacon lardons
250ml vegetable oil
4 banana shallots, sliced
2 garlic cloves, finely chopped
1 tsp thyme leaves
40g soft brown sugar
160ml sherry vinegar
2 tsp Dijon mustard
2 egg yolks
50ml single cream
1 tbsp chopped parsley
freshly ground black pepper

1 For the salad, heat the vegetable oil in a non-stick sauté pan over a high heat, and add the bacon. Cook for 3–4 minutes, until crisp, then tip the bacon into a sieve placed over a bowl. Keep the oil that drains into the bowl and place the lardons on kitchen paper to drain. Set them aside for garnishing the salad.

2 For the vinaigrette, cook the bacon in a non-stick sauté pan until crisp, with the oil from the reserved bacon oil plus 100ml of vegetable oil. Add the shallots, garlic and thyme and cook for 2 minutes, until they are just soft. Drain the bacon and shallots into the same bowl through a sieve, again keeping all the oil. Place the pan back on the stove, return the bacon, shallot and garlic mixture to it, and add the soft brown sugar and 100ml of the sherry vinegar. Simmer until the vinegar has all evaporated, then transfer the mixture to a bowl. Add the mustard, remaining vinegar, egg yolks and some freshly ground pepper and whisk for a minute, until it thickens. Add the oil from the cooked bacon and the remaining 150ml of vegetable oil. Whisk all the time; as it starts to thicken, you may need to add a little warm water to keep it to a dressing consistency. Add the cream and parsley at the end and adjust the seasoning, if necessary.

3 To cook the herring, mix 75ml of olive oil with the thyme, salt and pepper and brush over the fish. Put a non-stick sauté pan on to a medium high heat. When hot, add 50ml of olive oil then carefully add the herring pieces to the pan, skin-side down, and cook for 4 minutes. Flip over and cook the other side for 2 minutes. Leave the herrings in the pan, pour in the vinegar and cook, stirring until it has evaporated. Remove from the heat.

4 To finish the salad, put the spinach into a bowl with the spring onions, chopped walnuts and bacon. Add enough dressing to bind, then taste and add a little salt and pepper, if required. Mix the salad well and serve with the sautéd herring. Sprinkle the crispy bacon over the top.

FISH OPTIONS: mackerel, sea bass

Salads, Raw & Marinated

This oily fish can be a bit under-rated, but I personally feel they're the most tasty. By putting some simple ingredients together you can make a delicious, healthy meal out of herring.

Herring Fillets with Apple and Potato Salad

SERVES 4

1 x quantity Wholegrain Mustard Vinaigrette Dressing (see page 290)
1 tsp thyme leaves
1 tsp chopped tarragon
1 tsp Maldon salt
a large pinch of freshly ground black pepper
juice of 1 lemon
75ml olive oil
4 x 200g herring, filleted (see page 294)
30g unsalted butter

For the Charlotte potatoes:
300g Charlotte potatoes, washed and scrubbed
1 tbsp Maldon salt
8 sprigs of tarragon
4 garlic cloves, cut in half
2 spring onions, peeled and finely sliced
1 heaped tbsp chopped chives
1 heaped tbsp chopped tarragon
Maldon salt and freshly ground black pepper

For the salad:
1 bunch of watercress, picked and washed
12 sprigs of tarragon, leaves picked
2 Granny Smith or Braeburn apples, sliced thinly, each slice cut into very thin strips, tossed in a little lemon juice

1 Put the potatoes, salt, tarragon and garlic into a pan with 1.5 litres of cold water. Slowly bring to a simmer, and cook for 20 minutes, until the potatoes are just tender. Take them off the heat and leave to cool at room temperature in their cooking liquid. When they are cool, drain and leave to dry, then cut them into 4mm thick slices. You can peel off the skin before you slice them or not, as you prefer. Put the sliced potatoes into a bowl with the spring onions, herbs, salt and pepper, add enough of the dressing to bind, and mix gently.

2 Mix the herbs, salt, pepper, half the lemon juice and half the oil in a bowl and brush over the herring fillets. Put a non-stick sauté pan on the heat, and when hot add the remaining olive oil. Carefully add the herring fillets to the pan and cook for 2–3 minutes on the skin side first, then add the butter and flip the fish over with a spatula. Cook the other side for 2 minutes and finish with a squeeze of lemon.

3 Toss the watercress and tarragon with the apple strips and a little of the dressing. Serve the potato salad with the herring fillets on top and the apple salad alongside, and drizzle some more of the dressing over the fish, if you like.

FISH OPTIONS: sardines, mackerel, grey mullet

Spiced Rice Pilaff with Herring

100ml olive oil
juice and grated zest of 1 lemon
1 tbsp thyme leaves
2 garlic cloves, finely chopped
8 x 60g herring fillets,
  skin slashed
Maldon salt and freshly ground
  black pepper

For the spiced rice pilaff:
600ml White Chicken Stock
  (see page 282)
50g unsalted butter
150g onions, finely diced
4 garlic cloves, finely chopped
1 heaped tsp chopped thyme
3 bay leaves
6 cloves
4 cardamom pods, split
4 allspice berries, crushed
300g long-grain rice
2 strips of lemon zest
150ml white wine

1 Heat the chicken stock in a large pan and keep warm. Melt the butter in a second pan and add the onion, garlic, and thyme. Add the rest of the spices, tied up in a piece of muslin, and cook for 4 minutes, until the onions and garlic are soft. Add the rice and lemon zest and cook for a minute, then add the white wine and simmer until reduced by half. Pour in the hot chicken stock and bring back to a simmer. Place a piece of baking parchment over the top of the rice and cook for about 20 minutes, until the liquid is all absorbed, being careful that the rice does not catch on the bottom of the pan. Season with salt and pepper.

2 Mix the olive oil, lemon juice and zest, thyme leaves and garlic in a bowl and brush all over the herring fillets. Season each fillet with salt and pepper, then put them under a hot grill on a baking tray and cook for 4–6 minutes, leaving them slightly pink inside. Serve with the spiced rice pilaff.

FISH OPTION: mackerel

Salads, Raw & Marinated

It's hardly surprising this crab is called a spider crab given the look of the legs, but down on the Cornish coast before the First World War the crab was know as gran 'f'er jenkin, the gorwich or gaber.

Spider Crab with Orange and Fennel

SERVES 4

2 fennel bulbs
2 heads of red chicory
2 heads of white chicory
4 large navel oranges or
   6 blood oranges
2 spider crabs, cooked and
   prepared (see page 302)
Maldon salt and freshly
   ground black pepper

For the orange dressing:
250ml fresh orange juice
1 tsp grated orange zest
25g sugar
25ml white wine vinegar
1 tbsp honey
1 tbsp smooth French mustard
200ml sunflower oil
100ml olive oil
25g wholegrain mustard

1 Trim the fennel bulbs, removing any brown or bruised layers, and halve them down the centre. Using a mandoline, slice them very thinly and put them into a bowl. Cut the chicory in half, remove the core, and separate the leaves. Put them into the bowl with the fennel. Cut off the top and the bottom of the oranges, then carefully, with a paring knife, cut the peel away from the sides to reveal the flesh. Cut in between the membranes so you get nice orange segments, removing any seeds. Keep the juice to add to the dressing.

2 To make the dressing, put the orange juice, zest and sugar into a pan and simmer until reduced to 2 tablespoons. Allow to cool slightly, then put into the blender and blend with the vinegar, honey and mustard, slowly adding the oils. Add about 25ml of water if the dressing is too thick, and continue until emulsified, adding the wholegrain mustard last.

3 Mix the sliced fennel with the chicory, then add the crab meat and orange segments. Toss with the vinaigrette, season with salt and pepper and arrange in a salad bowl.

With an ever-soaring population, the demand for fish has increased hugely. There are now not enough wild stocks to meet this demand so fish farming, or aquaculture, is something we have come to rely on heavily. Some in the fishing industry have found the concept of farming upsetting and condemn everything about it but we have found ourselves in a position where we either have to embrace farmed fish or many people are just going to starve. The brief outline below and on pages 60 and 70 should give you an idea of what fish farming is, so that you can make up your minds about where you stand on this controversial issue.

The rearing of fish in captivity is by no means a recent enterprise. For centuries, people have raised fish and shellfish in ponds and coastal impoundments around the world. However, the recent explosive growth in large-scale industrial farming of carnivorous species of fish such as salmon has radically changed the nature of the industry, its impact on other wildlife and on the environment.

The Chinese were one of the first nations to begin fish farming. Farmers used to dig six miles of land into a paddy field and add 2000 carp fry to the pond. In a good year, with ample rainfall and moderate weather, these fry could produce thousands of eggs. The fish fed on the weeds and worms and helped to enrich the fertility of the water and soil, which helped stimulate the growth of rice plants and increase the grain yields by more than 10%. The emphasis on placing the two together was to enhance the growth of the rice plants but the advantages were seen on both sides as the production of both rice and fish increased.

This is a great dish for a light lunch served with wholemeal or granary bread and butter.

Crab Mayonnaise

SERVES 4

1 large live cock crab, weighing about 1.2kg
a large pinch of paprika
1 x quantity Mayonnaise (see page 289)
a large pinch of chopped dill
a large pinch of chopped chervil
a large pinch of chopped tarragon
juice and grated zest of 1 lemon
cayenne pepper
2 baby Little Gem lettuces, leaves separated

For the poaching liquid:
2 celery sticks, sliced
1 onion, sliced
2 leeks, sliced
½ fennel bulb, sliced
2 garlic cloves, sliced
2 bay leaves
6 star anise
16 pink peppercorns
12 sprigs of thyme
6 sprigs each of parsley, tarragon and chervil
4 long strips of lemon zest, taken off with a speed peeler
grated zest of 1 orange
250ml Noilly Prat vermouth
200ml white wine
juice of 1 lemon
2 heaped tsp Maldon salt
200ml white wine
3–4 litres water

1 First kill your crab (see page 302). Place all the ingredients for the poaching liquid in a large pan and bring to a simmer. Add the crab, adding more water if necessary to cover, and simmer for 10–12 minutes. Remove from the heat and leave the crab to cool in the liquid.

2 Mix the paprika into the mayonnaise. Remove the meat from the crab (see page 302). Place the white meat in a bowl and mix in enough mayonnaise to bind the meat together and make it deliciously moist. Add the dill, chervil and tarragon, plus a little lemon juice and zest and some black pepper. Place the brown crab meat in a second bowl and add cayenne pepper, lemon juice and just a little mayonnaise to bind it together.

3 Arrange the lettuce leaves on a serving plate. Place the brown and white crab meat on the lettuce leaves and serve with the remaining paprika mayonnaise. You can dip the claws into the mayonnaise as well as the large pincers and suck out all the juice.

Salads, Raw & Marinated

Curried Crab Salad

SERVES 4

300g cleaned white crab meat
(see page 302)
2 spring onions, sliced
1 red chilli, finely chopped
½ quite firm mango, cut into
small dice
juice and grated zest of 1 lime

For the vegetable salad:
100g Chinese leaves, finely
sliced
100g baby bok choy, finely
sliced
200g mizuna
4 spring onions, sliced
1 red pepper, deseeded and cut
into matchstick strips
1 yellow pepper, deseeded and
cut into matchstick strips
80g carrots, cut into matchstick
strips
a small handful of coriander
leaves

For the curry mayonnaise:
1 garlic clove, finely chopped
1 tbsp sugar
1 tsp Maldon salt
125ml Thai sweet chilli sauce
90ml lime juice
40ml rice wine vinegar
150g mango purée
1 red chilli, deseeded and finely
chopped
2 tbsp curry powder
1 tsp Thai curry paste
1 tsp ground turmeric
1 heaped tsp finely chopped
ginger
400g Mayonnaise (see page 289)

For the curry vinaigrette:
225ml Thai sweet chilli sauce
90ml lime juice
60ml rice wine vinegar
20g sugar
15ml soy sauce
30ml fish sauce
1 garlic clove, finely chopped
1 heaped tsp finely chopped
ginger
90ml vegetable oil

1 To make the curry mayonnaise, put all the ingredients into a bowl and whisk together until smooth.

2 To make the curry vinaigrette, put all the ingredients into a bowl except the vegetable oil. Gradually whisk in the oil in a steady stream so that the vinaigrette is emulsified.

3 Reserving some of the coriander leaves, mix together all the ingredients for the vegetable salad and toss with some of the curry vinaigrette. Season with salt and pepper. Arrange the crab meat on a serving plate or in a bowl and either toss the salad on top of the crab or simply mix the crab and salad together. Scatter over the spring onions, chilli, reserved coriander leaves and mango, and sprinkle with the lime juice and zest. Serve with the curry mayonnaise.

Salads, Raw & Marinated

For serving the dishes below you will need lobster crackers, picks, and a board each to serve the lobsters on.

Lobster Mayonnaise

4 x 500g lobsters, cleaned
    and cooked (see page 300)
juice and grated zest of
    1 lemon
2 spring onions, sliced
2 tbsp chopped chives
2 tbsp chopped tarragon
1 tbsp chopped dill
1 tbsp chopped chervil
1 tbsp chopped parsley
about 8 tbsp Mayonnaise
    (see page 289)
Maldon salt and freshly
    ground black pepper

1 Cut the lobster shells in half from the head to the end of the tail so you have two complete halves. Carefully remove the claws and take out the meat from the tail, claws and elbows.
2 Cut the lobster meat into small dice, about 0.5cm, and place in a bowl. Add the lemon juice and zest, spring onions, herbs, salt and pepper and enough mayonnaise to bind the lobster. Serve, perhaps with a green salad.

Lobster with Herb Mayonnaise

SERVES 4
4 x 500g lobsters, cleaned
    and cooked, left in the
    shell (see page 300)
wedges of lemon

For the herb mayonnaise:
1 tbsp chopped tarragon
1 tbsp chopped chives
1 tbsp chopped dill
1 tbsp chopped chervil
1 tbsp chopped parsley
1 x quantity Mayonnaise
    (see page 289)
1 tsp lemon juice

1 To make the herb mayonnaise, stir the herbs into the mayonnaise and add lemon juice to taste.
2 Cut the lobster shells in half from the head to the end of the tail so you have two complete halves. Serve the lobster on boards, accompanied by the herb mayonnaise and lemon wedges.

Depending on how elaborate you want to get with this you can either make it simple or very grand. You can build up the shellfish platter with crushed ice and blanched seaweed, or just serve it simply on a chilled plate with a few lemon wedges.

Shellfish Platter

SERVES 8–12
1 x 450g lobster, cooked
(see page 300)
12 langoustines, cooked
(see page 303)
1 x 1.2kg whole crab, cooked
(see page 302)
1 x 1kg spider crab, cooked
(see page 302)
14 cockles, cooked
(see page 305)
100g winkles, cooked
(see page 305)
12 prawns or shrimps, cooked
(see page 303)
20 Devon mussels, cooked
(see page 305)
12 native Colchester oysters

For the tarragon mayonnaise:
1 x quantity Mayonnaise
(see page 289)
1 tsp chopped tarragon

For the fresh aioli mayonnaise:
1 tsp English mustard
2 garlic cloves, finely chopped
1 tsp Maldon salt
a pinch of freshly ground
black pepper
1 tsp white wine vinegar
1 tsp lemon juice
3 egg yolks
300ml vegetable oil
100ml olive oil

For the cocktail sauce:
400ml Mayonnaise
(see page 289)
1½ tbsp Worcestershire
sauce
1 tbsp red wine vinegar
1 tsp Tabasco
30ml brandy
1 tsp Maldon salt
15g horseradish sauce
a squeeze of lemon juice
2 tbsp tomato ketchup

For the red wine and shallot
mignonette sauce:
300ml red wine vinegar
100ml sherry wine vinegar
1 tsp Maldon salt
a large pinch of freshly
ground black pepper
120g finely chopped shallots
50ml lemon juice
a little chopped tarragon

To serve:
optional: crushed ice
optional: blanched seaweed
2 lemons, cut into wedges

1 Cook and prepare all your seafood, apart from the oysters.
2 To make the tarragon mayonnaise, stir the tarragon into the mayonnaise. To make the aioli mayonnaise, place the mustard, garlic, salt, pepper, vinegar, lemon juice and egg yolks into a blender for a minute then slowly add all the oil (you may need to add a little water to the mix if it gets too thick). Check the seasoning.
3 To make the cocktail sauce, whisk all the ingredients together.
4 To make the red wine and shallot mignonette sauce, place the vinegars, salt and pepper in a saucepan and bring to a simmer. Add the shallots and set aside to cool. Once cool, add the lemon juice and tarragon.
5 Open the oysters. Arrange the seafood on a large platter of crushed ice and blanched seaweed, if you like, and serve the mayonnaises and sauces alongside. Accompany with lemon wedges.

Don't be squeamish about trying raw oysters. The clean, fresh taste is unlike anything you will have tried before.

Oysters with Red Wine Vinegar and Shallots

SERVES 4

16 native Colchester oysters, shucked (see page 304), shells kept

For the red wine and shallot mignonette sauce:

300ml red wine vinegar
100ml sherry vinegar
1 tsp Maldon salt
a large pinch of freshly ground black pepper
120g shallots, finely chopped
50ml lemon juice
1 tbsp chopped tarragon

1 To make the red wine and shallot mignonette sauce, place the two vinegars, salt and pepper in a pan and bring to a simmer. Add the shallots and set aside to cool. Once cool, add the lemon juice and tarragon.

2 Clean the oyster shells with a brush and cold water. Put the oysters back into the shells and spoon over a little of the mignonette sauce. The oysters can be served on crushed ice, if you like.

Mackerel Marinated in Soy

SERVES 4

4 x 300g mackerel, filleted, pin boned and skin removed (see pages 294, 296)
80ml light soy sauce
2 tsp soft brown sugar
3 tbsp olive oil
2 tbsp sesame oil
juice of 2 limes
2 tbsp rice wine vinegar
2 tbsp chopped coriander
2 spring onions, finely sliced
grated zest of 1 lime
1 small red chilli, deseeded and finely chopped
Maldon salt and freshly ground black pepper

1 Cut the mackerel into thin strips and then into small dice, about 0.5cm. Place in a bowl. In a separate bowl, whisk together the soy sauce, sugar, olive and sesame oils, lime juice and rice wine vinegar. Check the seasoning and add a little salt if need be.

2 Add the coriander, spring onions, lime zest and chilli to the mackerel, and stir in enough of the dressing to bind together. Check the seasoning.

3 You can serve this with toast or salad, and it would be great with avocado guacamole (see page 291).

FISH OPTIONS: sardines, herring

Over the centuries, oysters have been highly prized for their aphrodisiac qualities: even the Roman emperors sent thousands of slaves to British waters to gather the mollusks.

Oysters with Fresh Lemon Purée

SERVES 4
16 native Colchester oysters, shucked (see page 304), shells kept
a little lemon juice

For the lemon purée:
8 organic lemons
40g caster sugar
juice of 2 more lemons
50ml olive oil

1 To make the lemon purée, wash the 8 lemons and cut 5 of them into quarters, removing the pips. Remove the zest from the remaining 3 with a speed peeler, making sure you don't remove any of the white pith. Roughly chop the zest. Wrap all the 8 lemons in foil and put them into an oven preheated to 80°C/at the lowest possible gas mark for approximately 1–1½ hours until they have gone soft. While you are waiting for the lemons to cook, put the zest into a pan of cold water with 1 teaspoon of sugar. Bring to the boil, then refresh the zest in cold water and repeat the process twice more.

2 Once the lemons are soft, put them into a pan with the juice from the foil, add the blanched zest, and simmer over a medium heat, stirring regularly, until the liquid has reduced. Add the remaining sugar and the lemon juice. Place in the blender with the oil and purée until very smooth, then pass through a fine sieve. You may need to add more sugar or juice, depending on the strength of the lemons.

3 Clean the oyster shells with a brush and cold water. Put the oysters back into the shells and pipe a little of the lemon purée on top. Serve on crushed ice, with a little more lemon juice squeezed over.

TOM AIKENS

Make sure that the fish you use for this is extremely fresh – it needs to have been caught no more than a couple of days earlier, otherwise it will taste stale and the dish will not be as good.

Pollack Ceviche with Lemon and Thyme

SERVES 4

400g pollack, filleted and
  pin boned
80ml olive oil
finely grated zest of 2 lemons
juice of 1 lemon
1 heaped tbsp lemon thyme
  leaves
150g micro salad leaves, such
  as salad burnet, basil cress,
  bull's blood, sorrel
80g mixed fresh herb leaves,
  such as chervil, chives, dill,
  tarragon
Maldon salt and freshly
  ground black pepper

With a very sharp knife, slice the pollack very, very thinly at an angle away from you and down its length, discarding the skin. Straight away lay the slices, overlapping, on large serving plates. Drizzle the fish with the olive oil, then sprinkle with the lemon zest and juice. Season with salt and pepper and sprinkle with the lemon thyme, mini salad leaves and herbs. Drizzle with a little more olive oil and scatter over a bit more salt. Serve immediately.

FISH OPTIONS: mackerel, good-quality farmed salmon such as Loch Duart, line-caught sea bass

In the UK we have been fish farming for at least 30 years. We farm many species of fish but it is salmon farming that best demonstrates the impact and debate surrounding this issue. In less than two decades production of salmon on farms has grown enormously and by 1998 farmed production of salmon in coastal waters surpassed production from the wild fisheries.

Farming salmon has two phases. In the first phase eggs are hatched and kept indoors in shallow trays before being transferred to tanks on land. The hatchlings are then raised for 12–18 months until they undergo smoltification. On most farms the smolts are then transferred to net pens anchored in near-shore waters; there they are fed pelleted feed until they reach harvestable

size. The pens generally consist of a frame over which netting is stretched in order to confine the fish. The number of fish raised at a site depends on the total number of pens, the size of the pens, water depth, currents and any specific regulatory restrictions. Salmon farming emphasises increases in production and turnover and this has its problems, most notably a disregard for the growing concerns about impacts on the environment and wild salmon:

► Uneaten feed or faeces can enter surrounding waters and these wastes can pollute bottom habitats and organisms.
► Farmed salmon can escape due to damage to the pens and they can breed with wild salmon, weakening the latter's capacity to survive and damaging their natural antibiotic defences.

► Stocking a pen with as many fish as possible is common in some fish farms. This leaves very little room for the fish to use their muscles naturally nor convert their food into their omega-3 fatty acids, which means that farm-raised fish don't have the health benefits of truly wild fish.

Despite these problems, there are well-managed fish farms and those that are trying to produce a better quality product without damaging the environment should be given a chance. A lot has been learnt from the mistakes that have been made and we cannot disregard the need for farmed fish. Aquaculture is necessary for the future if we are to continue to satisfy the demand for fish as long as it is conducted in an environmentally and socially responsible way.

Salads, Raw & Marinated

Carpaccio of Bream with Lemon Dressing

SERVES 4

1 x 1kg bream, filleted and pin boned (see pages 294, 296)
4 spring onions
50ml olive oil
grated zest of 2 lemons
juice of 1 lemon
1 x quantity Lemon Dressing (see page290)
1 tsp lemon thyme leaves
8 sprigs of tarragon, leaves picked
1 tbsp chopped chives
1 tbsp dill leaves
Maldon salt and freshly ground black pepper

Slice the fish very thinly, discarding the skin, and arrange in a single layer straight on to serving plates. Slice the spring onions very thinly and at an angle and scatter over the fish. Drizzle with the olive oil and sprinkle with lemon zest. Squeeze over the lemon juice and season with salt and pepper. Drizzle the dressing around the fish and sprinkle with the herbs.

FISH OPTIONS: line-caught sea bass or mackerel

Bream are found in very shallow water and often much closer to shore than we realise. You can land them off the beaches at Brighton, Shoreham, Littehampton and the Isle of Wight, which offers both beach and rock- fishing for bream. The rocks and breakwaters in the Channel Isles also offer a shot at shore bream, while bream are taken off Pwllheli Beach, inside the Menai Straits and at Ilfracombe in Devon, from the rocks around St Ives in Cornwall and from the Gower coast. Look out for small outcrops of rock that jut out, but where the depth does not exceed 9m. Bream will congregate here, especially if the seabed is mixed, rough ground. Find a rock mark with an eel grass bed within casting range and you'll have found a really hot mark. Bream will take most baits if given a chance, but the best are scallop frills, squid or cuttlefish and ragworm. Ragworm tipped with scallop frills or squid can get those fish biting if they are finicky.

Salads, Raw & Marinated

Ceviche of Bream

SERVES 4

1 x 1kg bream, filleted, pin boned and skin removed (see pages 294, 296)

juice of 2 lemons and grated zest of 1

60ml extra virgin olive oil

2 tbsp fresh chopped coriander

2 tbsp fresh chopped dill

2 tbsp chopped chives

3 tbsp finely chopped banana shallots

Maldon salt and freshly ground black pepper

1 Place the bream on a cutting board and carefully slice into long thin strips about 0.5cm wide. Take a few strips at a time and cut them into small dice. Place in a bowl and put into the fridge while you prepare the rest of the ingredients. Add them to the bream, and season with salt and pepper.

2 Serve the bream with some avocado guacamole or tomato salsa (see page 291).

FISH OPTIONS: line-caught sea bass or mackerel

When I worked in Paris with the amazing Joël Robuchon, the chefs there could not believe that we got fresh live scallops and langoustines in the UK, as a lot of them had never seen shellfish alive. How could the English have better produce than the French?

Ceviche of Scallops, Chilli and Olive Oil

SERVES 4

12 large diver-caught scallops, cleaned (see page 304)

80ml olive oil

2 tbsp chopped coriander

2 tbsp chopped mint

3 tbsp finely chopped red onion

1 red chilli, deseeded and finely chopped

grated zest of 1 lime

juice of 2 limes

a pinch of sugar

Maldon salt and freshly ground black pepper

1 Slice the scallops thinly on a board, then cut them first into strips and then into small dice. Place them in a bowl and add the olive oil, coriander, mint, onion, chilli, lime zest and juice. Season with salt, pepper and a little sugar and leave to marinate for 1 hour.

2 Serve the scallops with avocado guacamole or tomato salsa (see page 291).

Salads, Raw & Marinated

Salad of Lobster and Artichokes

SERVES 4

2 x 500g lobsters, cooked
  (see page 300)
1 x quantity Lemon Dressing
  (see page 290)
2 tbsp chopped dill, plus
  6 sprigs, leaves picked
2 tbsp chopped tarragon,
  plus 6 sprigs, leaves picked
2 tbsp chopped chives
6 sprigs of chervil, leaves
  picked
1 head of frisée
1 small packet of baby mâche
  salad
1 small thinly sliced truffle
Maldon salt and freshly
  ground black pepper

For the artichokes:
400ml olive oil
5 shallots, thinly sliced
6 garlic cloves, thinly sliced
2 large sprigs of thyme
1 tsp coriander seeds
2 tsp Maldon salt
1 tbsp black peppercorns
400ml white wine vinegar
400ml white wine
8 large globe artichokes
1 x quantity of Truffle

1 Cut the lobster shells in half from the head to the end of the tail so you have two complete halves. Carefully remove the claws and take out the meat from the tail, claws and elbows.

2 Place the oil in a pan, add the shallots, garlic, thyme, coriander seeds, salt and pepper, and cook, covered, on a low heat for 3–4 minutes without letting the shallots and garlic colour. Add the vinegar and boil to reduce by half, then add the white wine and boil to reduce by half again.

3 Meanwhile, prepare the artichokes. Pull off the outer dark green leaves, then peel the stem down with a peeler until smooth, nice and white with no dark green leaves at all. Cut off the stem leaving 10cm of stalk attached. Cut the tops off next, then with a paring knife carefully cut around the artichoke until you get to the core and there are no outer leaves left. With a small spoon scrape out all the furry inside of the artichoke so it is nice and clean, giving it a rinse under the tap.

4 Add 2 litres of water to the boiling liquid. Bring to the boil and simmer for 5 minutes, then check the seasoning and place the artichokes immediately in the cooking liquid to stop them oxidising and going dark brown, which will happen quite quickly. Cook them for approximately 20 minutes, until they are just about tender, and leave to cool in the liquid with the pan standing in a bowl of ice. Take the artichokes out of the cooking liquid and dry on a paper towel. Cut each artichoke in half and then cut each half into four. Toss the pieces in the truffle vinaigrette and leave to marinate.

5 To assemble the salad, put the lobster meat into a bowl, season with salt and pepper, and add some of the lemon dressing, the chopped dill and half the chopped tarragon. Put the artichokes into another bowl with the truffle vinaigrette, the chopped chives and the remaining chopped tarragon. Arrange the lobster and artichokes on a serving platter. Put the chervil, frisée, mâche, sliced truffle, tarragon leaves and dill leaves into a bowl, season with salt and pepper, toss with some more of the lemon dressing and arrange on top of the lobster and artichokes.

Marinated Sea Bass with Orange and Lemon, Summer Herbs

SERVES 4

2 oranges
1 lemon
70ml olive oil
3 tbsp honey
2 tbsp wholegrain mustard
2 tbsp finely chopped banana
   shallots
1 x 1.4kg line-caught sea
   bass, filleted and pin boned
   (see pages 294, 296)
2 tbsp chopped chives
2 tbsp picked coriander
2 sprigs of dill, leaves picked
2 sprigs of chervil, leaves
   picked
Maldon salt and freshly
   ground black pepper

1 In a bowl, grate the zest from 1 orange and 1 lemon, squeeze the juice and set aside. In another bowl, whisk together the olive oil, honey, wholegrain mustard, 2 tablespoons each of orange and lemon juice, and the chopped shallots and season with salt and pepper.

2 Take the sea bass fillets one at a time, place them on a board and cut them into very thin slices. Arrange on a serving dish or plate, spreading out the fillets so they barely overlap, covering the whole area. Drizzle with some of the dressing and brush it over so that all the fish is covered. Cover with clingfilm and place in the fridge for an hour to marinate.

3 Remove the rind of the remaining orange carefully with a knife, then cut between the membranes of the orange so you get separate segments. Cut each segment into 5 or 6 smaller pieces.

4 Remove the plate of bass from the fridge, take off the clingfilm and scatter the orange segments over the top. Sprinkle with some of the orange and lemon zest (not too much, or it will taste bitter), and lastly scatter over the herbs and drizzle with the rest of the dressing.

FISH OPTION: black bream

Salads, Raw & Marinated

This recipe requires you to have a juicer to make the beetroot juice, as it is not yet possible to buy it ready-made. The beetroot dressing can be used in all sorts of salads, and with pickled or cured fish I like to serve the salmon with crème fraîche.

Beetroot Marinated Salmon

SERVES 4

grated zest of 1 orange
grated zest of 1 lemon
25g dill, roughly chopped
225g beetroot, grated
75g Maldon salt
50g caster sugar
1 heaped tbsp freshly ground
    black pepper
1 x 500g piece of salmon
    fillet, pin boned (see pages
    294, 296)
2 tbsp capers, drained and
    rinsed
2 banana shallots, finely diced
optional: crème fraîche

For the roasted beetroot:
600g medium-sized beetroot
50ml olive oil
50g unsalted butter
2 tsp soft brown sugar
1 tsp thyme leaves
3 sprigs of rosemary
250ml balsamic vinegar
Maldon salt and freshly
    ground black pepper

For the beetroot dressing:
150ml port
250ml beetroot juice
    (made in a juicer)
150ml olive oil
100g shallots, finely diced
1 tsp thyme leaves
80ml balsamic vinegar

1 Chop the orange and lemon zest and add the dill. Put the beetroot into a bowl, add the salt, sugar and pepper. Place half the mixture on a tray, making it into an oblong shape roughly the size of the salmon fillet. Lay the salmon skin-side down on the tray, on top of the beetroot. Place the rest of the beetroot on top of the salmon and cover with a flat tray. Place a weight on the tray and leave the salmon to marinate for 9 hours or overnight.
2 Meanwhile make the roasted beetroot. Toss the beetroot in the olive oil. Season, wrap in foil, place on a tray and bake in the oven for approximately 1½–2 hours, until cooked through but not soft. Cool, then peel off the skin. You will need 100g of roasted beetroot for the dressing, so cut this amount into small dice and set aside. Halve the remainder and cut each half into 4.
3 Melt the butter in a pan over a medium heat and add the pieces of roasted beetroot, 1 teaspoon of salt and a pinch of black pepper. Cook for 6 minutes, then add the sugar and cook for a further 5–6 minutes, stirring occasionally and adding the thyme and rosemary halfway through. Drain off the juices, then put the beetroot back into the pan and add the vinegar. Boil until the vinegar has reduced to a syrupy consistency.
4 To make the beetroot dressing, heat the port over a low heat and simmer until reduced to a syrup. Add the beetroot juice, raise the heat, and cook until reduced by two thirds. Put the olive oil into a second pan over a low heat, add the diced shallots and cook gently for 2–3 minutes, until soft. Add the thyme, diced roasted beetroot and balsamic vinegar. Bring to a simmer, cook for 2 minutes, then remove from the heat and set aside to cool.
5 When ready to serve, remove the salmon from the marinade, lightly wash in cold water, and pat dry with a clean cloth. Place the fish on a board, cut it carefully into thin slices, and arrange on a plate. Drizzle with the beetroot dressing, and sprinkle with the capers, shallots, and freshly ground black pepper.

Don't be daunted by the thought of curing your own fish; it's actually very simple. Curing prolongs the shelf life – it will keep for about 10 days in the fridge – and you can slice it whenever you like, making it a really quick and easy snack.

Cured Salmon with Celeriac Remoulade

SERVES 4

600g piece of salmon fillet, pin boned (see pages 294, 296)
zest of 3 oranges and 4 lemons, taken off in long strips with a speed peeler
60g dill, roughly chopped, stalks and all
75g caster sugar
150g Maldon salt
50g cracked black pepper
lemon wedges, to serve

For the celeriac remoulade:
1 celeriac, peeled and trimmed (approximately 300g trimmed weight)
120g Mayonnaise (see page 289)
25g capers, drained and rinsed
40g gherkins, chopped
4 tsp wholegrain mustard
1 tsp chopped parsley
50ml crème fraîche
2 tsp lemon juice
4 tbsp white wine vinegar
a pinch of sugar
Maldon salt
a large pinch of freshly ground black pepper

1 Place a double layer of clingfilm on a tray, leaving enough at the sides to wrap round the salmon later. Mix together the orange and lemon zest, dill, sugar, salt and pepper. Place half this mixture on the tray and make it into an oblong shape roughly the size of the salmon fillet. Lay the salmon skin-side down on the mixture, place the rest of the mixture on top, then bring the clingfilm up over the salmon and wrap very well. Place a flat tray and a weight on top and leave the salmon in the fridge for 9 hours or overnight.

2 For the remoulade, cut the celeriac into fine strips and put it into a bowl. Add all the remaining remoulade ingredients, mix well and check the seasoning. Leave to stand for 30 minutes before serving.

3 Remove the salmon fillet from the marinade and lightly wash and dry it, being careful not to bend or fold it. It is now ready to be sliced. With a very sharp knife, slice it very, very thinly at an angle away from you and down its length. Arrange on plates with wedges of lemon, and serve the remoulade on the side.

FISH OPTIONS: sea trout, sea bass, pollack

Salads, Raw & Marinated

Tartare of Salmon

SERVES 4
500g salmon fillet, skinned
   and pin boned (see pages
   294, 296)
1 cucumber, peeled, deseeded
   and cut into 0.5cm dice
80g crème fraîche
2 tbsp chopped dill
3 tbsp chopped chives
4 tbsp finely chopped banana
   shallots
1 tbsp wholegrain mustard
1 tsp honey
juice and grated zest of 1 lemon
Maldon salt and freshly ground
   black pepper

1 Place the salmon on a cutting board and with a sharp knife cut into thin strips. Cut the strips into 0.5cm dice and put them into a bowl. Place the cucumber in a colander, add a sprinkling of salt to draw out some of the water and leave for 30 minutes. Dry the cucumber with kitchen towel and add to the diced salmon, with the crème fraîche, herbs, shallots, wholegrain mustard, honey, lemon juice and zest. Season with salt and pepper.

2 This would be nice served with sourdough toast, avocado guacamole (see page 291) or, in the summer, a ripe tomato salad.

Loch Duart Ltd is an independent salmon farm in the northwest of Scotland. The winds and tides come from the northern Atlantic in one of the most beautiful and stunning sceneries, and the environment and conditions for rearing their salmon are exceptional. I have visited the farm and was completely bowled over by the work they do there and the sheer enthusiasm and environmental concerns that they display.

The farm produces a limited 3,600 tonnes of salmon per year in three separate sea sites and two hatcheries. If they wanted to, the farm could produce almost double this in the pens and space they have, but because they believe so much in the welfare of the salmon they do not want to farm factory-style fish.

Loch Duart have always had a strong commitment to the environment and Dawn Purchase, the Mariculture Officer at the MCS, has spent time at Loch Duart helping to prepare the critical guidelines that they are working towards. One of the many reasons for working with the MCS is that they know everything about the fish pellets that are fed to the salmon, including whether they are from sustainable fish stocks, and whether they contain growth promoters, antibiotics for enhanced growth or GM components. As a result, all the industrial fish that Loch Duart uses for their pellets comes from fisheries that are not used for fertilisers or for pig or chicken feed, but from fisheries that are used for human consumption. One of their initiatives is to focus the customer's mind on sustainability; not just of the food they are eating, but also in regard to the impact this food may have on the environment. Batches of feed are extensively tested and Loch Duart knows the types of fish used, where they were caught and which batches of feed were used to rear them. GM-free components, fishmeal and fish oil are also guaranteed through an independent feed supplier.

The waters in the Loch are like the Caribbean – crystal clear – and the farm is taking huge steps to protect the salmon's environment, looking at ways of keeping the waters around the pens clean. They grow sea urchins and seaweed next to the pens which helps filter out some of the impurities in the water that are produced by the feed and by the salmon.

You may or may not agree with the farming of salmon, but Loch Duart have been very successful at raising and farming salmon with the best possible methods. The farm's overall objective is to create as natural a life-cycle as possible, using skilled and experienced staff, with good husbandry – and I saw for myself the amazing achievements they have made.

Salads, Raw & Marinated

Sourdough toast makes a lovely accompaniment to this dish and turns into into a more substantial lunch.

Tartare of Mackerel with Roasted Beetroot

SERVES 4

4 x 300g mackerel, filleted,
    pin boned and skin removed
    (see pages 284, 296–7)
80g crème fraîche
2 tbsp chopped dill
2 tbsp chopped chives
2 tbsp chopped chervil
3 tbsp finely chopped shallots
2 spring onions, thinly sliced
1 tbsp wholegrain mustard
juice and grated zest of 1 lemon
salt and freshly ground black
    pepper

For the roasted beetroot:
400g medium-sized beetroot
50ml olive oil
1 tsp thyme leaves
Maldon salt and freshly ground
    black pepper

1 Toss the beetroot in olive oil, season with salt and pepper, and sprinkle with the thyme. Wrap in foil, place on a tray and bake in an oven preheated to 150°C/Gas Mark 2 for approximately 1½ to 2 hours, until cooked through but not soft. Leave to cool, then peel off the skin and cut into small dice, about 0.5cm.

2 Cut the mackerel into thin strips and then into small dice, the same size as the beetroot. Place in a bowl. Add the crème fraîche, herbs, shallots, spring onions, mustard, lemon juice and zest, and season with salt and pepper. Add the diced beetroot, fold into the mackerel, and serve immediately.

FISH OPTIONS: sardines, herring

Salads, Raw & Marinated

Mackerel Escabeche

SERVES 4

8 fillets of mackerel, pin
   boned and skin removed
   (see pages 294, 296–297)
2 tbsp chopped flatleaf parsley
12 large basil leaves, cut into
   fine strips
Maldon salt and freshly
   ground black pepper

For the poaching liquid:
200ml olive oil
3 garlic cloves, thinly sliced
180g banana shallots, thinly
   sliced
150g fennel, thinly sliced
150g carrots, sliced
2 bay leaves
2 pinches of saffron
4 heaped tsp sugar
3 teaspoons Maldon salt
a large pinch of freshly
   ground black pepper
1 tsp coriander seeds, lightly
   toasted and crushed
1 tsp fennel seeds, lightly
   toasted and crushed
4 star anise
300ml white wine
150ml orange juice
1 tsp grated orange zest
60ml white wine vinegar

1 Place a saucepan on a medium heat and add the olive oil, garlic, shallots, fennel and carrots, followed by the bay leaves, saffron, sugar, salt, pepper and spices. Cook for 2 minutes, then add the white wine, orange juice, zest and vinegar, and bring to a simmer. Cook for 4 minutes.

2 Season the mackerel fillets with salt and pepper and add them to the liquid. Poach for 2 to 3 minutes, then add the fresh herbs and either serve immediately or leave to cool to room temperature.

Nutritionists have known for years that seafood is a source of top-quality protein, and through the educational and promotional efforts of the seafood industry and government we all have a keener sense of the importance of seafood in a healthy diet. Fish, particularly cold-water oily fish, contain essential fatty acids (EFAs) and are said to be a rich source of a large number of minerals. There is increasing evidence that eating oil-rich fish containing omega-3 fatty acids can help protect against heart and circulatory disease and the Food Standards Agency now recommends we eat at least two portions of fish a week, one of which should be oil-rich, such as sardines, trout, mackerel or salmon.

Grilling & Barbecuing

Grilling your fish is a good method of cooking it if you are watching your weight or calorie intake. You are not cooking the fish in lots of oil or butter, simply brushing or lightly coating it in the fat, which means that it's a much healthier way of eating than frying, for example. It's also easier to control the cooking as you're not having to stand over a hot pan, which means there's less stress involved.

Grilling works well with many different varieties of fish and if you're quite new to fish cooking then it's a good way of starting to experiment with fish and learning what works and what doesn't.

Grilling & Barbecuing

Grilled Plaice with Roast Fennel

SERVES 4
8 x 75g plaice fillets
80ml olive oil
40g softened unsalted butter
1 tsp each fennel and cumin
    seeds, ground in a pestle
    and mortar
juice of ½ lemon
Maldon salt and freshly
    ground black pepper

For the roast fennel:
4 fennel bulbs, each cut
    into quarters
100ml olive oil
1 tsp chopped thyme
1 tsp chopped rosemary
2 bay leaves
juice and grated zest of
    1 lemon
4 garlic cloves, unpeeled,
    cut in half lengthways
¼ tsp mixed fennel and cumin
    seeds, ground in a pestle
    and mortar
Maldon salt and freshly
    ground black pepper

1 For the fennel, set the oven at 180°C/Gas Mark 4 and place a small roasting tin in it to heat up. Put a pan of salted water on to simmer, add the fennel wedges and blanch for 5 minutes, until slightly softened. Drain on some kitchen paper and place in a bowl. Add the olive oil, herbs, lemon juice and zest, garlic, fennel and cumin seeds and some salt and pepper and mix well. Place in the roasting tin and cook in the preheated oven for about 15 minutes, until lightly golden.

2 Meanwhile, cook the plaice. Brush the fillets with the olive oil, dab with the butter, season with salt and pepper and scatter over the fennel and cumin seeds. Place the fish under a hot grill and cook for 4 minutes on each side, carefully flipping them over with a spatula. When the plaice fillets are done, squeeze some lemon juice over them and serve with the fennel.

For grilled whole plaice

You will need 1 cleaned whole plaice, weighing about 1.4kg. Sprinkle both sides with the olive oil, dab with the butter, season with salt and pepper and then sprinkle on the fennel and cumin seeds. Put the plaice on a preheated ridged grill pan and cook for about 4 minutes per side, until golden brown. Transfer to an oven tray and place in an oven preheated to 180°C/Gas Mark 4. The fish will take about 10–12 minutes to cook. To test if it is done, gently insert a sharp knife near the bone; the fillets will start to come away from the bone.

FISH OPTIONS: monkfish, mackerel, sardines

Grilling & Barbecuing

Provençal Grilled Mullet with Grilled Aubergine

SERVES 4

1 tbsp black olive tapenade
4 x 300g red mullet, cleaned
    and skin slashed
    (see page 293)
1 lemon, peeled, divided into
    segments and roughly diced
16 green olives, chopped
1 garlic clove, chopped
8 basil leaves, roughly torn
2 tsp chopped thyme
2 tsp Maldon salt
a large pinch of freshly
    ground black pepper
100ml olive oil
juice of 1 lemon

For the grilled aubergine:

2 medium aubergines
    (about 200g each)
150ml olive oil
2 tbsp honey, warmed slightly
75ml balsamic vinegar
1 tsp chopped thyme
1 tsp chopped rosemary
2 garlic cloves, finely chopped
Maldon salt and freshly
    ground black pepper

1 Place a grill pan over a medium heat. Cut each aubergine lengthways in half and brush the cut side with the olive oil. Place on the grill, cut-side down, and cook for 3 minutes, until starting to caramelise. Turn over and cook for another 3 minutes. Place on a baking tray with the cut side facing up. Brush with the honey and drizzle with the balsamic vinegar. Sprinkle on the chopped herbs, garlic and some salt and pepper, then smear this mixture into the aubergine. Place in an oven preheated to 180°C/ Gas Mark 4 for 10–12 minutes, until just tender.

2 Smear the tapenade into the slashes on both sides of the mullet. Mix the lemon segments with the chopped olives, garlic, basil, thyme, salt and pepper and stuff this mixture into the slashes too. Brush the fish with the olive oil, then transfer to a preheated ridged grill pan. Cook over a low to medium heat for 6–8 minutes per side. Squeeze over the lemon juice and serve with the grilled aubergine.

FISH OPTIONS: line-caught sea bass, sardines, herring

The anise, lemony flavour of fennel makes it a good accompaniment to fish. You can serve it grilled as a vegetable side dish or use it in a fish stock, or make it into a salad, as here.

Grilled Mullet Fillets
with Fennel and Orange Salad

SERVES 4

¼ tsp each cumin, coriander and fennel seeds
100ml olive oil
juice and grated zest of 1 lemon, plus a little extra juice to finish
4 x 300g red mullet, filleted, pin boned and skin slashed (see pages 294, 296)
1 tsp Maldon salt
a pinch of freshly ground black pepper

For the fennel and orange salad:
200ml orange juice
150ml olive oil
a squeeze of lemon juice
1 tsp tarragon, cut into neat strips
2 large fennel bulbs
1 orange, peeled and segmented
Maldon salt and freshly ground black pepper

1 First prepare the fennel salad. Put the orange juice into a small pan and boil until reduced by three-quarters. Pour into a bowl and whisk in the olive oil while still warm, then add the lemon juice, tarragon and some salt and pepper. Cut each fennel bulb in half and slice very thinly, preferably on a mandoline. Place in a bowl and mix in the dressing. Add the orange segments and check the seasoning.

2 For the fish, lightly roast the seeds in a dry frying pan over a medium heat for 2 minutes, moving them around a little; this will release the flavours and oils. Transfer them to a coffee grinder and blitz very briefly until coarsely crushed (or use a pestle and mortar).

3 Mix the olive oil with the spices, lemon juice and zest, salt and pepper, and brush the skin side of the mullet with the mixture. Place on a hot grill pan, skin-side down, and cook for 3 minutes. Turn the fillets over very carefully with a palette knife and cook for another 2 minutes, until the fish is just done. Finish with a squeeze of lemon juice and serve with the fennel and orange salad.

FISH OPTIONS: sardines, mackerel, herring

Grilling & Barbecuing

Grilled Lemon Sole with Lemon Thyme

SERVES 4

150ml olive oil

100ml lemon juice, plus extra to serve

2 tsp lemon thyme leaves

4 x 400g lemon sole, cleaned, skin removed from the top, i.e. the dark side (see pages 293, 295)

40g unsalted butter

½ tsp Maldon salt

a large pinch of freshly ground black pepper

zest of 2 large organic lemons, taken off in long strips with a speed peeler (leaving behind all the bitter white pith)

1 Mix the olive oil, lemon juice and lemon thyme together in a bowl. Brush the lemon sole with a little of this mixture, dab with the butter and season with the salt and pepper. Put on to a medium-hot grill pan and cook for 4 minutes, until there are score marks underneath.

2 Arrange the lemon zest on 2 non-stick oven trays, then place the lemon sole on top and brush with the remaining olive oil and lemon juice mixture. Place in an oven preheated to 180°C/ Gas Mark 4 and cook for 8–10 minutes; the fish is done when the flesh comes away from the centre bone if you insert a sharp knife. Squeeze a little lemon juice over the fish and serve straight away.

FISH OPTIONS: plaice, flounder, mackerel

Grilled Herring with Bay Leaves

SERVES 4

75ml olive oil

1 heaped tsp thyme leaves

zest and juice of 1 lemon

4 x 400g herring, gutted and left whole (see page 293)

8 bay leaves

4 sprigs of rosemary

1 tbsp Maldon salt

a large pinch of freshly ground black pepper

Mix the olive oil, thyme, lemon juice and zest in a small bowl and brush over the outside and inside of each herring. Inside each fish place 2 bay leaves, a rosemary sprig, and some salt and pepper. Carefully place the herring on a grill pan, under a grill, or the edge of a barbecue, away from the direct heat of the open fire, and cook for about 3–4 minutes on each side, watching them to make sure the fish and herbs don't burn.

Grilled Lobster with Hollandaise Sauce

SERVES 4

4 x 400–500g lobsters
  – depending how hungry
  you are, half a lobster each
  may be enough
100ml olive oil
juice of ½ lemon
1 tsp thyme leaves
½ tsp Maldon salt
a pinch of freshly ground black
  pepper
1 x quantity Hollandaise Sauce
  (see page 305)

1 Kill and cook your lobsters (see page 300). Cut the tails in half and remove the meat from the claws.

2 Mix the olive oil with the lemon juice, thyme, salt and pepper. Season the lobster tail and claw meat with salt and pepper, then drizzle over the olive oil mixture. Place the tails, still in their shells, on a hot grill pan, cut-side down, and cook for 3 minutes, then turn and cook the other side for 3–4 minutes. Place the claws on the grill as well and cook for 2–3 minutes. Once they are all ready, serve with the hollandaise for dipping.

FISH OPTION: langoustines (allow 5 per person)

Barbecued Squid

SERVES 4

400g medium-sized squid
  bodies, cleaned (see page 305)

For the marinade:
1 heaped tbsp chopped
  coriander
2 heaped tbsp chopped basil
1 stem of lemongrass, bashed
  and chopped
zest of 2 limes
juice of 4 limes
2 large pinches of smoked
  paprika
a large pinch of cayenne pepper
1 red chilli, deseeded and finely
  chopped
3 garlic cloves, finely chopped
175ml olive oil
1 tbsp sugar

1 Mix all the marinade ingredients in a bowl. Add the squid and leave to marinate for at least 2 hours, or overnight for better flavour.

2 Put the squid on a barbecue grill in a row, so they are easy to turn over with a pair of tongs. Cook them for about 2 minutes each side, then slice them into rings and serve with the marinade as a dipping sauce.

Grilling & Barbecuing

I remember catching mackerel in large quantities as a child, in Devon. When my father went sailing, we'd throw lines out of the back of the boat with multicoloured feathers and lures – the mackerel were very easy to catch.

Grilled Mackerel with Crushed Broad Beans and Oregano

SERVES 4

80ml olive oil
juice of 1 lemon
a large pinch of oregano leaves
4 x 160g mackerel, cleaned and
   skin slashed (see page 293)
Maldon salt and freshly ground
   black pepper

For the crushed broad beans:
600g shelled fresh broad beans
75ml olive oil
80g shallots, finely chopped
1 garlic clove, finely chopped
½ tsp Maldon salt
a pinch of freshly ground black
   pepper
1 tsp thyme leaves
juice and grated zest of
   ½ lemon
1 tsp chopped oregano

1 Blanch the broad beans in a pan of boiling salted water for 30–60 seconds. Drain in a colander and transfer instantly to a bowl of iced water to cool. Leave for 3–4 minutes, then drain. Squeeze the beans between your thumb and finger so they pop out of their thin inner skin and then place on kitchen paper to dry. Put the olive oil in a small saucepan with the shallots, garlic, salt, pepper and thyme and cook over a low to medium heat for about 3 minutes, until the shallots are translucent and just soft. Then place in a bowl to cool. Add the broad beans, lemon juice and zest and oregano and crush lightly with a fork.

2 For the mackerel, mix the olive oil, lemon juice and oregano together in a bowl and brush them over the fish, rubbing them into the cuts on both sides. Season with salt and pepper. Place the mackerel under a hot grill and cook for 4–6 minutes. Turn the fish over carefully and cook for a further 4–6 minutes.

3 Divide the crushed broad beans between 4 plates and place the mackerel on top.

FISH OPTIONS: sardines, grey mullet

Grilling & Barbecuing

Sea Bass Grilled on an Open Fire with Cherry Tomato and Shallot Sauce and Balsamic Red Onions

SERVES 4

6 bay leaves, cut in half
6 garlic cloves, sliced
1 tsp thyme leaves
1 x 1.5–2kg sea bass,
    cleaned and skin slashed
    (see page 293)
100ml olive oil
grated zest of 2 lemons
juice of 1 lemon
a large pinch of Maldon salt
a large pinch of freshly
    ground black pepper

For the cherry tomato and
    shallot sauce:
75ml olive oil
80g onions, finely chopped
50g large shallots, finely
    chopped
4 garlic cloves, finely chopped
2 tbsp caster sugar
1 tsp chopped thyme
1½ tsp Maldon salt
a large pinch of freshly
    ground black pepper
100ml white wine
370g cherry tomatoes, cut
    in half
20g tomato paste

For the balsamic red onions:
400g red onions, peeled
100ml olive oil
½ tsp Maldon salt
1 tsp dried herbes de Provence
1 tsp chopped thyme
2 garlic cloves, sliced
30g light brown sugar
150ml balsamic vinegar
15g basil leaves

1 Put the bay leaves, garlic and thyme inside the slashes in the sea bass. Whisk the olive oil, lemon zest and juice together and rub this mixture all over the fish so it is well coated. Place in the fridge and leave to marinate for at least 2 hours; it's best left overnight, covered in clingfilm. Remove the fish from the fridge 30 minutes before cooking so it gets to room temperature.

2 To make the cherry tomato and shallot sauce, place a pan over a medium heat, add the olive oil, then add the onions, shallots, garlic, sugar, thyme, salt and pepper. Cook for 3–4 minutes, until the onions and shallots are translucent. Add the white wine and simmer until it has almost evaporated. Next add the cherry tomatoes and cook for 15–20 minutes, stirring now and again, until they have cooked down by half. Stir in the tomato paste and cook for a further 5 minutes.

3 For the balsamic red onions, cut the onions in half, remove the root, and slice each half into 4 or 5 pieces. Heat the olive oil in a sauté pan over a low to medium heat. Add the onions, salt, herbes de Provence, thyme and garlic and cook, uncovered, for 8–10 minutes. Add the sugar and cook slowly for another 8–10 minutes, stirring occasionally, until caramelised. Pour in the vinegar, stirring to deglaze the base of the pan. Cover with a lid and cook gently for 15 minutes, until all the liquid has evaporated and the onions are syrupy. Stir in the basil and cool.

4 Season the bass with the salt and pepper, then place it on a barbecue grill towards the edge of the fire, so it's not on the hottest part. Cook for 8–10 minutes, until crisp and golden. Turn the fish over very carefully with a pair of tongs; this will be easier if you place the fish inside a barbecue basket. Cook for a further 8–10 minutes. The onions and sauce can be reheated on the edge of the fire while the fish is cooking.

Variation: Baked Sea Bass

Season the fish with salt and pepper. Place a large sheet of foil on a baking tray and place the balsamic onions towards the bottom of it. Put the tomato sauce around the onions and place the bass carefully on top. Bring the foil loosely up around the fish and seal the edges. Bake in an oven preheated to 180°C/Gas Mark 4 for 12–14 minutes. Be careful when opening the foil – it will steam quite a lot.

Grilled Mackerel Fillets with
Roast Beetroot and Potato Salad

SERVES 4
100ml olive oil
juice and grated zest of 1 lemon
a large pinch of thyme leaves
2 garlic cloves, finely chopped
8 x 60g mackerel fillets, skin
   slashed (see page 293)
Maldon salt and freshly
   ground black pepper

For the roast beetroot:
4–5 raw beetroot
150ml olive oil
25g unsalted butter
½ tsp chopped thyme
2 large sprigs of rosemary
20g brown sugar
150ml balsamic vinegar
20ml lemon juice
Maldon salt and freshly
   ground black pepper

For the potato salad:
400g Charlotte potatoes,
   scrubbed
20g Maldon salt
a few sprigs of mint
4 garlic cloves, peeled and
   cut in half
1.5 litres cold water
1 tbsp chopped parsley
1 tbsp chopped dill
1 tbsp chopped chives
6 spring onions, finely sliced
1 x quantity of Herb
   Mayonnaise (see page 289)

1 First cook the beetroot. Toss them in 40ml of the olive oil, season with salt and pepper, then wrap each one in foil and place in a roasting tray. Bake in an oven preheated to 180°C/Gas Mark 4 for 1½ hours, until they are just cooked but not soft. Leave to cool, then remove the foil and peel the skin away. Cut each beetroot in half and each half into 4–6 small wedges. Set aside.

2 For the potato salad, place the potatoes, salt, mint and garlic in a pan, cover with the cold water and slowly bring to a simmer. Cook for 20 minutes or until only just tender. Take off the heat and leave the potatoes to cool to room temperature in their cooking liquid so they take on more flavour. Drain the potatoes and cut them into slices about 1cm thick. Add the herbs and spring onions, then fold in enough of the herb mayonnaise to bind everything together. Season with salt and pepper.

3 To finish the beetroot, place a sauté pan over a medium heat and add the rest of the olive oil. Once it is hot, add the butter and then the beetroot, thyme, rosemary, sugar, 1 teaspoon of salt, and a large pinch of pepper. Slowly cook the beetroot for 10–12 minutes, until they start to caramelise. Once they start to soften, add the vinegar and lemon juice. Simmer until they reduce to a sticky syrup and the beetroot is soft.

4 Finally, cook the mackerel. Mix the olive oil, lemon juice and zest, thyme and garlic together in a bowl and brush over the skin side of the fish. Season with salt and pepper and place on a baking tray. Cook under a hot grill, skin side up, for 4–6 minutes, keeping the flesh slightly pink.

5 To serve, divide the potato salad between 4 plates, put the mackerel on top and then the beetroot on top of that.

FISH OPTIONS: sardines, herring

Grilling & Barbecuing

Grilled Sardines with Garlic Potatoes

SERVES 4

100ml olive oil

juice of 1 lemon

2 garlic cloves, finely chopped

1 tsp chopped rosemary

8 x 80g sardines, cleaned and
skin slashed (see page 293)

Maldon salt and freshly
ground black pepper

For the garlic potatoes:

150ml olive oil

50g unsalted butter

400g medium-sized Charlotte
potatoes, scrubbed and cut
into quarters

4 sprigs of rosemary

2 bay leaves

½ tsp Maldon salt

a pinch of freshly ground
black pepper

12 garlic cloves, peeled and
bashed with the palm of
your hand

1 tbsp chopped parsley

6 spring onions, thinly sliced

1 First prepare the garlic potatoes. Place a large sauté pan over a medium heat and add the olive oil. When the oil has heated up, immediately add the butter and then the potatoes, rosemary, bay leaves, salt and pepper. Sauté over a medium heat for 15 minutes, until the potatoes start to colour, turning them every few minutes so they cook evenly. Add the garlic and cook for 5 minutes, until soft. Stir in the parsley and spring onions.

2 For the sardines, mix the olive oil in a bowl with the lemon juice, garlic and rosemary and season with salt and pepper. Place the sardines on a non-stick baking tray and smear the mixture all over them, then place under a hot grill and cook for 6–8 minutes, turning halfway through. Watch them carefully to make sure they don't burn. Serve with the garlic potatoes.

FISH OPTIONS: grey mullet, megrim sole

Throughout the sixteenth to nineteenth centuries, pilchards (sardines) were a very valuable product. They were cured for food and could then be exported over long distances, while their oil was used for lighting and heating. The life cycle of the pilchard requires them to come close to the shore in late summer, and this they did in huge shoals numbering in their millions. On sighting the pilchard shoals, lookouts would signal with a trumpet and guide boats out to land them. During the industry's *annus mirabilis* of 1871, 16,000 tonnes of pilchards were exported, while on one night in November 1905, 13 million fish were caught in a few hours. I imagine it was quite a sight. Sadly, I'm not sure it's something we will ever see again.

Grilling & Barbecuing

The French call sea bass the *loup de mer*, the 'wolf of the sea', because they work together to capture small fish that swim in huge shoals. It is this hunting that gives the predatory sea bass its high oil content and fabulous taste.

Grilled Sea Bass with Paprika
Red Pepper Relish and Sauce

SERVES 4
50ml olive oil
4 large pinches of smoked paprika
4 x 140g pieces of sea bass fillet, skin slashed
½ tsp Maldon salt
a large pinch of freshly ground black pepper
12 basil leaves, cut into fine strips

For the red pepper relish:
300ml olive oil
3 onions, very thinly sliced
2 tsp chopped thyme
25g caster sugar
20g Maldon salt
8 red peppers, peeled with a speed peeler (reserve the skins for the sauce if you like) and cut into fine strips
300ml white wine vinegar

For the red pepper sauce:
20ml olive oil
20g unsalted butter
2 red peppers, finely chopped (plus the reserved skins, if using)
a few sprigs of thyme
15g caster sugar
½ tsp Maldon salt
100ml lemon juice
100ml double cream

1 To make the relish, place the olive oil in a pan over a medium heat, add the onions, thyme, sugar and half the salt and cook for 5–8 minutes, being careful not to let the onions colour. Add the red pepper strips and the remaining salt. Cover and cook for 10–12 minutes over a medium to high heat, so the peppers cook down quickly; stir every minute to prevent them catching on the bottom of the pan. Add the vinegar and cook down rapidly until completely evaporated. Check the seasoning, remove from the heat and leave to cool.

2 For the red pepper sauce, place a pan on a medium heat and add the olive oil and butter. Stir in the red peppers, thyme, sugar and salt, then cover the pan and sweat until the peppers are soft. Stir in the lemon juice and cook, covered, for 2 minutes, then add the cream. Bring to a simmer and cook for 2 minutes. Place in a blender and purée until smooth, then pass through a fine sieve into a small pan. Cover with clingfilm to keep warm.

3 Whisk the olive oil and paprika together and brush them over the skin of the fish. Season with the salt and pepper. Place the bass, skin-side down, on a medium-hot ridged grill pan and cook for 8 minutes, until golden underneath. Turn the fish over very carefully with a pair of tongs and cook for 4–6 minutes, being careful not to let it get too dark. Serve with the relish and sauce, with the basil sprinkled over.

This is a fantastic way of spicing up a storecupboard emergency meal. Instead of canned sardines, use delicious fresh ones – the taste is phenomenal and I guarantee you won't want to go back to reaching for that can.

Barbecued Sardines on Toast
with Shallot Chutney and Basil

SERVES 4

40 basil leaves
2 garlic cloves, thinly sliced, plus 1 garlic clove, cut in half
8 large sardines, boned (see page 296), with the head and tail left on
100ml olive oil
4 slices of sourdough bread
1 lemon
Maldon salt and freshly ground black pepper

For the shallot chutney:
320g shallots, peeled and sliced
2 Anjou pears, peeled and diced
25g raisins
½ tsp Maldon salt
a large pinch of ground cinnamon
1 tbsp mustard seeds
a large pinch of mustard powder
a large pinch of ground ginger
1 tbsp finely chopped fresh ginger
200ml cider vinegar
70g dark soft brown sugar

1 Place all the ingredients for the chutney in a heavy-based pan and bring to a slow simmer. Cover and cook over a low heat for about 1 hour, stirring now and again, then remove the lid and continue to cook until most of the liquid has evaporated. Remove from the heat and leave to cool.

2 Place 5 basil leaves and a few slivers of garlic in the middle of each sardine. Close the sardines up around the basil and garlic, then tie them loosely with string around the middle, where the belly was – just loop the string around and tie it with a granny knot 4 times to hold the basil and garlic in.

3 Brush the sardines with the olive oil and season with salt and pepper. Place on a barbecue, under a grill or on a grill pan and cook for about 4 minutes on each side. Whilst they are cooking, brush the sourdough with a little olive oil and toast it on the grill until golden on both sides; it may burn slightly at the edges, which is fine as it all adds to the flavour. Rub the toast with the halved garlic clove and the whole lemon, then cut the lemon in half and squeeze some juice over the sardines. Once the sardines are cooked, spread the chutney over the toast, cut the string off the sardines, place them on top and eat.

FISH OPTIONS: red mullet, herring, mackerel

Barbecued Sardines
with Boulangère Potatoes

SERVES 4

8 large whole sardines, boned
  (see page 296), with the head
  and tail removed
80ml olive oil
juice of 2 lemons
8 strips of lemon zest, taken
  off in long strips with a speed
  peeler (leaving behind all the
  bitter white pith)
8 small sprigs of rosemary
8 sprigs of thyme
4 garlic cloves, thinly sliced
4 round shallots, thinly sliced
80g butter
1 tbsp chopped thyme
1 tbsp chopped rosemary
Maldon salt and freshly
  ground black pepper

For the boulangère potatoes:
12 large Charlotte potatoes,
  washed
8 round shallots, sliced
2 bay leaves
2 tbsp chopped thyme
1 tbsp chopped rosemary
4 garlic cloves, sliced
50ml olive oil
300ml White Chicken Stock
  (see page 282)
60g butter
Maldon salt and freshly
  ground black pepper

1 First make the boulangère potatoes. Cut the potatoes widthways into 5mm slices. Put them into a bowl with the shallots, bay leaves, thyme, rosemary and garlic, and season with salt and pepper. Brush 2 small ceramic ovenproof dishes or small non-stick loaf/cake pans with olive oil, and put in the potatoes, pushing them down so they are evenly spread out. Pour over the chicken stock, dab with butter and sprinkle with a little more salt and pepper. Cover the dish with foil and place on the edge of a barbecue grill. Cook for about 45 minutes to an hour, rotating the dishes several times so the potatoes bake evenly.

2 Season the inside of the sardines with salt and pepper and drizzle with some olive oil and lemon juice. Inside each of the sardines place a strip of lemon zest, a sprig each of rosemary and thyme, some sliced garlic and shallots and sprinkle with a little more salt, pepper and olive oil. Brush the outside of the sardines with olive oil, rub with butter, then sprinkle with salt, pepper and the chopped herbs. Place each sardine on a 25cm square of foil, squeeze over a little more lemon juice, and wrap the fish up in the foil.

3 Towards the end of the cooking time for the potatoes, place the foil parcels on the edge of the barbecue grill and cook for about 12 minutes, turning them round every few minutes.

4 Serve the grilled sardines with the boulangère potatoes.

Grilling & Barbecuing

Whole Barbecued Red Mullet with Fennel

SERVES 4

4 x 300g red mullet, cleaned
    (see page 293)
2 large fennel bulbs
150ml olive oil
Maldon salt and freshly
    ground black pepper

For the marinade:
150ml olive oil
juice and grated zest of
    1 lemon
6 sprigs of thyme
6 sprigs of tarragon
6 sprigs of dill
8 basil leaves
4 garlic cloves, sliced

1 For the marinade, whisk the olive oil, lemon juice and zest together and rub them all over the fish so they are well coated. Mix the herbs and garlic together and place inside the belly of the fish and over the outside. Leave to marinate for at least 2 hours, or even overnight.

2 Cut each fennel bulb across its width into 4–6 pieces approximately 1cm thick. Sprinkle with the olive oil and season with salt and pepper on both sides. Put the fennel on a barbecue grill and cook for 6 minutes on each side. After a few minutes, season the mullet with salt and pepper and add to the grill, moving the fennel nearer the centre of the barbecue if necessary. Cook the mullet for about 6 minutes per side, being careful that both the fennel and the mullet don't become too dark. Serve at once.

FISH OPTIONS: red gurnard, megrim sole

Barbecued Split Lobster
with Garlic and Rosemary

4 x 400–500g lobsters
   (depending how hungry
   you are, half a lobster each
   may be enough)
a little lemon juice
Maldon salt and freshly
   ground black pepper

For the garlic and rosemary
   butter:
250g softened unsalted butter
20g garlic, finely chopped
80g shallots, finely chopped
1 tsp chopped parsley
2 tsp chopped rosemary
finely grated zest of 1 lemon
2 tbsp lemon juice
1½ tsp Maldon salt
a large pinch of black pepper

1 Place all the ingredients for the garlic and rosemary butter in a bowl and beat until smooth.

2 Kill and cook your lobsters (see page 300). Cut them in half, leaving the claws attached to the body. Season the flesh with salt and pepper, spread some of the garlic and rosemary butter on the tails and place on a barbecue grill, cut-side down, making sure the claws are towards the middle of the fire and the tails nearer the edge. Cook for 3 minutes, then turn and cook the other side for 3–4 minutes.

3 Melt the remaining garlic and rosemary butter in a small pan. Once the lobsters are ready, crack open the claws and dip them into the warm melted butter, squeezing a little lemon juice over before eating.

FISH OPTION: langoustines (allow 5 per person)

Grilling & Barbecuing

Barbecued Langoustines
with Olive Oil and Garlic

SERVES 4
20 langoustines

For the marinade:
25ml olive oil
8 garlic cloves, finely chopped
juice and grated zest of 1 lemon
½ tsp Maldon salt
a large pinch of freshly ground
    black pepper
2 tsp finely chopped rosemary
2 large pinches of smoked
    paprika, plus extra to serve

1 Whisk all the ingredients for the marinade together in a large bowl. Add the langoustines, turning so they are well coated in the marinade, and leave for 30–60 minutes.

2 Place the langoustines on a barbecue grill in a row, so they are easy to turn over with a pair of tongs. Cook for about 3 minutes on each side. To remove the meat, you can crack the shells using shellfish crackers or you can press down on the back of the shell and pull the shell off. Sprinkle on some extra paprika, if liked.

FISH OPTIONS: lobsters, prawns

Langoustine, scampi, Dublin Bay prawn, Norway lobster, nephrop – these are all names for this shellfish. The name Dublin Bay was bestowed because the fishing boats coming into Dublin Bay often had these prawns on board, having caught them incidentally. Since they were not fish, the fishermen would dispose of them on the side to the Dublin Bay street vendors.

The main part of the clam's meat is at the foot – it's the part the clam pushes into the sand to hold itself in place. However, the top part, which is white, is where you will find the sweetest meat.

Barbecued Razor Clams with Soy Dressing

SERVES 4 AS A STARTER
20 razor clams, cleaned
   (see page 305)

For the soy dressing:
200ml soy sauce
2 garlic cloves, finely chopped
20g fresh ginger, finely chopped
1 small red chilli, deseeded
   and finely chopped
50g caster sugar
25ml rice wine vinegar
juice of 2 limes
50ml sesame oil
1 tsp chopped coriander

1 First make the dressing. Put the soy sauce, garlic, ginger, chilli, sugar and rice wine vinegar in a small pan, bring to the boil, then reduce the heat and simmer for 2 minutes. Remove from the heat and leave to cool to room temperature. Add the lime juice, sesame oil and chopped coriander. Place the razor clams in a bowl, toss with the dressing and leave to marinate for an hour or so.
2 Put the clams on a barbecue grill, arranging them in rows, as this will make it easier to turn them over with tongs. Cook them for about 2 minutes on each side, brushing the inside of each one with more of the soy dressing when they start to open. When they are ready, dip them into the dressing and serve.

FISH OPTIONS: scallops, squid

Grilled or Barbecued Scallops
with Garlic and Lemon

SERVES 4
12 scallops in their shells,
   cleaned, coral removed
   (see page 304)
150ml olive oil
1 tsp lemon thyme leaves
juice and grated zest of
   2 lemons, plus a little extra
   lemon juice to finish
4 garlic cloves, finely chopped
½ tsp Maldon salt
a large pinch of freshly ground
   black pepper

Make sure that the shells and scallops are thoroughly clean. Place the olive oil, lemon thyme, lemon juice and zest, garlic, salt and pepper in a bowl and mix well. Tip all this mixture over the scallops in their shells and place under the grill (or straight onto the coals of a hot barbecue) for 6–8 minutes, depending on their size. Finish with a little lemon juice.

Grilling & Barbecuing

Baking & Roasting

Baking or roasting fish in the oven is one of the simplest ways of preparing it – you can have a delicious meal with very little effort and without having to spend hours in the kitchen. By placing your fish on a baking tray, adding some aromatic herbs or vegetables, some oil and seasoning and putting it in the oven, you can have supper on the table in under half an hour. What's more, the simplicity of this cooking means you let the fish's natural flavour do the work.

When you want to do a little more with your fish, the recipes in this chapter will give you ideas for different flavour combinations and will help you serve up a really fantastic meal – in minutes.

Baking & Roasting

Gurnard Fillets with Caper and Parsley Crumb

SERVES 4
60ml olive oil
8 x 80g gurnard fillets, scaled,
    filleted and pin boned
    (see pages 293, 294, 296)
Maldon salt and freshly
    ground black pepper

For the parsley crumb:
a large handful of parsley,
    leaves picked
250g fresh white breadcrumbs
20g unsalted butter
juice and grated zest of
    ½ lemon
2 garlic cloves, finely chopped
a large pinch of freshly ground
    white pepper
1 tsp Maldon salt
20ml olive oil
½ tsp chopped rosemary
40g capers, drained, rinsed
    and chopped

1 To make the parsley crumb, put all the crumb ingredients, except the capers, into a blender or food processor and blitz until the crumbs are green and everything is coarsely chopped. Alternatively, you can place all the ingredients in a mixing bowl and rub together with your fingertips (though the crumbs may not become as green this way). Either way, when you have your crumbs, add the chopped capers.

2 Pour the olive oil on to a baking tray and sprinkle with salt and pepper. Add the gurnard fillets, season with salt and pepper, and cover with the parsley crumb mixture. Bake in an oven preheated to 180°C/Gas Mark 4 for 8–10 minutes, then remove from the oven and sprinkle with a little lemon juice.

FISH OPTIONS: line-caught sea bass, red mullet, sea trout

Baking & Roasting

Baked Gurnard with Chilli

SERVES 4

4 x 400g gurnard, scaled
    and gutted (see page 293)
100ml olive oil
60g unsalted butter
2 red chillies, deseeded and
    finely chopped
120g coriander, leaves picked
    and chopped, stems reserved
finely grated zest and juice of
    2 limes
2 tsp Maldon salt
a large pinch of freshly ground
    black pepper
zest of 2 limes, taken off in large
    strips with a speed peeler
8 lime leaves, cut in quarters
4 stems of lemongrass, chopped

1 Make 4 slashes down each side of the gurnard and rub the inside of the slashes with half the olive oil. Push the butter, finely chopped chillies, coriander leaves and grated lime zest into the slashes, and season with salt and pepper. Put the coriander stems, lime zest strips, lime leaves and lemongrass inside the belly of the fish, filling the cavity.

2 Cut 4 x 30cm squares of baking parchment and rub them with the rest of the olive oil. Place a gurnard on each piece of parchment and drizzle with a little lime juice. Carefully fold the parchment over and secure with staples or paper clips – you should end up with a little rectangle with the fish inside (see page 125 for picture).

3 Place the gurnard on a baking tray and bake in an oven preheated to 180°C/Gas Mark 4 for 16 minutes. When you tear open the paper be careful of the steam, as it will be very hot (and will smell amazing).

FISH OPTIONS: line-caught sea bass, red mullet, sea trout

Gurnard Baked with Dill

SERVES 4

4 x 400g gurnard, scaled,
    gutted and filleted
    (see pages 293, 294)
100ml olive oil
1 tsp Maldon salt
a large pinch of freshly ground
    black pepper
1 tbsp chopped dill
1 tsp dill seeds
1 tsp crushed fennel seeds
1 fennel bulb, very thinly sliced
60g unsalted butter
8 star anise
juice and finely grated zest
    of 1 lemon
100ml white wine

1 Brush the gurnard fillets on both sides with half the olive oil. Season with the salt and pepper, and sprinkle with the chopped dill, dill seeds and fennel seeds.

2 Cut 4 x 30cm squares of baking parchment and brush with the rest of the olive oil. Place some of the sliced fennel in the centre of each piece of parchment, then place 2 gurnard fillets on top. Dab with the butter, add the star anise, and sprinkle over the lemon juice and zest. Spoon the wine over the fish, then carefully fold over the parchment and secure with staples or paper clips – you should end up with a little rectangle with the fish inside (see page 125 for picture).

3 Place the gurnard on a baking tray and bake for 12 minutes in an oven preheated to 180°C/Gas Mark 4. Be careful when you tear open the paper, as the steam will be very hot.

FISH OPTIONS: red mullet, trout

Baking & Roasting

You may think the combination of fish and meat is a strange one, but I've always enjoyed it as the texture and taste complement each other very well. This dish is quite rich, but utterly delicious!

Scallops with Roast Pork Belly and Balsamic Jus

SERVES 4

8 scallops, out of the shell,
   roe removed (see page 304)
100ml olive oil
20g unsalted butter
juice of ½ lemon
Maldon salt and freshly
   ground black pepper

For the roast pork belly:
1 kg fresh pork belly
4 tsp Maldon salt
1 tsp sugar
1 tsp chopped thyme
1 tsp rosemary leaves
8 black peppercorns, crushed
2 garlic cloves
a large pinch of nutmeg
6 cloves
6 juniper berries
1 bay leaf, chopped

For the balsamic jus:
20g unsalted butter
250g shallots, finely chopped
2 garlic cloves, finely chopped
1 bay leaf
1 tsp chopped thyme
200ml balsamic vinegar
400ml Brown Chicken Stock
   (see page 282, or use
   good-quality bought stock
   such as Joubère)

1 Put the pork belly into a shallow dish. Place all the other pork belly ingredients in a blender or food processor and blitz to a coarse powder, then rub the mix liberally all over the pork and put into the fridge to marinate for 6 hours or overnight.

2 When you are ready to cook the pork, rub off the marinade, place the pork on a wire rack in an oven preheated to 120°C/Gas Mark ½, and cook for 3 hours, until the fat is nicely rendered and golden. If you want to crisp up the skin you can do this by carefully putting it under a hot grill, which will make the skin bubble up and become nice and crispy. Once the pork is cooked, with a sharp knife remove the crackling from the meat to make it easier to slice. Cut the pork into 1cm slices and set aside while you make the balsamic jus and cook the scallops.

3 Melt the butter in a pan and add the shallots, garlic, bay leaf and thyme. Cook for 2–3 minutes, until just soft, then add the balsamic vinegar and simmer until syrupy. Add the stock and simmer until reduced to the level of the shallots, then taste and add a pinch of salt and pepper.

4 Heat a large non-stick sauté pan, or a flat-top griddle if you have one, until it is nice and hot. Season the scallops with salt and pepper, drizzle them with olive oil and cook for about 3 minutes on one side, until golden. Add the butter, flip them over with a spatula, and cook for another 3 minutes. Finally, squeeze over a little lemon juice.

5 Serve the scallops with the roast pork belly, and with the balsamic jus poured over.

Salmon Baked on Parchment with Capers and Caper Beurre Noisette

SERVES 4

600g good-quality farmed salmon fillet such as Loch Duart, sliced very thinly, almost carpaccio style (see page 62)
100ml olive oil
1 tsp Maldon salt
a large pinch of freshly ground black pepper
40g capers, drained, rinsed and chopped
40g unsalted butter
juice and grated zest of 1 lemon

For the caper butter:
150g unsalted butter
100ml olive oil
250g banana shallots, sliced lengthways
4 garlic cloves, finely diced
2 tsp chopped thyme
2 bay leaves
1 tsp Maldon salt
a large pinch of freshly ground black pepper
80g capers, drained and rinsed
50ml white wine vinegar
50ml lemon juice
2 lemons, divided into segments
1 heaped tsp chopped flatleaf parsley

1 To make the caper butter, you first need to make a beurre noisette. Put the butter into a hot pan over a high heat. When it bubbles, keep it on the heat for a couple of minutes until it is golden brown in colour. Put the olive oil into another pan over a medium heat, add the shallots, garlic, thyme and bay leaves, and cook slowly for 2–3 minutes without letting the vegetables colour. Add the brown butter to the pan, stir in the salt and pepper, capers, vinegar, lemon juice and lemon segments, and heat gently. Finally, add the chopped parsley and set the sauce aside to keep warm while you cook the salmon.

2 Heat the oven to 200°C/Gas Mark 6 and put a baking tray in to get hot. Cut 4 pieces of baking parchment into 20cm squares and lay them out on a board. Drizzle the parchment with a little of the olive oil and sprinkle with salt and pepper and the capers. Lay the salmon slices on top, slightly overlapping, and season with more salt and pepper. Drizzle with more olive oil and sprinkle with the lemon zest and juice.

3 Open the oven and carefully place the salmon, still on its parchment squares, directly onto the hot tray. Close the oven quickly and cook for 2–3 minutes, until the fish is just cooked but still pink. Remove from the oven, take the salmon off the tray and flip it over on to dinner plates, peeling back the paper so that the capers are on the top. Spoon over the caper butter, and serve.

FISH OPTIONS: line-caught sea bass, halibut, sea trout

Baking & Roasting

This is a quick and easy dish which uses simple ingredients. It's pan-fried then baked, which I think adds flavour, but you can just bake it if you prefer and avoid the fuss of pan-frying.

Sea Bass with Ginger and Lime

SERVES 4

80ml olive oil
juice and grated zest of 2 limes
40g fresh ginger, finely chopped
2 garlic cloves, finely chopped
1 red chilli, deseeded and finely chopped
40g unsalted butter
4 x 160g sea bass fillets

For the lime and ginger vinaigrette:

2 banana shallots, finely chopped
1 garlic clove, finely chopped
1 tbsp sugar
1 tbsp clear honey
1 heaped tbsp finely chopped ginger
juice and grated zest of 2 limes
½ small red chilli, deseeded and finely chopped
2 tbsp chopped coriander

1 To make the lime and ginger vinaigrette, whisk all the ingredients together.

2 Put the oil, lime juice and zest, ginger, garlic and chilli into a bowl, season with salt and pepper, and whisk together. Add the sea bass fillets and put into the fridge for 1–2 hours to marinate.

3 Heat the oven to 180°C/Gas Mark 4 and heat an ovenproof frying pan on the stove. When it is hot, remove the sea bass fillets from their marinade and add to the pan, skin-side down. Cook on a medium high heat for 4–5 minutes, until the edges start to turn golden, pressing down on the skin for the first minute or so to prevent them shrinking and curling up. Transfer the pan to the hot oven and cook the sea bass for a further 6 minutes, then remove and add the butter and a squeeze of lime juice.

4 Serve the sea bass immediately, drizzled with the lime and ginger vinaigrette.

FISH OPTIONS: good-quality farmed salmon such as Loch Duart, red mullet

Sales of farmed fish have grown by 11 per cent a year since 1984, making it the world's fastest-growing food sector. In 2001 some 29 per cent of all fish and shellfish eaten were farmed and the UN's Food and Agriculture Organization has predicted that farming will have to grow sevenfold in the next 25 years just to maintain the world's consumption of fish.

However, we must encourage fisheries to take more responsibility for conserving coastal waters, developing operational practices that are environmentally friendly, and urge governments to look more holistically at aquaculture and its effects on marine ecosystems before it allows the practice to expand.

Baking & Roasting

Sea Bass Baked with Peppers and Thyme

SERVES 4
4 x 160g sea bass fillets
80ml olive oil, plus a little for
  the baking parchment
grated zest and juice of 1 lemon
2 garlic cloves, finely chopped
1 tbsp chopped thyme
1 tbsp chopped rosemary
2 sprigs of basil, leaves picked
  and finely sliced
100ml white wine
Maldon salt and freshly ground
  black pepper

For the peppers:
80ml olive oil
40g unsalted butter
1 medium onion, thinly sliced
4 garlic cloves, thinly sliced
1 bay leaf
1 tbsp thyme leaves
1 tsp chopped rosemary
1 tsp salt
a large pinch of freshly ground
  black pepper
2 red peppers, deseeded and
  thinly sliced
2 yellow peppers, deseeded
  and thinly sliced
25g sugar
150ml white wine vinegar
2 sprigs of basil, leaves picked
  and finely sliced

1 Put the sea bass fillets into a shallow dish. Mix the oil, lemon zest and juice, garlic and herbs in a bowl, then brush this all over the fillets and put into the fridge to marinate for at least 2 hours or overnight.

2 To cook the peppers, put the olive oil and butter into a sauté pan over a medium heat. Add the onion, garlic, bay leaf, thyme, rosemary, salt and black pepper and cook for 3 minutes with the lid on, without letting the onions colour. Add the red and yellow peppers and cook for 10 minutes, again without colouring, then add the sugar and vinegar and cook until nearly evaporated. Remove from the heat, leave to cool, and stir in the basil.

3 Cut a piece of baking parchment 30cm square and brush one third of it with olive oil. Sprinkle it with salt and pepper and lay the peppers on it in a rectangular shape. Remove the sea bass fillets from their marinade, season with salt and pepper and place on top of the peppers. Pour over the wine, then fold over the parchment and secure with staples or paper clips – you should end up with a little rectangle with the fish inside (see page 125 for picture). Bake in an oven preheated to 180°C/Gas Mark 4 for 10 minutes.

FISH OPTIONS: John Dory, black bream, grey mullet

Sea Bass Baked in Foil with White Wine and Peppercorns

SERVES 4

1 x 2kg sea bass, scaled,
    gutted and fins removed
    (see pages 293, 297)
1 tsp Maldon salt
50g unsalted butter
1 fennel bulb, very thinly sliced
a small bunch of dill
grated zest of 2 lemons
20 black peppercorns, finely
    crushed
6 star anise
juice of 1 lemon
6 thyme sprigs
2 bay leaves, cut in half
150ml white wine
100ml olive oil

1 Rub the sea bass inside and out with the salt. Take a piece of foil large enough to wrap round the fish and smear half the butter over it. Place half the fennel, dill, lemon zest, peppercorns and star anise on top, then place the fish on top of that. Squeeze the lemon juice over the fish and place the remaining fennel, dill, pepper and star anise on top, with the thyme sprigs and bay leaves. Drizzle with the white wine and olive oil. Bring the foil up around the fish and scrunch the edges to seal.

2 Place on a baking tray and cook for 20 minutes in an oven preheated to 180°C/Gas Mark 4. Be careful when opening the foil, as it will steam quite a lot. Serve with a crisp green salad.

FISH OPTIONS: pouting, gurnard, monkfish

Whole Sea Bass Baked with Basil

SERVES 4

2 x 1kg sea bass, scaled,
    gutted and fins removed
    (see pages 293, 297)
100ml olive oil
a bunch of basil, leaves
    picked, stems reserved
6 bay leaves, cut in half
8 garlic cloves, cut in half
1 tsp chopped thyme
1 tsp chopped rosemary
juice and grated zest of
    2 lemons
25g unsalted butter
Maldon salt and pepper

1 Give the sea bass a good rinse in cold water to remove any stray scales, and dry it on kitchen paper. Season the inside of the fish with salt and pepper, drizzle the inside with some of the olive oil, and place the basil stems inside the cavity.

2 Place the fish on its side and make 4 to 6 slashes on each side, spaced evenly apart, going from the head down to the tail. Push some of the basil leaves, bay leaves and garlic into each of the slashes, and rub the outside of the fish with more of the olive oil. Season with salt and pepper and rub with the thyme and rosemary, then scatter over the lemon zest and dab both sides of the fish with butter.

3 Place the fish on a baking tray brushed with olive oil and bake in an oven preheated to 180°C/Gas Mark 4 for 10 minutes. Flip the fish over and cook for a further 10 minutes, then remove from the oven and squeeze over some lemon juice before serving.

FISH OPTIONS: monkfish tail, sea trout

Baking & Roasting

Baked Sea Bass with Sesame

SERVES 4
4 x 160g sea bass fillets
60ml sesame oil
½ tsp pink peppercorns,
   crushed
2 tbsp toasted sesame seeds
2 limes
1 tbsp chopped coriander
Maldon salt

For the soy marinade:
300ml soy sauce
3 garlic cloves, finely chopped
40g finely chopped ginger
1 small red chilli, deseeded
   and finely chopped
80g soft brown sugar
juice and grated zest of
   2 limes
60ml sesame oil
1 heaped tbsp chopped
   coriander

1 To make the soy marinade, put the soy sauce, garlic, ginger, chilli and sugar into a small pan over a low heat and simmer until reduced by half and slightly syrupy. Take off the heat and set aside to cool to room temperature. When cool, add the lime juice and zest, sesame oil and coriander.

2 Cut 4 rectangular pieces of baking parchment a bit bigger than your fish fillets and brush them with sesame oil. Put the sea bass fillets on a board and cut them into thin slices at an angle. Place them on the parchment in neat rows, slightly overlapping. Brush the slices with the soy marinade, season with a little salt and crushed pink peppercorns, and leave to marinate for an hour or so.

3 Heat the oven to 180°C/Gas Mark 4 and put a baking tray in to get very hot. Put the slices of bass, still on their baking parchment, on the hot baking tray, put back into the oven and cook for about 6–8 minutes. While they are baking, brush them with the marinade a couple of times more so they get a nice coating of soy. Once they are cooked, remove from the oven and sprinkle with a few sesame seeds, a squeeze of lime juice and some chopped coriander. If you like you can serve the rest of the marinade alongside as a dipping sauce.

FISH OPTIONS: red mullet, gurnard

I'm afraid I had to include a few more complicated dishes and this is one of them. It is an extravagant dish – probably one for a special occasion – but I think you'll agree that both the work involved and the wait is definitely worth it.

Lobster Pancakes with Mustard and Gruyère Béchamel

SERVES 4

4 x 400–500g lobsters, cooked and prepared (see page 300)
1 tbsp each chopped chives, dill, parsley and chervil
80g grated Gruyère cheese
Maldon salt and freshly ground black pepper

For the pancakes:
100g plain flour
2 large eggs
250ml milk
25g unsalted butter, melted, plus a little for cooking the pancakes
1 tbsp vegetable oil
1 tbsp each chopped chives, dill, parsley and chervil
Maldon salt and freshly ground black pepper

For the white wine and grain mustard sauce:
80g unsalted butter
150g shallots, finely chopped
2 garlic cloves, finely chopped
1 bay leaf
150ml white wine
400ml Fish Stock (see page 280)
400ml double cream
2 tbsp chopped tarragon leaves
120g wholegrain mustard
10g Dijon mustard
5 spring onions, thinly sliced
25g Gruyère cheese, grated

1 To make the pancake batter, put the flour into a bowl with a little seasoning and stir to mix. Whisk the eggs and milk together, add to the flour, then pass the mixture through a fine sieve. Stir in the butter, oil and chopped herbs, set aside for 2 hours.
2 To make the pancakes, heat a small non-stick crêpe pan or sauté pan on a medium heat and add a teaspoon of butter, tipping the pan so it coats the bottom. Add a small ladle of batter and swirl this around the base of the pan to make a very thin layer. When the pancake starts to colour around the edges, which will take a minute or so, flip it over with a spatula and cook it for a minute longer. Slide the cooked pancake onto a piece of baking parchment, and repeat the process until you have used up all the batter, layering the cooked pancakes between more pieces of baking parchment. You should get about 12 pancakes from this quantity of mixture.
3 To make the sauce, melt the butter in a pan and add the shallots, garlic and bay leaf. Cook for 3 minutes, until soft, then add the white wine and reduce by two thirds. Add the fish stock and reduce by half. Add the cream and reduce by half again, then add the chopped tarragon and the wholegrain and Dijon mustards. Stir in the spring onions and grated cheese and set the sauce aside.
4 Cut the lobster meat into 1.5cm dice and place in a bowl. Add the herbs and stir in enough of the sauce to bind the lobster meat. Season with salt and pepper. Take one of the pancakes and place it on a board in front of you, then place a line of the lobster filling down the centre. Fold the pancake over and roll it into a cigar shape. Fill the rest of the pancakes the same way – you should be able to make about 8 altogether.
5 Brush an ovenproof dish with butter and spread with a thin coating of the sauce. Arrange the rolled pancakes on top, spread over the remaining sauce and sprinkle with the Gruyère. Bake in an oven preheated to 180°C/Gas Mark 4 for 10 minutes, then put the dish under a hot grill until golden and bubbling.

FISH OPTION: langoustines

This has only two main ingredients – fish and egg – but it's the sauce that makes it really special. Its fantastic flavour comes from the heat of the paprika and the acidity of the capers, which help cut through the hot spice and lighten the dish.

Whiting with Poached Eggs, Capers and Paprika

SERVES 4

2 x 800g whiting, filleted
   (see page 294)
100ml olive oil
1 tsp Maldon salt
a large pinch of freshly ground
   black pepper
4 large pinches of paprika
juice and grated zest of 1 lemon
1 tsp unsalted butter

For the poached eggs:
50ml white wine vinegar
3 heaped tsp Maldon salt
4 large organic or free-range
   eggs
a pinch of paprika
freshly ground black pepper

For the sauce:
100g unsalted butter
100g shallots, finely diced
4 pinches of smoked paprika
2 garlic cloves, finely chopped
60g capers, rinsed, dried and
   chopped
1 lemon, peeled, segmented
   and cut into little squares
1 tbsp chopped parsley
Maldon salt and freshly
   ground black pepper

1 Brush the whiting fillets with the olive oil and season with salt and pepper. Rub the paprika and lemon zest into the flesh and put a dab of butter on top of each fillet. Place the fish on a non-stick baking tray and bake in an oven preheated to 180°C/Gas Mark 4 for 8–10 minutes.

2 Meanwhile, poach the eggs. Fill a medium pan three-quarters full with water and bring to a simmer. Add the vinegar and salt – this will help hold the eggs together when poaching. Crack each egg into a small ramekin. When the water is simmering, whisk it in one direction in a circular motion, creating a whirlpool in the pan, and add the eggs one by one – they will spin round, which gives them an even round shape. They will gently settle at the bottom of the pan and you may need to move them slightly with a spatula so they do not stick to each other. Cook for 3–4 minutes, then remove with a slotted spoon and drain on kitchen paper. Season with salt, pepper and a little pinch of paprika.

3 For the sauce, place the butter in a pan over a medium heat and let it foam. After 3–4 minutes, it will start to go brown. As soon as the foaming begins to slow down, add the chopped shallots and paprika. Sauté for a couple of minutes, until the shallots are just cooked, then add the garlic, capers, lemon and parsley and season with salt and pepper.

4 When the fish is cooked, remove it from the oven and squeeze over the lemon juice. Place a poached egg in each serving dish, put the whiting on top and spoon the sauce over.

FISH OPTIONS: pollack, gurnard

Baking & Roasting

Baked Red Mullet with Artichokes and Basil

SERVES 4

4 x 250g red mullet, gutted
   and fins removed
   (see page 293)
20 basil leaves
4 garlic cloves, thinly sliced
100ml olive oil
Maldon salt and freshly
   ground black pepper
juice of ½ lemon

For the fresh pesto:
125g fresh basil
100g pine nuts
150g Parmesan cheese,
   grated
9 garlic cloves
a large pinch of freshly
   ground black pepper
1½ tsp Maldon salt
400ml olive oil

For the roasted artichokes:
16 baby artichokes
150ml olive oil
50g unsalted butter
1 tsp Maldon salt
a pinch of freshly ground
   black pepper
1 heaped tsp chopped thyme
2 small sprigs of rosemary
4 garlic cloves, cut in half
200ml White Chicken Stock
   (see page 282)
4 sprigs of basil, leaves
   picked and finely sliced

1 Everything must be as cold as possible before you start making the pesto, so put the blade of your food processor into the freezer for an hour or so beforehand. If you don't do this, the processor can get too warm when puréeing and the basil may discolour. Place all the pesto ingredients in the processor and purée for 30 seconds. Set aside in the fridge.

2 To prepare the artichokes, pull off the outer leaves and cut off the tops, leaving just the heart. Peel the hearts with a vegetable peeler until they are smooth and no dark green areas are left. Cut the stalk, leaving 8cm attached. Peel the stalks until they are nice and white, and cut the artichokes carefully in half.

3 Heat the olive oil and half the butter in a sauté pan over a medium heat and add the artichokes, putting them in alternately stalk up and stalk down so they fit tightly. Season with the salt and pepper and add the thyme, rosemary and garlic. Cook for 8–10 minutes, then turn the artichokes over and cook for another 8–10 minutes, until golden. Add the stock and simmer until reduced by two thirds. Add the remaining butter and the basil and keep the artichokes warm while you cook the fish.

4 Put 5 basil leaves inside each mullet and divide the sliced garlic between them. Tie the mullet round the middle with string. Brush with olive oil and season with salt and pepper. Place the fish on a non-stick baking tray and bake in an oven preheated to 190°C/Gas Mark 5 for about 15–16 minutes, brushing them from time to time with the cooking juices and turning them over halfway through.

5 When the mullet are cooked, remove them from the oven, squeeze over some lemon juice, cut off the string and serve with the roasted artichokes and pesto.

FISH OPTIONS: grey mullet, mackerel

Baking & Roasting

Baked Mullet Fillets with Oregano and Roast Chicory

SERVES 4

4 x 250g red mullet, gutted and
    filleted (see page 293, 294)
80ml olive oil
juice and grated zest of 1 orange
2 round shallots, finely chopped
2 garlic cloves, finely chopped
2 tbsp chopped oregano leaves
2 bay leaves, cut in half
Maldon salt and freshly ground
    black pepper

For the roast chicory:
4 whole chicory
40g brown sugar
1 tsp Maldon salt
a large pinch of freshly ground
    black pepper
60g unsalted butter 200ml
    orange juice

1 Peel a few outer leaves from the chicory and cut in half lengthways. Place a shallow pan on a medium heat and sprinkle the sugar in the bottom. Add the chicory and cook slowly for about 25 minutes, covered with a circle of greaseproof paper. When they are caramelised, add the salt and pepper and the butter and swirl it around the pan. Pour in the orange juice and cook slowly until the chicory are soft. Then turn up the heat and simmer until the liquid is reduced enough to coat the chicory.
2 Brush the mullet fillets with the olive oil and season with salt and pepper. Put them on a non-stick baking tray, squeeze over the orange juice and scatter the zest over the top. Add the shallots, garlic, oregano and bay leaves and bake in an oven preheated to 180°C/Gas Mark 4 for 8 minutes. Serve with the roast chicory.

FISH OPTIONS: grey mullet, sardines

The Romans loved the redness of red mullet and used to keep them alive for as long as possible, bringing them to the table in a huge glass bowl and then killing and cooking them pretty much to order. As soon as red mullet are killed, the red shade starts to fade quite quickly, with the fish going through a rapid and beautiful series of colour changes while dying. Considerable changes in colouration also occur depending on the time of day, stress and condition of the fish. Mullet can change to a darker pink when it is irritated or confronted with danger and the yellow banding along the sides of the fish tends to become mottled in the dark, with the whole body also taking on a more yellow hue.

Baked Plaice with Lemon Peel and Lemon Risotto

SERVES 4

80g unsalted butter

2 tsp thyme leaves

4 bay leaves, cut in half

4 garlic cloves, sliced

zest of 2 lemons, taken off in thin strips with a speed peeler

½ tsp Maldon salt

a large pinch of freshly ground black pepper

1 x 1.2kg plaice, cleaned (see page 293)

80ml olive oil

100ml white wine

juice of 1 lemon

For the lemon risotto:

550ml White Chicken Stock (see page 282)

50g unsalted butter

50ml olive oil

150g shallots, finely diced

1½ tsp Maldon salt

a large pinch of freshly ground black pepper

4 garlic cloves, finely chopped

½ tsp chopped thyme

1 bay leaf

zest of 1 lemon, taken off in large strips with a speed peeler

200g risotto rice

175ml white wine

finely grated zest of 1 lemon

1 tbsp lemon juice

50ml crème fraîche

50g Parmesan cheese, freshly grated

1 Use most of the butter to grease a large, shallow, non-stick baking tray. Scatter half the thyme, bay leaves, garlic, lemon zest strips, salt and pepper over it, then put the plaice on top. Put the rest of the seasonings on top of the fish, drizzle with the oil, white wine and lemon juice, then add a few specks of the remaining butter and some more seasoning. Cover the tray with foil and set aside while you start cooking the risotto.

2 Put the stock into a pan, bring to a simmer and keep warm. Heat the butter and oil in a heavy-based pan, add the shallots, half the salt and pepper, the garlic, thyme, bay leaf and lemon zest strips, then cover and cook gently until the shallots are soft, without letting them colour. Add the rice and cook for 2 minutes, stirring all the time, until the oil has been absorbed.

3 At this point, put the tray containing the plaice into an oven preheated to 180°C/Gas Mark 4 and bake for 15–20 minutes.

4 Add the white wine to the rice and cook for a minute or so, until it has all evaporated, then slowly add the hot stock over a fairly low heat, little by little, stirring every minute or so. After about 16–18 minutes, the rice should be almost cooked. Add the grated lemon zest, lemon juice, crème fraîche and Parmesan. Adjust the seasoning with the remaining salt and pepper if needed. Cook for 2 minutes and serve with the baked plaice.

FISH OPTIONS: lemon sole, flounder, halibut

Baking & Roasting

This is a very healthy way of cooking fish as it uses relatively little oil. Ideally I would serve it very simply with some steamed vegetables.

Flounder in a Bag with Baked Cherry Tomatoes and Basil

SERVES 4

150ml olive oil, plus extra
  for brushing
grated zest of 2 lemons
2 garlic cloves, finely chopped
1 tsp chopped thyme
1 tsp chopped rosemary
4 x 120g flounder fillets
12 basil leaves
Maldon salt and freshly
  ground black pepper

For the baked cherry tomatoes:
600g cherry tomatoes on
  the vine, cut in half
6 garlic cloves, finely sliced
1 tsp chopped thyme
20g icing sugar
200ml olive oil
2 tsp Maldon salt
a large pinch of freshly
  ground black pepper

For the tomato and caper sauce:
400ml Thick Tomato Sauce
  (see page 288)
50g unsalted butter, diced
60g capers, rinsed and dried
100g mixed green and black
  olives, dried on kitchen paper
  and roughly chopped
20ml lemon juice
10 basil leaves, finely sliced
80ml extra virgin olive oil

1 For the fish, mix the oil in a bowl with the lemon zest, garlic, thyme and rosemary. Drizzle the flounder fillets all over with this mixture and put into the fridge to marinate for at least 2 hours or overnight.

2 Place the tomato halves on a baking tray, add the garlic, thyme, icing sugar, olive oil, salt and pepper, and just lightly mix everything together, making sure the tomatoes are all facing cut-side upwards. Place in an oven preheated to 90°C (or the lowest possible gas mark) and bake for 1½–2 hours.

3 Take 4 sheets of baking parchment about 30cm square and lay them on a work surface. Brush half of each sheet with olive oil and sprinkle with salt and pepper. Season the flounder fillets with salt and pepper, lay some basil leaves over one half of each fillet, then fold them over so that the basil is enclosed. Arrange the baked tomatoes in a rectangle on the oiled parchment and place the fillets on top. Fold over the parchment to cover the fish, fold in each side and secure with staples or paper clips – you should end up with a little rectangle with the fish inside (see page 125 for picture). Place in an oven preheated to 180°C/Gas Mark 4 and bake for about 6 minutes.

4 Meanwhile, gently heat the thick tomato sauce and whisk in the butter a little at a time. Stir in the capers, olives, lemon juice and basil, then drizzle in the olive oil. Serve the fish and tomatoes still in their parchment, with the sauce on the side.

FISH OPTIONS: pollack, coley

Baking & Roasting

This recipe can really be made with any type of fish.
You could say it's a modern twist on fish and chips.

Flounder Fillets with Baked Charlotte Potatoes and Garlic

SERVES 4
100ml olive oil
4 x 120g flounder fillets
3 garlic cloves, finely chopped
1 tsp thyme leaves
juice of 1 lemon
Maldon salt and freshly
  ground black pepper

For the baked Charlotte
  potatoes:
16–20 medium Charlotte
  potatoes, washed, dried
  and cut into 3
80ml olive oil
12 garlic cloves, unpeeled
2 bay leaves
1 sprig of rosemary, leaves
  picked and chopped
1 tsp thyme leaves
2 tsp Maldon salt
a large pinch of freshly ground
  black pepper
40g unsalted butter, melted

1 Place the potatoes in a bowl and add the olive oil, garlic, herbs, salt and pepper. Mix well, then transfer to a baking tray or roasting pan and bake for 45–60 minutes in an oven preheated to 170°C/Gas Mark 3, rotating the tray every 15 minutes and giving the potatoes a stir so they bake evenly and do not burn.
2 Meanwhile, lay 4 x 25cm squares of foil on a baking tray and brush with olive oil. Place the flounder fillets on the foil squares, brush with olive oil and sprinkle with the garlic, thyme, salt and pepper. About 8 minutes before you think the potatoes are going to be ready, take them out of the oven and add the butter. Return the potatoes to the oven with the tray of flounder fillets and bake for the final 8 minutes. Finish the flounder with a squeeze of lemon juice, and serve with the baked Charlotte potatoes.

FISH OPTIONS: brill, megrim sole

There have been reports on fishing in which conservation groups have been quoted saying there will be no fish in the sea by 2045 and world seafood could run out by 2048. That is hopefully an exaggeration of the truth but we need to be putting measures in place now to guarantee this will not happen. Everyone in the UK has a right to expect that the sea will be managed for sustainability to ensure we can continue to enjoy every single species of fish.

Boat to buyer traceability can, and has, transformed parts of the industry's accountability: more and more of us are wanting stricter guarantees of where something has come from so that we know that the fish we are eating is not a species with low stock levels and has been reared in a manner that will not be harmful to ourselves, the planet or the livelihood of fishermen.

Would it not be best to give more ownership and responsibility of the industry's future to the people who are out at sea day in, day out – those who know what's in the sea and can see evidence of the declining stock levels? Seeking regional knowledge and working with fishermen has certainly given me a real insight into how some of the process works and what life is like for these hard-working men and women and I would urge others to seek it too.

It is up to the processors, caterers, chefs and consumers to demand better-sourced and traceable supplies and to use this information as a tool to promote sustainability.

Baking & Roasting

This is a really versatile dish that works well at any time of the day – even breakfast! You can prepare it in advance of when it's needed so it's ideal for picnics or for when unexpected guests drop by.

Smoked Haddock and Spinach Tart
with Grain Mustard

SERVES 6–8

For the pastry:
225g plain flour
½ tsp Maldon salt
a pinch of freshly ground black pepper
1½ tsp chopped thyme
100g cold unsalted butter, diced
1 egg, lightly beaten
25ml iced water
beaten egg, to glaze

For the smoked haddock:
700ml milk
10 sprigs of thyme
12 white peppercorns
2 garlic cloves, cut in half
2 bay leaves
a pinch of Maldon salt
300g smoked haddock fillet

For the spinach:
30g unsalted butter
2 garlic cloves, peeled and cut in half
6 spring onions, thinly sliced
300g baby spinach leaves
a pinch of freshly grated nutmeg
Maldon salt and freshly ground black pepper

For the custard:
2 eggs
3 egg yolks
50ml crème fraîche
125ml double cream
2 large tbsp wholegrain mustard
a pinch of freshly grated nutmeg
Maldon salt and freshly ground black pepper

1 First make the pastry. Sift the flour and salt into a large bowl and add the pepper, thyme and butter. Rub the butter in with your fingertips until the mixture looks like small breadcrumbs. Make a well in the centre, add the egg and the iced water, then stir until it all comes together into a dough, adding a little more water if necessary to bind. Wrap in clingfilm and leave in the fridge to rest for about 45 minutes.

2 Roll out the pastry on a lightly floured surface to 3–4mm thick. Pick it up by rolling it loosely around the rolling pin and lay it over a 24cm loose-bottomed tart tin. Using the back of one finger and the fingertips of your other hand, push the pastry all the way round the tin so it fits tightly into the edges. Trim the edge of the pastry so it comes half way over the sides of the tin (you need an overlap to trim off later). Leave in the fridge to rest for about 10 minutes.

3 Line the pastry case with baking parchment and fill with baking beans; this helps the pastry to hold its shape during baking. Place on a baking sheet in an oven preheated to 180°C/Gas Mark 4 and bake for 15 minutes, until the edges of the pastry are golden. Remove from the oven and leave to cool for 10 minutes, then lift out the beans and paper. Brush the pastry with beaten egg and return it to the oven for 5 minutes to dry out; if there are any cracks or little holes in the pastry, the egg will seal them. Remove from the oven and set aside.

4 To cook the smoked haddock, bring the milk to a simmer in a pan, then add all the rest of the ingredients. Bring back to a simmer, then take the pan off the heat and set aside for 5 minutes. Remove the smoked haddock to a plate with a slotted spoon, then strain the poaching liquid and set aside. When the fish has cooled to room temperature, flake it into large pieces, removing the skin and any bones.

5 To cook the spinach, melt the butter in a large pan, add the garlic and cook for a minute to bring out the flavour. Stir in the spring onions, cook for a minute longer, then add the spinach, nutmeg and some salt and pepper. Turn the heat up high and cook for a couple of minutes, until the spinach is just wilted. Transfer immediately to a colander and squeeze out the excess liquid. Place on a tray lined with kitchen paper to dry.

6 To make the custard, whisk the eggs and yolks together in a bowl, then whisk in the crème fraîche, cream and 125ml of the strained haddock poaching milk. Season with the wholegrain mustard, nutmeg and some salt and pepper.

7 Arrange the spinach in the pastry case so it just covers the base, and put the haddock on top. Pour the custard mixture over everything. Place in an oven preheated to 170°C/Gas Mark 3 and bake for 25–30 minutes, until the custard is just set but still a little wobbly when you move the tart tin – any more than that and it will be overcooked by the time it cools. Once the tart is ready, leave it to cool to room temperature, then carefully, with a knife, scrape away the excess pastry overhanging the edge. Remove the tart from the tin and it is ready to serve.

FISH OPTIONS: smoked salmon, smoked mackerel

A smoked sausage such as Morteaux really adds a distinct flavour to this dish. If you are unable to find smoked sausage, I suggest you leave it out altogether, as the flavour won't be the same.

Roast Cod with Choucroute and Morteaux Sausage

SERVES 4

4 x 160g MSC-certified or handline-caught cod fillets
40g plain flour
100ml olive oil
40g unsalted butter
150g shallots, finely diced
1 tbsp black peppercorns, finely crushed
1 heaped tsp demerara sugar
1 tsp chopped thyme leaves
150ml sherry vinegar
350ml Brown Chicken Stock (see page 282, or use good-quality bought stock such as Joubère)
Maldon salt and freshly ground black pepper

For the choucroute:

1 white cabbage, weighing about 750g
100g duck fat
200g onions, thinly sliced
4 tsp Maldon salt
1 smoked sausage, such as Morteaux
80g smoked back bacon, cut into thin strips
3 bay leaves
1 tsp thyme leaves
12 juniper berries, crushed
2 tsp black peppercorns
125ml white wine vinegar
650ml white wine
1 tsp caster sugar

1 Preheat the oven to 180°C/Gas Mark 4. Cut the cabbage into quarters, remove the core and slice as thinly as possible. Blanch the cabbage in a large pan of boiling salted water – it needs to go straight in and out, without being brought back to the boil. Drain and run under the cold tap to cool. Drain thoroughly.

2 Melt the duck fat in a large casserole over a medium heat. Add the onions, salt, the whole sausage, bacon, bay leaves and thyme. Tie up the juniper berries and black peppercorns in a small piece of muslin and add to the pan. Cook for 5 minutes, until the onions are slightly softened but not coloured. Add the cabbage and cook for a few minutes, then add the vinegar, white wine and sugar, stirring well. Place a sheet of greaseproof paper over the top, cover with a lid, then transfer to the oven lowered to 170°C/Gas Mark 3 and cook for about 2 hours, stirring the cabbage from time to time. Remove the lid and paper for the last 30 minutes so the liquid reduces. Remove the sausage from the casserole, peel and slice it and place it back among the cabbage.

3 About 20 minutes before the end of the casserole's cooking time, season the cod with salt and pepper and dust the skin side only with flour. Heat the olive oil in an ovenproof frying pan over a medium heat. Place the cod in the pan, skin-side down, then transfer to the oven and cook for 6–8 minutes.

4 Meanwhile, melt 20g of the butter over a medium heat. Add the shallots, pepper, sugar and thyme and cook for 2–3 minutes, until the shallots are soft. Add the sherry vinegar and simmer until evaporated. Add the stock and simmer until reduced by half, then add 15g of the remaining butter, stirring it until it has emulsified.

5 Remove the fish from the oven, add the remaining butter to the pan and turn the fish over. Cook for 2–4 minutes on the hob, basting the fish with the butter.

6 To serve, divide the cooked cabbage between 4 serving bowls, place the fish on top and pour the sauce around.

FISH OPTIONS: pollack, coley

Baking & Roasting

For this recipe you will need a juicer in order to make the beetroot juice, as it is not yet possible to buy it ready-made. If you can get beetroot with its leaves still on, keep the leaves to serve on top of the salad with a little tarragon and dressing. You could use ruby chard or red mustard leaves the same way.

Roast Sea Trout with Beetroot and Blood Orange Salad and Beetroot Dressing

SERVES 4 AS A STARTER
4 x 130g sea trout fillets
100ml olive oil
40g unsalted butter
juice of 1 lemon
Maldon salt and freshly
  ground black pepper

For the beetroot dressing:
800g raw beetroot
200ml port
1 golfball-sized cooked
  beetroot, roughly chopped
juice of ½ lemon
150ml olive oil
Maldon salt and freshly
  ground black pepper

For the beetroot salad:
500g raw organic baby beetroot,
  roughly 3–4cm in diameter,
  with leaves if possible
a little lemon juice
a large pinch of freshly ground
  black pepper
1 tbsp chopped tarragon
2 blood oranges, all peel and
  white pith removed, divided
  into segments

1 First make the beetroot dressing. Peel the beetroot and put them through a juicer. Remove the scum from the surface of the juice and strain the juice through a fine sieve; you will need 400ml. Place the juice in a pan over a low heat and heat until it is barely simmering, then skim off all the scum again and pass through a fine sieve into a clean pan. Add the port and chopped beetroot and simmer until the liquid is reduced by half. Leave to cool, then add the lemon juice and transfer the mixture to a blender. Purée for 30 seconds, then pour into a bowl and stir in the olive oil so that the dressing is emulsified. Season with a little salt and pepper.

2 For the salad, peel the beetroot, leaving the leaves on, and slice very thinly lengthwise. Place in a bowl, sprinkle with lemon juice and add enough of the beetroot dressing to bind. Season to taste and add the tarragon and the orange segments.

3 Season the sea trout fillets. Heat the olive oil in a large, non-stick sauté pan over a medium heat, and add the fillets skin-side down. Cook for 4–6 minutes, until they are starting to colour underneath, then flip them over with a spatula, add the butter and continue to cook for 2 minutes. Squeeze over the lemon juice.

4 To serve, arrange the beetroot salad on serving plates, put the fish on top and spoon over some of the dressing.

If you are cooking this dish for a dinner party, or want to cut down on preparation time, you can make the gnocchi the day before you need them and keep them in the fridge.

Baked Sea Trout with Peas and Chervil Gnocchi

SERVES 4

4 x 130g sea trout fillets
80ml olive oil
40g unsalted butter
juice and grated zest of 1 lemon
1 tbsp thyme leaves
2 tbsp chopped chervil
Maldon salt and freshly ground
   black pepper

For the peas:
400g fresh peas (shelled weight)
40g unsalted butter
1 tsp sugar
2 tbsp chopped chervil
juice of ½ lemon
Maldon salt and pepper

For the chervil gnocchi:
3–4 baking potatoes (Desiree,
   Yukon, Maris Piper are the
   best varieties for this)
2 egg yolks
100–120g '00' strong flour
3 tbsp chopped chervil
50g grated Parmesan cheese
olive oil
250ml White Chicken Stock
   (see page 282)
100g crème fraîche
a squeeze of lemon juice

1 Bake the potatoes in an oven preheated to 180°C/Gas Mark 4 for about 45–60 minutes. Scrape out the flesh from inside the skins and weigh it – you need about 400g. Put the potato flesh into a bowl, mash it with a fork, and add the egg yolks, flour, half the chervil and half the Parmesan. Mix well and season. Divide into four, dust a work surface with flour and roll each piece into a long sausage shape 3–4mm in diameter. Cut into 1cm lengths and place them on a plate – they will look like little barrels.

2 Bring a large pan of salted water to the boil. Add a drop of olive oil, then add the gnocchi. Once they float to the top, remove them from the pan with a slotted spoon and place them into iced water for 2 minutes to cool. Drain well, and place on a tray. Drizzle with a little olive oil and mix with your hands until all the gnocchi are coated, then set them aside while you cook the peas and fish.

3 Brush the sea trout fillets with olive oil and place on a non-stick baking tray. Divide the butter between the fish, putting a knob on top of each fillet, sprinkle with the lemon juice and zest, thyme and chervil, and season with salt and pepper. Put them into an oven preheated to 180°C/Gas Mark 4 and bake for 8–10 minutes, depending on the thickness of the fillets (the sea trout should still be pink).

4 Meanwhile cook the peas in boiling salted water for 5 minutes. Drain in a colander, then put back into the pan with the butter, sugar, lemon juice, chervil, salt and pepper and keep warm.

5 Bring the stock to the boil in a medium pan and add the crème fraiche and the remaining Parmesan and chervil. Add the gnocchi and lemon juice, simmer for a minute to warm through, and serve with the sea trout and peas.

FISH OPTIONS: good-quality farmed salmon such as Loch Duart, line-caught sea bass

Baking & Roasting

This is one of my favourite dishes. If you take the time to slice the fish neatly, laying it on the paper with fresh herbs, you will really see the benefits once it's cooked as it will look stunning.

Sea Trout Cooked in a Minute

SERVES 4

100ml olive oil
1 tsp Maldon salt
a large pinch of freshly
    ground black pepper
2 tbsp chopped dill
2 tbsp chopped chervil
2 tbsp chopped chives
600g sea trout, sliced very
    thinly, almost carpaccio
    style (see page 62)
grated zest of 1 lemon
juice of 2 lemons
40g unsalted butter

1 Preheat the oven to 200°C/Gas Mark 6 and put a baking tray in to get very hot. Cut 4 x 20cm squares of baking parchment, lay them side by side and brush them with olive oil. Sprinkle with salt and pepper and divide half the chopped herbs between them. Lay the sea trout slices on top of the herbs, slightly overlapping, season again with salt and pepper and drizzle with more olive oil. Sprinkle the lemon zest and a little juice over the fish, and finally top with the rest of the chopped herbs.
2 Open the oven and carefully place the sea trout, still on its parchment, directly on the hot tray. Dot each fillet with butter. Close the oven and cook for 2–3 minutes, until the fish is just cooked and still pink. Remove from the oven, flip on to dinner plates, peel back the paper and serve.

FISH OPTIONS: line-caught sea bass, halibut, good-quality farmed salmon such as Loch Duart

Bream Baked with Salt and Thyme

SERVES 4

1 whole 1.8-2kg bream,
    scaled and gutted, with
    the head and tail removed
    (see page 293)
3kg coarse sea salt
20g black peppercorns, crushed
3 tsp chopped thyme
1 tsp chopped rosemary
3 bay leaves, finely chopped
8 garlic cloves, sliced

1 Wash the bream in cold water and dry on kitchen paper. Place the salt in a bowl and stir in all the remaining ingredients. Place half the flavoured salt on the bottom of a baking tray and place the bream on top. Lay the rest of the salt on top of the fish and bake in an oven preheated to 180°C/Gas Mark 4, allowing 20 minutes cooking time per kilo.
2 Once the cooking time is up, remove the tray from the oven. The bream will have shrunk and there will be a gap between the fish and the salt, which should allow you to crack the crust open. Serve the bream still inside its salt crust.

Roast John Dory Baked with Sliced Charlotte Potatoes, Garlic and Thyme

SERVES 4

100ml olive oil
2 garlic cloves, finely chopped
1 tsp thyme leaves
1 tsp rosemary leaves
4 x 140g John Dory fillets
40g softened unsalted butter
Maldon salt and freshly
    ground black pepper

For the Charlotte potatoes:

600ml White Chicken Stock
    (see page 282)
80g unsalted butter
200g round shallots, cut in
    half and thinly sliced
6 garlic cloves, thinly sliced
2 bay leaves
1 tsp chopped thyme
400g Charlotte potatoes,
    cut into 3–4mm slices
Maldon salt and freshly
    ground black pepper

1 Put 50ml of the oil into a bowl and add the garlic, thyme and rosemary. Brush on to the fish and leave to marinate for an hour. To cook the potatoes, first put the chicken stock into a pan over a medium heat and simmer until reduced by two thirds. Melt half the butter in a sauté pan and add the shallots, garlic, bay leaves and thyme. Season with salt and pepper, put a lid on the pan and cook until the shallots are soft and opaque, without letting them colour. Leave to cool slightly. Use a little of the remaining butter to grease a shallow 34 x 27cm ovenproof dish. Arrange a layer of the sliced potatoes in the dish, seasoning with salt and pepper, then add a layer of shallots.

2 Repeat this process until you have three layers of potatoes and two layers of shallots, putting a few dabs of the remaining butter between the layers. Pour the reduced stock over the top, sprinkle with salt and pepper, and brush the top of the potatoes with melted butter. Cover with foil, bake in an oven preheated to 180°C/Gas Mark 4 for about 10 minutes, then remove from the oven.

3 Take the John Dory fillets from the marinade and spread with the 40g of softened butter. Lay the fish on top of the potatoes, put back into the oven for another 10 minutes, and serve immediately.

For whole roast John Dory

You can use the same method to cook whole fish. Marinate 2 whole 1.2kg John Dory as above, then place them in a shallow, greased, 34 x 27cm ovenproof dish and bake for 10 minutes in an oven preheated to 180°C/Gas Mark 4. Carefully take out the fish and arrange the potatoes in layers in the dish. Put the fish back on top of the potatoes, cover with foil, and return the dish to the oven for a further 20 minutes.

FISH OPTIONS: brill, pollack, sea bass

Baking & Roasting

Roast Monkfish with Red Wine and Lentils

SERVES 4

2 x 900g monkfish, bone in,
    skin removed (see page 297)
150ml olive oil
6 large sprigs of thyme
2 sprigs of rosemary
3 bay leaves, torn
6 garlic cloves, crushed
40g unsalted butter
juice of 1 lemon
Maldon salt and freshly
    ground black pepper

For the lentils:
250g green lentils, soaked
    overnight in cold water
400ml White Chicken Stock
    (see page 282)
1 shallot, cut in half
½ carrot, cut in half
1 celery stalk, cut in 3
2 bay leaves
8 sprigs of thyme
2 garlic cloves

To finish the lentils:
60g unsalted butter
150g shallots, finely chopped
100g celery, diced
100g carrots, diced
2 garlic cloves, finely chopped
1 heaped tsp chopped thyme
1 bay leaf
40ml sherry vinegar
2 tbsp chopped parsley
2 tbsp chopped tarragon

For the red wine sauce:
500ml red wine
300ml port
400g banana shallots, thickly
    sliced
10 black peppercorns, crushed
2 bay leaves
6 sprigs of thyme
500ml Brown Chicken Stock
    (see page 282, or use good-
    quality bought stock such
    as Joubère)
25g unsalted butter

1 Put the lentils into a large pan with cold water to cover and bring to a simmer. Drain and rinse the lentils, then put back into the pan and add the stock and enough water to cover. Add the vegetables, herbs and garlic and cook for about 14 minutes, until the lentils are tender. Drain the lentils and put aside until later. Pour the cooking liquid back into the pan and simmer until reduced by half.

2 To make the red wine sauce, put the red wine, port, shallots, peppercorns, bay leaves and thyme into a pan over a low heat and simmer until reduced by two thirds. Add the stock and simmer until reduced by two thirds. Set the sauce aside while you cook the fish.

3 Heat the oven to 190°C/Gas Mark 5 and place a roasting pan on the hob to get nice and hot. Season the monkfish with salt and pepper. Add the olive oil to the pan, then put in the fish and cook on one side until golden. Flip it over with a spatula, add the herbs and garlic, then transfer the pan to the hot oven and roast for 10–12 minutes. While the monkfish is roasting turn it over a couple of times, so it cooks evenly, and 2 minutes before the end of the cooking time, add the butter. Remove the monkfish from the oven and spoon over the butter, which will have melted by now, and finally squeeze over some lemon juice and leave the fish to stand for a few minutes.

4 While the monkfish is roasting, finish the lentils. Melt all but 1 teaspoon of the butter in a pan, add the shallots, celery, carrots, garlic, thyme and bay leaf, and cook on a medium heat until the vegetables are soft. Add the vinegar and simmer until reduced by half, then add the reserved cooking liquid and the lentils. Bring to a simmer and cook for 10 minutes – the liquid should reduce by a third. Stir in the parsley, tarragon and remaining butter, and season with salt and pepper.

5 Stir the remaining 25g of butter into the red wine sauce, and serve with the monkfish and lentils.

FISH OPTIONS: John Dory, pollack, halibut

Dab is a fish that is not seen very often but I hope that over the next few years that will change. Dab are a perfect portion size for one, and they are extremely moist and tasty.

Dab Baked with Parsley and Garlic

SERVES 4

4 x 300–350g dab, scaled and gutted (see page 293)
150ml olive oil
20g unsalted butter
20 garlic cloves, peeled and crushed
8 sprigs of thyme
80g parsley leaves
150ml white wine
juice and grated zest of 1 lemon
4–5 slices of lemon
150ml Fish Stock (see page 280)
Maldon salt and freshly ground black pepper

To finish:
½ garlic clove, finely chopped
1 tsp chopped parsley
50g unsalted butter, diced

1 Season the dab inside and out with salt and pepper and set aside. Put a large, heavy-based roasting tin on the hob over a medium heat and add the olive oil and butter. Once the butter is foaming, add the garlic, sprinkle over the thyme and some salt and cook slowly for 3–4 minutes, until the garlic is just golden. Add the parsley, white wine, lemon juice and zest.
2 Add the dab to the pan, put the lemon slices on top, and pour over the stock. Place in an oven preheated to 180°C/Gas Mark 4 and bake for 12–14 minutes – the flesh should start to come away from the bone when the fish is done.
3 Remove the tin from the oven and, holding the fish against the tin, tip all the cooking juices into a pan. Place on a medium heat and bring to a simmer. Add the finely chopped garlic and parsley, then mix in the butter a little at a time and blend in with an electric hand blender. Serve the sauce with the fish.

FISH OPTIONS: megrim sole, halibut, good-quality farmed salmon such as Loch Duart

Baking & Roasting

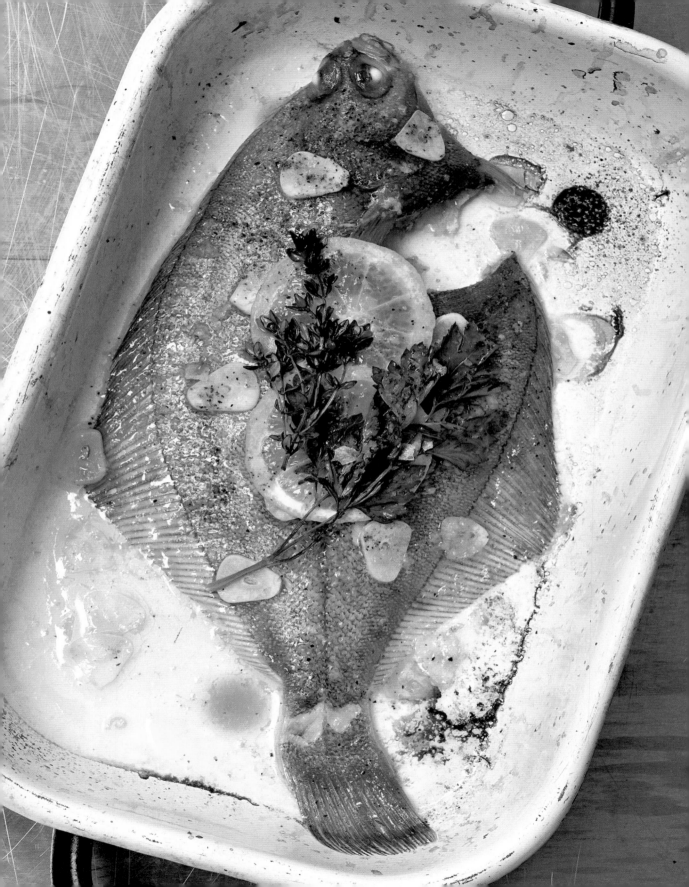

Dab with Roast Artichokes

SERVES 4
100ml olive oil
20g unsalted butter
1 tsp chopped thyme
1 tsp chopped rosemary
2 garlic cloves, finely chopped
4 x 200g dab, scaled and
    gutted (see page 293)
Maldon salt and freshly
    ground black pepper
juice of ½ lemon

For the roast artichokes:
16 baby artichokes
150ml olive oil
50g unsalted butter
1 tsp Maldon salt
a large pinch of freshly
    ground black pepper
4 garlic cloves, peeled
    and cut in half
1 tsp chopped thyme
2 small sprigs of rosemary
1 tsp chopped parsley
200ml Brown Chicken Stock
    (see page 282, or use
    good-quality bought
    stock such as Joubère)

1 First prepare the artichokes. Pull off the outer leaves and cut off the tops, leaving just the heart. Peel the hearts with a vegetable peeler until they are smooth and no dark green areas are left. Cut the stalk, leaving 8cm attached. Peel the stalks until they are nice and white, and cut the artichokes carefully in half.
2 Heat the olive oil and half the butter in a sauté pan over a medium heat and add the artichokes, putting them in alternately stalk up and stalk down so they fit tightly. Season with salt and pepper and add the garlic and all the herbs except the parsley. Cook for 8–10 minutes, then turn the artichokes over and cook for another 8–10 minutes, until golden. Add the stock and simmer until reduced by two thirds. Add the remaining butter and the chopped parsley, and keep the artichokes warm while you cook the fish.
3 Oil a baking sheet with olive oil and season with salt and pepper. Dot the baking sheet with butter and sprinkle over half the herbs and garlic. Place the dab on top, season with salt and pepper, put a few more specks of butter on top and sprinkle with the remaining herbs and garlic. Place in an oven preheated to 180°C/Gas Mark 4 and roast for 8 minutes. Remove from the oven and squeeze over a little lemon juice.
4 To serve, divide the artichokes between 4 serving plates and place the fish on top.

FISH OPTIONS: megrim sole, lemon sole, plaice

Baking & Roasting

Baked John Dory on the Bone
with Confit Tomatoes

SERVES 4

2 x 1.2kg John Dory, gutted,
  heads and fins removed
  (see page 293)
150ml olive oil
1 tsp chopped thyme
1 large sprig of rosemary
20g unsalted butter
1 x quantity Thick Tomato
  Sauce (see page 288)
juice of ½ lemon
1 x quantity Oven-dried
  Tomatoes (see page 291)
Maldon salt and freshly
  ground black pepper

1 Carefully rinse the John Dory inside and out under cold running water and dry well. Place the fish in a roasting tray and rub with the olive oil. Season with salt and pepper, sprinkle over the thyme, then pick off the leaves from the rosemary sprigs and scatter them over the fish. Dab it with butter, place into an oven preheated to 180°C/Gas Mark 4 and bake for 14–18 minutes.

2 Meanwhile, gently reheat the tomato sauce. Once the fish is cooked – it should be firm to the touch and starting to pull away from the backbone – remove it from the oven, squeeze over the lemon juice and scatter the confit tomatoes on top. Serve the fish from the roasting tray, with the tomato sauce on the side.

FISH OPTIONS: monkfish tail, gilthead bream

Whole Roast Langoustines
with Paprika and Fennel Seeds

SERVES 4

24 whole langoustines

For roasting:
150ml olive oil
1½ tsp smoked Spanish paprika
1 large pinch of cayenne pepper
1 red chilli, finely chopped with
  the seeds removed
4 star anise broken up
½ tsp crushed cumin seeds
1 tsp crushed coriander seeds
1 tbsp crushed fennel seeds
1 tsp chopped thyme
2 bay leaves, chopped
8 whole garlic cloves
Maldon salt and pepper

1 Place all the roasting ingredients in a bowl and mix well. Heat the oven to 190°C/Gas Mark 5 and put in a roasting tray big enough for all the langoustines to fit without being overcrowded. Once the tray is hot, remove it from the oven and spread the langoustines on it. Put the tray back into the oven and cook for 8 minutes.

2 Serve the langoustines hot, with garlic aioli alongside (see page 289).

Baking & Roasting

Roast Red Mullet with Tomato Salsa

SERVES 4

4 x 300g red mullet, gutted and
    fins removed (see page 293)
150ml olive oil
2 garlic cloves, finely chopped
juice and grated zest of 1 lemon,
    plus extra to squeeze
1 small red chilli, deseeded
    and finely chopped
4 sprigs of coriander, leaves
    picked and chopped
2 sprigs of basil, leaves picked
    and finely sliced
1 x quantity Tomato Salsa
    (see page 291)
Maldon salt and freshly
    ground black pepper

1 Make sure the mullet are quite dry inside before you start. Put the olive oil, garlic, lemon zest and juice, chilli and herbs into a bowl, stir together, and rub into the fish so that they are well coated, inside and out. Put into the fridge for at least 2 hours or even overnight to marinate.

2 Meanwhile, make the tomato salsa.

3 Heat the oven to 190°C/Gas Mark 5, then place a roasting pan on the stove and get it nice and hot. Take the mullet out of their marinade and season with salt and pepper. Add to the hot pan and cook on one side for about 4 minutes, until golden. Flip the fish over with a spatula, then place the pan in the hot oven and cook for 10–12 minutes, turning the fish over a couple of times so it cooks evenly. Remove from the oven, add a squeeze of lemon juice, and serve with the tomato salsa.

FISH OPTION: grey mullet

Roast Turbot with Roast Asparagus

SERVES 6–8

16–20 large English asparagus
    spears
180ml olive oil
1 heaped tbsp chopped thyme
2 garlic cloves, finely chopped
juice and grated zest of
    2 lemons
1 x 2kg turbot, filleted
    (see page 295)
60g unsalted butter
30ml balsamic vinegar
Maldon salt and freshly
    ground black pepper

1 Snap the woody ends off the asparagus and discard. Put the asparagus into a bowl with 100ml of the olive oil, the thyme, garlic, lemon zest, salt and pepper and mix well until the spears are coated with the oil. Set aside to marinate while you cook the fish.

2 Season the turbot fillets with salt and pepper. Put a large non-stick sauté pan to heat up on the hob, and add the rest of the olive oil. Add the turbot fillets and cook for 3 minutes on one side, then add half the butter and flip the fish over. Cook for another 3 minutes, finish with a squeeze of lemon juice, and keep warm while you cook the asparagus.

3 Heat a sauté pan on the hob over a medium heat and add the rest of the butter. Add the asparagus and sauté for 3–4 minutes, until they start to turn golden. Add the balsamic vinegar and a squeeze of lemon juice and serve with the turbot.

FISH OPTIONS: brill, John Dory

Baked Whole Turbot with Rosemary

SERVES 4

1 x 1.8–2kg turbot, gutted,
  with head, fins and tail
  removed (see page 293)
80ml olive oil
60g unsalted butter
6 sprigs of rosemary
8 garlic cloves, crushed
4 bay leaves
6 thyme sprigs
zest of 1 lemon, taken off
  in large strips with a
  speed peeler
100ml white wine
juice of 1 lemon
Maldon salt and freshly
  ground black pepper

For the Charlotte potatoes
  with mint and butter:
a small bunch of mint
400g Charlotte potatoes
1 whole head of garlic, cloves
  unpeeled and bashed with
  the back of a knife
20g butter
Maldon salt and freshly
  ground black pepper

1 Place the turbot on a non-stick baking tray and brush with the olive oil. Season with salt and pepper on both sides, then turn the fish so that the dark skin side is facing up. Dab the top of the fish with the butter, and scatter the rosemary, garlic, bay leaves, thyme and lemon zest on and around the fish. Drizzle with the white wine and lemon juice. Place the turbot in an oven preheated to 180°C/Gas Mark 4 for about 30 minutes, basting with the juices every 10 minutes or so.

2 Meanwhile, bring a large pan of salted water to the boil. Chop 2 sprigs of mint and set aside, and add the remainder to the pan with the potatoes and garlic. Bring back to a simmer and cook for about 20 minutes, until the potatoes are tender. Drain them in a colander, discarding the garlic, and put them back into the pan with the butter, salt, pepper and reserved chopped mint.

3 When the turbot is cooked, remove it from the oven and serve with the minted Charlotte potatoes.

Roast Turbot on the Bone
with Chicken

SERVES 6–8

1 x 2kg turbot, prepared and
    cut into darnes (see page
    298 – you should have
    8 x 100g portions)
150ml olive oil
1 tsp thyme leaves
40g unsalted butter
1 tsp Maldon salt
4 garlic cloves, halved
6 sprigs of rosemary
6 large sprigs of thyme
juice of 1 lemon

For the chicken legs:

2 tbsp flour
4 free-range chicken legs,
    cut through the joint
100ml vegetable oil
40g unsalted butter
80g carrots, roughly chopped
80g onions, roughly chopped
2 shallots, chopped
4 stems of celery, roughly
    chopped
2 bay leaves
1 tsp thyme leaves
4 sprigs of rosemary
6 garlic cloves, cut in half
250ml white wine
1 litre Brown Chicken Stock
    (see page 282, or use good-
    quality bought stock such
    as Joubère)
1 heaped tbsp chopped parsley
Maldon salt and freshly
    ground black pepper

1 Season and flour the chicken legs. Heat the oil in a deep-sided pan and add the butter. When it has melted, add the chicken legs and cook over a medium heat on all sides until they are golden all over and the skin is crispy – this should take about 8–10 minutes. Remove the chicken legs from the pan and set aside. Add the carrots, onions, shallots, celery, bay leaves, thyme, rosemary and garlic to the pan, season with a little salt and pepper, and cook until the vegetables are soft and golden, stirring now and again. Pour the wine into the pan, stir to deglaze, and simmer until the wine has reduced by half.

2 Put the chicken legs back into the pan, add the stock and bring to a simmer, skimming the top with a ladle to remove the scum. Simmer gently for 60–80 minutes, until the chicken is tender, then lift the legs from the stock with a slotted spoon and cool. Simmer the stock until it has reduced by two thirds, then strain it through a colander, pressing down on the vegetables to extract the maximum flavour. Pass it through a fine sieve, discarding the vegetables, and set aside. When the chicken legs have cooled, remove the meat from the bones in large pieces.

3 Heat the oven to 170°C/Gas Mark 3. Rub the turbot with 50ml of the olive oil and sprinkle with the thyme leaves. Heat a large ovenproof frying pan on the hob and add the remaining olive oil and the butter. Once the butter is melting and starting to turn golden, put in all the pieces of turbot with the garlic, rosemary and thyme sprigs. The butter should be foaming nicely, but make sure it doesn't burn. After 4 minutes or so, when the fish is starting to colour, flip the pieces over with a spatula, and transfer the pan to the oven for 6–8 minutes, until the fish is coming away from the bone. Squeeze over a little lemon juice.

4 When the fish is nearly ready, bring the chicken stock back to a simmer and skim off any scum. Add the chicken meat and warm through. Stir in the chopped parsley and serve with the turbot.

Baking & Roasting

I first made this while in Ibiza. I picked wild fennel and rosemary from the roadside, mixed it with salt, added the spices and baked the fish in the mixture. It was one of the most delicious meals I have ever had – simple, but outstanding.

Salt-crusted Whole Baked Turbot

SERVES 4

1 x 1.8–2kg turbot, gutted, with head, fins and tail removed (see page 293)
3kg coarse sea salt
zest of 3 lemons, taken off in large strips with a speed peeler
zest of 2 oranges, taken off in large strips with a speed peeler
4 garlic cloves, sliced
4 tsp chopped dill
1 tsp thyme leaves
1 tbsp dill seed
1 tbsp fennel seed
4 star anise, crushed
20g black peppercorns, crushed

1 Wash the turbot in cold water and dry on kitchen paper. Place the salt in a bowl and stir in all the remaining ingredients. Place half the flavoured salt on the bottom of a baking tray and place the turbot on top. Lay the rest of the salt on top of the fish and bake in an oven preheated to 180°C/Gas Mark 4, allowing 20 minutes cooking time per kilo.

2 Once the cooking time is up, remove the tray from the oven. The turbot will have shrunk and there will be a gap between the fish and the salt, which should allow you to crack the salt crust open. Serve the fish still inside its salt crust.

Turbot has been held in high regard in Europe for at least 2000 years. By the eighteenth century, turbot was already being sold in London's Billingsgate Fish Market, and during much of the nineteenth century the price that it fetched at market could vary from week to week by a factor of 100, due to the large quantity that was landed by fisherman. It can still cost anything from £12 to £22 per kg.

Turbot is a very good source of protein and B3 and B12 vitamins. It also contains the mineral selenium, which is important for immune system functioning; magnesium, which plays a part in metabolism; and phosphorous, which helps to build strong bones and teeth.

You should avoid buying small turbot as they have very thin fillets and not right from a conservation standpoint.

The turbot is fished by heavy bottom gear– by beam trawling (see pages 9–10) – which is doing a huge amount of damage to the sea floor and I would not have buy turbot from the North Sea at all. The best way of catching the turbot is either handline or static net. For more information see pages 343–4.

Baking & Roasting

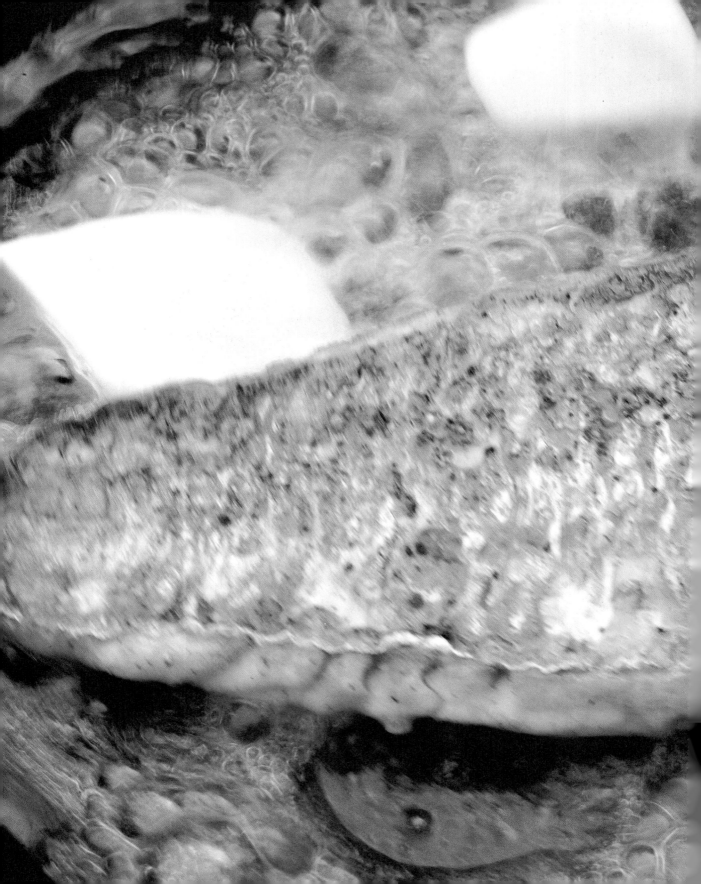

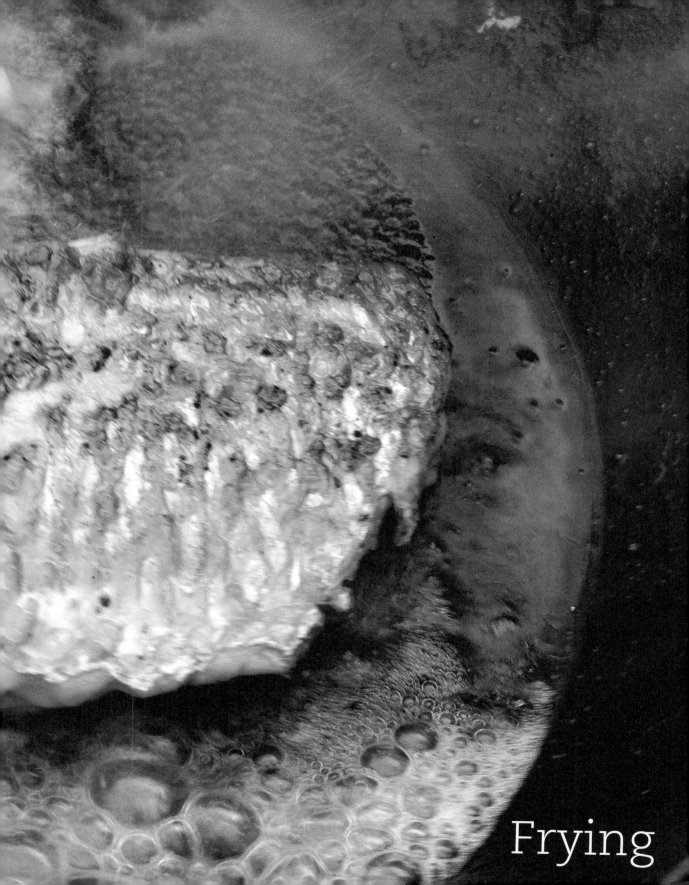

Frying

Pan-frying fish is another easy way of preparing it, but some people shy away from it because they get nervous about having to stand over a pan and watch it. It's true that one of the main problems with this method of cooking is timing – a lot of people tend to overcook their fish – but if you try and stick to the timings in my recipes you should end up with moist, tasty fish. Don't get disheartened if you do overcook your fish a few times, it's only through trial and error that you'll become more confident.

It's the same with deep-frying: you might be a little daunted by the prospect of standing over a pan of hot oil but if you follow the instructions in these recipes, you should end up with a beautiful piece of fish.

Frying

HASTINGS FM 001
HASTINGS FM 001
HASTINGS FISHMARKET, ENGLAND.
HS001FM
HS001FM

When you are choosing your smoked haddock do make sure that it is genuinely smoked rather than dyed. There is a chemical called E104 (quinoline yellow) that can be used to dye the haddock, which gives the fish its yellow, smoked look, without the processor actually having to go through the entire process.

Smoked Haddock Omelette

SERVES 4
150ml whipping cream
150ml milk
1 bay leaf
3 sprigs of thyme
2 garlic cloves
a pinch of Maldon salt
8 whole black peppercorns
2 x 100g smoked haddock
   fillets

For the omelettes:
60g unsalted butter
9 large eggs, lightly beaten
4 tbsp crème fraîche
2 tbsp chopped chives
Maldon salt and freshly
   ground black pepper

1 Place the cream, milk, bay leaf, thyme, garlic, salt and peppercorns in a shallow pan and slowly bring to a simmer. Add the smoked haddock fillets, then take the pan off the heat and set aside for 6 minutes.

2 Remove the haddock from the liquid, let it cool a little, and flake it into big pieces, removing any bones. Reserve 100ml of the cooking liquid, strain, and let it cool to room temperature.

3 Warm a non-stick omelette pan on the stove. When it is hot, add the butter, and when that has melted add a quarter of the eggs. Cook gently over a low heat, stirring every few seconds with a spatula at first, then let the eggs sit in the pan without moving them so that they will cook on the bottom but remain runny on top. Raise the pan so that it is at an angle and tap the edge so that the omelette slides towards the front. Add a quarter of the flaked haddock, a quarter of the reserved cooking liquid, a tablespoon of crème fraîche and some chopped chives, and use a spatula to fold over the top of the omelette so that the haddock is enclosed. Flip over the omelette onto a warmed plate so that the fold is now underneath.

4 Make three more omelettes the same way, and serve with a fresh green salad.

FISH OPTION: smoked salmon

There are various different styles of smoked haddock that you can buy. One of the best, in my opinion, is the Arbroath smokie. The Arbroath smokie originally came from the small fishing village of Auchmithie, three miles from Arbroath. Local legend has it that a building caught fire one night, destroying barrels of haddock preserved in salt. The following morning, the people of Auchmithie came to clean up the debris and found that some of the barrels had caught fire, cooking the haddock inside. Further inspections revealed the haddock was edible and quite tasty.

Frying

Eggs Benedict with Smoked Haddock

SERVES 4

400ml milk
2 bay leaves
5 sprigs of thyme
6 white peppercorns
2 garlic cloves
200g smoked haddock fillet
20g unsalted butter
4 English muffins, cut in half,
   lightly toasted and spread
   with a little butter
1 x quantity Hollandaise
   Sauce (see page 288)
Maldon salt

For the poached eggs:
8 large eggs
100ml white wine vinegar
a pinch of Maldon salt

1 Bring the milk to a simmer and add the bay leaves, thyme, peppercorns, garlic and a pinch of salt. Add the smoked haddock and gently simmer for 2 minutes, then take the pan off the heat and set aside for 5 minutes. Remove the smoked haddock from the pan and let it cool a little, then flake it into large pieces, removing any bones. Reserve 50ml of the milk, and let it cool to room temperature.

2 Meanwhile, poach the eggs. Fill a medium pan three-quarters full with water and bring to a simmer. Add the vinegar and salt – this will help hold the eggs together when poaching. Crack each egg into a small ramekin. When the water is simmering, whisk it in one direction in a circular motion, creating a whirlpool in the pan, and add the eggs one by one – they will spin round, which gives them an even round shape. They will gently settle at the bottom of the pan and you may need to move them slightly with a spatula so they do not stick to each other. Cook for 3–4 minutes, then remove with a slotted spoon and drain on kitchen paper. Season with salt and pepper.

3 Put a small pan on the heat and add the butter and the reserved milk. Add the flaked smoked haddock and warm through. Serve on the toasted muffin halves, with the poached eggs and hollandaise sauce on top.

FISH OPTION: smoked salmon

Arbroath smokies are still prepared using traditional methods. The fish are salted overnight to preserve them, then tied in pairs using hemp twine and left overnight to dry. They are then hung over a triangular-shaped length of wood above a fire in barrel to smoke. The top of the barrel is covered with a lid and sealed around the edges with wet jute sacks. All of this serves to create a very hot and humid fire which is devoid of flames. The intense heat and presence of thick smoke is essential if the fish are to be cooked, not burned, and to have the strong smoky taste and smell people expect from Arbroath smokies.

This is a very easy dish to prepare – it can be cooked and on the table in under 15 minutes, served with a simple green salad. The combination of hot horseradish with the oiliness of the sardines is a fantastic combination.

Sardines with Horseradish

SERVES 4

8 large whole sardines, boned (see page 296)
140ml olive oil
2 tsp grated fresh horseradish
1 tsp thyme leaves
1 sprig of rosemary, leaves picked
15g unsalted butter
juice of 1 lemon
Maldon salt and freshly ground black pepper

For the horseradish cream:

120g double cream
100g crème fraîche
1 tsp Maldon salt
a large pinch of freshly ground black pepper
50g spring onions, finely sliced
1 tsp chopped chives
2 tbsp freshly grated horseradish
juice of 1 lemon

1 Put all the ingredients for the horseradish cream into a bowl and stir well to combine. Whisk until light and fluffy and set aside.

2 Brush the sardines with 60ml of the olive oil and season with salt and pepper. Put a little grated horseradish on each one, followed by a little thyme and rosemary. Heat a non-stick sauté pan on a medium heat and add the remaining olive oil. When it's hot, add the seasoned sardines and cook for 2 minutes, until the fish is golden around the edges. Add the butter, then flip over the fillet and cook on the other side for 2 minutes. Finally, squeeze over the lemon juice.

3 Serve the sardines with a spoonful of the horseradish cream on top and let it melt over the fish.

FISH OPTIONS: red mullet, herring, mackerel

Even if fish do look strange or have an odd name, they can be worth trying out. We have even seen some fish names changed so they can become more marketable and popular. The change from pilchards to Cornish sardines proved this as there was a visible uplift in sales.

The slimehead is now known as orange roughy and the Patagonian toothfish sells much better as Chilean sea bass while rockfish is now being sold as Pacific red snapper, dogfish as rock salmon and there are now moves to have the megrim sole renamed as Cornish sole. Sadly, however, the change is not always for the better. The popularity of orange roughy and Chilean sea bass has increased so much that they are now endangered.

Frying

Peppered Sardines with Sherry Vinegar and Braised Shallots

SERVES 4

8 large whole sardines,
   boned (see page 296)
1 tsp Maldon salt
1 tsp crushed black
   peppercorns
80ml olive oil
40g unsalted butter
100g shallots, finely sliced
2 garlic cloves, finely chopped
1 tsp thyme leaves
5 tsp demerara sugar
150ml sherry vinegar

For the braised shallots:

25g unsalted butter
8 sprigs of thyme
2 bay leaves
1 heaped tsp sugar
1 tsp Maldon salt
a large pinch of freshly
   ground black pepper
16 shallots
50ml sherry vinegar
300ml White Chicken Stock
   (see page 282)

1 For the braised shallots, melt the butter in a pan over a medium heat and add the thyme, bay leaves, sugar, salt and pepper. Add the shallots and cook for 2–3 minutes, until starting to colour, then put a lid on the pan and cook over a low to medium heat for 15 minutes. Add the vinegar and stock, and simmer until reduced and syrupy. Keep the shallots warm while you cook the sardines.

2 Season the sardines with the salt and the crushed black peppercorns. Heat the oil in a large sauté pan over a medium to high heat, add the sardines and cook for 2 minutes on each side. Remove the fish from the pan and set aside.

3 Put the pan back on a lower heat and add the butter. When it is hot, add the shallots, garlic and thyme, and cook for about 4 minutes, until the shallots are soft. Add the sugar and turn the heat up high so that it starts to caramelise, then add the vinegar and simmer until reduced by two thirds and slightly syrupy. Put the sardines back into the pan and cook for a further minute on each side, until the sardines are nicely glazed with the syrup.

4 Serve the sardines with the braised shallots.

FISH OPTIONS: red mullet, herring, mackerel

Herring with Puy Lentils and Ham

SERVES 4

1 x quantity Ham Hock
   (see page 162)
150ml olive oil
1 tsp thyme leaves
juice and grated zest of
   1 lemon
1 tsp Maldon salt
a large pinch of freshly
   ground black pepper
4 x 150g herring fillets

For the lentils:

200g Puy lentils, soaked
   overnight in cold water
1 banana shallot, peeled,
   or 2 round shallots,
   cut in half
1 small carrot, cut in half
1 celery stick, cut in 3
2 garlic cloves
2 bay leaves
8 sprigs of thyme

To finish the ham and lentils:

60g unsalted butter
100g shallots, finely chopped
75g carrots, diced
2 garlic cloves, finely chopped
4 rashers of smoked bacon,
   cut in large slices (optional,
   but will give extra flavour)
a pinch of chopped rosemary
1 heaped tsp chopped thyme
1 bay leaf
150ml Madeira (optional)
80ml sherry vinegar
1 tbsp chopped parsley
a little Maldon salt

1 Cook the ham hock according to the instructions on page 162 and leave to cool in the liquid. Once it has cooled, carefully lift it out with a slotted spoon and place on a tray. Pass the stock through a fine sieve and reserve. Remove the fat, gristle, and bone from the ham, leaving it in medium-sized pieces.

2 Meanwhile, rinse the lentils in a sieve under a cold running tap, place in a pan and add cold water to cover. Put the pan on to a high heat and bring the lentils up to a simmer, then drain in a sieve, rinse under cold water and put back into a clean pan. Cover with the reserved ham stock, add the shallots, carrot, celery, garlic and herbs, and simmer for about 35–40 minutes, until the lentils are just soft. Set aside, still in their liquid.

3 In a pan, melt half the butter on a low to medium heat. Add the shallots, carrots, garlic, bacon, rosemary, thyme and bay leaf and cook slowly without letting the vegetables colour for about 3 minutes, until they are soft. Add the Madeira and half the vinegar, and simmer until reduced by half. Drain the lentils, reserving the liquid, and add the lentils to the pan. Stir in 300ml of the lentil liquid and simmer until reduced by half, then add the pieces of ham and the parsley. Stir in the remaining butter at the end, and check the seasoning. Keep the lentils warm while you cook the fish.

4 Mix 100ml of the olive oil in a bowl with the thyme, lemon juice, salt and pepper, and brush over the fish. Place a non-stick sauté pan on a low to medium heat, and when hot add the remaining oil. Carefully add the herring fillets to the pan and cook for 2–3 minutes on the skin side, then flip over with a spatula and cook the other side for 2 minutes. Finish with a little fresh lemon zest and a squeeze more lemon juice.

5 Serve the ham and lentils in a bowl with the sautéed herring fillets on top.

FISH OPTION: sardines

Frying

Pouting with Capers and Lemon

SERVES 4

2 x 500g pouting, filleted
   and pin boned (see pages
   294, 296)
150ml olive oil
160g unsalted butter
juice of 2 lemons
100ml white wine
160g shallots, finely sliced
2 garlic cloves, finely sliced
1 bay leaf
1 tsp thyme leaves
80g capers, drained and rinsed
grated zest of 1 lemon
1 lemon, peeled, divided into
   segments and roughly diced
4 sprigs of parsley, leaves
   picked and chopped
Maldon salt and freshly
   ground black pepper

1 Season the pouting fillets with salt and pepper, and place a large non-stick sauté pan on the stove to heat. Add 50ml of the olive oil and once it is hot, add the pouting fillets, cooking the skin side first and pressing down on the fish lightly with a spatula so the skin will get nice and crispy. After 4 minutes or so, when the fish is golden, add 60g of the butter, flip the fillet over on to the other side and cook for a further 4 minutes. Squeeze over the juice of half a lemon, then remove the fish from the pan and keep warm. Pour the white wine into the pan, stirring to deglaze, and set these pan juices aside for the sauce.

2 Heat the remaining oil in a pan and add the shallots, garlic, bay leaf, thyme, salt and pepper. Cook on a medium heat without letting the shallots colour too much, then add the remaining butter and turn the heat up so they start to turn golden. Add the rest of the lemon juice and the capers and cook for a minute, and finally add the lemon zest, lemon segments and parsley. Add the reserved cooking juices to the sauce and serve immediately with the pouting.

FISH OPTIONS: pollack, coley

Frying

Pan-fried Mackerel with
Split Garlic and Bay Leaf

SERVES 4

100ml olive oil, plus 1 tbsp
for frying
juice and grated zest of 1 lemon
2 garlic cloves, finely chopped
2 bay leaves, chopped
1 tsp thyme leaves
8 x 60g mackerel fillets, sides
slashed
Maldon salt and freshly
ground black pepper

For the split roasted garlic:
40ml olive oil
2 heads of garlic, separated into
cloves, outer layers removed
10 sprigs of fresh thyme
3 bay leaves
20g unsalted butter
Maldon salt and freshly
ground black pepper

1 For the roasted garlic, heat a roasting pan to medium heat. Add the olive oil, garlic, thyme and bay leaves and season with salt and pepper. Toss the pan every few minutes until the garlic starts to colour, then add the butter. Transfer the pan to an oven preheated to 160°C/Gas Mark 2, and roast slowly for 30 minutes, until the garlic is very tender and soft. Keep it warm while you cook the mackerel.

2 Mix the oil, lemon juice and zest, garlic, herbs, salt and pepper together in a bowl and brush over the mackerel fillets. Heat a tablespoon of oil in a non-stick sauté pan, add the mackerel and cook for 2 minutes on the skin side. Flip over and cook the other side for another 2 minutes, leaving the flesh slightly pink.

3 Serve the mackerel with the split roasted garlic.

FISH OPTIONS: sardines, herring

Pan-fried Fillets of Plaice
with Tartare Sauce

SERVES 4

80g plain flour
2 large eggs, lightly beaten
140g white breadcrumbs,
brioche crumbs or Japanese
panko crumbs
4 x 190g or 8 x 100g plaice
fillets, skinned (see page 297)
150ml vegetable or
groundnut oil
20g unsalted butter
½ lemon
1 x quantity Tartare Sauce
(see page 00)
Maldon salt and freshly
ground black pepper

1 Put the flour on a plate and the eggs and crumbs into two separate shallow bowls. Make sure the plaice fillets are free from any bones. Season them with salt and pepper and lightly dust them with the flour, patting it on gently. Place one fillet at a time in the beaten egg, then lift it out vertically, let it drip for a minute, and wipe the excess egg down the fillet with your thumb and forefinger. Place the fillet in the breadcrumbs and roll it over so it is well coated. Transfer to a clean plate or tray.

2 Heat the oil in a large frying pan over a medium heat, then add the plaice fillets and cook for 3 minutes, until they start to go golden around the edges. Add the butter, cook for another minute and turn the fillets over. Cook for 2 more minutes, until the fish is just done. Add a squeeze of lemon juice and serve straight away, with the tartare sauce.

FISH OPTIONS: megrim sole, witch sole, gurnard, pollock

Truffles are expensive, so if you don't want to make the truffle vinaigrette just make an ordinary vinaigrette (see page 290) and add a little truffle oil.

Scallops with Ham and Leeks

SERVES 4

8 leeks, split lengthways but with the root kept together and washed
12 scallops, out of the shell, roe removed (see page 304)
100ml olive oil
40g unsalted butter
juice of ½ lemon
1 x quantity Truffle Vinaigrette (see page 290)
Maldon salt and freshly ground black pepper

For the ham hock:

1 ham hock, soaked in cold water for 24 hours
2 celery sticks, washed
2 banana shallots, cut in quarters
6 garlic cloves, cut in half
1 small nugget of fresh ginger, sliced
1 onion, cut in quarters
1 leek, halved
4 plum tomatoes, halved
12 sprigs of thyme
1½ tsp Maldon salt
4 star anise
½ cinnamon stick
1 tsp juniper berries
1 tsp coriander seeds
1 tsp fennel seeds
12 black peppercorns
10 cloves
4 sprigs of parsley
2 sprigs of rosemary
40g honey

1 Place the ham hock in a large pan, add cold water to just cover it and bring to a simmer. Drain the ham, rinse it under cold water and put it into a clean pan with all the vegetables, tomatoes and spices. Top up with water to cover the ham, and add the honey. Bring back to a simmer on a medium heat, and cook for approx 2½ hours, until the ham is coming away from the bone. Take the pan off the heat and leave the ham hock to cool in the liquid. Once it has cooled, carefully lift it out with a slotted spoon and place on a tray. Pass the stock through a fine sieve and keep for another recipe. Remove the fat, gristle, and bone from the ham, leaving it in medium-sized flaked pieces, and set aside.

2 Cut the green tops off the leeks. Bring a large pan of salted water to the boil, add the leeks, and cook until they are tender, about 12–15 minutes. Drain, place in iced water for 5 minutes, then drain again and cut them in half. Place the leeks on a small baking tray and rub all over with the vinaigrette. Season with salt and pepper and place under the grill to warm through for a few minutes.

3 Warm the ham gently in a small pan with a little vinaigrette.

4 Heat a large non-stick sauté pan, or a flat-top griddle if you have one. Season the scallops with salt and pepper, drizzle them with olive oil and cook for about 3 minutes on one side, until they are golden. Add the butter, flip them over with a spatula, and cook for another 3 minutes on the other side. Finally, squeeze over a little lemon juice.

5 To serve, place some leeks on each plate, with the ham pieces scattered over. Put the scallops on top and drizzle with the vinaigrette.

Frying

TOM AIKENS

Coley with Orange Butter Sauce and Roast Chicory

SERVES 4
80ml olive oil
4 x 140g coley fillets
40g unsalted butter
juice and grated zest of
   1 orange
Maldon salt and freshly
   ground black pepper

For the orange butter sauce:
250ml fresh orange juice
2 oranges, peeled, divided
   into segments and
   roughly diced
juice of ½ lemon
80g unsalted butter
1 tbsp chopped tarragon
Maldon salt and freshly
   ground black pepper

For the roast chicory:
4 whole chicory
40g unsalted butter
20g brown sugar
200ml orange juice
1 tsp Maldon salt
a large pinch of freshly
   ground black pepper

1 Place the orange juice and segments in a pan over a medium heat and simmer until reduced by two thirds. Add the lemon juice, then whisk in the butter. Add the chopped tarragon and season with a little salt and pepper. Set aside.

2 Peel a few outer leaves from the chicory, cut in half lengthways and remove the core at the base. Place a pan on a medium heat and add the butter and sugar. Lay the chicory in the pan, cover with a circle of greaseproof paper, and cook slowly for about 10 minutes. When the chicory are caramelised, add the orange juice, salt and pepper and continue to cook slowly until they are tender and the liquid has become syrupy, coating the chicory.

3 Meanwhile, heat a non-stick pan and add the olive oil. Season the coley fillets with salt and pepper, add to the pan, and cook on one side for about 4 minutes, until golden. Add the butter, and once it starts to foam flip the fillets over and cook the other side for 4 minutes. Pour the orange juice and zest into the pan and stir to deglaze.

4 Serve the coley with the chicory and the orange butter sauce.

FISH OPTIONS: pollack, MSC-certified cod, line-caught sea bass

Fish is an international commodity. The global trade is worth over $60 billion more than the combined export values of coffee, cocoa, sugar and tea. Developing countries produce over half of this, while 82% of the markets are in developed countries.

Yet at the same time, 52% of world fish stocks are fully exploited, which means that they are being fished at their maximum biological capacity; 24% are over exploited, depleted or recovering from depletion and 21% are moderately exploited.

Wood chips from fruit trees are more suitable for cooking fish than hardwood as they give off a sweeter flavour. Soak the wood chips in water for 10 minutes before using. I like to pan-fry the pollack as well – it puts back some of the moisture lost during the smoking, adds flavour and gives the fish a crispier skin.

Smoked Pollack with Poached Egg

SERVES 4
4 x 140g pollack fillets
100ml olive oil
1 heaped tsp thyme leaves
1 sprig of rosemary, leaves
    picked and chopped
40g unsalted butter
juice of 1 lemon
Maldon salt and freshly
    ground black pepper

For the poached eggs:
4 large eggs
50ml white wine vinegar
a pinch of Maldon salt

For the grain mustard butter
    sauce:
125g unsalted butter, cut
    into small cubes
140g shallots, finely diced
250ml white wine
300ml Fish Stock
    (see page 280)
400ml double cream
2 tbsp wholegrain mustard
juice of 1 lemon
2 tbsp chopped tarragon
Maldon salt and freshly
    ground black pepper

1 Brush the pollack fillets with 40ml of the olive oil and season with salt and pepper. Sprinkle with the thyme and rosemary.
2 Heat the smoker on the grill, or use a roasting tray, and add enough chips to cover the base of the pan. Once they start to catch and smoke, place the fish fillets inside and put the top on. Smoke the fillets for 20 minutes; enough to give them a smoky flavour.
3 Meanwhile, poach the eggs. Fill a medium pan three-quarters full with water and bring to a simmer. Add the vinegar and salt; this helps hold the eggs together. Crack each egg into a small ramekin. When the water is simmering, whisk it in one direction to create a whirlpool. Add the eggs one by one – they will spin round, which gives them an even round shape. They will gently settle at the bottom of the pan and you may need to move them slightly with a spatula so they do not stick to each other. Cook for 3–4 minutes, then remove with a slotted spoon and drain on kitchen paper. Season and set aside to keep warm.
4 For the sauce, place a shallow pan on a low to medium heat and add 25g of the butter. Once it has melted, add the shallots and cook slowly until translucent, about 2–3 minutes, then add the white wine and simmer until reduced by two thirds. Add the fish stock and reduce by half. Add the cream and reduce by half again, then whisk in the remaining butter, then the wholegrain mustard and lemon juice. Season with salt and pepper, and lastly add the chopped tarragon. Keep the sauce warm.
5 Once the pollack is smoked, you can sauté it in a little olive oil and butter if you like. Heat a non-stick sauté pan and add the remaining olive oil. When it starts to smoke, add the pollack skin-side down and cook for 4 minutes, until the skin is crispy. Add the butter, and when it starts foaming, flip the pollack over and cook for 4 minutes. Finish with a squeeze of lemon juice.
6 Place a poached egg on each serving plate, with a pollack fillet on top, and serve with the grain mustard butter sauce.

Frying

Eels need to be approached with caution (see page 314). If you do treat yourself to this precious fish, make sure that you are buying farmed eel – I would recommend Brown & Forrest.

Pan-fried Smoked Eel with Roast Apple and Rosemary

SERVES 4

4 Granny Smith apples
40g demerara sugar
80g unsalted butter
1 tsp chopped rosemary
juice of 1 lemon
150ml cider
4 x 80g pieces of smoked eel, cleaned
a little olive oil
Maldon salt and freshly ground black pepper

1 Peel and halve 2 of the apples, then remove the core and cut each half into 3 wedges. Heat a large non-stick sauté pan until very hot. Add the apple wedges and sugar, but do not move the apples around or stir otherwise they will not colour. The apples will smoke a lot in the hot pan, so you will need to watch them closely and flip them over once they have started to caramelise. After 4–5 minutes, when the apples are turning a nice golden brown, add 40g of the butter and sprinkle in half the rosemary and a squeeze of lemon juice. Add the cider and simmer until syrupy and sticky, then set aside while you cook the eel.

2 Season the eel fillets with plenty of black pepper. Melt the remaining butter in a non-stick sauté pan, and once it is foaming add the eel and the rest of the rosemary. Cook the eel for 2 minutes on one side, until golden, then flip over and cook the other side.

3 Peel and core the remaining apples and slice thinly. Cut each slice into very thin strips and toss in a little olive oil and lemon juice. Serve the eel with the roasted apples, with the crisp apple strips scattered over the top.

Eels were smoked in Britain from the early 1900s when many Jewish refugees settled in London and, keen on their salmon and blinis, brought with them the craft of smoking.

Frying

Pan-fried Whiting with White Wine and Mustard

SERVES 4
4 x 110g whiting fillets
1 heaped tsp Maldon salt
2 tsp crushed yellow
   mustard seeds
80ml olive oil
40g unsalted butter
juice of 1 lemon
50ml white wine

For the white wine and grain
   mustard sauce:
80g unsalted butter
150g shallots, finely chopped
2 garlic cloves, finely chopped
1 tsp thyme leaves
1 bay leaf
150ml white wine
400ml Fish Stock (see page 280)
400ml double cream
1 tsp chopped tarragon
120g wholegrain mustard
2 heaped tsp Dijon mustard

1 Melt the butter in a pan over a medium heat and add the shallots, garlic, thyme and bay leaf. Cook for 3 minutes, until the shallots and garlic are soft, then add the wine and simmer until reduced by two thirds. Add the fish stock and simmer until reduced by half, then add the cream and simmer until reduced by half again. Finally, add the tarragon and the wholegrain and Dijon mustards, and keep the sauce warm while you cook the fish.

2 Season the whiting fillets all over with the salt and mustard seeds. Heat a non-stick sauté pan on a medium heat and add the olive oil. Add the whiting to the pan, skin-side down, and cook for 4 minutes, until the fish is golden around the edges. Add the butter and then flip over the fish and cook the other side for 2 minutes. Squeeze over the lemon juice and drizzle with the white wine.

3 Serve the whiting with the white wine and wholegrain mustard sauce.

Dab with Butter and Samphire

SERVES 4
4x 200g whole dab, scaled,
   gutted, head and tail
   removed (see page 293)
100ml olive oil
20g unsalted butter
1 tsp chopped thyme
juice of 1 lemon
Maldon salt and freshly
   ground black pepper

For the samphire:
200g prepared samphire
30g unsalted butter
juice of ½ lemon
freshly ground black pepper

1 Bring a medium pan of salted water to the boil, add the samphire and cook for 3–4 minutes, until tender but still with a slight crunch. Drain in a colander, then put back into the pan and add the butter, thyme, lemon juice and pepper. Set aside and keep warm while you cook the dab.

2 Place a large pan on a medium heat and add the oil. When it is hot add the butter, and once it starts to foam add the dab. Cook them skinned side down for about 4 minutes, spooning over the foaming butter while they cook and making sure the butter does not burn, then turn the dab over and cook on the other side for a further 4 minutes. Finish with a little lemon juice and serve with the samphire.

Frying

Escalopes of Monkfish Fried with Parsley and Garlic, and Lyonnaise Potatoes

SERVES 4

1 x 1.8kg monkfish, cleaned, filleted and cut into 8–12 escalopes (see page 299)
100ml olive oil
juice of 1 lemon
Maldon salt and freshly ground black pepper

For the parsley and garlic butter:

190g unsalted butter, softened
8 garlic cloves, finely chopped
8–12 anchovy fillets in oil, chopped finely
1 tbsp Pernod
75g finely chopped shallots
3 heaped tbsp chopped parsley
juice and grated zest of 1 lemon
1 tsp Maldon salt
a large pinch of freshly ground black pepper

For the Lyonnaise potatoes:

400g Charlotte potatoes, washed
1 tsp Maldon salt
6 sprigs of thyme
3 bay leaves
4 garlic cloves
20g unsalted butter
300g Spanish onions, thinly sliced
1 tsp thyme leaves
60g duck fat or olive oil
2 sprigs of flatleaf parsley, leaves picked and chopped
a large pinch of freshly ground black pepper

1 To make the parsley and garlic butter, put the softened butter into a bowl and add all the other ingredients. Beat until well combined (you can do this in a blender or processor), then set aside.

2 Put the potatoes into a pan of cold water with the salt, thyme sprigs, 2 of the bay leaves and the garlic. Bring to a simmer, then cook for 5 minutes and drain in a colander. Place the potatoes on a tray and leave to cool to room temperature. Peel and cut into 0.5cm slices.

3 Heat a large frying pan and add the butter. When it is foaming add the onions and cook, stirring from time to time, until they start to colour. Add the thyme leaves and remaining bay leaf, season with salt and pepper and continue cooking for about 15–20 minutes, until the onions are golden. Remove them from the pan and set aside.

4 Wipe the pan, add the duck fat and place over a medium heat. Add the sliced potatoes and sauté until golden, then add the fried onions and the chopped parsley. Keep the potatoes warm while you cook the monkfish.

5 Season the monkfish escalopes with salt and pepper, then heat a non-stick sauté pan and add the olive oil. Once the pan is hot, add the escalopes and cook over a high heat for 2 minutes, then add the parsley and garlic butter and turn the monkfish over. Cook the other side for a further 2 minutes and finish with a squeeze of lemon juice. Serve the monkfish with the Lyonnaise potatoes.

FISH OPTIONS: good-quality farmed salmon such as Loch Duart, line-caught sea bass

Monkfish is not really the name of this fish. It was always known as angler fish until retail and marketing demands changed it, possibly because the deep-sea variety of angler fish was so menacing and fierce-looking.

Pan-fried Monkfish, Cooked on the Bone
with Brown Butter, Celeriac Mash

SERVES 4

2 x 1.4kg monkfish tails,
    cleaned (see page 293)
80ml olive oil
100g shallots, finely sliced
1 bay leaf
1 tsp thyme leaves
140g unsalted butter
juice and grated zest of
    1 lemon
2 sprigs of flatleaf parsley,
    leaves picked and chopped
Maldon salt and freshly
    ground black pepper

For the celeriac mash:

35g unsalted butter
400g celeriac, peeled
1 heaped tsp Maldon salt
a large pinch of freshly
    ground black pepper
juice of 1 lemon
a large pinch of chopped
    thyme
2 tsp caster sugar

1 To make the mash, place a pan on a medium heat and add the butter. When it has melted, add the celeriac, salt, pepper, half the lemon juice and the thyme. Put a lid on the pan and cook slowly for 15–20 minutes, until soft, stirring now and again. Add the sugar and the remaining lemon juice and cook for a further 5 minutes, uncovered, then mash with a potato masher and keep warm.

2 Preheat the oven to 180°C/Gas Mark 4. Season the monkfish with salt and pepper and put a large ovenproof frying pan or roasting tray on the heat to get nice and hot. Add the olive oil to the pan, and when it's hot add the monkfish and cook on one side for 4 minutes, until golden. Flip the fish over and cook the other side for 2 minutes, then transfer the pan to the oven for approximately 10 minutes.

3 Remove the monkfish from the pan and set aside. Put the pan on the hob, add the shallots, bay leaf and thyme, and season with salt and pepper. Cook for 2 minutes on a high heat, until the shallots are slightly coloured, then add the butter and cook until it goes a nice golden brown. Take the pan off the heat and add the lemon juice, zest, parsley and more salt and pepper.

4 Put the monkfish back into the pan and roll it in the sauce for a minute, then place it on a chopping board and carefully remove the fillets from the bone with a knife, cutting down each side of the backbone. Slice the fish and serve with the celeriac mash and brown butter.

FISH OPTIONS: darnes of brill or turbot (see page 298)

Dover sole can often be the victim of chefs' elaborate creations but my feeling is that the best way to cook it is just to let the flavour of the fish come through. I tend to serve it with nothing more than a simple sauce and some vegetables.

Dover Sole with Peas and Pea Shoots

SERVES 4
500g fresh peas (shelled weight)
100g unsalted butter
3 large banana shallots, finely
  diced
150ml White Chicken Stock
  (see page 282)
200ml double cream
1 tbsp chopped parsley
1 tbsp chopped chervil
1 soft English lettuce, cut into
  fine strips
5 spring onions, thinly sliced
150ml olive oil
4 x 450g Dover sole,
  cleaned, skin removed
  (see page 293, 297)
Maldon salt and freshly
  ground black pepper

For the pea shoot salad:
100g fresh pea shoots
a little olive oil
lemon juice
Maldon salt and freshly
  ground black pepper

1 Bring a large pan of salted water to the boil, add the peas, and cook for 2 minutes, until tender. Refresh them in iced water, then drain in a colander.

2 Melt 25g of the butter in a pan over a low to medium heat, add the shallots and cook gently, without letting them colour, until almost soft. Add the chicken stock and cream, bring to the boil, cook for 2 minutes, then add the peas. Stir in the remaining butter, add the herbs, lettuce and spring onions and cook for a minute, then check the seasoning. Keep warm.

3 Place the pea shoots in a bowl and sprinkle with a little olive oil, lemon juice and seasoning.

4 Place a large frying pan on a medium heat and add the oil. When it's hot, add the remaining butter, and when it starts to foam add the Dover sole. Cook them skinned side up first, spooning the foaming butter over the fish as it is cooking and making sure it doesn't burn. After 6–8 minutes, turn the fish over and cook on the other side for a further 5–6 minutes. Finish with a little lemon juice.

5 Serve the Dover sole with the peas, and sprinkle with the pea shoot salad.

Variation: Baked Dover Sole
Instead of pan-frying, you can bake the sole in the oven. Cook the prepared sole skinned side up for a few minutes, then place it on a baking tray and bake in an oven preheated to 180°C/Gas Mark 4 for about 12 minutes. Serve with the peas and salad as above.

FISH OPTIONS: megrim sole, witch sole, flounder

Frying

Dover Sole Meunière

SERVES 4

4 x 500g Dover sole, skinned
   (see page 297)
100ml olive oil
150g unsalted butter
150g shallots, finely sliced
2 garlic cloves, sliced
2 bay leaves
1 tsp thyme leaves
100g capers, drained and rinsed
40g sultanas
juice of 2 lemons
grated zest of 1 lemon
2 lemons, peeled, divided into
   segments and roughly diced
2 tbsp chopped parsley
Maldon salt and freshly
   ground black pepper

1 Season the Dover sole with salt and pepper. Heat the olive oil in a large non-stick pan, and once it starts to smoke slightly, add the sole, skinned side up, and cook for 4 minutes on a medium heat. Once golden add the butter, cook for a minute or two, then very carefully flip the sole over with a large spatula and add the sliced shallots, garlic, bay leaves and thyme. Cook for 4 minutes, then add the capers and sultanas and cook for another 2 minutes.

2 Turn the heat up to brown the butter, and add the lemon juice and zest, basting the sole with the foaming butter as this will add more flavour and colour to the fish. After a couple more minutes add the lemon segments and the chopped parsley and serve immediately.

Pan-fried Witch Sole with Parsley and Caper Mash

SERVES 4

4 x witch sole, skinned
   (see page 297)
150ml olive oil
80g unsalted butter
juice and grated zest of 1 lemon
80g capers, drained and rinsed
a small bunch of chopped
   parsley
Maldon salt and fresh ground
   black pepper

For the parsley and caper mash:
500g potatoes, peeled
3 tsp Maldon salt
100g unsalted butter
100g milk, warmed
50g double cream, warmed
a large pinch of freshly
   ground black pepper
a little nutmeg to taste
1 tbsp chopped parsley
30g capers, drained, rinsed
   and roughly chopped

1 Put the potatoes into a pan with 1 litre of water and 2 teaspoons of salt and bring to the boil. Turn the heat down and simmer for about 30 minutes, until the potatoes are tender, then tip them into a colander and drain really well. Place the potatoes back in the pan and dry out on a low heat for 1 minute, then mash with the butter, remaining salt, warm milk and cream. Season with pepper and nutmeg, and finally add the parsley and capers and keep the mash warm while you cook the fish.

2 Heat a large non-stick sauté pan until it is good and hot, and season the sole with salt and pepper. Add the oil to the pan, then the butter, and when melted add the sole, skinned side up. Cook on a low to medium heat for 5–6 minutes on each side, until golden. Add the lemon juice, zest, capers and parsley and serve with the mash.

FISH OPTIONS: lemon sole, brill fillets

Frying

You can buy the chestnuts for this recipe from most large supermarkets. They come roasted and peeled and are ready for use straight away.

John Dory with Chestnuts, Bacon and Lettuce

SERVES 4
200g smoked bacon
4 x 140g John Dory fillets
100ml olive oil
40g unsalted butter
juice of 1 lemon
Maldon salt and freshly
    ground black pepper

For the chestnut sauce:
60g unsalted butter
1 tsp chopped thyme
350g shallots, finely chopped
200g ready-roasted
    chestnuts, diced
1 tsp salt
a large pinch of freshly
    ground black pepper
2 tsp lemon juice
175ml Madeira
50ml white wine
500ml White Chicken Stock
    (see page 282)
175ml double cream
2 garlic cloves, finely chopped
1 tbsp finely chopped sage

For the buttered gem lettuce:
80g unsalted butter
4 heads of baby gem lettuce,
    trimmed and cut in half
1 tsp sugar
1 tsp Maldon salt
a large pinch of freshly
    ground black pepper
400ml White Chicken Stock
    (see page 282)
1 bay leaf
1 tsp thyme leaves

1 Heat a sauté pan and add the bacon. Cook slowly for about 5 minutes, letting the fat run out, until the bacon is crispy, then drain off the fat, chop or crumble the bacon and set aside.

2 For the sauce, place a pan on a medium heat and add half the butter. Add the thyme and 100g of the shallots and cook for a few minutes without letting them colour, then add 75g of the chestnuts and cook for a minute longer. Stir in the salt, pepper, lemon juice, Madeira and white wine, and simmer until nearly all the liquid has evaporated. Then add the stock and cream and simmer for 10 minutes. Put the sauce into a blender and purée until smooth, then pass it through a fine sieve into a bowl and set aside.

3 To make the buttered lettuce, melt the butter in a wide shallow pan and add the lettuce, sugar, salt and pepper. Cook slowly until golden and caramelised, then add the chicken stock, bay leaf and thyme and continue to cook for about 20 minutes, until the lettuce is tender. When the lettuce is cooked, remove it from the pan with a slotted spoon. Simmer the liquid until reduced to a glaze, then return the lettuce to the pan and keep warm.

4 To finish the sauce, put a pan on a medium heat, add the remaining butter, and once it has melted add the garlic, sage and the rest of the shallots and season with salt and pepper. Cook over a medium heat for 4 minutes, without letting the vegetables colour, then add the rest of the chestnuts. Stir in the sauce, along with the crispy bacon, and gently warm through.

5 Season the John Dory fillets with salt and pepper. Heat a non-stick sauté pan on a medium heat and add the olive oil. When the oil is hot, add the John Dory to the pan and cook for 3 minutes, until the fish is golden around the edges. Add the butter, then flip over the fillets and cook the other side for 2 minutes. Finally, squeeze over the lemon juice, and serve with the buttered lettuce and the chestnut sauce.

John Dory has quite a bland taste so it can take potent flavours – this dish definitely gives it some punch.

John Dory with Spiced Couscous

SERVES 4

150ml olive oil
juice and grated zest of 2 limes
2 garlic cloves, finely chopped
1 red chilli, deseeded and finely
   chopped
1 large pinch each of turmeric,
   ground coriander, ground
   cumin, fennel seed and
   curry powder
2 tsp grated fresh ginger
1 heaped tbsp chopped
   coriander
1 heaped tbsp finely sliced
   basil leaves
1 stem of lemon grass,
   bashed and chopped
4 x 140g John Dory fillets
Maldon salt and freshly
   ground black pepper

For the spiced couscous salad:
300g instant couscous
75ml olive oil
80g chopped black olives
grated zest of 1 orange
grated zest of 1 lemon
a large pinch each of turmeric,
   ground coriander, ground
   cumin and ground ginger
50g dried apricots, diced
50g sultanas
50g raisins
1 heaped tsp chopped coriander
1 heaped tsp chopped mint
25ml lemon juice
1 tsp Maldon salt
a large pinch of freshly ground
   black pepper

1 Mix the oil, lime juice, garlic, chilli, spices, ginger, herbs and lemon grass in a bowl and add the John Dory fillets. Put into the fridge to marinate for at least 2 hours or overnight.

2 Place the couscous in a bowl and add the oil, olives, citrus zest, spices and dried fruit. Add 250ml of boiling water, cover with clingfilm and leave to stand for 15 minutes. Fluff up the couscous with a fork and add the herbs, lemon juice, salt and pepper. Set aside while you cook the fish.

3 Remove the John Dory fillets from the marinade, place on a grill tray, and season with salt and pepper. Put the fish under a hot grill and cook on one side for 4–5 minutes, then turn over carefully and cook for a further 4–5 minutes on the other side.

4 Serve the John Dory with the spiced couscous salad.

FISH OPTIONS: line-caught sea bass, red mullet, good-quality farmed salmon fillet such as Loch Duart

Frying

Pan-fried Red Mullet with Pistachio Risotto

SERVES 4

4 x 400g red mullet, filleted and pin boned (see pages 294, 296)
100ml olive oil
15g unsalted butter
15g pistachio nuts, finely chopped
a little lemon juice
Maldon salt and freshly ground black pepper

For the pistachio oil:
250ml pistachio oil or plain nut oil
100g pistachio nuts (as bright green as possible)

For the pistachio risotto:
150g shallots, finely diced
1 garlic clove, chopped
1 tsp chopped thyme
1 bay leaf
1 tsp Maldon salt
a large pinch of freshly ground black pepper
30g unsalted butter
200g Arborio risotto rice
150ml white wine
500ml White Chicken Stock (see page 282)
35g crème fraîche
40g grated Parmesan cheese
80g chopped pistachio nuts
1 tsp lemon juice

1 Place the pistachio oil and nuts in a blender and purée until fine. Set aside.

2 To make the risotto, put the shallots, garlic, thyme, bay leaf, salt and pepper into a pan with the butter and cook gently on a low heat until the shallots are soft and opaque. Add the rice and cook for 2 minutes, stirring all the time. Pour in the white wine and cook for a minute or two, until absorbed, then slowly add the hot chicken stock to the rice little by little, stirring every minute or so. This will take around 16–18 minutes, and the rice should be soft but still with a little bite.

3 About 5 minutes before the risotto is due to be finished, season the mullet fillets with salt and pepper. Heat a non-stick sauté pan, and once it is hot add the olive oil. Carefully put the fish skin side down into the pan and sauté for 3 minutes on a high heat, until golden around the edges. Flip the fish over with a spatula, then add the butter and when it starts to foam sprinkle on the pistachio nuts. Cook for a further 2 minutes, spooning the foaming butter over the fish. Sprinkle with the lemon juice.

4 When the risotto is ready, stir in the crème fraîche, Parmesan and chopped pistachios and check the seasoning. Serve the risotto with the mullet on top, and drizzle over the green pistachio oil.

FISH OPTIONS: halibut, gurnard

Frying

Sea Trout with Caramelised Beetroot

SERVES 4

4 x 130g sea trout fillets
100ml olive oil
40g unsalted butter
1 lemon
Maldon salt and freshly
    ground black pepper

For the caramelised beetroot:
600g beetroot, washed
100ml olive oil
1 tsp Maldon salt
a large pinch of freshly
    ground black pepper
20g unsalted butter
5 heaped tsp brown sugar
2 bay leaves
4 sprigs of thyme
1 tsp rosemary leaves
100ml balsamic vinegar
40ml lemon juice
1 tsp thyme leaves

1 Toss the beetroot in the oil and season with the salt and pepper. Wrap them in foil, place on a baking tray and bake in an oven preheated to 170°C/Gas Mark 3 for approximately 1 hour, until just cooked. Leave to cool, then remove the foil, peel off the skin and cut the beetroot into small wedges.

2 Place a sauté pan on a medium heat, and once hot add the butter and sugar, followed by the beetroot, bay leaves, thyme sprigs and rosemary. Season with salt and pepper and cook the beetroot for 10–12 minutes, with the butter just foaming and not burning, until they are starting to caramelise and soften. Add the balsamic vinegar and lemon juice, and simmer until the juice is sticky and reduced down to almost nothing and the beetroot are cooked through. Remove the thyme sprigs and add the thyme leaves. Keep the beetroot warm while you cook the fish.

3 Season the sea trout fillets with salt and pepper. Heat a large non-stick sauté pan on a medium heat, add the olive oil, and when it is hot add the fillets skin-side down, one at a time. When they are starting to colour, after 4–6 minutes or so, flip them over on to the other side with a spatula and add the butter. Cook for another 2 minutes, then squeeze over a little fresh lemon juice and serve with the caramelised beetroot.

FISH OPTIONS: good-quality farmed salmon fillet such as Loch Duart, line-caught sea bass

Because this dish is so simple, I think it's really important to ensure that the quality of the three main ingredients are the best you can find to ensure maximum flavour.

Sea Bream with Lemon, Thyme and Olives

SERVES 4

4 x 120g sea bream fillets
100ml olive oil
juice and grated zest of
    1 lemon
2 tbsp thyme leaves
60g unsalted butter
1 lemon, peeled, divided into
    segments and roughly diced
100g pitted green olives, cut
    into quarters
Maldon salt and freshly
    ground black pepper

1 Brush the sea bream fillets with a little olive oil and season with salt and pepper. Sprinkle with the lemon zest and half the thyme.

2 Heat a large sauté pan, add the rest of the olive oil, and when it is hot add the fillets, skin-side down. Cook for 4 minutes, until the edges start to turn golden, then add the butter and flip the fish over. Cook for another 3 minutes, then add the lemon juice, lemon segments, olives and the rest of the thyme. Cook for 1 more minute and serve immediately, with boiled or mashed potatoes.

FISH OPTIONS: line-caught sea bass, mackerel

Stir-fried Squid with Salt and Pepper Spring Onion

SERVES 4

60ml olive oil
juice and grated zest of 1 lime
1 tsp sugar
2 garlic cloves, finely chopped
30g fresh ginger, finely chopped
1 small red chilli, deseeded
    and finely chopped
120ml sesame oil
500g medium squid bodies,
    cleaned (see page 305)
1 bunch of spring onions,
    thinly sliced
1 tbsp chopped coriander
2 tbsp sesame seeds, lightly
    toasted
Maldon salt and freshly
    ground black pepper

1 Put the olive oil into a bowl with the lime juice and zest, sugar, garlic, ginger, red chilli and 50ml of the sesame oil, then add the squid and put into the fridge to marinate for at least 2 hours or overnight.

2 When you are ready to cook the squid, remove them from the bowl, reserving the marinade. Heat a large sauté pan and add the remaining sesame oil. When it starts to smoke, add the squid to the pan and toss or stir with a wooden spoon, working very quickly so that they do not catch on the bottom. Season with salt and pepper, sauté for 1 minute, then add the reserved marinade and the spring onions and cook for another minute. Finally add the chopped coriander, sprinkle with the sesame seeds, and serve immediately.

FISH OPTIONS: scallops, langoustines

Pan-fried Scallops with Chorizo and Chickpeas

SERVES 4

12 scallops, out of the shell,
   roe removed (see page 304)
100ml olive oil
40g unsalted butter
juice of ½ lemon
Maldon salt and freshly
   ground black pepper

For the chorizo and chickpeas:
100ml olive oil
80g chorizo sausage, diced
60g smoked bacon, cut into
   lardons
10 round shallots, quartered
2 large pinches smoked paprika
a pinch of cayenne pepper
1 bay leaf
1 heaped tsp chopped thyme
3 garlic cloves, finely chopped
1 red chilli, deseeded and
   finely chopped
150g red pepper, peeled and
   diced
a large pinch of saffron
1 tsp Maldon salt
a large pinch of freshly
   ground black pepper
150ml white wine
8 plum tomatoes, peeled,
   deseeded and diced
1 tsp caster sugar
1 tbsp tomato purée
200g tinned chickpeas
200ml Fish Stock (see page 280)
juice and grated zest of 1 lemon
25g unsalted butter
1 tbsp finely sliced basil leaves

1 Place a pan on a medium heat and add the olive oil. When it is hot add the chorizo and cook until the oil turns pink, which will take about 2 minutes. Add the bacon, shallots, paprika, cayenne, bay leaf and thyme and cook on a medium heat for 6–8 minutes, without allowing the shallots to colour, until they are soft. Add the garlic, chilli, red pepper, saffron, salt and pepper. Cook for a further 3 minutes, then add the white wine and simmer until reduced by half. Add the chopped tomatoes, sugar, tomato purée and chickpeas, then pour in the stock and cook on a low heat at a slow simmer for 15 minutes. Finally, add the lemon zest, a little lemon juice, the butter and the basil, and keep the stew warm while you cook the scallops.

2 Heat a large non-stick sauté pan, or a flat-top griddle if you have one. Season the scallops with salt and pepper, drizzle them with olive oil and place them on the griddle pan. Cook them for about 3 minutes on one side and then, once they are golden, add the butter, flip the scallops over with a spatula and cook again for another 3 minutes. Squeeze over a little lemon juice and serve with the chorizo and chickpea stew.

FISH OPTIONS: red mullet, monkfish medallions

The scallop shell is the traditional emblem of St James the Greater, the first of the Twelve Apostles to be martyred. He is very popular with pilgrims who visit his shrine at Santiago de Compostela in Spain. His association with the scallop can be traced back to the legend that he once rescued a knight covered in scallops, although another version tells that after he was martyred in Jerusalem his servant brought his body back to Galicia by sea. As the boat neared the shore, a startled horse threw its rider to the ground, and the man drowned. The servant prayed, and miraculously the man emerged alive from the water, covered in cockleshells – hence scallops are sometimes known as 'James's shell'. Medieval Christians often wore a scallop shell symbol on their hats or clothes when on pilgramage, or carried a scallop shell, which they would present at churches, castles and abbeys. In return they would receive as much financial support or food as they could pick up with one scoop of the shell – often oats, barley, and perhaps beer or wine.

Frying

These chips are proper thick-cut chips. You cook them three times, blanching them in water then frying them twice at two different temperatures. Make sure the oil is hot enough for the second frying, otherwise they will not colour properly or become crisp.

Pollack and Chips

SERVES 4

4 x 140g pollack fillets
vegetable or groundnut oil
   (or beef dripping) for
   deep-frying

For the batter:
300g self-raising flour
60g cornflour
15g caster sugar
1½ tsp Maldon salt
¼ tsp freshly ground white
   pepper
15g fresh yeast or 1 sachet
   of dried yeast
250ml sparkling water
250ml Heineken or other lager

For the thick-cut chips:
700g Maris Piper potatoes
vegetable or groundnut oil
   for deep-frying
Maldon salt

To serve:
malt vinegar
1 x quantity Tomato Ketchup
   (see page 288)

1 To make the batter, place the flour, cornflour, sugar, salt and pepper in a bowl and make a well in the centre. Crumble the yeast into the well, then pour in the sparkling water and beer and leave for a good 10 minutes. Whisk until smooth, gradually drawing in the flour from around the sides. It needs to be whisked very well in order to prevent lumps. Leave to stand for 15–20 minutes, but no longer.

2 Peel the potatoes and cut them into 1cm thick batons the length of the potato. Rinse the starch off the potatoes under cold running water, then place them in a pan of slightly salted cold water and bring to a rapid boil. Reduce the heat and simmer for 1 minute, then drain. Chill in a bowl of ice-cold water to stop them cooking any further, then drain and dry them very well on a tea towel.

3 Heat some oil to 140°C in a deep-fat fryer or a large, deep saucepan (it should be no more than half full). Plunge the chips into the hot oil, cooking them in batches so as not to overcrowd the pan. Cook for 4–5 minutes, until soft but not coloured, and drain on kitchen paper.

4 Bring the temperature of the oil up to 180°C. Plunge the chips in again and cook for 4–5 minutes, until golden brown. Drain well, season them with salt and keep them warm in an oven heated to 140°C/Gas Mark 1 while you cook the fish .

5 Heat a fresh batch of oil to 170°C. Place the fish fillets in the batter one at a time, then, holding them by the tail end, let the excess drip off. Fry in the hot oil for about 8 minutes, until golden and crisp, and drain on kitchen paper. Serve with the chips, plus some salt, malt vinegar and tomato ketchup.

FISH OPTIONS: MSC-certified cod, gurnard

Frying

Fishcakes with Tomato Sauce

SERVES 6

3–4 large baking potatoes
  (Desiree, Yukon, Maris Piper)
500g pollock fillet, pin boned
  (see page 296)
200g good-quality farmed
  salmon, such as Loch Duart
40g unsalted butter
300g onions, finely sliced
1 bay leaf
1 tsp chopped thyme
2 tbsp chopped parsley
50g gherkins, chopped
50g capers, drained, rinsed
  and chopped
150g white crabmeat
3 egg yolks
80g flour
4 eggs, beaten with 1 tbsp milk
200g white breadcrumbs or
  Japanese panko breadcrumbs
vegetable or groundnut oil for
  deep-frying
1 x quantity Thick Tomato
  Sauce (see page 288)
Maldon salt and freshly
  ground black pepper

For the poaching liquid:
800ml milk
3 garlic cloves, cut in half
4 bay leaves
2 small sprigs of thyme
12 black peppercorns
3 tsp Maldon salt

1 Bake the potatoes in an oven preheated to 180°C/Gas Mark 4 for about 45–60 minutes. Scrape out the flesh from inside the skins and weigh it – you need about 400g. Put the potato flesh into a bowl and mash it with a fork.

2 Place all the ingredients for the poaching liquid into a large, shallow pan, bring to a simmer and leave to simmer gently for 5 minutes. Lower the heat, add the pollock and poach for 7–10 minutes, turning the fish over halfway through to cook it evenly. When it's ready, the fish will flake if you lift it. Remove the pollock from the pan and place on a wire rack set over a plate to drain and cool. Poach the salmon in the same way and leave to cool on the rack alongside the pollack. Flake both fish into large pieces, removing the skin and any bones, and chill.

3 Place the butter in a medium saucepan over a low to medium heat, add the onions, bay leaf, thyme and a good pinch of salt, then cover and sweat for 5–7 minutes, until soft but not coloured. Remove from the heat and leave to cool. Mix in the potato, parsley, gherkins and capers, then fold in the crabmeat and the poached fish. Finally, stir in the egg yolks and season to taste.

4 Put the flour on a plate and the eggs and crumbs into two shallow bowls. Mould the mixture into fishcakes – you should be able to make about 12 – and dip them first into the flour, then into the egg wash and finally into the breadcrumbs.

5 Heat the oil to 180°C in a deep-fat fryer or a large, deep saucepan (it should be no more than half full). Add the fishcakes to the oil and deep-fry for 3–4 minutes, until golden brown. Drain well, then transfer to a baking tray and place in an oven preheated to 180°C/Gas Mark 4 for 2–3 minutes to heat through. Serve immediately, with the tomato sauce.

Frying

Spicy Crab Cakes

SERVES 4

3–4 baking potatoes (Desiree, Yukon, Maris Piper)

20g butter

5 banana shallots, peeled and finely diced

2 garlic cloves, crushed

1 stem of lemongrass, peeled down to the tender inner part and very finely chopped

400g fresh white crabmeat

1 heaped tbsp chopped coriander

1 large red chilli, deseeded and finely diced

1 large green chilli, deseeded and finely diced

grated zest of 1 lemon

2 pinches of smoked paprika

a pinch of cayenne pepper

4 egg yolks

80g plain flour

3 eggs, lightly beaten with 1½ tbsp milk

150g white breadcrumbs or Japanese panko crumbs

vegetable or groundnut oil for deep-frying

1 x quantity Tomato Salsa (page 291) or Guacamole (page 291)

Maldon salt and freshly ground black pepper

1 Bake the potatoes in an oven preheated to 180°C/Gas Mark 4 for about 45–60 minutes. Scrape out the flesh from inside the skins and weigh it – you need about 300g. Put the potato flesh into a bowl and mash it with a fork.

2 Heat the butter in a pan, add the shallots and 1 teaspoon of salt, then cover and cook gently for 2–3 minutes, until soft but not coloured. Stir in the garlic and lemongrass and cook for 2 minutes. Transfer to a large bowl and leave to cool. Mix in the crabmeat, mashed potato, coriander, chillies, lemon zest, paprika, cayenne and a large pinch of black pepper, then add the egg yolks. Check the seasoning.

3 Put the flour on a plate and the eggs and crumbs into shallow bowls. With floured hands, shape the mixture into about 16 golfball-sized balls and lightly roll them in the flour. Dip them one at a time into the egg wash, let the excess drain off, then transfer them to the bowl of crumbs, rolling them over so they are well coated. Place on a clean plate or tray.

4 Heat the oil to 190°C in a deep-fat fryer or a large, deep saucepan (it should be no more than half full). Add the crab cakes to the oil and fry until golden brown, then drain and transfer to a baking tray. Place in an oven preheated to 180°C/Gas Mark 4 for 5–8 minutes, until heated right through. Serve with tomato salsa or guacamole.

FISH OPTIONS: any white fish, good-quality farmed salmon fillet such as Loch Duart

Frying

The smoked eel for this recipe can be ordered from suppliers such as Brown & Forrest.

Eel and Chive Cakes with Horseradish Cream

SERVES 4 AS A STARTER

25g unsalted butter
200g leeks, finely sliced
400g smoked eel, cut into rough 1cm dice (mind the small, fine bones)
2 tbsp creamed horseradish
2 tsp grated fresh horseradish
15g sorrel leaves, finely sliced
juice and grated zest of 1 lemon
2 heaped tbsp chopped chives
1 tsp chopped parsley
2 eggs, boiled for 10 minutes, then shelled and coarsely chopped
80g flour
4 eggs, lightly beaten with 2 tbsp milk
150g white breadcrumbs or Japanese panko crumbs
1.5 litres vegetable or groundnut oil
Maldon salt and freshly ground black pepper

For the horseradish cream:

2 tbsp creamed horseradish
10g fresh horseradish, grated
150g double cream, lightly whipped
50ml crème fraîche
1 tbsp chopped chives
juice and grated zest of 1 lemon

1 To make the sauce, fold the creamed and grated horseradish into the whipped cream, then add the crème fraîche, chives, lemon zest and some freshly ground black pepper and salt to taste. It may just need a squeeze of lemon juice to lift the flavour. Stir gently until combined.

2 Melt the butter in a shallow pan over a medium heat. Add the leeks, cover the pan and cook slowly for 3 minutes until just softened. Season with a good pinch of black pepper and a little salt. Add the smoked eel and cook, uncovered, for a minute. Remove from the heat and add the creamed and grated horseradish, followed by the sorrel, lemon zest, chives and parsley. Leave to cool, then add the chopped hard-boiled eggs and mix lightly. Adjust the seasoning with salt and pepper, if necessary, and add a squeeze of lemon juice.

3 Put the flour on a plate and the eggs and crumbs into shallow bowls. Divide the mixture into 12 balls and then, using 2 palette knives, squash and mould them on a floured work surface into small cake shapes. Place them in the fridge to firm up, then re-flour and dip them first into the beaten egg and then into the crumbs. Pat them back into shape if necessary. Deep-fry in the vegetable or groundnut oil at 180°C for 2–3 minutes, until golden brown. Drain on kitchen paper and serve with the horseradish cream.

FISH OPTION: smoked haddock

You might not think it necessary to coat these croquettes in breadcrumbs twice, but believe me it's worth doing as it guarantees they will hold together when you deep-fry them and it will give them a crispier coating.

Salmon and Grain Mustard Croquettes

SERVES 4

2–3 baking potatoes (Desiree, Yukon, Maris Piper)
1 x quantity Poaching Liquid (see page 204)
500g good-quality farmed salmon fillet, skinned and any bones removed (see page 297)
40g unsalted butter
200g onions, finely sliced
1 tsp Maldon salt
a few sprigs of thyme
1 bay leaf
6 spring onions, sliced
40g capers, drained, rinsed and chopped
1 heaped tbsp wholegrain mustard
1 heaped tbsp chopped parsley
150g flour
5 eggs, beaten with 4 tbsp milk
160g white breadcrumbs or Japanese panko crumbs

1 Bake the potatoes in an oven preheated to 180°C/Gas Mark 4 for about 45–60 minutes. Scrape out the flesh from inside the skins and weigh it – you need about 250g. Put the potato flesh into a bowl and mash it with a fork.

2 Place the poaching liquid in a large pan and bring to a simmer. Simmer for 10 minutes, then add the salmon and cook for 2–3 minutes on a low heat. Remove the pan from the heat and leave the salmon to cool in the liquid. Flake the salmon into large pieces and place in a bowl.

3 Heat the butter in a medium pan, add the onions, salt, thyme and bay leaf, then cover the pan and cook over a low to medium heat for 5–7 minutes, without allowing the onions to colour, until soft. Stir in the spring onions, cook for a minute longer, then remove from the heat and cool. Mix in the mashed potato, salmon, capers, wholegrain mustard and parsley and check the seasoning.

4 Mould the mixture into croquettes – you should get about 12 – and roll them on a floured surface into small barrel shapes, using a palette knife to shape them, tapping the ends and rolling at the same time. There should be no visible cracks in the ends. Put them into the fridge for 30 minutes to firm up.

5 Put the flour on a plate and the eggs and crumbs into two shallow bowls. Coat the croquettes in the flour, then dip them first into the egg wash and then into the crumbs. Gently reshape them if necessary and put them back into the fridge for about 20–30 minutes. Then egg wash and crumb them again.

6 Heat the oil to 180°C in a deep-fat fryer or a large, deep saucepan (it should be no more than half full) and deep-fry the croquettes for 3–4 minutes, until golden brown. Drain on kitchen paper, then transfer them to a baking tray and place them in an oven preheated to 180°C/Gas Mark 4 for 2–3 minutes to make sure they are heated right through.

7 Serve with home-made tomato ketchup (see page 288).

Frying

In the Catholic countries of southern Europe, dried fish fulfilled an important and valuable product as a protein-rich food for people who were not allowed to eat meat on as many as 120 days a year. Bacalhau became an important and staple part of the Portuguese diet and was nicknamed *Fiel amigo* (faithful friend).

Salt Cod Beignets

SERVES 4 AS A STARTER

3–4 baking potatoes (Desiree, Yukon, Maris Piper)
200ml olive oil
400g ready-prepared or home-made salt cod (see page 35), soaked in cold water for a day, then dried on kitchen paper
200g shallots, finely diced
8 garlic cloves, finely diced
a large pinch of freshly ground black pepper
2 heaped tbsp chopped parsley
a little plain flour for dusting
juice of 1 lemon
1 litre vegetable or groundnut oil for deep-frying

For the beer batter:
170ml warm milk
30g caster sugar
15g yeast or 1 sachet of dried yeast
120g plain flour
a pinch of Maldon salt
35ml beer

1 Bake the potatoes in an oven preheated to 180°C/Gas Mark 4 for about 45–60 minutes. Scrape out the flesh from inside the skins and weigh it – you need about 250g. Put the potato flesh into a bowl and mash it with a fork.

2 Pour the olive oil into a pan and heat until very hot. Add the cod and sauté for 3–4 minutes, then drain in a colander and set aside for a minute or so to cool. Add the shallots and garlic to the pan and cook for 1 minute, then add the black pepper.

3 Place the cod in a bowl with the mashed potato and mix together with a fork, adding the shallots and garlic, the rest of the olive oil and the parsley. Check the seasoning, leave to cool, then chill.

4 Meanwhile, make the batter. Mix the milk with the sugar and yeast and leave to stand for 15 minutes. Place the flour and salt in a bowl, make a well in the centre and pour in the yeasted milk. Add the beer and whisk to a smooth batter.

5 Divide the salt cod mixture into balls (you should be able to make about 20, golfball size) and roll them in flour to coat lightly. Heat the oil to 180°C in a deep-fat fryer or a large, deep saucepan (it should be no more than half full). Using a fork, dip the salt cod balls into the batter, then fry them in the hot oil until golden brown. Drain on kitchen paper, season with salt and a little lemon juice and serve straight away.

Tartare sauce is great with deep-fried fish, as it cuts through the richness of the batter.

Langoustine Tempura
with Tartare Sauce

SERVES 4 AS A STARTER

1 litre vegetable oil for
  deep-frying
12–16 langoustines, shelled
  (see page 303)
1 quantity Tartare Sauce
  (see page 290)
Maldon salt

For the batter:
300g self-raising flour
150g cornflour
75g baking powder
1 tsp Maldon salt
400ml chilled sparkling water
2 ice cubes

1 First make the batter. Sift the flour, cornflour and baking powder into a bowl, add the salt and then whisk in the water a little at a time until smooth. Add the ice cubes and set aside for 30 minutes.

2 Heat the oil to 180°C in a deep-fat fryer or a large, deep saucepan (it should be no more than half full). Dip the langoustines into the batter, let any excess drain off, and add them to the hot oil, cooking them in batches if necessary. Cook for 2–3 minutes, until golden, then remove and drain on kitchen paper. Sprinkle with salt and serve immediately, with the tartare sauce.

FISH OPTIONS: lobster, plaice, squid, megrim sole, witch sole

The first fish and chip stalls were set up 170 years ago and there are now approximately 12,000 fish and chip stalls in the UK serving around 200–250 million meals a year.

The humble fish and chip meal was not rationed at all during the war and it has been argued that because of this, it helped us win the war. The fish-and-chip shop soon became a typical family business, run by and for working people, in London to some extent, but especially in the north of England. Where there were no shop premises, the trade would be carried on from people's front rooms, a practice hardly likely to be approved by today's environmental health and safety inspectors. Over time, practically every working community had at least one chip shop, fortifying factory employees and other shift workers through the lengthy working day.

The traditional wrapping for a portion was old newspaper, a thrifty custom that is still recalled when people scornfully refer to the press as 'tomorrow's fish-and-chip wrapping'. In fact, on hygiene grounds alone, chip shops haven't been allowed to use real newspaper since the 1980s, when it was decided that the possible absorption of newsprint by the food wasn't a good idea.

It has often been said in recent years that fish and chips may well be entering a period of decline. Dwindling stocks of the fish that the northern chippies, in particular, dealt in (mainly cod and haddock) have sent prices up and there are health concerns as well arising from the type of oil used for deep-frying. However, despite all of these challenges, the humble chippie remains an enduring feature of many towns and city streets.

Deep-fried Paprika Squid with Lime

SERVES 4 AS A STARTER
1 litre vegetable or groundnut
  oil for deep-frying
200g plain flour
½ tsp paprika, plus a little
  extra for serving
grated zest of 2 limes
400g medium squid, cleaned
  (see page 305), bodies cut
  into 5mm rings, tentacles
  left whole
juice of 1 lime
Maldon salt and freshly
  ground black pepper

For the batter:
300g self-raising flour
150g cornflour
75g baking powder
a pinch of paprika
juice of 2 limes
ice-cold water
Maldon salt and freshly ground
  black pepper

1 First make the batter. Sift the dry ingredients into a bowl, season with salt and pepper and mix in the lime juice. Whisk in enough ice-cold water to give the consistency of double cream.

2 Heat the oil to 180°C in a deep-fat fryer or a large, deep saucepan (it should be no more than half full). Place the flour, paprika and lime zest in a bowl and add the squid. Toss well to coat, then shake off the excess flour. Remove the squid from the bowl and dip into the batter. Cook in the hot oil, in batches, for about 3 minutes, until golden.

3 Drain well on kitchen paper, sprinkle with the lime juice and a little more paprika and season with salt and pepper. Serve straight away – in paper cups, if you like.

Beer-battered Coley Strips
with Gremolata

4 x 160g coley fillets, cut
  into 2cm strips
1.5 litres vegetable or
  groundnut oil
1 x quantity Beer Batter
  (see page 184)

For the gremolata:
100g flatleaf parsley, cut
  into fine strips
6 garlic cloves, finely chopped
grated zest of 5 lemons
juice of 1 lemon
150ml olive oil

1 Mix all the ingredients for the gremolata together and set aside.

2 Season the coley strips with salt and pepper. Dip the strips into the batter and deep-fry in vegetable or groundnut oil at 180°C for 3–4 minutes. Drain on kitchen paper. Add a squeeze of lemon juice and serve with the gremolata.

FISH OPTIONS: gurnard, witch sole, flounder

Frying

Floured Squid with Aioli

SERVES 4 AS A STARTER
400g medium squid, cleaned
    (see page 305), bodies cut
    into 5mm rings, tentacles
    left whole
4 garlic cloves, finely chopped
grated zest of 1 lemon
½ tbsp finely chopped rosemary
100ml olive oil
1 litre vegetable or groundnut
    oil for deep-frying
200g self-raising flour
a squeeze of lemon juice
1 x quantity Aioli Mayonnaise
    (see page 289)
Maldon salt and freshly
    ground black pepper

1 Put the squid into a bowl and add half the garlic, the lemon zest, rosemary and olive oil. Season with salt and pepper. Stir well and put into the fridge to marinate for a day.
2 Heat the oil to 180°C in a deep-fat fryer or a large, deep saucepan (it should be no more than half full). Mix the flour with the remaining garlic in a bowl. Toss the squid in the flour and then deep-fry, in batches, for about 3 minutes, until golden. Sprinkle with the lemon juice and serve immediately, with the aioli mayonnaise.

Megrim Sole Goujons with Tartare Sauce

SERVES 4
150g plain flour
4 eggs, lightly beaten with
    4 tbsp milk
150g coarse white breadcrumbs
    or Japanese panko crumbs
4 x 160g fillets of megrim sole,
    cut into 2cm strips
1.5 litres vegetable or
    groundnut oil
1 x quantity Tartare Sauce
    (see page 290)
Maldon salt and freshly
    ground black pepper

1 Put the flour on a plate and the eggs and crumbs into two shallow bowls. Season the sole goujons lightly with salt and pepper. Dust them lightly with the flour, then dip them into the egg wash, wiping off any excess. Finally dip them into the crumbs, turning to coat them well.
2 Heat the oil to 180°C in a deep-fat fryer or a large, deep saucepan (it should be no more than half full). Add the goujons in batches, so as not to overcrowd the pan, and deep-fry for 3–4 minutes, until golden brown. Drain on kitchen paper and serve with the tartare sauce.

FISH OPTIONS: lemon sole, plaice, witch sole

After World War Two we wanted more convenience food, and soon after the war ended the humble fish finger was invented by a Mr Clarence Birdseye. After five decades on shop shelves, 114 packets are thought to be sold every minute in supermarkets in the UK. Traditionally made from cod and coated in breadcrumbs, the fingers are also made from haddock and pollock as North Sea cod supplies continue to fall. While often thought of as children's food, unbelievably two-thirds are eaten by adults. Birds Eye's new Omega-3 fish fingers use 100 per cent fish fillet and are made from wild Alaskan pollock. Alaskan pollock is certified as sustainable and meets the MSC environmental standard for well-managed fisheries.

Frying

Steaming and poaching can often be thought of as boring methods of cooking but by marinating your fish and using plenty of herbs and spices your dishes can become very flavoursome. These are very healthy ways of cooking as you don't lose the nutrients in the way that you can when cooking at high temperatures and there is very little mess involved which means clean food and, I hope, a clean kitchen!

Steaming & Poaching

PLEASE
SUPPORT THOSE
WHO RISK THEIR
LIVES TO FEED
THE NATION

The plaice that you've eaten is most likely to have been grilled or fried so you might like to try poaching it to ring the changes a little. This taste of the fish will be very different to your previous experiences.

Poached Plaice with Leeks and Grain Mustard

SERVES 4

1 x quantity Poaching Liquid (see page 204)
4 x 450g plaice, cleaned and filleted (see page 297)

For the leeks:
6 medium leeks
60g unsalted butter
150ml White Chicken Stock (see page 282)
1 tsp thyme leaves
Maldon salt and freshly ground black pepper

For the white wine and grain mustard sauce:
80g unsalted butter
150g shallots, finely chopped
2 garlic cloves, finely chopped
1 bay leaf
150ml white wine
400ml Fish Stock (see page 280)
400ml double cream
2 tbsp chopped tarragon leaves
120g wholegrain mustard
10g Dijon mustard
juice of 1 lemon

1 Put the poaching liquid into a large pan over a low heat.
2 To make the sauce, melt the butter in a pan and add the shallots, garlic and bay leaf. Cook for 3 minutes, until soft, then add the white wine and reduce by two thirds. Add the fish stock and reduce by half. Add the cream and reduce by half again, then add the chopped tarragon and the wholegrain and Dijon mustards. Set the sauce aside.
3 To cook the leeks, cut off the green top part and peel off two outer layers. Split each leek in half, then wash under cold running water to remove any sand or grit and cut crossways into thin strips. Put the butter and chicken stock into a small pan over a medium heat and bring to a simmer, then add the thyme. Stir in the leeks, season with salt and pepper, and simmer gently for 5 minutes, until the leeks are nice and tender and the cooking liquid has reduced. Keep warm while you cook the fish.
4 Bring the poaching liquid to a gentle simmer. Season the plaice fillets with salt and pepper and fold them in half. Carefully place them in the liquid and cook for 4 minutes. Meanwhile, gently reheat the sauce. Remove the fillets carefully from the pan with a slotted spoon and serve with the leeks and sauce.

FISH OPTIONS: megrim sole, lemon sole, Dover sole

Whole Poached Fish in a Court Bouillon

SERVES 4–6

1 x 1.8kg sea trout, scaled
    and gutted (see page 293)
Maldon salt and freshly
    ground black pepper

For the court bouillon:
3 celery sticks, sliced
1 onion, sliced thinly
2 leeks, sliced
1 fennel bulb, sliced
4 shallots, sliced
2 garlic cloves, sliced
3 bay leaves
6 star anise
12 whole black peppercorns
16 pink peppercorns
4 thyme sprigs
a few sprigs each of parsley,
    tarragon and chervil
juice and grated zest of
    1 lemon
3 heaped tsp Maldon salt
300ml white wine

1 A salmon-poaching kettle is ideal for this, or you can use a large roasting pan. Season the sea trout and place in the kettle or pan first, then add the rest of the court bouillon ingredients. Add enough water to cover the fish, and bring to a slow simmer. Cook for 15 minutes, then remove from the heat and leave to stand for 5 minutes.

2 Carefully remove the vegetables from the liquid, discarding them, then lift the trout out carefully and place on a serving plate. Serve with a green salad and boiled new potatoes.

FISH OPTIONS: line-caught sea bass, turbot

Keeping an eye on the level of the fish stock in the North Sea is about as achievable as a magician pulling a white rabbit out of his hat. It takes an enormous amount of effort to gather all the necessary data and is virtually impossible to get real readings of what we have taken out of the sea and what is left. The spawning stock of the cod is said to be around 50,000 but when factors such as fish migration, the quantity of fish that is caught as bycatch or discarded and therefore potentially not included in the count, and the EU quota system are taken into consideration, it's easy to see how unlikely it is that this figure is accurate.

Prawn stocks in the North Sea and are generally thought to be exploited at sustainable levels and may even be under-exploited in the northern North Sea, but many of the wonderful fish that we all enjoy eating – cod, plaice, sole and monkfish, for example – are now outside safe biological limits and listed by the ICES as being endangered, which essentially means that the population of the fish is so low that they could suffer breeding failure on a very large scale. Of course, it is impossible to instil a ban on the fishing of a certain species of fish: you can't stop cod coming into your net, for example. Nevertheless, there are different mesh sizes and escape panels in some nets that would aid the release of certain types fish and there are moves towards the development of further no-go areas in the North Sea. These are positive steps for the future.

Poached Coley with Grain Mustard and Lemon Butter

SERVES 4

80ml olive oil
juice and grated zest of
1 lemon
2 tsp yellow mustard
seeds, crushed
4 x 140g coley fillets
Maldon salt and freshly
ground black pepper

For the poaching liquid:
8 whole black peppercorns
grated zest of 1 lemon
juice of ½ lemon
a pinch of Maldon salt
150ml white wine
4 banana shallots, roughly
sliced
400ml Fish Stock
(see page 280)

**For the grain mustard
butter sauce:**
125g unsalted butter, cut
into small cubes
140g shallots, finely diced
200ml double cream
1 tbsp wholegrain mustard
2 tbsp mustard seeds, soaked
in cold water
juice and grated zest of
1 lemon
1 large pinch of chopped
tarragon
1 heaped tsp chopped chives
Maldon salt and freshly
ground black pepper

1 Put the oil, lemon juice and zest, mustard seeds, salt and pepper into a bowl. Stir well and brush over the coley fillets. Leave to marinate for at least an hour – and for 2 hours if possible.

2 Place all the ingredients for the poaching liquid into a pan, bring to a simmer and cook for 5 minutes. Add the seasoned coley and cook gently for 4–6 minutes, then turn the fillets over and cook for another 3–4 minutes. Remove with a slotted spoon to a warm plate, cover with butter paper or foil and keep warm while you make the sauce.

3 Place a shallow pan on a low to medium heat and add 25g of the butter. Once melted, add the shallots and cook slowly until translucent – about 2–3 minutes. Add 200ml of the poaching liquid, bring to a simmer and cook until reduced by half. Add the cream and simmer until reduced by half, then whisk in the remaining butter, the wholegrain mustard, mustard seeds, lemon juice and zest. Season with salt and pepper, then add the cooked coley fillets, bring to a simmer and add the herbs.

FISH OPTIONS: pollack, MSC-certified cod, line-caught sea bass

Steaming & Poaching

Poached Salmon with Dill and Pernod

SERVES 4

4 x 160g salmon fillets, skin
    removed (see page 297)
300ml double cream
100g unsalted butter
juice of ½ lemon
½ a small bunch of dill,
    leaves picked and chopped
Maldon salt and freshly
    ground black pepper

For the poaching liquid:
8 whole black peppercorns
grated zest of 1 lemon
juice of ½ lemon
a pinch of Maldon salt
150ml white wine
4 sprigs of thyme
8 sprigs of dill
100ml Pernod
4 star anise
4 banana shallots, roughly
    sliced
approx. 400ml Fish Stock
    (see page 280)

1 Place all the poaching liquid ingredients into a pan, bring to a simmer and cook for 5 minutes. Season the salmon fillets with salt and pepper and add to the pan, adding more stock if necessary so that the fish is covered. Poach gently for 3–4 minutes, then turn the fillets over and cook for another 3–4 minutes. Remove from the poaching liquid to a warm plate and cover with butter paper or foil.

2 Pass the liquid through a fine sieve into a clean saucepan and simmer until reduced by two thirds. Add the cream and simmer until reduced by half. Whisk in the butter, add a squeeze of lemon juice and the dill, and season with salt and pepper. Add the salmon fillets carefully to the sauce, warm through for a minute or so, and serve.

FISH OPTIONS: line-caught sea bass, sea trout, monkfish

As chefs we are creative in the way we use seasonal vegetables and are managing to encourage consumers to try vegetables they may not have heard of, so why are we not all doing the same with fish? In order for fish stocks to remain stable and sustainable, fish should not be bought during their breeding period. This period differs according to the fish and explains why species should not be available all year round. I remember a time when, owing to its quality and rarity, the king of the waters was the wild Atlantic salmon. It was a seasonal product – only available for six weeks of the year – and as such it was hard to get hold of. Now it's a fish that is commercially available because it is farmed, yet for the wild stock to sustain itself we should only be buying it during those six weeks of the year.

As chefs I do feel we have a responsibility to try and engage with consumers and encourage them to learn about when the different species of fish are in season. If chefs can be open-minded about what they should or should not be serving it could help to make a change in how the consumer chooses and thinks about fish.

Steaming & Poaching

Plaice Poached in Red Wine
with Parmentier Potatoes

SERVES 4

4 x 450g plaice, filleted
(see page 295)
Maldon salt and freshly
ground black pepper

For the poaching liquid:
150ml vegetable oil
30g unsalted butter
3 celery sticks, cut into
small dice
4 shallots, cut into small dice
1 leek, cut into small dice
½ fennel bulb, cut into
small dice
1 large carrot, cut into
small dice
4 garlic cloves, peeled and
crushed
1 tsp caster sugar
1 tsp black peppercorns,
crushed
2 bay leaves
4 sprigs of thyme
4 star anise
2 tsp Maldon salt
800ml red wine
250ml Madeira
400ml Brown Chicken Stock
(see page 282, or use
good-quality bought
stock such as Joubère)
1 tbsp chopped parsley

For the Parmentier potatoes:
4 large Maris Piper or Desiree
potatoes, peeled and rinsed
150ml olive oil
4 garlic cloves, crushed
60g unsalted butter
2 tsp thyme leaves
1 tbsp chopped parsley
300ml Brown Chicken Stock
(see page 282, or use
good-quality bought
stock such as Joubère)
Maldon salt and freshly
ground black pepper

1 To make the poaching liquid, place a large shallow pan on a high heat and add the oil and 20g of the butter. Once it starts to foam, add the vegetables, garlic, sugar, peppercorns, bay leaves, thyme, star anise and salt and cook for 6–8 minutes until the vegetables are golden, stirring now and again until nicely caramelised. You may need to turn down the heat to medium so they do not get too dark. Add the red wine and Madeira, and simmer until reduced by half. Add the stock and cook for a further 15 minutes at a simmer. Keep the poaching liquid warm.

2 To make the Parmentier potatoes, take one potato at a time, place it on a cutting board and cut off the sides to make a rectangle or square shape. Cut the potato into even slices about 1.5cm thick, then cut the slices into 1.5cm squares so they are nice and even and rinse in cold water to remove the starch. Repeat with the rest of the potatoes.

3 When you are ready to cook the potatoes make sure you drain and then dry them very well, otherwise when you cook them they will stick together and the oil will spit and could burn you. Place a large non-stick sauté pan on the heat and add half the olive oil and 2 of the garlic cloves. When the oil is hot, add half the potatoes, season with salt and pepper and sauté until the potatoes are light golden in colour. Tip them into a colander to drain off the oil. Repeat the process again with the second batch and again drain the potatoes when light golden in colour.

4 Wipe the pan out and heat it up again, adding the butter. When it starts foaming, add the potatoes and cook until they are a nice golden colour. Add the thyme and check the seasoning. Pour in the stock and simmer until the stock has reduced and the potatoes are nicely glazed. Sprinkle with the parsley.

5 Bring the poaching liquid to a gentle simmer. Season the plaice fillets, fold them in half, add them to the poaching liquid and cook for 6–8 minutes, depending on their size. Remove with a slotted spoon and place on a warmed plate. Turn the heat up and cook until the liquid has reduced down to below the level of the vegetables, then add the remaining butter with the chopped parsley and serve with the plaice and the Parmentier potatoes.

Gurnard with Orange
and Lemon in a Paper Bag

SERVES 4

4 x 400g whole gurnard, scaled,
    heads removed, gutted and
    filleted (see pages 293, 294)
100ml olive oil
40g unsalted butter
2 tsp Maldon salt
a large pinch of freshly ground
    black pepper
2 tsp lemon thyme leaves
4 sprigs of rosemary
8 bay leaves, cut in quarters
1 orange, peel removed in large
    strips with a vegetable peeler
2 lemons, peel removed in large
    strips with a vegetable peeler
½ bunch of dill
juice of 1 orange
juice of 1 lemon

1 Take the gurnard and lay them on their sides. Make 4 slashes down each side and rub in the olive oil, butter, salt and pepper. Inside the slashes put the thyme, rosemary and bay leaves. Open the belly and fill the cavity with half the orange and lemon peel and half the dill.

2 Cut 4 x 30cm squares of baking parchment. Take a square and rub with olive oil, then place some of the remaining orange and lemon peel and dill on each one, just off centre. Put a gurnard on top of each one and drizzle with orange juice and a little lemon juice. Carefully fold the paper over and secure with staples or paper clips – it should look like a little rectangle with the fish inside. (See page 125 for picture.)

3 Place the packages on a baking tray and bake for 16 minutes in an oven preheated to 180°C/Gas 4, and when you tear open the paper be careful of the steam (it will smell amazing).

FISH OPTIONS: line-caught sea bass, red mullet, sea trout

Steaming & Poaching

Poached Turbot with Chervil Sauce

SERVES 4

1 x quantity Poaching Liquid
   (see page 204)
1 x 1.6kg turbot, filleted
   (see page 295)
Maldon salt and freshly
   ground black pepper

For the chervil sauce:
80g unsalted butter
100g shallots, finely sliced
1 bay leaf
300ml white wine
600ml White Chicken Stock
   (see page 282)
400ml double cream
2 bunches of chervil, leaves
   picked and roughly chopped
juice of ½ lemon
Maldon salt and freshly
   ground black pepper

1 Put the poaching liquid into a large pan over a low heat.
2 To make the chervil sauce, melt 30g of the butter over a low heat and add the shallots and bay leaf. Cook for 4 minutes, until the shallots are soft, then add the white wine and simmer until reduced by two thirds. Add the chicken stock and simmer until reduced by half. Lastly, add the cream and simmer until reduced by half again. Pass the sauce through a fine sieve, discarding the shallots, then put the sauce into a blender, add the remaining butter, the chervil and the lemon juice and purée until smooth. Keep the sauce warm while you cook the fish.
3 Bring the poaching liquid to a gentle simmer. Season the turbot fillets with salt and pepper, place them in the liquid and cook them for 3 minutes. Remove them from the pan with a slotted spoon and serve immediately with the chervil sauce.

FISH OPTIONS: good-quality farmed salmon such as Loch Duart, brill, Dover sole

Poached Monkfish Tail with Saffron and Capers

SERVES 4

1 x 1.6kg monkfish tail
100g tomatoes, diced
100g capers, drained and rinsed
1 tbsp chopped parsley
Maldon salt and freshly
   ground black pepper

For the saffron sauce:
80g unsalted butter
200g shallots, sliced
400ml white wine
800ml Fish Stock (see page 280)
300ml double cream
4 large pinches of saffron
juice of 1 lemon
1 heaped tsp Maldon salt
1 tsp sugar

1 To make the saffron sauce, place a pan on a medium heat and add half the butter. Once melted, add the shallots and cook for 3–4 minutes until semi-soft. Add the white wine and simmer until reduced by two thirds, then add the fish stock and reduce by two thirds again. Add the cream and saffron and simmer until reduced by half. Add the lemon juice and salt, then transfer to a blender and add the sugar and the rest of the butter. Blend for about a minute, then pass the sauce through a fine sieve.
2 Cut the monkfish into thin medallions or escalopes (see page 299) and season them with salt and pepper. Place them in the saffron sauce and poach for 4–5 minutes, adding the diced tomato, capers and chopped parsley for the final minute of cooking. Serve immediately.

Steaming & Poaching

Poached Sea Trout with Chantenay Carrots and Sauternes

SERVES 4

500ml Fish Stock (see page 280)
6 sprigs of tarragon
6 sprigs of thyme
1 bay leaf
2 banana shallots, sliced
juice of ½ lemon
200ml Sauternes
40g unsalted butter
Maldon salt and freshly ground
    black pepper
4 x 160g pieces of sea trout,
    skin removed (see page 297)

For the carrots:
80ml olive oil
300g Chantenay carrots
80g unsalted butter
1 tsp sugar
1 tbsp thyme leaves
2 tbsp chopped tarragon leaves
150ml Sauternes
200ml Fish Stock (see page 280)
juice of ½ lemon
grated zest of 1 lemon

1 Place the fish stock, herbs, shallots, lemon juice, Sauternes, butter, salt and pepper into a shallow saucepan and bring to a simmer. Keep warm over a low heat.

2 Heat a non-stick sauté pan on the hob and add the olive oil. When it is slightly smoking add the carrots with some salt and pepper and toss them in the pan so they get a nice golden colour. Add 40g of the butter and when it starts foaming add the sugar, thyme and tarragon. When the carrots are nicely caramelised, pour the Sauternes into the pan, standing back when you do this as it will splash up. Simmer to deglaze the pan and reduce the wine by two thirds, then add the fish stock. Finally, add the rest of the butter with the lemon juice and zest.

3 Season the fish with salt and pepper, then add to the warm fish stock and poach for 4 minutes. Remove from the liquid and serve with the roasted carrots.

FISH OPTIONS: good-quality farmed salmon such as Loch Duart, monkfish, line-caught sea bass

Sea Trout with Sorrel Sauce

SERVES 4

4 x 130g sea trout fillets
  (see page 294)
100ml olive oil
40g unsalted butter
juice and grated zest of
  1 lemon
Maldon salt and freshly
  ground black pepper

For the sorrel sauce:
80g unsalted butter
100g finely sliced shallots
200ml white wine
500ml Fish Stock
  (see page 280)
500ml double cream
juice of ½ lemon
1 bunch of sorrel,
  leaves picked
Maldon salt and freshly
  ground black pepper

1 To make the sorrel sauce, melt the butter in a pan, add the sliced shallots and cook on a low heat for 4 minutes until they are soft. Add the white wine and simmer until reduced by two thirds, then pour in the fish stock and simmer until reduced by half. Add the cream and reduce by another third, then season with salt and pepper, add a squeeze of lemon juice and the sorrel leaves and cook for 1 minute. Once cooked you can either use a hand blender to blend the sauce directly in the pan, or use an upright blender for a smoother texture. Keep the sauce warm while you cook the fish.

2 Season the sea trout fillets with salt and pepper. Heat a large non-stick sauté pan on a medium heat and add the olive oil. When it's hot, add the fish skin-side down, one fillet at a time. When they are starting to colour, after 4–6 minutes or so, flip them over to the other side with a spatula, add the butter and continue to cook for another 2 minutes. Squeeze over a little lemon juice and zest, and serve with the sorrel sauce.

FISH OPTIONS: good-quality farmed salmon such as Loch Duart, line-caught sea bass

Steaming & Poaching

Sea Trout Mousse with Chervil Butter

SERVES 4

300g sea trout fillets, cleaned,
　skinned and pin boned,
　flesh roughly chopped
1 egg white
300ml double cream
1 tsp Maldon salt
a pinch of freshly ground black
　pepper
750ml Fish Stock (see page 280)
2 tbsp chopped tarragon
3 tbsp chopped chervil

For the chervil butter:
160g unsalted butter
150g shallots, finely sliced
1 bay leaf
1 bunch chervil, leaves picked
　and chopped, stems reserved
300ml white wine
400ml double cream
juice of ½ lemon

1 You will need a food processor for this recipe, as the mousse needs to be very smooth. Everything must be as cold as possible before you start, so put the processor blade into the freezer well beforehand, and place the chopped trout on a plate in the freezer for 15–20 minutes. If you don't do this, the processor can get too warm when puréeing and the mousse may split.
2 Once the blade and trout are cold, purée the fish for a minute until smooth. Add the egg white and purée until incorporated, scraping the bowl with a spatula. Slowly add half the cream, scrape the bowl again and add the salt and pepper. Switch the processor on and slowly add the rest of the cream, puréeing until smooth.
3 Pass the mousse through a fine sieve and place in a metal bowl over ice. Beat with a spatula for a minute to make sure all the cream is mixed in. You need to do a test now, to check the seasoning and smoothness of the mousse. Place the stock in a pan and bring to a bare simmer at around 80°C. Take a small spoonful of the mousse, place in the stock and cook until it floats – this will take about a minute. Remove with a slotted spoon and taste the mousse – if the seasoning is okay, add the chopped herbs to the mixture. With 2 dessertspoons, one in each hand, make quenelle shapes with the rest of the mousse and poach them in the stock for about 4 minutes. When they float, remove them with a slotted spoon, set aside and reserve the stock.
4 To make the chervil butter, place 40g of the butter in a non-stick saucepan, add the shallots, bay leaf and chervil stems, and cook for 4 minutes on a low heat without letting the shallots colour. Add the white wine and simmer until reduced by two thirds, then add the fish stock you poached the quenelles in, and simmer until reduced by half. Finally add the cream and reduce by half again. Whisk in the remaining butter little by little, and lastly add the chopped chervil leaves and lemon juice. Add the poached quenelles to the sauce and warm through.

FISH OPTION: good-quality farmed salmon such as Loch Duart

Sea Trout Poached in Olive Oil
with Pickled Cucumber

SERVES 4
2 English cucumbers
4 x 160g pieces of sea trout,
    skin removed (see page 297)
400ml extra virgin olive oil
6 garlic cloves, crushed
3 bay leaves
12 sprigs of thyme
8 sprigs of dill
2 sprigs of rosemary
2 sprigs of basil
18 black peppercorns, crushed
4 star anise
6 juniper berries, crushed
2 tsp each fennel and cumin
    seed
Maldon salt

For the pickling liquid:
400ml distilled vinegar
175ml water
30g caster sugar
½ cinnamon stick
4 all spice berries, crushed
12 black peppercorns
½ tsp mustard seed
6 whole cloves
2 tbsp sliced root ginger
1tsp fennel seed
2 star anise
4 juniper berries, crushed

1 Place all the ingredients for the pickling liquid in a pan and bring to a simmer, then take off the heat. Leave to infuse for 3 hours, then pass through a muslin cloth into a large bowl.

2 Peel the cucumbers and cut them in half down the middle. Scoop out the seeds with a teaspoon, then cut each half into three pieces and slice into thin strips. Sprinkle a little salt over the cucumber and leave for 20 minutes to remove some of the water. Gently squeeze the cucumber to remove as much water as possible, then add to the pickling liquid and leave for 1 hour.

3 To poach the sea trout, put the olive oil in a heavy-based pan with the garlic, herbs, spices and salt and heat to 80°C. Place the sea trout in the pan, remove from the heat immediately and leave for 30 minutes – by now the trout should be at room temperature and if you stick in a cocktail stick it should come out clean.

4 Drain the pickled cucumber in a colander and serve with the trout.

FISH OPTIONS: good-quality farmed salmon such as Loch Duart, monkfish

You can buy the won ton wrappers used in this recipe from most large supermarkets or Asian food shops.

Poached Prawn Dumplings with Chilli

SERVES 4

1 packet of small won ton
   wrappers
1 egg, beaten
olive oil for cooking
1 x quantity Sweet and Sour
   Sauce (see page 287)

For the prawn filling:
50g unsalted butter
2 tbsp sesame oil
40g ginger, finely chopped
8 garlic cloves, finely chopped
60g shallots, finely sliced
1 small red chilli, deseeded
   and finely chopped
4 spring onions, finely sliced
400g prawns, peeled and
   deveined (see page 303)
2 egg whites
4 tbsp soy sauce
juice and grated zest of 1 lime
1 heaped tbsp chopped
   coriander
50ml coconut milk
30g cornflour, sifted
Maldon salt and freshly
   ground black pepper

1 Melt the butter in a sauté pan over a low heat. Add the sesame oil, ginger, garlic, shallots and chilli and cook on a low heat for 3–4 minutes, until soft. Add the spring onions, cook for 2 more minutes, and set aside to cool.

2 Put the prawns, egg whites, soy sauce, lime juice and zest into a food processor and pulse on low speed until they make a coarse purée. Transfer the purée to a mixing bowl and add the coriander and coconut milk. Stir in the cooled ginger and garlic mixture, and lastly mix in the cornflour. Season with salt and pepper. (If you want to make sure that the seasoning is okay, cook a small piece in a non-stick sauté pan for a couple of minutes each side and taste.)

3 Lay 4 of the wrappers at a time on a board. Place a tablespoon of the prawn mixture in the centre of each wrapper, then, using a pastry brush, brush the edges with the egg wash. Fold each wrapper over itself so you have a triangular-shaped dumpling and press down along the edges, sealing in the filling. Make 4–6 dumplings per person, depending on how hungry you are.

4 To cook the dumplings, bring a large pan of salted water to the boil and add a little olive oil. Lower the dumplings into the pan and cook for 5 minutes on a gentle simmer. Meanwhile, put the sweet and sour sauce into a small pan and warm gently over a low heat. Using a vegetable spider, carefully lift the dumplings out of the pan and into a colander, being careful not to tear them. Serve immediately, with the sweet and sour sauce.

FISH OPTION: langoustines

Salmon Confit with Duck Confit in Red Wine Sauce

SERVES 4

750ml duck fat for poaching the salmon (alternatively, this is good made with olive oil)
2 bay leaves
1 heaped tsp thyme leaves
4 sprigs of rosemary
1 tsp black peppercorns
2 heaped tsp Maldon salt
4 garlic cloves, peeled and cut in half
zest of 1 lemon, taken off in strips with a speed peeler
4 x 160g organic salmon fillets, skinned

For the duck confit:
150g Maldon salt
1 heaped tsp thyme leaves
1 tsp rosemary leaves
2 bay leaves
4 garlic cloves, cut in half and crushed
1 heaped tbsp black peppercorns, crushed
½ tsp juniper berries
2–3 duck legs, depending on how hungry you are
600–800ml duck fat (you need enough to cover the duck legs completely)

For the red wine sauce:
500ml red wine
300ml port
400g banana shallots, thickly sliced
10 black peppercorns, crushed
4 sprigs of thyme
2 bay leaves
500ml Brown Chicken Stock (see page 282, or use good-quality bought stock such as Joubère)
25g unsalted butter

1 First prepare the duck confit. Place the salt, herbs, garlic, peppercorns and juniper berries in a bowl and add the duck legs. Mix well, and leave to marinate in the fridge overnight. The next day, wipe off the excess seasoning. Place the duck fat in a shallow casserole, or even a small roasting tin, and melt on the hob. Add the duck legs to the fat, making sure they are completely covered. Transfer to an oven preheated to 90°C (or the lowest possible gas mark) and cook for 3–4 hours. The duck is ready when it is tender to the touch and the meat is falling away from the bone. Once the duck legs are cooked, carefully remove them from the oven and set aside to cool. Remove the legs from the fat with a slotted spoon, then take all the meat off the bone and shred it into large pieces.

2 To confit the salmon, put the duck fat or olive oil into a heavy-based pan with the herbs, peppercorns, salt, garlic and lemon zest and heat to 80°C. Place the salmon in the pan, remove from the heat immediately and leave for 30 minutes – by now the salmon should be at room temperature and if you stick in a cocktail stick it should come out clean.

3 For the red wine sauce, put the red wine, port, shallots, peppercorns, thyme and bay leaves into a pan over a low heat and simmer until reduced by two thirds. Add the stock, bring back to a simmer and reduce by two thirds again. Add the butter, a little at a time, then add the duck confit and warm through over a low heat. Place on serving plates, with the salmon on top.

FISH OPTIONS: monkfish, halibut

Steaming & Poaching

Poached Dover Sole with Champagne Sauce

SERVES 4

1 x quantity Poaching
Liquid (see page 204)
4 x 500g Dover sole,
cleaned, trimmed and
filleted (see page 295)
Maldon salt and freshly
ground black pepper

For the Champagne sauce:
80g unsalted butter
200g shallots, sliced
1 tsp Maldon salt
a large pinch of freshly
ground black pepper
200ml white wine
300ml Champagne
500ml Fish Stock
(see page 280)
400ml double cream
80ml lemon juice
1 tsp caster sugar

1 Put the poaching liquid into a large pan over a low heat.
2 To make the champagne sauce, place a pan on a medium heat and add half the butter. When it has melted, add the shallots, salt and pepper and cook for 3–4 minutes, without letting the shallots colour, until slightly soft. Add the white wine and Champagne and simmer until reduced to the level of the shallots. Next add the fish stock, simmer until reduced down to the level of the shallots again, then add the cream and simmer gently for a further 10 minutes. Pour the sauce into a blender, add the lemon juice, sugar and the rest of the butter, and blend for about a minute. Pass the sauce through a fine sieve and keep warm while you cook the fish.
3 Bring the poaching liquid to a gentle simmer. Season the fish fillets with salt and pepper and fold them in half. Place them in the poaching liquid and cook for 3 minutes, then remove with a slotted spoon and serve immediately, with the Champagne sauce.

FISH OPTIONS: lemon sole, megrim sole, salmon fillet

Dover Sole Véronique

SERVES 4

4 x 500g Dover soles,
filleted and skin removed
(see page 00)
Maldon salt and freshly
ground black pepper
80g unsalted butter
100g shallots, finely sliced
250ml dry vermouth
500ml Fish Stock (see page 280)
400ml double cream
juice of 1 lemon
25–30 green seedless grapes,
cut in half
1 tbsp chopped tarragon

1 Fold the sole fillets in half and season with salt and pepper.
2 Melt 40g of the butter in a pan, add the shallots and cook for 4 minutes on a medium low heat until soft. Add the vermouth and simmer until reduced by two thirds, then add the fish stock and simmer until reduced by half. Add the cream and reduce by a third again, then place in a blender, add the lemon juice and purée until smooth. Pass the sauce through a fine sieve, check the seasoning and put back into a shallow pan.
3 Bring the sauce back to a simmer, add the sole fillets and poach gently for 3–4 minutes. Add the grapes and tarragon, and serve immediately.

Steaming & Poaching

Poached Megrim Sole with Shallot Butter

SERVES 4

1 x quantity Poaching Liquid
  (see page 204)
4 x 500g megrim sole
Maldon salt and freshly
  ground black pepper

For the shallot butter:

150g unsalted butter
200g shallots, finely chopped
1 bay leaf
2 tsp thyme leaves
300ml white wine
300ml double cream
juice of ½ lemon
Maldon salt and freshly
  ground white pepper

1 Put the poaching liquid into a large pan over a low heat.
2 To make the shallot butter, melt 50g of the butter in a pan over a low heat. Add the shallots, bay leaf and thyme, and cook for 4 minutes, until the shallots are soft and opaque. Add the white wine and simmer until reduced by two thirds, then add the cream and reduce by half. Once reduced, start adding the remaining butter little by little, whisking all the time so that it blends into the cream. Season with salt and pepper and the lemon juice, and keep warm while you cook the fish.
3 Bring the poaching liquid to a gentle simmer. Season the fish fillets with salt and pepper and fold them in half. Place them in the poaching liquid and cook for 3 minutes, then remove and serve immediately with the shallot butter.

FISH OPTIONS: Dover sole, lemon sole, John Dory

Semi-poached Brill with Leeks

SERVES 4

1 x quantity Poaching Liquid
  (see page 204)
4 x 140g brill fillets
  (see page 295)
Maldon salt and freshly
  ground black pepper

For the leeks:

8 medium leeks
150ml White Chicken Stock
  (see page 282)
60g unsalted butter
1 tsp thyme leaves
Maldon salt and freshly
  ground black pepper

1 Put the poaching liquid into a large pan over a low heat.
2 To cook the leeks, cut off the green top part and peel off two outer layers. Split each leek in half, then wash under cold running water to remove any sand or grit and cut crossways into thin strips. Bring the stock to a simmer in a small pan and add the butter, thyme and leeks. Season with salt and pepper, and simmer gently for 10 minutes, until the leeks are nice and tender and the cooking liquid has reduced.
3 Bring the poaching liquid to a gentle simmer. Season the brill fillets with salt and pepper, place in the liquid and cook for 3 minutes. Remove with a slotted spoon and serve immediately with the leeks.

Brill Poached in Red Wine

SERVES 4

4 x 140g brill fillets
  (see page 295)
Maldon salt and freshly
  ground black pepper

For the poaching liquid:
150ml vegetable oil
30g unsalted butter
3 celery sticks, cut in small dice
4 shallots, cut in small dice
1 leek, cut in small dice
½ fennel bulb, cut in small dice
1 large carrot, cut in small dice
4 garlic cloves, peeled and
  crushed
2 bay leaves
1 tsp thyme leaves
1 tsp crushed black
  peppercorns
1 tsp caster sugar
4 star anise
2 tsp Maldon salt
600ml red wine
250ml Madeira
300ml Brown Chicken Stock
  (see page 282, or use
  good-quality bought
  stock such as Joubère)
1 tbsp chopped parsley

1 To make the poaching liquid, heat a large shallow saucepan and add the oil and 20g of butter. As soon as it starts to foam, add the vegetables, garlic, bay leaves, thyme, sugar, black pepper, sugar and star anise and cook for 6–8 minutes, stirring now and again, until nicely caramelised – you may need to turn down the heat to medium so it does not get too dark. Add the red wine and Madeira and bring to a simmer. Reduce this by two thirds, then add the chicken stock, bring back to a simmer, and cook for 15–20 minutes.

2 Season the brill fillets and poach them in the simmering stock for 7–10 minutes, depending on their size, turning them over halfway through. Remove the fish with a slotted spoon and place on a warmed plate. Turn up the heat and simmer the liquid until it has reduced down to below the level of the vegetables, then stir in the remaining butter and chopped parsley and serve with the fish.

Brill is often considered a second-class citizen in comparison to its cousin, the turbot, yet some chefs do prefer brill because it is not as meaty or as chewy as turbot. Despite its reputation it is still very much one of the luxury flat fish. You can distinguish it from turbot by looking at its dorsal fin: turbot has a frilly edge to its fin while brill does not. And unlike turbot, the brill's upper body surface is covered in scales. Brill has a creamy-white underside and like many flatfish it is capable of camouflage and can change its colour to match the seabed.

Brill has a firm bite and its bones make a very tasty fish stock.

Steaming & Poaching

Steamed Brill with Grain Mustard Butter Sauce

SERVES 4

4 x 140g brill fillets
   (see page 295)
Maldon salt and freshly
   ground black pepper

For the grain mustard butter
   sauce:
150g shallots, chopped
1 bay leaf
6 sprigs of thyme
300ml white wine
300ml White Chicken Stock
   (see page 282)
200ml double cream
150g unsalted butter
a squeeze of lemon juice
60g wholegrain mustard
1 tsp smooth Dijon mustard
Maldon salt and freshly
   ground black pepper

1 To make the sauce, melt 20g of the butter in a pan and add the shallots, bay leaf, and thyme. Cook on a low heat for 4 minutes, without letting the shallots colour, until soft, then add the white wine and simmer until reduced by two thirds. Add the chicken stock and simmer until reduced by half. Next add the cream and simmer until reduced by half again. Keep warm while you cook the fish.

2 Place a bamboo steamer over a pan of simmering water. Season the brill fillets with salt and pepper and place each one on a piece of baking parchment just slightly larger than the fillet (if you are cooking for just two people you can put both in together). Place them in the steamer and steam for 8–10 minutes, depending on the size of the fillets.

3 Whisk the butter into the sauce little by little, being careful not to add it too quickly otherwise it could split. Once all the butter is added, pass the sauce through a fine sieve into a clean pan. Add a squeeze of lemon juice, then whisk in the mustards and finally season with salt and pepper. Serve with the brill fillets.

FISH OPTIONS: turbot, sea bass, monkfish

Steaming & Poaching

Poached Brill with Crayfish

SERVES 4

24 crayfish, cooked and
   cleaned, heads and shells
   reserved (see page 303)
400ml double cream
juice of ½ lemon
40g unsalted butter
4 x 140g brill fillets (see
   page 295)
3 tbsp chopped tarragon
2 tbsp chopped chives
Maldon salt and freshly
   ground black pepper

For the crayfish stock:
150ml olive oil
the reserved crayfish heads
   and shells
3 tsp Maldon salt
3 banana shallots, chopped
1 large carrot, cut into 1cm dice
½ a bulb of fennel, cut into
   1cm dice
4 star anise
1 tbsp fennel seeds
1 tbsp coriander seeds
1 tbsp dill seeds
20 black peppercorns
1 tsp pink peppercorns
a small bunch of thyme
a small bunch of tarragon
50g tomato purée
500ml white wine
200ml brandy
4 plum tomatoes, quartered
1 litre Fish Stock (see page 280)

1 To make the crayfish stock, heat a large pan and add the olive oil. Add the crayfish shells and some Maldon salt and sauté over a high heat until nice and golden. Drain the shells in a colander and pour the oil back into the pan. Heat the pan again over a medium heat, add the shallots, carrots, fennel and a pinch of salt, and cook for 6–8 minutes, until the vegetables are golden. Add all the spices and herbs. Add the crayfish shells and tomato purée and cook for 2–3 minutes. Add the white wine and brandy and simmer until reduced by half. Add the tomatoes and cook for a further 5 minutes. Cover with the fish stock and bring to a simmer. Skim the scum off the top with a ladle, then simmer gently for 1 hour.

2 Tip the crayfish stock into a colander, pressing the shells and vegetables well to get maximum juice and flavour out of them. Pass the liquid through a fine sieve, put back on the heat, and simmer until reduced by half. Add the double cream and simmer until again reduced by half. Add a squeeze of lemon juice and whisk in the butter.

3 Season the brill fillets with salt and pepper, add to the sauce and cook for 3–4 minutes. Add the crayfish and herbs and warm through for 30 seconds. Remove the fillets carefully with a spatula, place on serving plates, and serve the crayfish and sauce alongside.

FISH OPTIONS: turbot, hake

You can of course use any selection of mushrooms you like for this – the ones listed below are only a suggestion.

Pouting with Sautéed Wild Mushrooms and Summer Herbs

SERVES 4
2 x 1.2kg pouting, filleted
    (see page 294)
Maldon salt and freshly
    ground black pepper

For the poaching liquid:
2 celery sticks, chopped
2 shallots, chopped
1 leek, chopped
½ fennel bulb, chopped
4 garlic cloves, cut in half
2 bay leaves
4 star anise
12 black peppercorns
16 pink peppercorns
4 sprigs of thyme
a few sprigs each of parsley,
    tarragon, dill and chervil
grated zest of 1 lemon
juice of 1 lemon
200ml white wine
500ml water
2 tsp Maldon salt

For the wild mushrooms:
80g chanterelle mushrooms
60g each of shiitake, oyster
    and trumpet mushrooms
250ml olive oil
40g unsalted butter
1 tsp mixed chopped thyme
    and rosemary
1 tsp Maldon salt
a large pinch of freshly
    ground black pepper
2 bay leaves
6 garlic cloves, finely chopped
150ml brandy
200ml White Chicken Stock
    (see page 282)
100ml double cream
juice of 1 lemon
a large pinch each of chopped
    parsley, chives, tarragon
    and chervil

1 Place all the ingredients for the poaching liquid in a pan and bring to a simmer. Cook for 10 minutes, then leave on a low heat for the flavours to infuse.

2 Wipe the mushrooms and trim the stalks. Slice the shiitakes and tear the oyster and trumpet mushrooms into quarters. Place a large frying pan over a fairly high heat. When it is hot, add the olive oil, followed by half the butter. Add half the mushrooms, then the thyme, rosemary, salt, pepper, bay leaves (cut in half lengthways) and garlic, and cook for a minute or two. Remove from the frying pan to a plate and repeat with the rest of the mushrooms, adding a little more oil and butter if necessary. Don't try to cook all the mushrooms at the same time, otherwise they will stew as opposed to being sautéed.

3 When the mushrooms are all cooked, transfer them to a shallow pan and add the brandy. Simmer until the brandy has reduced by half, then add the chicken stock and cream. Reduce by half again, then add the remaining butter and the lemon juice, followed by the parsley, chives, tarragon and chervil. Correct the seasoning if necessary, and keep warm while you cook the fish.

4 Bring the poaching liquid to a gentle simmer. Season the fish fillets and fold them in half. Lower them carefully into the liquid, poach for 3–4 minutes, then remove with a slotted spoon.

5 Divide the mushrooms and sauce between 4 serving plates and put the poached fish on top.

FISH OPTIONS: flounder, halibut, plaice

Steaming & Poaching

I've chosen to use mullet for this dish but lots of other white fish suit the light, fresh oriental flavours that are used in this recipe.

Steamed Grey Mullet with Ginger, Sesame and Soy Bok Choy

1x 1.2 kg grey mullet, scaled, gutted and filleted (see page 293, 294), cut into 4 x 140g pieces
6 bok choy, cut in half
1 lime, thinly sliced

For the soy marinade:
300ml soy sauce
3 garlic cloves, finely chopped
40g ginger, finely chopped
1 small red chilli, seeds removed, finely chopped
80g soft brown sugar
juice and grated zest of 2 limes
60ml sesame oil
1 tbsp chopped coriander

1 Place the soy sauce, garlic, ginger, chilli and sugar in a small saucepan and bring to a simmer. Cook until reduced by half and slightly syrupy, then take off the heat and leave to cool to room temperature. Add the lime juice and zest, sesame oil and chopped coriander. Place the mullet fillets in a bowl, pour over the marinade, and leave for 30 minutes.

2 Place a steamer over a pan of simmering water. Dip the bok choy into the marinade, lay them in the bottom section of a two-tier bamboo or wooden steamer, and steam for 2–3 minutes. Place each mullet fillet on a piece of baking parchment just slightly larger than the fish (if you are cooking for just 2 people you can put the 2 fillets in together) and lay them side by side in the next tier of the steamer, above the bok choy. Place a lime slice on each fillet. The fish will take about 8–10 minutes to cook, depending on their size.

3 Serve the fish with the bok choy, with the marinade as a dipping sauce if you like.

FISH OPTIONS: red mullet, gilthead bream, line-caught sea bass

Steaming & Poaching

Jellied Ray with Parsley and Egg

SERVES 4

4 free-range or organic eggs
1 x 1.5kg ray wing, filleted and
   skinned (see pages 295, 297)
1 litre Fish Stock (see page 280)
80g shallots, finely chopped
1 tbsp chopped parsley
1 tbsp chopped chives
1 tbsp chopped chervil
4 tbsp capers, drained, rinsed
   and chopped
juice and grated zest of 1 lemon
3 leaves of gelatine, soaked in
   cold water
Maldon salt and freshly
   ground black pepper

1 Bring a pan of water to a simmer, add the eggs, and cook in gently simmering water for 8 minutes. Put them into an ice bath until cold, then remove the shells and chop the eggs roughly. Place the chopped egg in a bowl and season with salt and pepper. Divide between four 250ml ramekins.

2 Bring the fish stock to a slow simmer. Season the ray wing with salt and pepper, then place it in the stock and poach for 6–8 minutes, until just cooked. Remove it from the stock and place on a tray to cool. Once cooled, carefully shred, pulling apart the flesh along the natural lines of the ray so you have long strands, and put them into a bowl.

3 Add the shallots, herbs, capers, lemon juice and zest to the shredded ray, seasoning with salt and pepper, then place this on top of the chopped eggs and level the top. Make sure you do not pack the ray in too tightly – you need to leave room for the jelly to seep through to the bottom.

4 Warm 600ml of the fish stock in a pan. Add the soaked gelatine and stir until melted. Pass through a fine sieve into a bowl, season with salt and pepper, then place the bowl over iced water to cool, stirring slowly all the time so that the liquid will not set. When cool enough, carefully spoon the jelly into the ramekins until the mixture is covered, and place in the fridge for at least 1 hour to set.

5 Serve as a starter, with sourdough toast and butter.

Steaming & Poaching

Flounder Poached with Peas, Broad Beans and Chervil

SERVES 4

400g fresh peas (shelled weight)
400g fresh broad beans (shelled weight)
80g unsalted butter
100g shallots, finely chopped
1 bay leaf
500ml Fish Stock (see page 280)
100ml white wine
250ml double cream
4 x 140g flounder fillets
1 bunch of chervil, leaves picked and chopped
juice of 1 lemon
Maldon salt and freshly ground black pepper

1 Put the peas and beans into a colander and rinse under a cold tap. Bring a pan of water to the boil and add some salt. Add the peas, blanch for 2 minutes, then remove them from the water with a slotted spoon and put them into iced water to cool. Add the beans to the water and blanch for a minute – again, cool them in iced water. Once the peas are cool, simply drain them in a colander. Remove the skins from the broad beans by squeezing them between your thumb and forefinger. Set the peas and beans aside until later.

2 Melt the butter in a shallow saucepan, add the shallots and bay leaf, and cook on a low heat for about 4 minutes, until the shallots are soft. Add the fish stock and white wine, bring to a simmer, and cook until the liquid has almost evaporated. Add the cream and simmer until reduced by a third. Season the sauce with salt and pepper.

3 Fold the flounder fillets in half and season with salt and pepper. Add the fillets to the sauce and cook them for 2 minutes, then add the peas and broad beans and cook for a further 2 minutes on a gentle simmer. Finally add the chopped chervil and a squeeze of lemon juice and serve immediately.

FISH OPTIONS: Dover sole, pollack

Flounder Fillets in Foil with Noilly Prat, Soft Shallots and Thyme

SERVES 4
100ml olive oil
80g unsalted butter
2 tsp thyme leaves
juice and grated zest of
    2 lemons
4 x 140g flounder fillets
3 tsp chopped dill leaves
4 bay leaves
200ml Noilly Prat vermouth
Maldon salt and freshly
    ground black pepper

For the soft shallots:
12–16 round shallots
150ml vegetable oil
80g unsalted butter
1 tsp thyme leaves
1 bay leaf
1 tsp caster sugar
250ml Noilly Prat vermouth
1 tsp chopped chervil
Maldon salt and freshly
    ground black pepper

1 To cook the shallots, very carefully cut the top and the base from just above the root line and peel off the first two layers with no green or brown outer skin layers, then cut them in half lengthways. Place a shallow pan on a low to medium heat and add the oil and half the butter. When it has melted, add the shallots, thyme, bay leaf, sugar and a little salt and pepper. Cover the pan and leave to cook gently, stirring occasionally, for at least 8–10 minutes without allowing the shallots to colour. Take off the lid, add the Noilly Prat and simmer until reduced by two thirds.

2 Cut 4 x 30cm squares of tin foil. Brush each square with olive oil and smear with a little butter. Sprinkle with salt and pepper and scatter some thyme and lemon zest over each one. Put the fish on top, season with salt and pepper, and sprinkle with the dill. Dot the remaining butter on top, sprinkle with a little lemon juice and place a bay leaf on each one.

3 Drizzle over the Noilly Prat, bring the corners of the foil into the middle, and secure them by just folding over the edges. Place the pouches on a baking tray and cook in an oven preheated to 180°C/Gas Mark 4 for 10–12 minutes (be very careful when you open them, as there will be a lot of steam).

4 Stir the remaining butter and the chervil into the shallots, and add a squeeze of lemon juice. Check the seasoning and serve with the flounder.

FISH OPTIONS: pouting, dab

Steaming & Poaching

If you'd like an alternative to mayonnaise to serve with these langoustines, you could try the slightly lighter option of my Sweet and Sour sauce on page 287.

Steamed Whole Langoustines
with Tarragon and Fennel

SERVES 4
16 x 60g langoustines
1 x quantity Mayonnaise
    (see page 289)
1 tsp chopped tarragon

For the tarragon and fennel
    salad:
2 medium fennel bulbs,
    sliced very thinly
100ml extra virgin olive oil
1 tsp tarragon leaves
1 tbsp chopped dill
freshly grated zest of 1 lemon
80g shallots, finely chopped
a squeeze of lemon juice
Maldon salt and freshly
    ground black pepper

1 To make the salad, place the fennel in a bowl and add the rest of the salad ingredients. Season with salt and pepper. Put the mayonnaise into a bowl and stir in the tarragon.
2 Steam the langoustines for 6–8 minutes in a bamboo or wooden steamer, and either eat them hot straight out of the steamer or cold, refreshing them in iced water for 2–3 minutes to stop them cooking.
3 Serve the langoustines and salad together, dipping the sweet-tasting tails in the tarragon mayonnaise.

FISH OPTION: crayfish

Oysters Poached in Red Wine Sauce
with Duck Confit and Celeriac

SERVES 4

12 native oysters, shucked
   (see page 304), shells kept
25g unsalted butter
1 x quantity Red Wine Sauce
   (see page 285)
1 x quantity Duck Confit
   (see page 216)
a little chopped parsley

For the celeriac mash:
35g unsalted butter
400g celeriac, peeled weight
1½ tsp Maldon salt
a large pinch of freshly
   ground black pepper
juice of 2 lemons
a large pinch of thyme leaves
2 tsp caster sugar

1 To make the celeriac mash, melt the butter in a medium pan and add the celeriac, salt, pepper, lemon juice and thyme and sugar. Place a lid on the pan and cook slowly for 15–20 minutes, stirring now and again, until the celeriac is soft. Remove the lid, cook for a further 5 minutes, then mash with a potato masher until finely crushed. Keep the celeriac warm.

2 Clean the oyster shells with a brush and cold water and warm through in the oven at 160°C/Gas Mark 2 for just 3 minutes.

3 Add the butter to the red wine sauce and remove the thyme sprigs. Put two thirds of the sauce into a separate pan, add the shredded duck meat and reheat over a low heat.

4 Heat the remaining sauce, add the oysters, and poach for no more than 90 seconds, otherwise they will go tough. To serve, place some crushed celeriac in the bottom of each oyster shell, put the oysters on top, and pour the red wine sauce and shredded duck over the whole thing. Sprinkle with a little chopped parsley.

Soups, Stews & Pot food

The one-pot dishes in this chapter cover every type of occasion. Most of the soups are great for a mid-week supper – quick and easy while also being a little more interesting than a vegetable-based soup, which is what we can often resort to. There are also a few that are a little more elaborate and are perhaps best saved for a dinner party.

The pasta dishes, pies and bakes are all crowd-pleasers – they make for easy entertaining and are guaranteed to provide a hearty meal but many of them are also easy to whip up when you get home from work.

Soups, Stews & Pot food

Leek and Oyster Soup

SERVES 4–6

80g unsalted butter
200g shallots, finely sliced
4 garlic cloves, finely chopped
150g fennel, finely sliced
400g leeks, chopped
a pinch of cayenne pepper
150ml brandy
300ml Fish Stock (see page 280)
300ml double cream
12 native Colchester oysters,
   shucked, juices reserved
   (see page 304)
2 bay leaves
8 sprigs of thyme
1 tbsp tarragon leaves
1 tbsp chopped parsley
1 tbsp chopped chervil
juice of 1 lemon
Maldon salt and freshly
   ground black pepper

1 Melt the butter in a shallow saucepan over a medium heat. Add the shallots, garlic, fennel, leeks, salt, pepper and cayenne, and cook, covered, over a low heat for 5 minutes until they are soft, but without letting them colour. Add the brandy and simmer until reduced by half, then add the fish stock and cream and simmer the soup for 10 minutes.

2 Add the oysters and juice and cook for a further 3 minutes, then add all the herbs and the lemon juice. Remove the bay leaf and thyme sprigs and serve.

FISH OPTIONS: cooked clams or mussels

If you've ever eaten oysters in a restaurant or seen an oyster farm you've most likely encountered the Pacific oyster, also known as the Portuguese oyster. Pacific oysters are currently the preferred aquaculture species in Scotland because they grow faster than native oysters. Yet farming native oysters could help replenish the wild population in this area.

Commercial cultivation of the oyster involves growing oysters on the seabed or in mesh bags laid on trestles on the lower shoreline, where they are only exposed to the air at low tide. The longer the period of immersion, the better the growth rate of the oyster, although some exposure is required to promote shell hardness before they are harvested. These oysters are available in a variety of size grades, usually from 4–30mm shell length. The size grade quoted by suppliers generally refers to the size of mesh used to sort the oyster seeds – as the oysters grow, the size of the mesh in the bags is increased progressively.

Soups, Stews & Pot food

Smoked Eel and Apple Soup

SERVES 4–6

400g smoked eel fillet, cleaned
80g unsalted butter
150g fennel, chopped
100g shallots, chopped
2 garlic cloves, chopped
100g leeks, washed and
   chopped
1 bay leaf
1 heaped tsp chopped thyme
30g sugar
3 Granny Smith apples, cut in
   quarters, cored and chopped
juice of 1 lemon
400ml apple juice
500ml Fish Stock (see page 280)
350ml double cream
80ml Calvados
Maldon salt and freshly
   ground black pepper

1 Dice three-quarters of the smoked eel fillet and set aside for serving.

2 Put the butter into a pan, add the fennel, then cover the pan and cook on a low heat for 3 minutes without allowing it to colour. Add the shallots, garlic, leeks, bay leaf, thyme, salt, pepper and apples and cook for a further 3 minutes until soft. Add the remaining smoked eel, cook for a minute, then add the sugar, lemon juice, apple juice and fish stock and bring to a simmer. Cook for 10 minutes, then add the cream and Calvados and transfer to a blender. Purée to a fine consistency, then pass through a fine sieve, pressing well. Check the seasoning, add the reserved diced eel fillet and serve.

Smoked Salmon Soup

SERVES 4–6

500g smoked salmon
80g unsalted butter
150g shallots, chopped
150g leeks, washed and
   chopped
150g fennel, chopped
1 bay leaf
2 garlic cloves, sliced
2 large pinches of smoked
   paprika
600ml Fish Stock (see page 280)
50ml Pernod
300ml double cream
100g crème fraîche
juice of 1 lemon
1 tbsp chopped dill
Maldon salt and freshly
   ground black pepper

1 Dice 100g of the smoked salmon and set aside for serving.

2 Melt the butter in a saucepan on a low to medium heat and add the shallots, leeks, fennel, bay leaf and garlic. Season with salt, pepper and paprika and cook for 3 minutes until soft. Add the remaining salmon, cook for a minute, then add the fish stock and Pernod and bring to a simmer. Cook for 10 minutes, then add the cream, crème fraîche and lemon juice. Transfer to a blender and purée to a fine consistency, then pass through a fine sieve, pressing well. Check the seasoning, add the diced smoked salmon and chopped dill, and serve.

Soups, Stews & Pot food

Prawn Soup with Ginger and Lime Leaf

SERVES 4

80g unsalted butter
200g shallots, finely sliced
20g fresh ginger, finely chopped
4 garlic cloves, finely chopped
1 red chilli, finely chopped
1 tbsp Thai curry paste
1 tsp turmeric
1 stem of lemongrass, end
  removed, cut into three and
  tied with string
150g shiitake mushrooms,
  sliced
4 star anise
6 kaffir lime leaves
750ml Fish Stock (see page 280)
2 tbsp Thai fish sauce
4 tsp caster sugar
2 heaped tsp Maldon salt
4 tbsp light soy sauce
2 tins of coconut milk
250ml double cream
150g baby bok choy, sliced
6 spring onions, sliced
1 heaped tsp chopped coriander
  leaves
1 heaped tsp finely sliced basil
  leaves
300g cooked peeled prawns
juice of 2 limes

Melt the butter in a saucepan and add the shallots, ginger, garlic, chilli, Thai curry paste, turmeric and lemongrass. Cook on a low heat for 3 minutes. Add the shiitake mushrooms, star anise, lime leaves, fish stock, Thai fish sauce, sugar, salt, soy sauce, coconut milk and cream. Bring to a simmer and cook for 10 minutes, until the liquid has reduced by a third, removing any scum with a ladle. Add the baby bok choy, spring onions, coriander, basil, prawns and lime juice, cook for 1 minute, then check the seasoning and serve.

Spiced Red Mullet Soup

SERVES 4–6

250ml olive oil
2 fennel bulbs, sliced roughly
60g chorizo sausage, sliced
1 level tsp crushed black
    peppercorns
2 banana shallots, sliced finely
3 cloves garlic
2 red peppers, chopped roughly
1 red chilli pepper, chopped finely
3 tsp Maldon salt
800g white fish, langoustine
    or lobster bones
200ml white wine
5 plum tomatoes, chopped
    roughly
100g tomato purée
2 level tsp caster sugar
a large pinch of cayenne
2 pinches of smoked paprika
80g unsalted butter
juice of 1 lemon
3 red mullet, cleaned
    (see page 293) and cut into
    2.5cm darnes (see page 298),
    approx. 4 pieces each
100ml olive oil

Variation: Chickpeas and Mullet

100ml olive oil
60g chorizo sausage, cut into
    approx. 2–3 mm dice
4 banana shallots, cut into
    0.5cm dice
2 pinches of smoked paprika
1 pinch of cayenne pepper
3 garlic cloves, finely chopped
150g canned chickpeas
200ml Spiced Red Mullet Soup
    (see above), made up to *
300ml cream
12 canned piquillo peppers,
    left whole
3 red mullet, prepared as above
25g unsalted butter
Maldon salt and freshly
    ground black pepper

1 Put the olive oil into a large pan on a medium heat. Once it is hot, add the sliced fennel, chorizo and black pepper and cook for 2–3 minutes without allowing the fennel to colour. Add the shallots, garlic, red peppers, chilli and salt, and cook for another 2–3 minutes, with a lid covering the pan. Add the fish bones, white wine and tomatoes and add just enough water to cover the bones by 2.5cm. Bring to a simmer and skim all the scum off, then add the tomato purée, sugar and spices, giving it a good stir. Bring back to a simmer and cook for 60 minutes, until it has reduced by about one third.

2 Using a hand blender (or you can use a normal blender), blend until very fine and smooth, then pass through a fine sieve into a bowl, pressing really well so that all the flavour and juice comes out of the fish bones. Repeat, and this time just tap the soup through the sieve. Blend again, adding the butter and lemon juice, then check the seasoning and pass through a fine sieve once more.*

3 Place the olive oil in a frying pan over a medium high heat. Season the mullet with salt and pepper and cook for about 2 minutes each side. Lower the heat and add a squeeze of lemon. Put some of the fish pieces into each serving bowl and pour the soup over.

FISH OPTION: grey mullet

Variation: Chickpeas and Mullet

Put the oil into a medium-sized pan on a low to medium heat and add the chorizo. Cook for 2 minutes until the oils have been released, then add the shallots, spices and garlic. Add the chickpeas and stir in the mullet soup and cream. Bring to a simmer and cook for 2–3 minutes, add the piquillo peppers then season the red mullet with salt and pepper, place in the pan and cook for 3–4 minutes, moving the fish around the pan so they get cooked evenly. Stir in the butter and serve in 4 shallow soup bowls.

Soups, Stews & Pot food

I work with a fisherman in Newlyn called Richard Ede who is one of the last remaining willow-pot makers. He crafts withy pots by hand and, as far as he knows, he's the only person that still makes them and uses them for lobster and crab fishing. It's amazing to watch him – it certainly takes a lot of patience.

Crab and Lemon grass Soup

SERVES 4–6

3kg crab bones and shells
300ml olive oil
2 large fennel bulbs, finely
  chopped
1 head of garlic, cut in half
200g shallots, chopped
1 red chilli, deseeded and
  chopped
4 kaffir lime leaves
3 level tsp Maldon salt
8 star anise
2 level tbsp fennel seeds
1 tbsp pink peppercorns
800ml white wine
200ml Pernod
a bunch of tarragon
a bunch of basil, roughly
  chopped
2 tins of coconut milk
1 litre double cream
12 stems of lemon grass,
  smashed, and 8 of them
  chopped
juice of 6 lemons
8 level tsp caster sugar
80g unsalted butter
optional: fresh crabmeat
  and lemon zest to finish

1 Put all the crab bones and shells into a large bowl and break up into small pieces with the end of a rolling pin. Put the olive oil into a large pan over a medium heat and add the broken-up bones and shells. Cook gently for 3–4 minutes, then add the fennel and cook for a further 3–4 minutes without allowing it to colour.

2 Add the garlic, shallots, red chilli and lime leaves, and stir in the salt and all the spices. Pour in the white wine and Pernod and cook until reduced by two thirds, then add water to cover. Bring to a slow simmer, skim off all the scum, and add the tarragon, basil, coconut milk and cream. Bring this back up to a simmer, and add the 8 chopped lemongrass stems. Cook for 45–60 minutes, then pass through a fine sieve into a clean pan. Chop the 4 remaining lemongrass stems and add half of them to the pan with the lemon juice and sugar. Bring to a simmer and cook for 15 minutes. Purée in the blender with the last of the lemon grass and the butter, and check the seasoning.

3 If you like, this can be finished with some fresh white crabmeat, warmed through in the soup, and a little lemon zest grated on top.

Soups, Stews & Pot food

Crustacean Soup

SERVES 4–6
For the mussels:
1kg mussels, cleaned
    (see page 305)
150ml white wine
2 shallots, sliced
2 bay leaves
8 sprigs of thyme

For the clams:
1kg clams, cleaned
    (see page 305)
200ml white wine
150ml Noilly Prat
50ml Pernod
2 shallots, sliced
2 garlic cloves, sliced
2 bay leaves
8 sprigs of thyme

For the soup:
80g unsalted butter
2 small fennel bulbs, chopped
6 round shallots, peeled and
    sliced
a large pinch of saffron
6 garlic cloves, peeled and
    chopped
3 leeks, chopped
2 bay leaves
8 sprigs of tarragon
4 sprigs of basil
a small bunch of chervil
4 star anise
1 tsp fennel seeds
the reserved clams and mussels
    and their cooking juices
500ml double cream
juice of 2 lemons
1 tsp chopped tarragon
Maldon salt and freshly
    ground black pepper

1 Place the mussels in a hot pan and add the white wine, shallots, bay leaves and thyme. Cover the pan and steam for 3 minutes until the mussels have opened. Put them into in a colander, reserving their juices, then transfer the mussels to a tray so they cool quicker. Take the mussels out of their shells, discarding the shells. Put the mussels into cold water to rinse out any grit or sand, then lift out and dry on kitchen towel. Pass the juice through a fine sieve.

2 Cook the clams the same way, adding the garlic with the shallots.

3 Melt the butter in a large pan. Add the fennel and cook for 3 minutes, covered, on a low heat without allowing it to colour. Add the shallots, saffron, garlic and leeks, and the herbs and spices, tied in muslin. Cook for a further 5 minutes, covered, then add the cooking liquid from the mussels and clams and bring this to a simmer. Remove the scum with a ladle and cook for 10 minutes at a slow simmer. Add half the cleaned clams and mussels, then stir in the cream and simmer for 5 minutes.

4 Purée the soup in a blender until smooth, then pass through a fine sieve into a clean saucepan. Bring back to a simmer and check the seasoning (you may only need the pepper). Add the lemon juice and the rest of the mussels and clams, and finish with some chopped tarragon.

Soups, Stews & Pot food

Soups are a fantastic way of serving up a nourishing one-pot meal in very little time. This shellfish soup is so easy to make yet it's packed with flavour. All you need to put on the table is the pot, a ladle and some really fresh bread to soak up every last drop.

Shellfish Soup

SERVES 4–6

1.5kg lobster shells, just the heads
1.5kg langoustine bodies and heads
200ml olive oil
40g flour
200ml brandy, plus 2 tbsp to finish
100g unsalted butter
1 fennel bulb, chopped
1 medium white onion, chopped
6 banana shallots, chopped
10 garlic cloves, chopped
2 leeks, split in half, chopped
6 sprigs of tarragon
8 sprigs of basil
1 heaped tsp thyme
2 bay leaves
4 star anise
1 tbsp fennel seeds
1 tsp black peppercorns
4 plum tomatoes
80g tomato purée
300ml white wine
1.5 litres Fish Stock (see page 280)
500ml double cream
juice of 2 lemons
Maldon salt and freshly ground black pepper

1 Place the lobster shells and langoustines in a large bowl and crush slightly with the end of a rolling pin. Add the olive oil and toss until coated, then put them into a roasting tray in an oven preheated to 200°C/Gas Mark 6 for 30 minutes. Add the flour, stir, and cook for another 5 minutes. Remove from the oven and pour the brandy into the tray, stirring to deglaze.

2 Put a large saucepan over a low heat and add the butter. Once it has melted and starts foaming, add the fennel and cook for 2 minutes. Add the onion, shallots, garlic and leeks, turn up the heat, and cook for about 8 minutes so that the vegetables get some colour. Next add the herbs and spices, fresh tomatoes and tomato purée, and cook for 3 minutes. Pour in the white wine and fish stock, bring to a simmer, remove any scum from the top with a ladle and cook for 30 minutes until it has reduced by a third. Add the cream and cook for a further 15 minutes.

3 Pass the soup through a colander, then pour it through a fine sieve back into the saucepan. Bring back up to a simmer and add the lemon juice and a couple of tablespoons of brandy.

Crayfish Soup

200ml olive oil
200g fennel, chopped
150g shallots
8 garlic cloves, chopped
2 sweet red peppers, deseeded
   and chopped
1 tsp Maldon salt
1 tsp smoked paprika
a large pinch of cayenne pepper
1 red chilli, chopped
1kg crayfish bones, tail meat
   reserved and cooked
   (see page 303)
300ml white wine
150ml brandy
2 bay leaves
1 heaped tsp chopped coriander
2 sprigs of basil, leaves picked
1 heaped tsp thyme leaves
4 tomatoes, chopped
40g tomato purée
1 litre Fish Stock (see page 280)
juice of 2 lemons
80g unsalted butter
300ml double cream
freshly ground black pepper

1 Put the olive oil into a large pan on a medium heat. Once it is hot, add the sliced fennel and cook for 2–3 minutes without letting it colour. Add the shallots, garlic, red peppers, salt, paprika, cayenne and chilli, then cover the pan and cook for another 2–3 minutes. Add the crayfish bones, white wine, brandy, herbs, tomatoes and tomato purée, and cover with the fish stock. Bring to a simmer, skim off all the scum, and cook for 60 minutes, until the liquid has reduced by about a third.

2 Using a hand blender (or you can use a normal blender), blend the soup until very smooth, then pass it through a fine sieve into a bowl, pressing really well so that all the flavour and juice comes out of the bones. Repeat, and this time just tap the soup through the sieve. Add the lemon juice. Add the butter and blend again, then return it to the pan and add the cream and the cooked crayfish meat. Check the seasoning and serve.

FISH OPTION: langoustines

John Dory with Dill Spaghetti

SERVES 4

400g dried spaghetti or linguine
2 x 1.2kg John Dory, filleted
   (see page 297)
2 tsp crushed fennel seeds
100ml olive oil
40g unsalted butter
a squeeze of lemon juice
Maldon salt and freshly
   ground black pepper

For the dill cream:

25g unsalted butter
200g shallots, finely chopped
4 garlic cloves, finely chopped
1 bunch of dill, leaves chopped,
   stems reserved
1 bay leaf
250ml white wine
400ml Fish Stock (see page 280)
400ml double cream
juice of 1 lemon
Maldon salt and freshly
   ground black pepper

1 First make the dill cream. Melt the butter in a saucepan, add the shallots, garlic, dill stems and bay leaf (tie the herbs together with a piece of string so they will be easier to take out at the end), and cook for 3 minutes until they are soft. Add the white wine and reduce by two thirds, then add the fish stock and reduce by two thirds again. Add the cream and reduce by another third, then add the chopped dill and the lemon juice and season with salt and pepper. Keep the dill cream warm while you cook the pasta and fish.

2 Cook the pasta in salted boiling water according to the packet instructions. While it is cooking, season the John Dory with salt and pepper and the crushed fennel seeds. Heat a non-stick sauté pan, add the olive oil, and when hot add the fish. Once it starts to go golden around the edges, after about 2 minutes, add the butter and flip the fillets over. Cook the other side for another 2 minutes or so, depending on their size. When the fish are done, add a squeeze of lemon juice to the pan.

3 Drain the pasta, stir into the dill cream and serve with the John Dory.

Soups, Stews & Pot food

In many countries, particularly in Europe, mussels are served with alcohol; cider and Calvados are natural partners in a sauce for them.

Mussels with Cider

SERVES 4

2kg mussels, washed
  and beards removed
  (see page 305)
300ml cider
1 bay leaf
1 sprig of rosemary, leaves
  picked and chopped
120g unsalted butter
juice of 1 lemon
40ml Calvados
1 heaped tbsp chopped parsley
freshly ground black pepper

For the shallot mix:
250g finely diced shallots
1 bay leaf
1 tsp chopped rosemary leaves
3 garlic cloves, finely chopped
250ml cider
50ml Calvados

1 Put all the ingredients for the shallot mix into a saucepan over a medium heat and cook until most of the wine has evaporated. Set aside to cool.

2 Place the mussels in a hot pan and add the cider, bay leaf, rosemary and shallot mix. Cover the pan with a lid so that the mussels steam, and cook for 3 minutes over a medium heat until they open. Stir in the butter, pepper, lemon juice, Calvados and parsley and serve.

The smell of this cooking in any kitchen is glorious and the mussels have an incredibly sweet taste, especially with the butter added to the sauce to enrich it.

Moules Marinières

SERVES 4

2kg mussels, washed
  and beards removed
  (see page 305)
300ml white wine
120g unsalted butter
juice of 1 lemon
1 heaped tbsp chopped parsley
freshly ground black pepper

For the shallot mix:
250g finely diced shallots
1 bay leaf
1 heaped tsp chopped thyme
3 garlic cloves, finely chopped
250ml white wine

1 Put all the ingredients for the shallot mix into a saucepan over a medium heat and cook until most of the wine has evaporated. Set aside to cool.

2 Place the mussels in a hot pan and add the white wine and the shallot mix. Cover the pan with a lid so that the mussels steam, and cook for 3 minutes over a medium to high heat until they open. Stir in the butter, pepper, lemon juice and parsley and serve.

Baked Parsley Mussels
with Parmesan and Mustard

SERVES 4

1.6kg large Devon mussels,
    washed and debearded
    (see page 305)
250ml white wine
a few sprigs of parsley
2 bay leaves
1 heaped tsp thyme
4 banana shallots, thinly sliced
3 garlic cloves, thinly sliced

For the green parsley crumbs:
100g white breadcrumbs
grated zest of 1 lemon
1 tbsp olive oil
1 garlic clove, finely chopped
a handful of parsley leaves,
    chopped
30g Parmesan cheese, grated
30g Gruyère cheese, grated
Maldon salt and freshly
    ground black pepper

For the grain mustard and
    Parmesan sauce:
200ml milk
100ml double cream
50g unsalted butter
5 banana shallots, cut into
    0.5cm dice
35g plain flour
50g Parmesan cheese, grated
50g Gruyère cheese, grated
6 spring onions, sliced
2 tbsp wholegrain mustard
2 heaped tsp Dijon mustard
2 egg yolks
Maldon salt and freshly
    ground black pepper

1 Place the mussels in a large pan over a fairly high heat. Add the white wine, herbs, shallots and garlic, then cover the pan and leave to steam for about 4 minutes, until the mussels open. Pour them into a colander set over a bowl to drain, reserving the juice. Leave the mussels to cool to room temperature. Remove them from their shells, discarding any that haven't opened, and place them in the bowl with the cooking liquor.

2 For the green parsley crumbs, place the breadcrumbs in a food processor with the lemon zest, oil, garlic, parsley and some salt and pepper and blitz for 20–30 seconds, just until coarsely chopped. Place in a bowl, add the Parmesan and Gruyère, and set aside.

3 To make the sauce, put the milk and cream in a saucepan and bring to a simmer, then remove from the heat and set aside. Meanwhile, melt the butter in another pan on a low heat, add the shallots and cook gently for 3–4 minutes until they are just becoming soft. Add the flour and cook for 5 minutes, stirring regularly. Add the hot milk and cream little by little, stirring all the time – do this over a low heat so it doesn't burn on the bottom of the pan.

4 Drain the mussels in a sieve over a bowl and add 100ml of the juice to the sauce. Bring to a simmer, cook for 5 minutes, then stir in the Parmesan, Gruyère, spring onions and both types of mustard. Remove from the heat and stir in the egg yolks and the drained mussels. Check the seasoning and transfer the mixture to a shallow earthenware dish. Sprinkle the breadcrumbs on top and place in an oven preheated to 180°C/Gas Mark 4 for 15 minutes, until golden brown.

FISH OPTION: scallops

Cockles with White Wine, Garlic and Herbs

SERVES 4

80g unsalted butter
100ml olive oil
200g shallots, sliced
6 garlic cloves, finely chopped
2 bay leaves
1 tsp chopped thyme
300ml white wine
100ml Noilly Prat vermouth
50ml Pernod
juice of 2 lemons
1.2kg cockles, cleaned
   (see page 305)
1 tbsp chopped parsley
1 tbsp chopped tarragon
1 tbsp chopped chervil
1 tbsp chopped chives
freshly ground black pepper

Put the butter and oil into a large, heavy-based pan over a medium heat and add the shallots, garlic, bay leaves and thyme. Cook for about 2 minutes, until the shallots and garlic are just soft but not coloured. Add the white wine, Noilly Prat, Pernod and lemon juice and simmer until reduced by half. Add the cockles, cover the pan and steam for 6–8 minutes, until they just open. Stir in the rest of the herbs and season with black pepper. Serve immediately, with some good bread.

FISH OPTIONS: mussels, clams

The song 'Cockles and Mussels' has acquired the status of an Irish classic, becoming the unofficial anthem of Dublin. It tells the tale of a beautiful fishmonger, Molly Malone, who plied her trade on the streets of Dublin from the back of cart and died young. In Dublin there is a statue that portrays Molly as a busty young woman in seventeenth-century dress and claims to represent the real person on whom the song is based. However, there is no evidence that the song is based on a real woman, though of course back in those days, that's how all the fish and shellfish were sold.

Soups, Stews & Pot food

Palourde Clams with Girolles and Parsley

SERVES 4

2kg palourde clams, washed
    (see page 305)
250ml white wine
6 sprigs of parsley
4 garlic cloves, chopped
2 bay leaves
12 sprigs of thyme
80g unsalted butter
80ml olive oil
450g girolle mushrooms,
    cleaned
Maldon salt and freshly
    ground black pepper

To finish the dish:
80g unsalted butter
200g shallots, finely chopped
4 garlic cloves, finely chopped
1 bay leaf
1 heaped tsp chopped thyme
250ml white wine
400ml double cream
2 tbsp chopped chives
2 tbsp chopped tarragon
1 heaped tbsp chopped parsley
juice of 1 lemon
20ml truffle oil

1 Place the clams in a hot pan and add the white wine, parsley, garlic, bay leaves and thyme. Cover the pan with a lid so that the clams steam, and cook for 3 minutes over a medium heat until they open. Stir in the butter and pepper and pour the clams into a colander over a bowl, reserving the juice. Pick the clams out of the shells and give them a rinse in cold water to remove any grit, then drain them and dry on kitchen towel.

2 Heat the olive oil in a pan over a high heat. Once the pan is very hot, add the girolles, season with salt and pepper and toss the pan so that the mushrooms cook evenly – they will only take 3–4 minutes or so. Once cooked, drain them in a colander, reserving the juices, and leave to cool.

3 To finish the clams, melt the butter in a large saucepan. Add the shallots, garlic, bay leaf and thyme and cook for 3 minutes, until they are soft. Add the white wine and simmer until you have about 1 tablespoon of liquid left in the pan, then add the reserved cooking juices from the clams and mushrooms and reduce by a third. Add the cream and reduce by another third – by now you will be left with a creamy sauce. Stir in the mushrooms, warm through for a minute, then add the clams, chives, tarragon, parsley, lemon juice and truffle oil and serve.

Fish, Chickpea and Chorizo Stew

SERVES 4

250ml olive oil
80g chorizo sausage, cut
   into 0.5cm dice
4 banana shallots, cut into
   0.5cm dice
3 garlic cloves, finely chopped
1 red pepper, deseeded and
   cut into 0.5cm dice
2 leeks, cut into 0.5cm dice
150g canned chickpeas,
   drained and rinsed
1 tsp thyme leaves
1 large pinch of saffron
300ml double cream
3 x 500g bream, cleaned and
   each cut into 4 x 2.5cm
   darnes (see page 298)
juice of ½ lemon
1 heaped tsp chopped tarragon
2 basil sprigs, leaves picked
   and cut into fine strips
Maldon salt and freshly
   ground black pepper

For the fish stock:
olive oil for cooking
1 fennel bulb, roughly sliced
2 banana shallots, sliced finely
3 garlic cloves
2 red peppers, roughly chopped
2 heaped tsp Maldon salt
1 red chilli, finely chopped
800g white fish bones, roughly
   chopped
200ml white wine
6 plum tomatoes, roughly
   chopped
100g tomato purée
4 sprigs of basil
4 sprigs of tarragon
2 large pinches of saffron
1 heaped tsp caster sugar
juice of 1 lemon
80g unsalted butter
a large pinch of freshly
   ground black pepper

1 To make the fish stock, put the olive oil into a large pan on a medium heat, and once it is hot add the fennel and black pepper. Cook for 2–3 minutes without colouring, then add the shallots, garlic, red peppers, salt, and red chilli and cook for another 2–3 minutes, with a lid covering the pan. Add the fish bones, white wine and tomatoes, then add enough water to cover the bones by about 2.5cm. Bring to a simmer, skim all the scum off, and stir in the tomato purée, herbs, spices and sugar. Bring back to a simmer and cook for an hour, until the liquid has reduced by about a third. Take a stick blender and blend until very fine and smooth, then pass the mixture through a fine sieve, pressing really well so that all the flavour and juice comes out of the bones. Pass again, this time just tapping the soup through the sieve. Add the lemon juice and put back into the blender with the butter. Blitz again, check the seasoning and pass again through a fine sieve.

2 Put the oil into a medium-sized pan on a low to medium heat and add the chorizo. Cook until the oil has been released from the sausage, then add the shallots and garlic and cook for 3 minutes until soft. Add the red pepper and leeks and cook for 1 minute, then add the chickpeas, thyme and saffron. Season with a little salt and pepper. Add 750ml of the fish stock and the cream, bring to a simmer and cook for 8 minutes.

3 Season the bream with salt and pepper and add to the pan. Simmer, moving the pieces of fish around the pan so they get cooked evenly, for 3–4 minutes. Add the lemon juice, tarragon and basil, pour the soup into bowls and enjoy.

The combination of the spices and the alcohol makes this a hearty, warming dish for a wintry day – perfect after a day's fishing!

Crayfish with Bacon and Brandy

SERVES 4
**20 live crayfish, cleaned
(see page 303)**

For the sauce:
**150ml vegetable oil
50g unsalted butter
200g smoked bacon, cut
into lardons
300g banana shallots, sliced
8 garlic cloves, finely sliced
2 heaped tsp chopped thyme
3 bay leaves
1 tsp Maldon salt
a large pinch of freshly
ground black pepper
a pinch of cayenne pepper
2 pinches of paprika
1 tbsp pink peppercorns
6 star anise
1 tsp fennel seeds
300ml brandy
400ml double cream
½ bunch of tarragon sprigs**

1 Put a large saucepan over a medium heat and add the oil and butter. Once the butter has melted, add the bacon and cook for 5 minutes, until it is slightly crisp; you may need to drain off a little of the fat if there is too much. Add the shallots, garlic, thyme, bay leaves, salt, pepper, cayenne, paprika, pink peppercorns, star anise and fennel seeds and cook over a low heat for about 5 minutes, until the shallots are just soft.
2 Pour in the brandy and simmer until reduced by two thirds, then add the cream and tarragon sprigs and bring back to a simmer. Add the crayfish, cover with a tight-fitting lid and cook over a low heat for 8–10 minutes, stirring occasionally. Check the seasoning and serve instantly.

FISH OPTION: langoustines

Soups, Stews & Pot food

Fresh Water Crayfish with Anise and Vermouth

SERVES 4

40 raw crayfish, cleaned
  (see page 303)

For the vegetable broth:
2 sticks celery, chopped
1 onion, chopped
1 leek, chopped
½ fennel bulb, chopped
2 bay leaves
12 star anise
12 whole black peppercorns
16 pink peppercorns
4 sprigs of thyme
a few sprigs each of parsley,
  tarragon and chervil
zest and juice of 1 lemon
3 heaped tsp Maldon salt
300ml sweet vermouth

For the sauce:
80g unsalted butter
½ fennel bulb, sliced
  (approx. 200g)
4 star anise
2 tsp fennel seeds
200g round shallots, sliced
150g leeks, thinly sliced
3 garlic cloves, finely chopped
1 bay leaf
1 heaped tsp chopped thyme
300ml sweet vermouth
50ml Pernod
200ml double cream
1 heaped tsp chopped tarragon
1 heaped tsp chopped dill
juice and grated zest of 1 lemon

1 Place all the ingredients for the vegetable broth in a pan and add water to cover. Bring to a simmer, cook for 10 minutes, then add the crayfish, cook for 2 minutes, and leave to cool in the broth.

2 To make the sauce, melt the butter in a large saucepan. Add the fennel, star anise and fennel seeds and cook for 2 minutes over a medium heat. Add the shallots, leeks, garlic, bay leaf and thyme and cook for 3 more minutes, until soft. Add the vermouth and Pernod and simmer until the liquid is just below the level of the vegetables, then add the reserved cooking broth and reduce by half. Finally, add the cream and reduce again by half – by now you will be left with a creamy sauce.

3 Remove the tails and shells from the crayfish and add to the sauce with the tarragon, dill, lemon zest and juice. Simmer for 30 seconds to reheat the crayfish, and serve.

Soups, Stews & Pot food

Darnes of Grey Mullet with Thick Tomato Sauce

SERVES 4

80ml olive oil
juice and zest of 1 lemon
2 garlic cloves, finely chopped
1 heaped tsp thyme leaves
4 x 350g grey mullet, cleaned
　　and cut into darnes
　　(see page 298)
Maldon salt and freshly
　　ground black pepper

For the thick tomato sauce:
150ml olive oil
400g onions, diced
20 garlic cloves, chopped
2 tbsp Maldon salt
35g caster sugar
2 tsp thyme leaves
300ml white wine
1kg tomatoes, chopped
100g tomato purée
4 tsp finely sliced basil leaves
a large pinch of freshly
　　ground black pepper

To finish the sauce:
150ml olive oil
1 fennel bulb, cut in medium
　　dice
4 banana shallots, diced
1 small onion, diced
4 garlic cloves, finely sliced
1 red pepper, deseeded and
　　diced
60g capers, rinsed and drained
80g pitted green olives, cut in
　　quarters
160g Oven-dried Tomatoes
　　(see page 291)
20 basil leaves, cut into fine
　　strips
2 sprigs of tarragon, leaves
　　picked and chopped

1 Place the oil, lemon juice and zest, garlic, thyme, salt and pepper in a bowl and stir well. Add the fish and leave to marinate for 30 minutes.

2 To make the thick tomato sauce, place a pan on a medium heat and add the olive oil, onions, garlic, salt, sugar and thyme. Cook for about 5 minutes without allowing the onions to colour, then add the white wine and simmer until it has evaporated. Add the tomatoes and tomato purée, and the basil tied in muslin, and bring to a simmer, stirring now and again. Leave to simmer for 25 minutes more, then remove the basil, transfer to a blender, purée and pass through a fine sieve.

3 To finish the sauce, heat the olive oil in a medium saucepan. Once hot, add the fennel and cook without colouring for 3 minutes, then add the shallots, onion, garlic and red pepper, and cook for 3 more minutes. Add the thick tomato sauce and bring slowly to a simmer. Cook for 10 minutes, then add the pieces of mullet. Stir in the capers and green olives and cook for 4 minutes, until the fish is cooked. Add the cherry tomato confit, basil and tarragon just before serving.

FISH OPTIONS: line-caught sea bass, red mullet, grey mullet

Although you might think that this classic French dish, originally from Marseille, looks quite rich, it's eaten in France all year round and the summery vegetables do give it a refreshing, lighter taste which works in any season – even under the Provençal sun.

Bouillabaisse

SERVES 4–6

250ml olive oil
2 fennel bulbs, chopped
5 red peppers, deseeded and chopped
4 garlic cloves, chopped
6 level tsp Maldon salt
a large pinch of freshly ground black pepper
3kg fish bones
12 plum tomatoes, chopped
100g tomato purée
3 large pinches of saffron
50g unsalted butter
150ml double cream
50ml lemon juice
4 medallions of monkfish
12 mussels, washed and debearded (see page 305)
4 red mullet fillets, cut in half
4 gurnard fillets, cut in half
150g tomatoes, diced
1 heaped tsp finely sliced basil
1 heaped tsp chopped fresh tarragon

1 Place the olive oil in a large saucepan over a medium heat. Once hot, add the fennel and cook for 3–4 minutes without colouring. Add the red peppers, garlic, salt and black pepper and cook for another 2–3 minutes. Add the fish bones and tomatoes, then cover with 3 litres of water and bring to a simmer.
2 Skim the scum off with a ladle, then add the tomato purée and saffron and cook for 45 minutes to one hour, until the liquid has reduced by approximately a third. Using a hand blender, blend until very fine. Pass the sauce first through a vegetable mouli or coarse sieve, pressing really well, then through a fine sieve. Whisk in the butter, cream and lemon juice.
3 Season the fish with salt and pepper, and add the fish and mussels to the pan – they will take no longer than 4 minutes to cook. Add the tomatoes and herbs, and serve.

Mussels are wonderfully nutritious: they contain many vitamins and minerals, such as magnesium, copper, selenium and zinc, and are rich in protein and omega-3 fatty acids, yet low in fat and cholesterol. Mussels contain more polyunsaturated omega-3 fatty acids than most shellfish, and more than many fish.

We source all our mussels for the restaurants from Demlane on the Isle of Shula. They are cultivated in the warm plankton-rich streams surrounding the Scottish West Coast and the Shetland Islands. They grow the mussels on long lines and were the first supplier to sell mussels boxed and iced. The rope-grown mussels are cultivated in a sustainable manner, making as little impact to the surrounding areas as possible. Because of this, the Isle of Shuna has almost year-round mussel production – they are a lot plumper than other mussels and they taste delicious as well.

Curried Cuttlefish with Spiced Basmati Rice

SERVES 4
150ml olive oil
2 x 800g cuttlefish

For the marinade:
juice and zest of 2 limes
1 heaped tsp chopped coriander
2 garlic cloves, finely chopped
2.5cm piece of ginger root,
   finely chopped
½ small red chilli, finely
   chopped
100ml olive oil

For the curry sauce:
1 litre Fish Stock (see page 280)
100ml vegetable oil
50g unsalted butter
200g onions, finely diced
100g shallots, finely chopped
85g ginger root, finely chopped
15 garlic cloves, finely chopped
1 small red chilli, deseeded
   and finely chopped
2 stems of lemon grass, cut in
   half lengthways, crushed
   and finely sliced
3 kaffir lime leaves
1 tbsp curry powder
1 tsp Maldon salt
a large pinch of freshly ground
   black pepper
2 tsp ground turmeric
2 tsp ground ginger
1 tsp ground cumin
400ml coconut milk
150ml double cream
80g spring onions, thinly sliced
juice of 2 limes
160g natural yogurt
1 heaped tsp chopped coriander

For the spiced basmati rice:
800g basmati rice, soaked in
   water for 30 minutes
60g unsalted butter
300g onions, finely diced
40g ginger root, finely chopped
40g garlic, finely chopped
a pinch of saffron
2 bay leaves
1 cinnamon stick, cut in half
8 cloves
8 cardamom pods, crushed
6 lime leaves
2 lemon grass stems, chopped
900ml water

500ml coconut milk
2 tbsp fish sauce
100g palm sugar
1 tsp turmeric
1 tbsp Maldon salt

Optional:
100g chopped pistachios
100g golden raisins
100g almonds, lightly toasted
1 tbsp chopped coriander
70g desiccated coconut, lightly
   toasted

1 To prepare the cuttlefish, see page 305. Cut the tentacles into 5cm pieces, and the main body into 2cm rings or strips. Mix all the marinade ingredients together in a bowl. Add the cuttlefish and leave to marinate for 2 hours in the fridge.

2 To make the curry sauce, first put the fish stock into a pan on a fairly high heat and boil until reduced by half. Put a second pan on a medium heat, add the oil, butter, onions, shallots, ginger, garlic, red chilli, lemon grass, lime leaves and curry powder, and cook for 5 minutes. Stir in the salt, pepper and spices and cook for another 5 minutes, then pour in the reduced fish stock, coconut milk and double cream. Bring to a simmer and cook for 15 minutes. Set aside.

3 Drain the soaked rice and rinse in a fine sieve under a cold running tap. Melt the butter in a saucepan and add the onions, ginger and garlic. Add all the spices and the lemon grass (you can tie these in a little muslin bag, or you can pick them out at the end, which will be more difficult) and cook for 5 minutes without allowing the vegetables to colour. Add the rice, water,

coconut milk, fish sauce, palm sugar, turmeric and salt. Bring to a simmer, then turn down the heat to its lowest setting and cook the rice, covered, for 10 minutes. Take off the heat and let it sit for a further 10 minutes in the pan. If you like you can stir in the chopped nuts, fruit, chopped coriander and toasted coconut for a nice finish.

4 Heat half the oil in a large non-stick sauté pan and when very hot add the cuttlefish, in batches. Sauté for 1 minute, stirring all the time, and put into a colander to cool. Continue until you have cooked all the cuttlefish, adding more oil as necessary.

5 Reheat the curry sauce gently and add the spring onions, lime juice and natural yogurt. Add the sautéed cuttlefish and cook for a further 2 minutes to warm through. Add the chopped coriander just before serving with the rice.

FISH OPTION: squid

For this dish I would recommend buying prepared and cleaned crabmeat, otherwise it could take some time to cook and clean the crab. You will still need to go through the crabmeat in case of bones.

Crab Pie

SERVES 4

600g cleaned crabmeat, checked for bones

For the grain mustard sauce:
45g unsalted butter
300g onions, finely chopped
1 bay leaf
55g flour
700ml milk
100ml white wine
80g wholegrain mustard
1 tsp English mustard
5 spring onions, sliced
100ml double cream
a large pinch of freshly ground black pepper
1 tsp Maldon salt

For the parsley crumb topping:
2 heaped tbsp roughly chopped parsley
200g fresh white bread, crusts removed, cut into 0.5cm cubes
1 garlic clove, finely chopped
20ml olive oil
zest of 1 lemon
1 tsp salt
a large pinch of freshly ground white pepper
80g Parmesan cheese, grated
20g Gruyère cheese, grated

1 To make the wholegrain mustard sauce, melt the butter in a pan on a low heat. Add the onions, bay leaf and a pinch of salt, and cook gently for 5 minutes without allowing the onions to colour. Take the pan off the heat, sprinkle over the flour and stir in. Meanwhile, place the milk in a pan and bring to just below a simmer. Pour the wine over the onion and flour mix and simmer until reduced by two thirds, then add the hot milk little by little, stirring all the time to prevent it burning or becoming lumpy. Add the mustards, spring onions and cream and season with salt and pepper. Simmer for 2 minutes, stirring all the time, then turn off the heat.

2 To make the parsley crumb topping, put the parsley, bread, garlic, olive oil, lemon zest, salt and pepper into a blender and blitz to coarse breadcrumbs. Place in a bowl and add the Parmesan.

3 Once the sauce is made, remove the bay leaf and mix in the crabmeat and place in a suitable pie dish. Sprinkle over the crumb topping, and then scatter the Gruyère on top. Bake in an oven preheated to 180°C/Gas Mark 4 oven for 25 minutes, until golden.

One of the fishermen I use at the restaurant makes all his own withy pots to catch crabs and lobsters, and he often notes the large amount of bream attracted to the smell of the squid bait when the baskets are disturbed and hoisted out of the water. Like with any fish, if something is being moved or disturbed there will usually be an opportunity for a snack somewhere, so he has a few rods on the back of his boat, just in case.

Langoustine Risotto

SERVES 4

1.2 litres Langoustine Stock
(see page 280)
80g unsalted butter
200g banana shallots, finely
diced
4 garlic cloves, finely chopped
1 heaped tsp thyme leaves
2 bay leaves
400g risotto rice
250ml white wine
16 langoustines
100ml olive oil
juice of 1 lemon
100g crème fraîche
100g grated Parmesan cheese
2 heaped tsp chopped
tarragon leaves
2 tbsp chopped chives
40ml brandy
Maldon salt and freshly
ground black pepper

1 Put the stock into a pan, bring to a simmer, and keep warm over a low heat. Melt the butter in a second pan over a low heat and add the shallots, garlic, thyme and bay leaves. Cook gently for a few minutes without allowing them to colour, then add the rice and cook for 2 minutes, stirring all the time. Add the white wine and cook until absorbed (it will take a minute or so), then slowly add the hot stock little by little, stirring every minute or so. The risotto will take around 16–18 minutes to cook. The rice should be soft, but still with a little bite.

2 When the risotto is nearly ready, cook your langoustines. Season them with salt and pepper, and place them in a hot sauté pan with the olive oil. Cook for 2 minutes on one side, then flip them over and cook them for a further 2 minutes. Finish with a squeeze of lemon juice.

3 Add the crème fraîche, Parmesan, tarragon, chives, lemon juice and brandy to the risotto and season with salt and pepper. Serve in bowls, with the langoustines on top.

FISH OPTION: prawns

Crab Risotto

SERVES 4

1.2 litres Crab Stock
(see page 280)
80g unsalted butter
100ml olive oil
200g banana shallots, peeled
and finely diced
4 garlic cloves, finely chopped
1 tsp thyme leaves
2 bay leaves
400g risotto rice
250ml white wine
400g cooked white crab meat
100g crème fraîche
40ml brandy
100g Parmesan cheese, grated
1 heaped tsp chopped
tarragon leaves
2 tbsp chopped chives
juice of 1 lemon
Maldon salt and freshly
ground black pepper

1 Put the stock into a pan, bring to a simmer, and keep warm over a low heat. Put the butter and olive oil into a second pan over a low heat, add the shallots, garlic, thyme and bay leaves, and cook gently until soft, without letting them colour. Add the rice and cook for 2 minutes, stirring all the time, then add the white wine and cook until absorbed – it will take a minute or so. Add the hot stock to the rice little by little, stirring every minute or so. The risotto will take around 16-18 minutes to cook. The rice should be soft, but still with a little bite.

2 When the risotto is nearly ready, add the crab meat, crème fraîche, brandy, Parmesan, tarragon, chives and lemon juice. Season with salt and pepper and serve.

Fish Pie

SERVES 4–6

250g monkfish fillet, sliced at
    an angle into 0.5cm thick
    escalopes, each slice cut in
    half (see page 299)
4 megrim sole fillets, cut in half
200g salmon fillet, cut into
    25g pieces
4 diver-caught scallops, cut
    into three crossways
20 cooked mussels
2 tbsp chopped chives
2 spring onions, thinly sliced
Maldon salt and freshly
    ground black pepper

For the white sauce:
45g unsalted butter
55g flour
700ml milk
1 bay leaf
1 tsp Maldon salt
a pinch of freshly ground
    black pepper

To finish the sauce:
30g unsalted butter
200g onions, finely chopped
100ml white wine
100ml double cream
juice of 1 lemon
Maldon salt and freshly
    ground black pepper

For the parsley crumb topping:
100g white breadcrumbs
zest of 1 lemon
1 garlic clove, finely chopped
a small handful of parsley
    leaves, roughly chopped
1 tbsp olive oil
20g Gruyère cheese, grated
10g Parmesan cheese, grated
Maldon salt and a little freshly
    ground black pepper

For the mashed potato
500g potatoes, cut into
    2.5cm dice
2 tbsp salt
80g unsalted butter
100g warm milk
a little nutmeg to taste
2 egg yolks
freshly ground black pepper

1 To make the white sauce, melt the butter in a pan on a low heat. Add the flour and cook for 5 minutes, stirring regularly. Meanwhile, place the milk in a pan with the bay leaf and bring to just below a simmer. Pour the milk little by little into the flour and butter mix, stirring all the time and keeping the heat low to prevent it becoming lumpy or burning. Add the salt and pepper and simmer for 8 minutes at a low heat.

2 To finish the sauce, melt the butter in a pan on a low heat and add the diced onions. Cook for 5 minutes without letting the onions colour, then add the wine and simmer until reduced by two thirds. Add the white sauce and the cream and simmer for 2 minutes, stirring all the time, then take off the heat.

3 To make the parsley crumb topping, put the crumbs in a food processor with the lemon zest, garlic, parsley, oil, salt and pepper. Blitz until coarsely chopped, no more than 20–30 seconds, then transfer to a bowl and add the cheeses.

4 To make the mashed potato, pour 1 litre of cold water into a large pan. Add the diced potato and the salt. Place on the heat and bring to the boil, then turn the heat down and simmer for 30 minutes. Drain the potatoes really well in a colander. Put the potato back into the pan and dry out on a low heat for 1 minute, then mash, adding the butter, ½ tsp of salt and the warm milk to bring it together. Off the heat, add the nutmeg and egg yolks. Put the mash into a piping bag with a large star nozzle, if you have one.

5 To cook the fish, add it to the hot sauce a little at a time. Start with the monkfish and cook it for 30 seconds, then add the megrim sole and cook for 30 more seconds more. Next add the salmon and the scallops, and cook for a further 30 seconds. Lastly add the mussels, chives and spring onions and let them warm through for a few seconds, then place the mixture in a suitable pie dish and pipe or spread over the warm mashed potato. Sprinkle over the parsley crumb topping, and bake in an oven preheated to 180°C/Gas Mark 4 oven for 15 minutes, until golden on top.

6 You can make the pie ahead of time if you like, up to the point where you have spread on the mashed potato. Remove it from the oven 30 minutes before you want to reheat it, add the crumb topping, and bake it at 180°C/Gas Mark 4 for 25 minutes (it will take longer because you are cooking it from cold).

This classic Italian risotto is a stunning dish to serve when you're entertaining, as the colour of the rice always makes an impression.

Squid Ink Risotto

SERVES 4

750ml Fish Stock (see page 280)
50ml olive oil
75g unsalted butter
200g shallots, finely diced
8 garlic cloves, finely chopped
1 tsp chopped thyme leaves
1 bay leaf
300g risotto rice
250ml white wine
4–5 small packets of squid ink (from supermarkets or your fishmonger)
250g small squid bodies, sliced into circles (see page 305)
1 tbsp lemon juice
40g crème fraîche
40g Parmesan cheese, grated
2 tsp Maldon salt
a large pinch of freshly ground black pepper

1 Heat the fish stock in a pan. Heat the oil and butter in a shallow pan, add the shallots, garlic, thyme and bay leaf, and cook over a low heat without letting the vegetables colour for about 2 minutes, until just soft. Add the rice and cook for 2 minutes, stirring all the time, until the oil has been absorbed. Add the white wine and cook until it has all evaporated (this will take a minute or so), then slowly add the hot fish stock and 4 packets of the squid ink, stirring every minute or so. The risotto will take 16–18 minutes to cook.

2 When the risotto is almost ready, add the squid rings and cook for just 2–3 minutes more. Finally, add the lemon juice, crème fraiche, and Parmesan, season and serve. If it needs any more squid ink to make it darker (it should be a grey-black colour), add the remaining squid ink at the end.

Soups, Stews & Pot food

Squid Stuffed with Saffron Rice

SERVES 4

1kg medium squid, cleaned
  (see page 305)
1 x quantity Cherry Tomato
  Shallot Sauce (see page 287)
a little grated zest of lemon

For the saffron rice:
750ml Fish Stock (see page 280)
50g unsalted butter
150g onions, finely diced
1 red pepper, deseeded and
  finely diced
4 garlic cloves, finely chopped
3 large pinches of saffron
2 bay leaves
2 strips of lemon zest
1 tsp chopped thyme leaves
400g long-grain rice
200ml white wine, plus extra
  to finish
200g white crab meat
1 tsp chopped coriander
2 sprigs of basil, leaves picked
  and cut into fine strips
6 sprigs of tarragon, leaves
  picked and chopped
50m olive oil
1 lemon
Maldon salt and freshly
  ground black pepper

1 For the saffron rice, put the fish stock into a pan, bring to a simmer, and keep warm over a low heat. In a second pan, melt the butter. Add the onions, red pepper, garlic, saffron, bay leaves, lemon zest and thyme, and cook for 4 minutes, until the onions and garlic are soft. Add the rice and cook for a minute, then add the white wine and simmer until reduced by half. Pour in the hot fish stock and bring up to a simmer. Place a piece of parchment paper over the top of the pan and cook for about 15 minutes, until all the liquid is absorbed, making sure that the rice does not catch on the bottom of the pan. Once the rice is cooked, spread it out on a baking tray lined with parchment paper. Cover with clingfilm, pierce some holes in the top, and leave to cool.

2 Once the rice is cool, place it in a bowl and mix in the crab meat and herbs. Season with salt and pepper and stir in the olive oil. The squid bodies are used for this dish, but you can either keep the heads for another use (such as the Deep-fried Paprika Squid with Lime on page 194), or mix them into the rice stuffing. (To use them in the stuffing, sauté them in a little olive oil, salt and pepper, finish with a squeeze of lemon juice and a knob of butter, then chop them up and mix them into the rice.) Take the squid bodies one at a time and place them on a board. Using a teaspoon, fill them with the rice so they are nice and plump – do not overfill, though, as the squid will shrink slightly when cooking. Skewer the ends with cocktail sticks so that the rice cannot come out. Brush the outside of the squid with olive oil and grate over some lemon zest. Season with salt and pepper.

3 Brush a non-stick baking tray with olive oil and lay the squid on it in rows. Sprinkle with lemon juice and 3 tablespoons of white wine, and cover the tray with tin foil. Cook the squid in an oven preheated to 180°C/Gas Mark 4 for 15 minutes. Be careful when you remove the tray from the oven, as there will be quite a lot of steam. Serve with the cherry tomato shallot sauce.

I ventured to all the seaside resorts in north Norfolk as a kid and we used to go crab fishing at the end of piers with a piece of string, some smoked bacon tied on the end and a little weight attached. We weren't exactly going to catch any gigantic crabs, but it was a lot of fun and it gave me my first taste of fishing.

Chilli Crab Linguine

SERVES 4
100ml olive oil
100g unsalted butter
150g shallots, chopped
4 garlic cloves, finely chopped
1 red chilli, finely chopped
200ml white wine
400ml Crab Stock (see page 280)
400g Cherry Tomato and Shallot
    Sauce (see page 287)
400g dried linguine or spaghetti
400g cleaned white crab meat
juice of 1 lemon
2 tsp chopped parsley
Maldon salt and freshly ground
    black pepper

1 Heat the oil with half the butter in a pan. Add the shallots, garlic and chilli, sauté until soft without letting them colour, then pour in the white wine and simmer until reduced by half. Add the crab stock and the tomato and shallot sauce, bring to a simmer, and keep warm.

2 Cook the pasta in salted boiling water according to the packet instructions and drain. Add to the sauce with the crab meat, lemon juice and parsley. Stir in the remaining butter and season with a little salt and pepper. Serve sprinkled with chopped parsley.

Creamed Cockles and Parsley Pappardelle

SERVES 4
1.2kg cockles
300ml white wine
100ml Noilly Prat vermouth
50ml Pernod
6 garlic cloves, sliced
8 sprigs of parsley
2 bay leaves
1 heaped tsp thyme
320g dried pappardelle or
    tagliatelle

For the cockle cream:
30g unsalted butter
200g shallots, finely chopped
4 garlic cloves, finely chopped
1 bay leaf
1 heaped tsp chopped thyme
250ml white wine
400ml double cream
1½ heaped tbsp chopped parsley
juice of 1 lemon
Maldon salt and freshly ground
    black pepper

1 Put a pan on the heat and when it is hot add the cockles, white wine, vermouth, Pernod, garlic, parsley, bay leaves and thyme. Cover the pan with a lid and cook for 3 minutes over a medium heat until the cockles are open. Pour them into a colander and leave to cool, straining the juice through a fine sieve. Pick the cockles out of the shells and give them a rinse in cold water to remove any grit, then drain them and dry on kitchen paper.

2 To make the cockle cream, melt the butter in a saucepan and add the shallots, garlic, bay leaf and thyme. Cook for 3 minutes until they are soft, then add the white wine and simmer until you are left with approximately 2 tablespoons of liquid. Add the cooking juices from the cockles and reduce by a third, then add the cream and reduce by another third – by now you will be left with a creamy sauce. Stir in the chopped parsley and lemon juice and keep the sauce warm.

3 Cook the pasta in salted boiling water according to the packet instructions and drain. Stir into the cockle cream and serve.

Spaghetti Vongole

SERVES 4

2kg clams, cleaned
   (see page 305)
550ml white wine
200ml Noilly Prat vermouth
40ml Pernod
10 garlic cloves, 6 of them
   sliced and the remainder
   chopped
2g sprigs of thyme
a few sprigs of parsley
50g butter
20g olive oil
2 shallots, chopped
1 red chilli, finely chopped
1 x quantity Cherry Tomato
   and Shallot Sauce
   (see page 287)
400g dried spaghetti
juice of 1 lemon
1 tbsp chopped parsley,
   plus a little for serving
freshly ground black pepper

1 Put a large pan on a high heat, and when it is hot add the clams, 400ml of the white wine, the vermouth, Pernod, sliced garlic and herb sprigs. Put a lid on the pan and cook for 3–4 minutes, until the clams have opened, then transfer them to a colander over a bowl to drain, discarding any that have remained shut. Pass the juices through a fine sieve and set aside.

2 Melt half the butter in a pan over a medium heat, add the olive oil, and sauté the shallots, chopped garlic and chilli for a few minutes, until the shallots are soft. Add the remainder of the white wine and simmer until reduced by half, then add 150ml of the reserved clam juices and the cherry tomato shallot sauce.

3 Cook the pasta in salted boiling water according to the packet instructions and drain. Add to the sauce with the clams, lemon juice and parsley, stir in the rest of the butter and season with a little pepper. Serve in a large bowl, with a little more chopped parsley sprinkled on top.

FISH OPTION: mussels

Soups, Stews & Pot food

Stocks

Fish Stock

This stock can be used for poaching and as a base for sauces and risottos.

MAKES 3.5 LITRES
2kg fish bones
40g butter
300g onions, chopped
150g fennel, sliced
200g celery, chopped
200g leeks, sliced
500ml white wine
a small bunch of parsley
a small bunch of thyme
2 bay leaves
1 tsp fennel seeds
6 star anise
1 tbsp white peppercorns
2 strips of lemon zest, taken off with a speed peeler
2 tsp Maldon salt

1 Wash the fish bones well under cold water and drain them in a colander. Melt the butter in a large pan, add the vegetables, and cook without letting them colour for 3–4 minutes. Add the fish bones, wine, herbs, spices and lemon zest and pour in about 5 litres of water, enough to cover the bones. Bring to the boil, skimming off any scum with a ladle, and cook on a gentle simmer for 20 minutes.
2 Leave to cool, then remove the vegetables and bones from the stock with a large spider or slotted spoon and pass the stock through a fine sieve.

Langoustine Stock

Both this stock and the crab version are great for poaching shellfish and for making sauces and risottos.

MAKES 3–4 LITRES
200ml olive oil
3kg langoustine shells
1 tbsp Maldon salt
2 carrots, chopped
4 banana shallots, chopped
1½ fennel bulbs, chopped
1 tsp thyme
1 tsp tarragon
1 small bunch of curly parsley
5 star anise
1 tbsp fennel seeds
1 tbsp coriander seeds
1 tsp dill seeds
2 tsp black peppercorns
80g tomato purée

500ml white wine
250ml brandy
4 plum tomatoes, halved

1 Heat the olive oil in a large sauté pan, and add the langoustine shells in batches, seasoning them with salt. Cook the langoustine shells for approximately 5 minutes per batch until they become a dark pink colour. Remove them from the pan and drain in a colander. Put any oil that drains from them back into the pan, add the carrots, and cook for 5–8 minutes, until they start to take on a little colour. Sprinkle with salt, then add the shallots, fennel and all the herbs and spices. Cook for another 8–12 minutes, until the vegetables are soft and golden.
2 Return the langoustine shells to the pan and cook for 2–3 minutes more, then add the tomato purée and cook for another 3–5 minutes on a low heat. Add the white wine and brandy and simmer until reduced by half, then add the tomatoes and cook for another 5 minutes. Transfer everything into a large pot and add enough cold water to cover. Bring to the boil, skimming off any scum with a ladle, then turn the heat down to a simmer and cook for 2½ hours. Strain in a colander, pressing the shells and vegetables down well to extract their maximum juice and flavour. Pass the liquid through a fine sieve into a clean pan, bring back to a simmer, then skim and pass through a fine sieve again.

Crab Stock

MAKES 3 LITRES
shells from 3 large cooked crabs
250ml olive oil
2 large fennel bulbs, chopped
1 onion, chopped
6 banana shallots, chopped
4 leeks, chopped
8 garlic cloves, chopped
50g fresh ginger, thinly sliced
8 sprigs of of tarragon
8 sprigs of of chervil
8 sprigs of of parsley
8 sprigs of thyme
1 tbsp Maldon salt
1 tsp black peppercorns
1 tsp pink peppercorns
1 tbsp fennel seeds
8 star anise
1 tbsp coriander seeds
500ml white wine
juice of 2 lemons

1 Crush the crab shells in a bowl with the end of a rolling pin. Heat 100ml of the olive oil in a large pan and sauté the shells in batches for 3–4 minutes per batch until they are pink but not too dark in colour. Add the remaining oil to the pan, and once hot add the fennel and cook for a couple of minutes. Add the onions, shallots, leeks, garlic and ginger and cook for another 2 minutes, then add the herbs, salt and spices.
2 Return the crab shells to the pot, cook for 3 more minutes, then add the wine and simmer until reduced by two thirds. Pour in enough water to cover the bones, bring back to a simmer, skimming off any scum with a ladle, then cook for 1½ hours. Drain in a large colander, pressing the shells and vegetables down well to extract their maximum juice and flavour. Pass through a fine sieve then add the lemon juice. If you like, you can whiz the stock in a blender and pass it through a fine sieve a second time.

Brown Chicken Stock

MAKES 3 LITRES

2kg chicken wings
300ml vegetable oil
100g butter
6 large carrots, cut in 2cm pieces
2 sprigs of thyme
4 garlic cloves, cut in half
4 banana shallots, peeled and cut in 2cm pieces
4 large onions, peeled and cut in 2cm pieces

1 Cut each chicken wing into 2 or 3 pieces. Heat the oil in a large saucepan. When smoking add a third of the butter and a third of the chicken wings. Cook for approximately 12 minutes, until caramelised then place in a colander to get rid of excess fat. Add another third of the butter to the pan (you can reuse the oil) and cook another third of the chicken wings. Repeat with the final third.
2 Once all the wings have been coloured, return them to the pan and add the carrots, thyme and garlic. Cook for 5–8 minutes, then add the shallots and onions. Continue to cook until golden brown all over. Drain the chicken and vegetables in a colander over a bowl.
3 Place the chicken and vegetables i a large saucepan and cover with cold water. Bring to a simmer, skimming off any scum with a ladle, then cook over a very low heat for 4 hours, skimming regularly.
4 Pour into a colander over a bowl, pressing the chicken wings down well to extract their maximum

juice and flavour. Pass the liquid through a fine sieve into a clean pan, and simmer, skimming off any scum, until reduced by a quarter. Finally pass the stock through a fine sieve once more.

White Chicken Stock

MAKES 4 LITRES

1 x 1.5kg chicken carcass
2 tbsp Maldon salt
3 tbsp thyme
140g leeks, cut in half
160g celery sticks, cut in half
300g onions, quartered
25g garlic cloves, peeled and left whole
2 tsp black peppercorns, crushed

1 Put the chicken carcass into a large pan and add the salt and about 4 litres of water, enough to cover the chicken. Bring to a simmer over a medium heat and skim any scum off the top with a ladle. Add the thyme, vegetables, garlic and peppercorns, then turn the heat up and bring back to a simmer, skimming the stock all the time. Cook the stock for 1½ hours, continuing to skim, then leave to cool for 30 minutes.
2 Remove the vegetables and chicken from the stock with a large spider or slotted spoon, so that all you have left is the liquid, and pass it through a fine sieve.

Vegetable Stock

MAKES 2.5 LITRES

2 celery sticks, washed and sliced
1 onion, thinly sliced
1 leek, sliced
½ fennel bulb, sliced
1 garlic clove, sliced
1 bay leaf
3 star anise
12 whole black peppercorns
16 pink peppercorns
4 sprigs of thyme
a few sprigs each of parsley, tarragon and chervil
grated zest of 1 lemon
juice of ½ lemon
2 tsp Maldon salt
150ml white wine

1 Put all the ingredients into a pan and add enough water just to cover. Bring to a simmer, cook for 10 minutes, then leave to cool. Pass the stock through a fine sieve.

Stocks & Sauces

Sauces and Dressings

Caper Beurre Noisette

Great with roasted or pan-fried fish such as ray, salmon or any kind of sole.

150g butter
100ml olive oil
250g banana shallots, sliced lengthways
4 garlic cloves, finely chopped
2 tsp chopped thyme
2 bay leaves
1 tsp Maldon salt
a large pinch of freshly ground black pepper
80g whole baby capers
50ml white wine vinegar
50ml lemon juice
50g lemon segments
1 tsp chopped flatleaf parsley

Put the butter into a pan and cook over a low heat until it is golden brown (this is known as beurre noisette). Put a second pan on a medium heat and add the olive oil, shallots, garlic, thyme and bay leaves. Cook slowly, without allowing the shallots to colour, for 2–3 minutes. Add the beurre noisette to the pan with the salt and pepper, capers, vinegar, lemon juice and lemon segments. Finally, stir in the chopped parsley.

Dill Cream Sauce

Good with baked or poached fish, particularly salmon.

25g butter
200g shallots, finely chopped
2 garlic cloves, finely chopped
1 bay leaf
4 tbsp chopped dill leaves chopped, stems reserved
250ml white wine
400ml Fish Stock (see page 280)
200ml double cream
juice of 1 lemon
Maldon salt and freshly ground black pepper

Melt the butter in a pan and add the shallots, garlic, bay leaf and dill stems (tied together with a piece of string). Cook for 3 minutes, until soft, then add the white wine and simmer until reduced by two thirds. Add the fish stock and simmer until reduced by two thirds again, then add the cream and reduce by another third. Stir in the chopped dill and the lemon juice, and season with salt and pepper.

Grain Mustard Sauce

This sauce can be served with smoked or poached fish, and can be used to make the base of a fish pie.

80g unsalted butter
150g shallots, finely chopped
2 garlic cloves, finely chopped
1 bay leaf
150ml white wine
400ml Fish Stock (see page 280)
400ml double cream
2 tbsp chopped tarragon leaves
120g wholegrain mustard
10g Dijon mustard
5 spring onions, thinly sliced

Melt the butter in a pan and add the shallots, garlic and bay leaf. Cook for 3 minutes, until soft, then add the white wine and reduce by two thirds. Add the fish stock and reduce by half. Add the cream and reduce by half again, then add the chopped tarragon and the wholegrain and Dijon mustards and finally stir in the spring onions.

Grain Mustard Butter Sauce

This butter sauce has a lovely mustard flavour and is lovely served with poached white fish. You can finish it with some chopped tarragon if you like.

150g butter
150g shallots, finely chopped
1 bay leaf
6 sprigs of thyme
300ml white wine
300ml White Chicken Stock (see page 282)
200ml double cream
a squeeze of lemon juice
3 tbsp wholegrain mustard
1 tsp smooth Dijon mustard
Maldon salt and freshly ground black pepper

1 Melt 20g of the butter in a pan and add the shallots, bay leaf and thyme. Cook on a low heat for 4 minutes, without allowing the shallots to colour, until they are soft, then add the wine and simmer until reduced by two thirds. Add the chicken stock and simmer until reduced by half. Next add the cream and simmer until reduced by half.
2 Using a whisk, add the rest of the butter little by little, being careful not to add it too quickly otherwise the sauce may split. Pass the sauce through a fine sieve into a clean saucepan, add a squeeze of lemon juice, then whisk in the mustards and finally season with salt and pepper.

Red Wine Sauce

This is excellent with roast salmon and monkfish.

500ml red wine
300ml port
400g banana shallots, thickly sliced
10 crushed black peppercorns
2 tsp thyme leaves
2 bay leaves
500ml Brown Chicken Stock (see page 282)
25g butter

Put the red wine, port, shallots, peppercorns and thyme into a pan over a low heat and simmer until reduced by two thirds. Add the stock and simmer until reduced by two thirds, then stir in the butter.

Red Wine and Shallot Mignonette Sauce

A perfect accompaniment for raw oysters.

300ml red wine vinegar
100ml sherry vinegar
a large pinch of freshly ground black pepper
1 tsp Maldon salt
120g finely chopped shallots
50ml lemon juice

Place the wine and sherry vinegars, salt and pepper in a saucepan and bring to a simmer. Add the shallots and set aside. Once cool, add the lemon juice.

Saffron Sauce

You can use this sauce for poaching small escalopes or darnes of fish, and you can replace the parsley with tarragon or dill if you prefer.

80g butter
200g shallots, sliced
200ml white wine
400ml Fish Stock (see page 280)
200ml double cream
4 large pinches of saffron
juice of 1 lemon
1 tsp Maldon salt
1 tsp sugar
100g baby capers
100g tomatoes, diced
1 heaped tbsp chopped parsley

Melt half the butter in a pan over a medium heat and add the shallots. Cook for 3–4 minutes, until semi-soft, then add the white wine and simmer until reduced by two thirds. Add the fish stock and simmer until reduced by two thirds again, then add the cream and saffron and simmer until reduced by half. Add the lemon juice and salt, then put into a blender with the sugar and the rest of the butter. Blend for a minute, then pass the sauce through a fine sieve. Before serving, stir in the capers, tomatoes and parsley.

Sauce Vierge

This is a great sauce for the summer, when tomatoes are nice and ripe; it's excellent with any kind of grilled or roasted fish (shown opposite).

6 ripe plum tomatoes, skinned, deseeded and cut
    into 0.5cm dice
150g shallots, finely chopped
4 garlic cloves, finely chopped
200ml olive oil
1 tsp chopped chives
1 tsp chopped tarragon
1 tsp sliced basil leaves
100g pitted green olives, cut into quarters
juice of 2 lemons
1 tsp sugar
Maldon salt and freshly ground black pepper

Put the tomatoes into a bowl and add the rest of the ingredients. Leave for 10 minutes to marinade, then place in a pan and warm slightly before serving.

Shallot and Black Peppercorn Sauce

Try this sauce with any roasted or pan-fried fish.

40g butter
150g shallots, finely diced
1 tbsp finely crushed black peppercorns
2 tsp Demerara sugar
1 tsp chopped thyme leaves
150ml sherry vinegar
350ml Brown Chicken Stock (see page 282)

Place a small pan on a medium heat and add half the butter. When it has melted, add the shallots, peppercorns, sugar and thyme and cook for 2–3 minutes, without allowing the shallots to colour. Add the vinegar and simmer until it has evaporated, then add the chicken stock and simmer until reduced by half. Stir in the remaining butter.

Sorrel Sauce

Try this sauce with sea trout or monkfish.

80g butter
100g shallots, finely sliced
200ml white wine
500ml Fish Stock (see page 280)
500ml double cream
juice of ½ lemon
1 bunch of sorrel, leaves picked
Maldon salt and freshly ground black pepper

Melt the butter in a saucepan, add the sliced shallots and cook on a low heat for 4 minutes, until they are soft. Add the white wine and simmer until reduced by two thirds, then add the fish stock and simmer until reduced by half. Next add the cream and simmer until reduced by a third. Season with salt and pepper, add a squeeze of lemon juice, then add the sorrel leaves and cook for 1 minute. Purée in a blender and serve immediately, as the green colour fades quickly.

Sweet and Sour Sauce

This can be served as a dipping sauce, and makes a great accompaniment to grilled scallops or langoustines.

40g butter
2 shallots, sliced
2 garlic cloves, sliced
1 small red chilli, deseeded and finely chopped
1 red pepper, deseeded and chopped
200ml orange juice
200ml pineapple juice
50g sugar
100ml rice wine vinegar
100g tomato ketchup

Melt the butter in a saucepan and add the shallots, garlic and chilli. Cook on a low heat for 4 minutes, until soft, then add the red pepper and cook for a further 4 minutes. Add the orange and pineapple juices, sugar, vinegar and ketchup. Cook for 20 minutes on a slow simmer, until the sauce is reduced by a third, then place in the blender and purée until smooth. Check the consistency, and if it is still too thin put back on the heat and simmer to reduce further.

Cherry Tomato and Shallot Sauce

Good with grilled or roasted red and grey mullet, salmon or scallops.

75ml olive oil
80g onions, finely chopped
8 large shallots, finely chopped
4 garlic cloves, finely chopped
1 tsp chopped fresh thyme
1½ tsp Maldon salt
a large pinch of freshly ground black pepper
100ml white wine
370g cherry tomatoes, cut in half
2 tbsp caster sugar
1 heaped tbsp tomato purée

1 Heat the olive oil in a pan over a medium heat. Add the onions, shallots, garlic, thyme, salt and pepper and cook for 3–4 minutes without letting the vegetables colour, until translucent. Add the wine and simmer until it has almost evaporated.
2 Add the cherry tomatoes and cook for 15–20 minutes, stirring now and again, until they have cooked down and reduced by half. Finally add the tomato purée and cook for a further 5 minutes.

Thick Tomato Sauce

Great with poached salmon or roasted white fish, such as sole, coley or MSC-certified cod.

75ml olive oil
100g onions, diced
7 garlic cloves, chopped
2 heaped tsp Maldon salt
2 large pinches of freshly ground black pepper
1 tsp thyme leaves
150ml white wine
250g plum tomatoes, chopped
40g tomato purée
2 tsp caster sugar
10 basil leaves, tied in a square of muslin

Heat the oil in a pan over a medium heat and add the onions, garlic, salt, a large pinch of pepper and the thyme. Cook for about 5 minutes, until the onions are softened but not coloured, then add the wine and simmer until it has almost all evaporated. Stir in the tomatoes, tomato purée, sugar and basil and bring to a simmer. Cook for 25 minutes, stirring now and again, until the sauce has reduced in quantity and is very thick. Place in a blender and purée until smooth, then pass through a fine sieve and add another large pinch of pepper.

Smooth Tomato Ketchup

MAKES 1 LITRE

1.5 kg tomatoes
300g onions, chopped
175g red peppers, chopped
2 garlic cloves, chopped
½ tbsp Maldon salt
50g light brown sugar
100ml cider vinegar
½ tsp mustard powder
1 cinnamon stick
½ tsp allspice berries
½ tsp cloves
½ tsp mace
½ tsp celery seeds
½ tsp black peppercorns
1 bay leaf
1 tsp smoked sweet paprika
30g tomato purée

Put the tomatoes, onions, red peppers, garlic and salt into a large pan and cook gently for about an hour, until reduced by half and of a thick consistency. Place in a blender and purée until smooth, then pass the sauce through a fine sieve and place back in the saucepan with the rest of the ingredients. Bring to a simmer over a low heat and cook, stirring every few minutes, until it has reduced by a third. Leave to cool, then store in a plastic container in the fridge until needed.

Hollandaise Sauce

This is good with any grilled or barbecued fish.

500ml clarified butter (see below), warmed
5 egg yolks
1 tsp Maldon salt
a large pinch of freshly ground black pepper
2 tbsp warm water
juice of ½ lemon

For the hollandaise reduction:
250g sliced banana shallots
2 sprigs of thyme
1 large sprig of tarragon
2 tbsp black peppercorns, crushed
700ml white wine vinegar
300ml white wine

1 Place all the ingredients for the reduction in a pan over a low heat and simmer until the liquid has reduced to just below the level of the shallots.

Leave to cool, then pass through a sieve into a small plastic container. The reduction will keep for a few weeks in the fridge.

2 To make the hollandaise, put 3 tablespoons of the reduction into a metal bowl with the egg yolks, salt, pepper and water. Place the bowl over a pan of simmering water and whisk until the mixture is light and fluffy. Be very careful not to overcook the egg yolks, otherwise they will scramble and you will have to start again. If it gets too thick, add a little of the water. Take the pan off the heat and slowly, a little at a time, whisk in all the warm butter. Finally add a squeeze of lemon juice and check the seasoning.

To make clarified butter:
Chop a couple of packs of unsalted butter into cubes and melt over a very low heat. The milk solids will separate from the butter and you will be left with the clarified butter at the top. Very slowly, tilt the pan and pour the clarified butter through a sieve into a measuring jug, leaving the milk solids behind in the pan.

Lemon Hollandaise

Make the hollandaise as above, adding the juice and finely grated zest of 1 lemon at the end. Again, good with any grilled or barbecued fish.

Mayonnaise

This mayonnaise can be varied by stirring in different herbs (see below), and can be used as a base for many sauces, such as tartare sauce and cocktail sauce. It can be kept in the fridge for up to five days.

1 ½ tsp English mustard
½ tsp Maldon salt
a large pinch of freshly ground black pepper
½ tbsp white wine vinegar
1 ½ tbsp lemon juice
grated zest of ½ lemon
2 egg yolks
300ml vegetable oil
1 tbsp water

Whisk together the mustard, salt, pepper, vinegar, lemon juice, zest and egg yolks in a bowl. Slowly whisk in all the oil, a little at a time, adding a little of the water if the mayonnaise becomes too thick.

Herb Mayonnaise

This is delicious served with cold poached salmon or baked fish.

1 x quantity Mayonnaise (see above)
1 tbsp chopped tarragon
1 tbsp chopped chives
1 tbsp chopped dill
1 tbsp chopped chervil
1 tbsp chopped parsley

Make the mayonnaise as above, and stir in the chopped herbs.

Fresh Aioli Mayonnaise

2 tsp English mustard
2 garlic cloves, finely chopped
1 tsp Maldon salt
a pinch of freshly ground black pepper
3 tbsp white wine vinegar
2 tbsp lemon juice
3 egg yolks
300ml vegetable oil
100ml olive oil
15ml water

Put the mustard, garlic, salt, pepper, vinegar, lemon juice and egg yolks into a blender. Whiz for a minute, then slowly add all the oil. You may need to add a little water if the mayonnaise gets too thick.

Tarragon Mayonnaise

5 tsp Dijon mustard
2 tsp Maldon salt
a pinch of freshly ground black pepper
3 tbsp lemon juice
1 tbsp white wine vinegar
3 egg yolks
350ml vegetable oil
1 tbsp water
1 tsp chopped tarragon

Whisk the mustard, salt, pepper, lemon juice, vinegar and egg yolks in a bowl. Slowly pour in the oil a little at a time, while whisking, adding a little water if the mayonnaise gets too thick. Stir in the tarragon.

Cocktail Sauce

This is excellent as a dipping sauce for cooked and raw shellfish.

1 x quantity Mayonnaise (see page 289)
1½ tbsp Worcestershire sauce
1 tbsp red wine vinegar
1 tsp Tabasco
30ml brandy
1 tsp salt
1 tbsp horseradish sauce
a squeeze of lemon juice
2 tbsp tomato ketchup

Make the mayonnaise as above, and stir in the remaining ingredients.

Tartare Sauce

1 x quantity Mayonnaise (see page 289)
1½ tsp white wine vinegar
35g gherkins, finely chopped
35g capers, drained, rinsed and finely chopped
1 tbsp chopped parsley
35g shallots, finely chopped

Make the mayonnaise as before, and stir in the remaining ingredients.

Simple Vinaigrette

This is a basic vinaigrette that can be used for any salad, and you can add herbs or different mustards to change the flavour if you wish.

30g Dijon mustard
45g honey
90ml white wine vinegar
2 tsp salt
a large pinch of freshly ground black pepper
300ml vegetable oil
120ml olive oil

Whisk the mustard, honey, vinegar, salt and pepper together in a bowl. Slowly whisk in the two oils until the vinaigrette is emulsified.

Wholegrain Mustard Vinaigrette

160g wholegrain mustard
90g honey
90ml white wine vinegar
80g shallots, chopped
1 tbsp sugar
1 tsp salt
a large pinch of freshly ground black pepper
180ml vegetable oil
80ml olive oil

Whisk the mustard, honey, vinegar, shallots, sugar, salt and pepper together, then slowly whisk in the two oils until the vinaigrette is emulsified.

Lemon Dressing

This citrus dressing is nice with any salad, or with roasted or grilled fish.

juice and grated zest of 2 lemons
2 tsp caster sugar
2 egg yolks
1 tbsp Dijon mustard
300ml olive oil
100ml water

Put the lemon juice, most of the zest and the sugar into a pan over a low heat and simmer until reduced by half. Place in a blender with the egg yolks and mustard, and switch on. Slowly add the oil, and when half of it is added, add half the water so it does not get too thick . Continue to add the rest of the oil until the dressing is emulsified. Add the rest of the water until the dressing is the consistency of double cream. Finally add a little more lemon zest.

Orange Dressing

Like the lemon dressing, this is nice with roasted or grilled fish, or any salad.

250ml fresh orange juice
1 tsp grated orange zest
25g sugar
25ml white wine vinegar
1 tbsp honey
1 tbsp smooth French mustard
200ml sunflower oil
100ml olive oil
25g wholegrain mustard

1 Put the orange juice, zest and sugar into a pan and simmer until reduced to a syrupy consistency (approximately 4 tablespoons of liquid). Allow to cool slightly, then put into a blender and add the vinegar, honey and mustard, slowly adding the oils. Add about 25ml water if the dressing is too thick, and continue until emulsified, adding the wholegrain mustard last.

Truffle Vinaigrette

Expensive to make, so save for a special occasion. Perfect with roasted scallops or lobster.

150ml olive oil
200g shallots, finely chopped
1 tsp Maldon salt
2 large pinches of freshly ground white pepper
20g black truffle, finely chopped
1 tsp chopped thyme
150ml balsamic vinegar
250ml Madeira
150ml vegetable oil
50ml truffle oil

Warm the olive oil in a pan and add the shallots. Cook gently for a few minutes without allowing them to colour, and add the salt, pepper, truffle and thyme. Add the balsamic vinegar and simmer until reduced to almost nothing, then add the Madeira and simmer until reduced by two thirds. Add the remaining oils and bring to a simmer, then check the seasoning and set aside to cool.

Accompaniments

Oven-dried Tomatoes

4 vine-ripened plum tomatoes
250g cherry tomatoes on the vine
4 garlic cloves, very finely sliced
1 tsp chopped thyme
½ tsp chopped rosemary
3 tbsp icing sugar, sieved
150ml olive oil
2 tsp Maldon salt
a large pinch of freshly ground black pepper

Cut the plum tomatoes into quarters. Leave half the cherry tomatoes whole, with the stalks on, and cut the rest in half. Place all the tomatoes on a tray lined with baking parchment or greaseproof paper. Mix the rest of the ingredients together in a bowl and sprinkle them over the tomatoes. Place in an oven preheated to 90–100°C (or the lowest possible gas mark) and bake for 1½ hours, until the tomatoes have shrunk to half their original size. Remove from the oven and set aside to cool.

Tomato Salsa

1 small red onion, diced
1 garlic clove, finely diced
400g tomatoes, peeled, deseeded and diced
2 tbsp lime juice
1 tbsp chopped red chilli
1 heaped tbsp chopped coriander
8 basil leaves, finely sliced
100ml olive oil
2 tsp caster sugar
2 tsp Maldon salt
a large pinch of freshly ground black pepper

Mix all the ingredients together in a bowl and taste for seasoning.

Guacamole

Excellent with grilled and barbecued fish, and with raw and marinated fish too.

3 ripe avocados
juice of 3 limes
1 small red onion, diced
5 spring onions, sliced
1 tbsp diced green chilli
4 tomatoes, skinned, deseeded and diced
1 heaped tbsp chopped coriander
2 tsp Maldon salt
1 tsp caster sugar

Peel and stone the avocados, then mash them in a bowl with the lime juice. Mix in all the rest of the ingredients, then taste and adjust the seasoning.

CLEANING AND GUTTING FISH

If you are cooking a fish with its skin on, you will need to remove the scales, especially if it is a large-scaled fish such as sea bass. Smaller-scaled fish such as Cornish mackerel and flounder, or red mullet, can have the scales left on.

The scales on a fish are arranged in overlapping rows, a bit like roof tiles, and can be scraped off with the back of a large knife or a fish scaler, which you can buy from a fishmonger. They are easier to scrape off when the fish is whole.

Put the fish into a sink full of water or inside a large plastic bag to prevent the scales getting everywhere, and hold the fish firmly by the tail with a cloth.

1 Place your knife or scaler against the skin at an angle, starting at the tail, and push it towards the head in a steady action. Once the scales start to come off it will get easier. Make sure you remove all the smaller scales around the belly and fins. Give the fish a good rinse under cold water and check to make sure no scales remain.

2 To gut the fish, lay it on its side with the tail towards you, so that you can see the fish's anus. Insert a sharp knife into the gills and make a cut all the way down to the anus, cutting no deeper than 0.5cm, otherwise you will pierce the intestines.

3 To remove the guts, put your fingers in through the cut and pull them out. With smaller fish they should come out easily in one piece, but with larger fish you may need to use scissors or a knife to detach them. If you see a long black line running down the backbone of the fish, remove it, using your finger or a small knife.

4 Rinse the fish under cold running water, then dry inside and out with kitchen paper. The fish is now ready to cook.

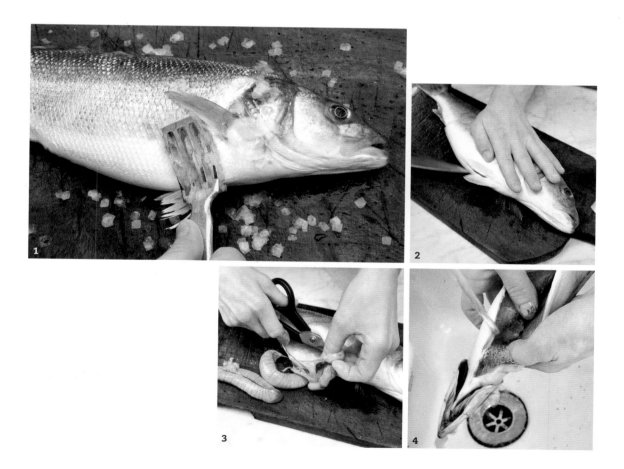

FILLETING FISH

ROUND FISH

This method applies to round fish such as salmon, sea bass and mackerel. Remember that the more times you fillet fish the easier it will get. First make sure you have a very sharp knife – you may want to buy a fish filleting knife, which has a long, narrow and very flexible blade for cutting round the curve of the fish. You will also need a heavier knife, such as a chef's knife, for cutting through the backbone. Keep the bones you remove for fish stock (see page 280).

1 Lay the fish flat on a large board and insert the knife along the belly and then remove all the guts, then remove the blood tract which runs along the inside next to the spine.

2 Wash the fish to remove any scales and slime and make it easier to hold. If you want to remove the head, make a cut through the flesh to the backbone, using your chef's knife, then hit the knife with a rolling pin or heavy object to make a clean cut through the bone.

3 Insert your knife at the head end and make a cut all the way along the backbone. Flip the fish over and do the same on the other side.

4 With the head end of the fish to the left, slide your filleting knife in between the flesh and the bones and cut along the whole length of the fish to loosen the fillet, working in short strokes, using the line of the backbone as a guide and keeping as close to the bone as you can. As you go, lift up the fillet with your other hand so that you can see how you are getting on.

5 Cut through the ribcage and pin bones into the belly of the fish, starting at the head end and working your way down to the tail. A knife with a stiff blade or a serrated edge is useful here, or just a pair of scissors. When you have cut away the fillet, insert the knife between the rib bones and the fillet and cut down between the two.

6 Cut through the fillet at the tail, releasing the fillet. Then turn the fish over and repeat the whole filleting process, but start at the tail this time.

7 Cut away any loose or uneven pieces of skin or flesh from the fillet so it looks neat and tidy. Trim away some of the excess belly if need be – this can be quite fatty in larger fish.

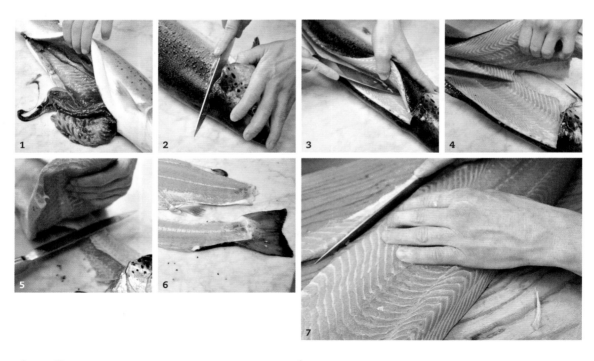

Fish preparation

FLATFISH

The method is the same for any kind of flatfish – sole, brill, or larger fish such as turbot or halibut.

1 The top of a flatfish is a lot plumper than the belly, and is camouflaged to resemble the seabed in order to avoid predators. Place the fish on a cutting board with the head facing away from you and the darker, camouflaged side facing up.

2 When you look down at the fish you will see its lateral line, which runs down the centre and is a good cutting guide. The head lies off-centre to the right, and you will have a slightly larger fillet on the left. Start at the top of the fish, by the head, and make a cut a couple of millimetres either side of the lateral line from the head to the tail.

3 Hold your filleting knife flat and make a few long sideways slices down the length of the fillet. Peel back and hold the fillet with your other hand so you can see what you are doing. Then once you get to the edge of the fillet, where the frilly fins are, cut and pull away at the same time until you have completely removed the fillet. Turn the fish the other way round so the head is facing you, and remove the second fillet in the same way.

4 Once you have removed the top two fillets, flip over the fish to reveal the white belly and remove the other two fillets in the same way, so you end up with four nice clean fillets of fish. Skin and trim all the fillets (see page 297).

1

2

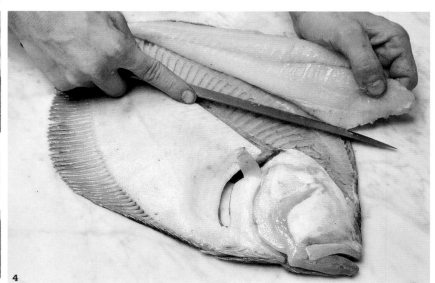

3

4

PIN BONES

You will find pin bones in all types of fish. They run down the centre of the fillet from the head to about halfway down, getting smaller towards the tail, and range from hair thickness, as in red mullet, to 3–4mm thick in a salmon fillet.

1 For larger fillets it may be easier to cut the pin bones out altogether in one piece. Smaller pin bones can be pulled out with fish tweezers. To find the bones, feel along the centre of the fillet with your fingertips. Pull the bones out one at a time with a firm tug, and if they snap, insert the tweezers carefully into the fish and remove the broken ends.

BONING SMALL FISH

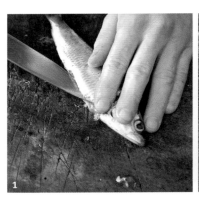

The bones of small fish, like sardines, would be very difficult to remove with tweezers, so a different method is used.

1 Lay the gutted fish on its side and cut down the belly all the way down to the tail.

2 Lay the fish on its belly and spread it out. Press firmly downwards along the whole length of the backbone, to loosen it. The backbone will come away from the flesh.

3 Turn the fish over and use scissors to cut through the backbone at the base of the tail. Carefully pull the backbone away from the flesh, then cut through the bone as close to the head as possible and remove it, with the ribcage bones attached. If any bones remain, remove them with tweezers.

Fish preparation

SKINNING FISH

FILLETS

To remove the skin from fish fillets, first remove the pin bones.

1 Lay the fish on a board, with the head end facing away from you. Holding the tail end of the fillet with a cloth, take a sharp knife in your right hand and cut under the flesh of the fillet, right against the skin. Using a sawing action, start removing the flesh from the skin.

2 When you have released a few centimetres you should be able to get a better grip on the fish. Hold the knife steady and pull the skin towards you while moving the knife blade slightly from side to side. Once you get halfway down, you may find it easier to fold the loosened fillet over and just follow through with the knife until you have removed all the skin.

3 With the skinned side facing upwards, check for any grey tissue and remaining scraps of skin, and remove them.

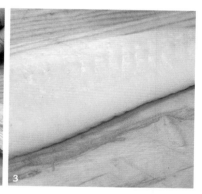

DOVER SOLE AND OTHER FLAT FISH

1 Lay the fish on a board, with the dark side facing upwards and the head pointing away from you, and make a score horizontally across the middle of the tail, just enough to cut through the skin. With a small sharp knife, scrape the skin up towards the head and push your finger underneath to make a small flap.

2 Wipe the skin to make it easier to get a good grip, then take the tail in your left hand and the flap of skin in your right. With a quick tug you should be able to pull the skin away. If it tears, push your finger underneath again to make another flap.

3 Once the top is done, flip the fish over and do the same on the other side.

4 Using a pair of sharp scissors, snip away the frilly bits from around the edge of the fish.

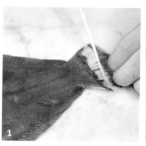
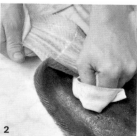

CUTS OF FISH

DARNES OR CUTLETS

1 To cut round fish like salmon and sea bass into darnes, lay the scaled and gutted fish on its side with the head to the right. Starting at the head of the fish and using a heavy sharp knife, cut straight downwards through the flesh. You will need to apply some pressure when you reach the backbone, then continue until you have cut all the way through.

2 Cut the rest of the fish the same way, making the darnes 4–5cm wide at the head end; when you get towards the tail, where the fish is thinner, cut them a little wider so that they will all be similar in weight.

3 For flat fish such as Dover or megrim sole, lay the skinned and gutted fish flat and start from the head end in the same way, but cut the darnes 3cm wide.

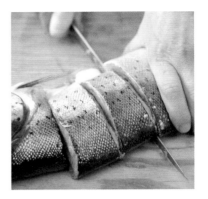

TRANCHES

1 This is a useful method for portioning large flatfish, such as brill, turbot or halibut. Place the fish belly down on a chopping board and remove the fins or frills with scissors. Using a large sharp knife, remove the tail and head.

2 Now cut along the backbone of the fish, cutting through the flesh down to the bone. To cut through the bone, hit the knife with a rolling pin or heavy object, then continue cutting through the fish. To remove the backbone, start at the head end and place the knife on one side of the bone, with the middle of the blade resting on it. Hit the knife with the rolling pin, and continue down the rest of the fish until you are able to remove the bone.

3 To cut the fish fillet into tranches, start at the head end where the flesh is plumpest, cutting the slices about 4cm wide, and work your way down the fish, making them wider at the thinner tail end so that they will all be of similar weight. You will end up with rectangular pieces of fillet plus a triangular tail piece. Give the tranches a rinse under the cold tap to remove any blood or broken bones, and dry on kitchen paper.

Fish preparation

SKINNED FILLETS

1 Regardless of whether you've cut your own fillets from a whole fish or have asked your fishmonger to do it for you, skinned fillets form the basis of preparing other cuts, such as the ones that follow.

ESCALOPES

2 Escalopes are taken from a skinned fillet. Starting at the tail end, cut the fillet at right angles into slices about 3-4 cm wide.

MINUTE STEAKS

3 Minute steaks are taken from escalopes. Slice through the middle of the escalope until your knife is 1cm from the other edge. Flip the top half over so that it is lying alongside the other and gently press each side down.

DICE FOR TARTARE

4 Dice are taken from a skinned fillet. Lay the salmon fillet lengthways in front of you. Slice the salmon into 0.5cm strips then turn it by 90 degrees and cut it into strips of the same width to make the dice.

FILLETS WITH SKIN

5 Fillets with skin are particularly good for pan-frying as you can get a good colour on the skin and a crispy texture.

LOBSTER

1 To kill your lobster, first place it in the freezer for an hour so that it goes to sleep. Place the lobster on a wooden board, then insert a large needle, or a thin sharp knife, into the middle of the head all the way through the skull. Cook the lobster in simmering salted water for 8 minutes, then plunge it into iced water.

2 When cool, remove the lobster from the water and pull the head away from the tail. You can use the head for a soup or stock (see page 280). Next pull the claws away from the head, and then the elbows from the claws. To clean the tail, first lay it on a board and gently press down on it so that the shell cracks, making sure you do not apply too much pressure and squash the tail meat.

3 Hold the tail in both hands with its back facing you and pull the shell apart, revealing the tail meat inside. Remove the tail meat, rinse in cold water and dry on kitchen paper.

4 With a sharp knife, cut through the flesh of the lobster all the way down the centre; you will be able to see the intestinal tract, which runs down the whole tail, so it will be easy to pull out. Rinse the tail under cold water again, and dry on kitchen paper. The tail can now be cut into small medallions of meat about 1cm thick.

5 Place the claw on a board and carefully insert a knife down the centre, then crack it all the way round the circumference. Very gently, pull the two broken sections of claw apart, revealing the meat inside. To remove the meat from the claws, wiggle the small pincer from left to right, then carefully pull it all the way down as though you are

dislocating a joint. Pull away the small piece of cartilage attached to the pincer. To get the claw meat out without tearing it you may need to use a small paring knife to loosen it from the edge of the shell.

6 Place the elbow joints on the board and apply a little pressure with the side of a knife or a heavy object to crack the shell. Take a small knife, cut down the length of the elbow, and gently pull away the shell. Prise out the elbow meat, wash in cold water and dry on kitchen paper.

7 Wash all the meat in cold water and dry on kitchen paper.

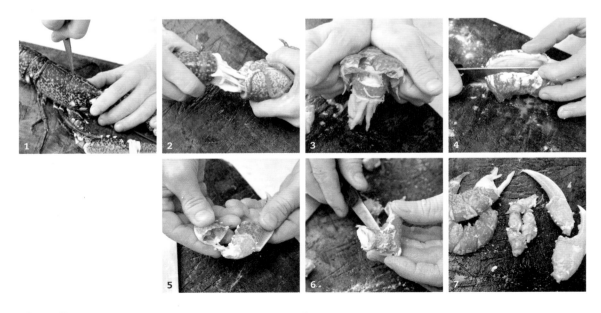

Fish preparation

TO PREPARE LOBSTER FOR THE GRILL OR BARBECUE

1 Kill the lobster as explained on the opposite page and lay it belly down on a board. Take a large chef's knife and insert it into the centre of the body of the lobster. Push down until you have cut through the lobster, then cut it in half, working towards the tail and following the clear line you will see down the centre.

2 When you get to the tail, turn the lobster round and cut through the rest of the body so you end up with two clean halves.

3 Using a teaspoon, remove the stomach sac, a slightly clear pouch which will now be in two halves, then the gills, or dead men's fingers, and the liver, which is a greenish colour. Next pull out the intestinal tract, which runs the whole length of the tail.

4 The claws of the lobster can be left attached to the body, as they will be cooked on the grill this way, and once cooked they can be cracked open with a pair of lobster crackers.

CRAB

1 To kill your crab, insert a sharp knife or skewer into the flap at the bottom of the crab. Cook the crab in simmering water for 15–25 minutes, depending on its size.

2 Place the cooked crab on a board and twist off the legs and claws. Holding the shell in your hands, press your thumb firmly into the mouth cavity just below the eyes and with your other hand push the main body part upwards away from the hard back shell. You will feel the shell start to come away and you will be able to pull them apart.

3 Remove the gills, or dead men's fingers, from the central body.

4 Cut the central body into four or six pieces with a sharp knife, then pick out all the meat from the leg sockets with a lobster pick. Clean out the remaining inner shell pieces with the pick as well. The hard back shell needs to be scraped of all the pinky brown meat with a spoon, making sure you get right into the corner of the shell.

5 Pull the claw and knuckle apart. Using the back of a large knife, crack the large claw. Take out all the white meat in the large legs with a skewer.

6 Twist the smaller legs at the joints and pull them apart, then take out all of the meat from each part with a lobster pick.

7 Separate the crabmeat into brown and white.

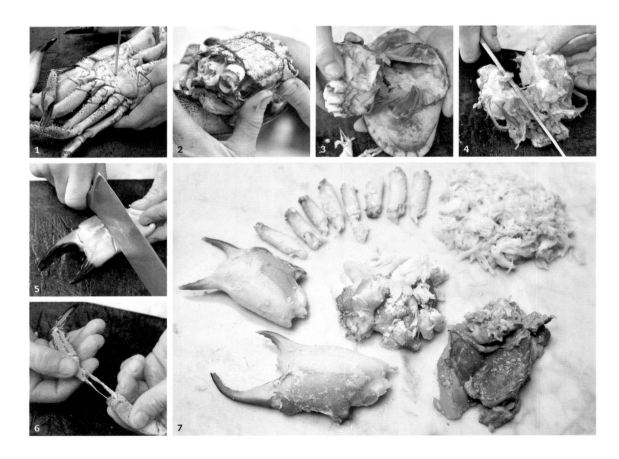

COOKING PRAWNS, LANGOUSTINES AND CRAYFISH

It is quite difficult to buy these live, as they do not live very long after being caught, but if you do manage to do so, put them into the freezer for an hour, which will send them to sleep. Then kill them by plunging them into boiling water for 20 seconds, and drain. If you are going to finish cooking them on the grill or barbecue, immediately plunge them into iced cold water to stop the cooking process. Otherwise, cook them in salted boiling water: prawns and langoustines for 1–2 minutes, crayfish for about 4 minutes. Prawns and shrimps are best peeled with your fingers. First pull off the head, then work your way down the body, peeling the shell away. When you get towards the tail, give it a wiggle or bend it slightly and you should be able to pull the meat out in one piece.

1 To peel langoustines and crayfish, first twist off the heads.

2 Press the shell inwards with your fingers until you feel it break or crack under the pressure.

3 Take the middle part of the tail fin and twist it at a right angle. Slowly pull the fin away from the rest of the tail. The intestinal tract should come with it but if it doesn't, you can cut it out with a knife.

4 Take the tail in both hands and with your thumbs and forefingers pull back the shell. Rinse in cold water and dry on kitchen paper; reserve any heads and shells for stock (see page 280).

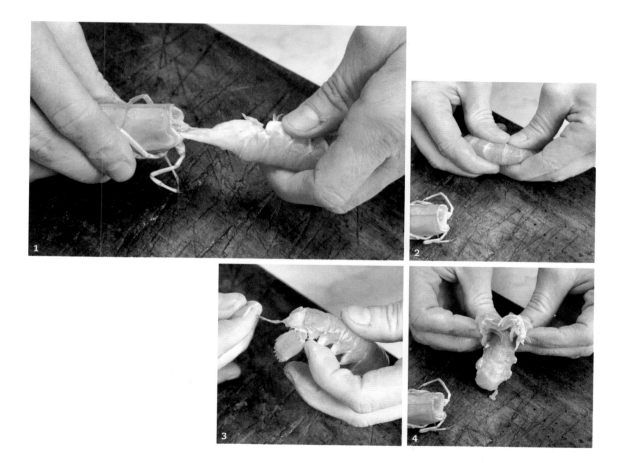

SHUCKING OYSTERS AND SHELLING SCALLOPS

OYSTERS

1 For shucking oysters you will need an oyster knife, which you can get at most kitchen stores. Wrap your hand in a cloth and hold the oyster with the flat side of the shell facing up and the hinge facing you. Put the point of the knife into the hinge, wiggling it slightly up and down so the shell is forced open.

2 Run the blade under the flat part of the shell and lift it up, then cut through the small muscle that holds it to the top shell.

3 Lift off the top shell, then hold the half shell containing the oyster over a bowl and tip out the juice. Flip the meaty part of the oyster over and you will see that it is attached by another muscle. Cut through this as close to the shell as possible, releasing the oyster into the bowl.

4 Check there is no shell in the oyster and clean the shells, then put the oyster back into the shell, ready to serve.

  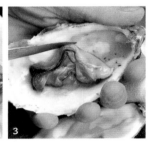

SCALLOPS

1 For scallops you need a knife that is flexible, though it need not be very sharp. Push the point in just above the hinge of the scallop and prise the two shells wide enough apart to insert the blade. Scrape the blade against the flat side of the shell at a slight angle until you have cut through the ligament holding the shells together.

2 To remove the scallop from the shell, use a spoon. Starting from the right-hand side, and holding the scallop shell in your left hand and the spoon in your right, place the spoon under the scallop meat and detach it from the base of the shell in a couple of firm but quick downward strokes.

3 Next, holding the scallop in your left hand, start by the white muscle and slowly work your way round with your right thumb and forefinger until it is released from the roe, the black stomach sac, and the frilly bits around the edge.

4 Rinse the scallops very carefully in cold water, and dry them on kitchen paper.

  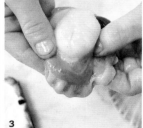 

CLEANING CUTTLEFISH OR SQUID

1 Working over a bowl, pull the head away from the body. Pull out and discard the quill, which is located at the top of the body and looks like a clear piece of plastic.

2 Remove the thin membrane on the outside of the body.

3 Discard the innards, which are in the body of the cuttlefish or squid.

4 Cut the tentacles away from the head just in front of the eyes, discarding the beak-like mouth and the rest of the head.

5 Pull away the two wings attached to the body, and set aside for now. Rinse the body under cold water to remove the membrane that covers it and any remaining innards or ink. The best way to get everything out is to turn it inside out. Rinse the body and tentacles in cold water.

6 Discard the wings if they are very small; if they are larger, trim the thick edge where they were attached to the body and rinse them under cold water to remove the membrane.

The cuttlefish or squid is best cut into rings while still inside out. If you want long strips, cut in a straight line from the opening where the head was down to the base, then open it out flat and cut to the size and shape you want.

For squid, you will need to remove the ink sac, which is a blue-white pouch at the head of the squid. If it has any ink inside, you could keep it to make the squid risotto on page 272, otherwise discard it

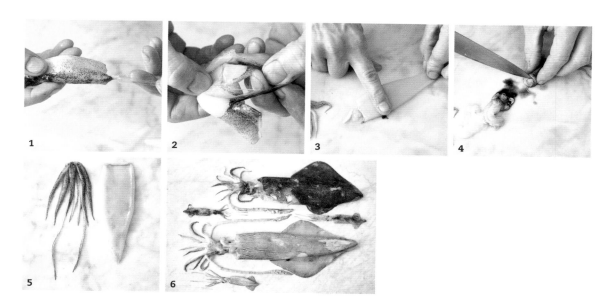

CLEANING MUSSELS, COCKLES AND CLAMS

1 Rinse the shells in cold water, discarding any that are broken, and scrub well to remove any sand, mud or grit. If any shells are open, give them a light tap; if they do not close, discard them as they are probably dead and will be dangerous to eat.

2 Leave them in clean water (sea or tap) for several hours to get rid of any grit inside.

3 Before you cook mussels you will need to remove the beard, a bunch of tough little fibres that the mussel uses for clinging on to the rocks. Hold the fibres with your thumb and forefinger and pull them away, or scrape them away with a not-too-sharp knife. Use your knife to remove any barnacles from the shell, and give them another rinse in cold water.

CLAMS

PALOURDE CLAM (*Tapes decussatus*)

The clam, carpet shell clam or *palourde*, as the French call it, are extremely delicious and do have one over the common cockle with their much sweeter and slightly fatter meat. These clams are adored by the French and other surrounding European countries, such as Spain, Italy and Portugal. If you ever get the opportunity of going to Barcelona's main market in Las Ramblas, you'll see a huge amount of clams for sale.

Along much of the coast of France, particularly from Brittany to the Charente-Maritime region around La Rochelle, you will find lots of great little seaside villages that have a fish market on the weekend and sell lots of clams. It must be such a treat to be able to buy such great produce from a fish market with the knowledge that they have most likely just come off the boat that morning or the day before. Clams are not often seen in our fish markets and definitely not in the supermarkets. I do, however, have very fond memories of when we used to go down to Noss Mayo and Newton Ferrers in Devon and find clams just by the shore line.

Fishing Clams have symmetrical shells and a mouth, but no head. They characteristically lie buried from just beneath the surface to depths of about 0.5m. They grow best in temperatures of 18°C to 25°C, but can live in temperatures as low as 6°C. They move around by using a foot, like most other bivalves, and are filter feeders – using 2 syphon tubes that catch all the particles that go past them while they are buried in the sand, out of sight.

Eggs from the clam are usually shed by the female into the water and fertilised there by sperm released from the male. Eggs develop into larvae that swim briefly before settling permanently on the bottom.

Capturing clams is done by hydraulic dredging or dredging involving a suction tube, which is not the best way of catching the clams as they take many other things up with them. The more traditional method of harvesting clams is by hand and involves nothing more than a few rakes. Clams collected just by hand do no damage to the seabed or any other marine life and are the best ones to buy. All species are widely distributed throughout the UK and temperate waters and they have a 1 rating from the MCS, so eat more of these please so we can stop exporting them and giving them away to our neighbours.

Cooking The palourde clam is a favourite among chefs and is, in a way, reminiscent of the British seaside. They taste very much of the sea and are best eaten instantly once cooked and fresh. Ever so slightly chewy, they have a great texture and are easily knocked back with a glass of dry white wine. With such a sweet taste, there is not a lot that you really need to do with clams except steam them in a little white wine with garlic and a few fresh herbs and make it into a sauce with butter and a hint of lemon. Clams also go very well with simply poached fish and some sorrel, and they make a delicious soup or stew. Once cooked, they are reminiscent of smoked bacon and so are great with spaghetti, chilli and masses of garlic. So whatever you want to do with them, enjoy the moment and savour the flavour of their sweet juices.

RAZOR CLAMS (*Ensis ensis*)

Fishing Razor clams are found all around the coasts of Britain and from Norway to the Atlantic coasts of Spain, as well as parts of the Mediterranean. They live at the lower shore in sand, lying buried with only a siphon protruding from their burrow. Razor shells can burrow faster than a man can dig and they bury themselves into the sand as deep as a metre or more. However, even the siphon is rarely seen, as razor shells are vibration- and light-sensitive, and with their fast movement they rapidly retreat into their burrow before you can get close and nab them. Normally the only sign of their location is a small spout of water as the razor shell burrows or the figure of eight in the sand formed by a razor shell that had laid on the surface and uprighted itself before burrowing.

Maturity is reached after three years and breeding takes place during spring. Spawning occurs in the summer and the fertilised eggs develop into mobile larvae hours after fertilisation. Being long-lived, they may survive for 16–18 years, if they are not caught, of course.

Razor clams are now being harvested by SCUBA divers in Scotland and supplied live to markets abroad, mostly in Europe and the Far East. At present, market preference is for the large pod razor clam (*Ensis siliqua*), which can reach up to 24cm in length, however, larger individuals of the smaller curved razor clam (*Ensis arcuatus*), which reaches a maximum of 18cm, are also favoured. Size does really seem to matter since these razor clams are often served whole in restaurants and it seems the longer they are, the more impressive they are for the customer. The large quantities caught by the dredgers that have now flooded the market have significantly reduced prices, making the smaller species an unprofitable catch for the divers.

Clams are rated 1 by the MCS and their MLS is 4cm. Choose clams harvested in the wild by sustainable methods only, such as hand-gathering, and avoid the spawning season from April to June. If you want your fishmonger to order you some, I would not think that it should be too much trouble; they might simply need a couple of days' notice.

Cooking To keep the razor shells alive while out of water for any length of time, you should collect them together like a bunch of pencils and place a couple of elastic bands around them so they are unable to open. Otherwise the muscles relax, the liquid escapes and the valve dies. If you want to eat them a day or so after they have been caught, keep them in a bucket of seawater and they will be okay for a few days. Wash them thoroughly first in cold water, then put them in a pan with a drop of salted cold water, a little white wine, parsley, garlic, thyme, a bay leaf and a wedge of butter. Turn up the heat until the shells just open and leave for 1 minute. If using butter and garlic, give them a little stir to mix the liquid into the meat, then enjoy. You can also lightly grill them on an open fire, brushed with a little mixed soy sauce, honey, chilli and garlic.

COCKLES (*Cerastoderma edule*)

Cockle is the common name for bivalve molluscs of the family *Cardiidae*. There are over 200 cockle species around the world, with eleven species found around the British Isles, of which the common cockle is the most commercially important and has been collected and sold for hundreds of years.

Fishing The common cockle is up to 50mm in length and is found mainly in sandy, gravelly estuaries and on beaches. Cockles are hermaphroditic – meaning that they have both sets of female and male organs so they reproduce quickly. Spawning is from May to August, which is when the cockle population is at its most vulnerable, and adults will begin to spawn in their second summer at a length of around 15 to 20mm and at an age of about 18 months.

Mechanised forms of collecting cockles use tractors

Glossary

and hydraulic dredges, but concerns about over-collecting have led to measures to control the numbers of cockles harvested and the methods used. In Scotland, for example, dredging with vehicles is banned, while traditional hand-gathering is the only method allowed in some parts of England and Wales. At the Bury Inlet cockle fishery, there is a minimum landing size to protect cockles, and only hand-gathering with the use of rake and sieve is allowed. The level of fishable stock is also set at around 2500 to 3000 tonnes, representing 25–33 per cent of the total biomass.

Cockles are hand-gathered using a long plank that is rocked from side to side on the sand. This brings all the cockles to the surface and they are raked and riddled to leave the small cockles behind on the bed. The cockles are then collected in net bags. The main areas for fishing for cockles are the Wash, Morecambe Bay and the Bury Inlet. Morecambe Bay has seen one of the largest increases in the numbers of cockles and cockle fishermen over the last couple of years, and the management of the fishery has had to change radically in response, including a seasonal closure from 1 April to 31 August each year. It was at Morecambe Bay that terrible tragedy struck in 2004 when at least 21 cockle workers drowned. The potential profits from cockling had been driving those involved to take bigger and bigger risks and the cocklers in Morecambe were going further and further out to reach the more profitable beds. In the past, anyone could rock up and fish for cockles and the environment was the last thing that was considered, but now only licensed holders can fish commercially for cockles. Other stricter measures have also come in, including a new permit system that now makes it compulsory for holders to have completed a one-day safety course before going out into the bay.

The export market for the cockle is huge and thousands of tonnes are exported abroad every year, especially to Spain and Holland, creating millions of pounds of income for the fisheries. I really do think we should be using more cockles too.

Cockles have a MSC rating of 2.

Cooking Cockles are sold, along with mussels, whelks and eels, from seafood stalls, or by the beach and are usually eaten with vinegar. We had a lot of cockles in Blakeney up on the north Norfolk coast. The mud there is really dense and thick and I remember squelching it through my feet as we used to go collecting samphire at low tide. Of course, you would find the cockles nestled in between the samphire, and a dish of those two things together with a little butter and parsley would be yummy. Cockles do have to be eaten fresh and are better cooked in the shell. They are quite gritty, but the meat is very smooth and the taste is mild, as is the smell. There is an almost floral sweetness to the flavour and it does not really need all that much in the flavouring department. Wash them very well and leave them in a bucket of cold water just for a day. Chucking in a few handfuls of breadcrumbs will also help a lot with the cleaning. I would cook them with garlic, spices, fresh herbs and white wine or vermouth in a pot with a tight lid so they steam with a little. Add a little butter and chopped parsley at the end, and eat instantly.

COD (*Gadidae* Family)

Cod is generally a lazy fish, and the fact that it has the most sluggish of muscle tissue is what makes its flesh the whitest of the white fish. There are three main species of cod: Atlantic, Pacific and Greenland.

Fishing Several other closely related fish share the same features as the cod – the pollock, saithe, bib, hake, pouting and ling – but the cod is more heavily built and is distinguished by a pale curved line, which runs along the side of its body. In colour, the cod can range from greenish brown through to dirty yellow or even red. The skin possesses a striking marbled pattern and it has a dark mottled brown back fading to a cream underbelly, which sets cod apart from the mainly battleship-grey pelagic fish.

Cod is a cold temperature demersal species. It is generally found in the Northern Atlantic and lives in climates of cold winters and warm summers, swimming through most UK waters. Areas with the greatest amount of cod fishing include the North Sea, Newfoundland, Labrador, New England, Nova Scotia, Iceland, Alaska, Indian Ocean, Mediterranean Sea, Gulf of Valdez and Florida.

Cod is expected to weigh more than 90kg and live over 20 years. It reaches maturity at about 50cm in length and at about 3–4 years of age. The older the cod is allowed to live, the more eggs it will lay. A three-year-old female can produce 250,000 eggs, while an eight-year-old female of 5kg can produce 2.5 million eggs per year. Spawning occurs between January and April at a depth of 200m in specific spawning grounds. The temperature of the water is important, needing to be around 2–3°C for successful mass fertilisation. British waters only fall to these temperatures in winter months (the spawning season for cod) and in recent times temperatures in these spawning grounds have tended to be around 4°C or above, which means fertilisation on a mass scale has been poor.

Cod are targeted mainly by otter trawl and gill net vessels, with gill net vessels better able to target their efforts towards just cod. The fishery is all year-round, although some of the fleets have seasonal fishing patterns. The big trawlers usually catch cod as part of a mixed fishery with haddock and whiting, however, cod are also a bycatch in the beam trawl fisheries, which target plaice and sole, and in the otter trawl fisheries which target prawns and langoustines.

In the late 20th and early 21st centuries, cod fishing off the coasts of Europe and America has severely depleted cod stocks. The stocks have declined from a level of approximately 250,000 tonnes of spawning stock in 1970 to just 40,000 tonnes today. To give you an idea of the severity of this situation and the resulting risk to this species, the sustainable level for cod, i.e. when there is enough spawning cod to reproduce and sustain their existence, is 150,000 tonnes. Cod fishing has now become a big political issue with the necessity to restrict catches to allow fish populations to recover (explained over the page) coming up against opposition from fishermen.

In 1995, we were warned by ICES that we had to reduce the catch by at least 40 per cent for cod to be sustainable. The EU fishing nations listened with closed ears and came up with a proposed reduction of just 3 per cent, with the politicians reluctant to approve any measures that resulted in either job losses or decommissioning. Nevertheless, since 2000 the EU has implemented restrictive catch quotas and as an emergency measure, in 2001 it closed parts of the North Sea to fishing. The closed area covered approximately one fifth of the North Sea and was intended to protect the adult cod during its spawning season. Yet langoustine trawling and beam trawling of other species were allowed to continue in nearly all of the closed area, meaning there was still a significant amount of cod being fished as bycatch (and then thrown away...). The quotas also led to the development of illegal practices. Fishermen landed cod and declared them as dogfish, or they simply landed them when there were no inspectors around. One Grimsby trader said: 'The quotas aren't policed properly and there's no control over the amount of fish being taken out. If there are no rules, human nature takes over and they [fishermen] just take out as much as they can.'

The cod levels in the North Sea have been said to be showing signs of recovery recently, and for the first time in 6 years, the annual report on fish stocks in the North East Atlantic by the ICES has not called for a complete ban on North Sea fishing. Yet there are still huge strides to be taken. There is hardly any cod being allowed to grow to more than 4 years old, so it cannot reach sexual maturity. Cod can produce 9 million eggs at a time, but half the cod is removed from the sea before they are old enough to spawn, ensuring that only 5 per cent make it to their fourth year. The ICES report also stated that fishing pressure is still very high. Martin Pastoors, the chairman of the Advisory Committee on Fishery Management (ACFM), which reviewed the ICES findings, said: 'Our scientific surveys show that the number of young fish has increased, although only to half of the long-term average. These young fish could contribute substantially to the recovery of the North Sea cod stock. To continue this recovery, ICES has recommended that catches be limited to less than 50 per cent of the 2006 catches in the North Sea and Eastern Channel'.

Supermarkets are now better at stocking sustainable fish species than ever before and are improving all the time. You can now buy labelled fish that comes with an organic stamp of approval. giving its origin and traceability. However, the cod you should be purchasing is MSC-certified fish, which has a blue oval label with a fish on it that guarantees the fish has come from a sustainable source or line-caught, again from a sustainable source. At Tom's Place, we use creamy-tasting MSC cod from the Pacific and some cod from the North Sea that is handline-caught by a boat that is part of the Responsible Fishermen's Scheme. It is a small 10-metre boat that is fished out of Lowesoft by two brothers who are passionate about their work and are very committed to fishing sustainably. You may ask why I am using fish from the North Sea at all, particularly cod, and the simple answer is trust and first-hand experience. I trust these fishermen because I have been out to sea with them and have watched them fish with no bycatch at all; if there were, it would be put straight back, along with any undersized cod.

One strategy for helping cod is to try and wean the British off their age-old preference for it by using other species, such as line-caught pollock and gurnard. I would urge you to try these and any other of the fish from my favourite fish list on page 25.

THE ATLANTIC COD (*Gadus morhua*)

The Atlantic cod is the world's largest population of cod. More than 6 million tonnes of cod are caught each year and over half of these are Atlantic cod, with the cod fishery in the Barents Sea among the largest and economically most important fisheries in the world.

Fishing Atlantic cod can grow to 2m in length, with an average weight of 4.5–11.3kg, though cod as big as 90kg have been caught. The Northwest Atlantic cod has been stated as having been heavily over-fished. This resulted in a crash in the fishery in the United States and Canada during the early 1990s, after commercial fishing and targeting of larger, older cod diminished the number of fertile females. Today, this stock is reported to have decreased by 96 per cent since the 1850s (see Newfoundland cod *below*).

In the northeast Atlantic, Norway, Russia and Iceland are by far the largest producers of Atlantic cod. In 2007, quotas were reduced for all three of the major producers. Iceland wants to maintain its good reputation for sustainability and, for what is probably the first time ever in Europe, it is following the advice of its scientists and is drastically cutting its cod quotas. This reduction will cut about 1 per cent off the GDP growth. Similarly, efforts to crack down on illegal fishing in the Barents Sea are gaining strength in Norway due to extreme public pressure.

Newfoundland cod

The collapse of the cod fishery on the Grand Banks of Newfoundland was one of the biggest fishing disasters of the twentieth century. An abundance of cod was discovered there some 500 years ago by John Cabot, who said that all he had to do was lower baskets set with stones over the side of the boat and then scoop them up full of fish. By the late 1700s, the catch had reached as high as 200,000 tonnes annually, and prior to 1900 the entire catch was preserved by salting.

In the twentieth century, technological changes heralded a new era for the cod fisheries and new fishing gear increased the catching efficiency of the fishing fleet. Landings of cod began to decline dramatically during the 1970s – to below 500,000 tonnes in 1977. In 1974, all of the cod stocks in the northwest Atlantic, and in particular those of the Canadian area, were placed under quota regulation. At first the TACs were not effective in curbing the overexploitation, partly because they were established at too high a level, and partly because enforcement was not effective and catches exceeded them in many cases. The other problem was that fishermen were high-grading the cod, which is where they keep throwing fish away until they get the larger, higher grade, premium fish. In the mid 1980s, millions of pounds' worth of fish were destroyed needlessly and thrown over the side of boats, and by the winter of 1992, the cod just seemed to have disappeared and gone elsewhere. By the end of that year, some 45,000 people in the fishing industry had been put out of work and now all that remains in Newfoundland – previously the biggest population of cod in the world – are small pockets of fish in Bonavista Bay and Trinity Bay.

THE PACIFIC COD (*Gadus macrocephalus*)

The Pacific cod resembles a young Atlantic cod in appearance. There is some debate about whether it is a separate species, as it is fished in the North Atlantic.

Fishing The Pacific cod rarely exceeds 37cm in length and may weigh up to 15kg. Pacific cod in the Bering Sea are known to grow rather rapidly and reach an average length of 19cm by the age of one, and may exceed 89cm by the age of 12 – but this is rare.

Glossary

TOM AIKENS

A relatively small fraction of the Bering Sea Pacific cod begins to mature at two, but the vast majority of females mature between the ages of three and six. The Pacific cod is a faster-growing variety of cod then the Atlantic, reaching maturity earlier and breeding sooner as a result. The fish producers are therefore able to use the larger, mature fish from the stocks and ensure that the smaller fish are left in the ocean to breed more.

The Pacific cod fishery provides approximately a quarter of the world's cod supply and Pacific cod stocks appear to be more stable than the Atlantic cod; catches are tightly regulated and although the harvest has declined in the last decade, with the 2008 quota for allowable catch in the Bering Sea and Aleutian Islands reflecting that trend, the decline has been modest. The Bering Sea and Aleutian Islands Freezer Longline Fishery for Pacific cod was certified as an environmentally responsible fishery by the MSC in 2006. It joins 10 Pacific cod fisheries which are currently MSC-certified, with the result that the Pacific cod is given a rating of 1 by the MCS.

GREENLAND COD (*Gadus ogac*)
In colour, the Greenland cod is generally sombre, ranging from a tan to brown to silvery. Its appearance is similar to that of other cod species and is generally heavy-bodied and elongated. They can grow to a length of 80cm. Greenland cod are bottom dwellers, inhabiting the inshore waters and continental shelves up to depths of 200m plus. They are found in the Arctic Circle.
Fishing Greenland cod was heavily fished for from as early as 1952 then, in 1960 and 1961, fishing increased sharply to their present level of just over 1,300,000 tonnes. Trawlers from at least 10 different countries take part in the fishery, in addition to the line fisheries of Greenland itself. The physical conditions at Greenland seem to be more delicately balanced than in most of the other cod fisheries, and in fact fishable concentrations have not always been present off Greenland.

After a long period of very low stock size, there are now signs of slightly improved abundance of cod around Greenland, however, it's still well below the historical levels and the distribution area is very limited.

ICES advises abstinence from fishing so that a spawning stock can be re-established. There is no information on stock status of Greenland cod at present, so the MCS has rated the Greenland cod, 3.

ARCTIC COD (*Arctogadus glacialis/Boreogadus saida*)
The deepwater polar or Arctic cod is a small relative of the Atlantic cod and one of several species of the cod-like fish scientifically named as gadoids.
Fishing The Arctic cod occurs farther north than any other marine fish, spanning the western part of the Arctic basin and Arctic seas off northern Russia, Alaska and Canada. Arctic cod are most common near the water's surface, but they also occur at depths below 900m. It's a small cod and will be found congregating in large numbers. While it resembles other members of the cod family, it can be told apart by its more slender body, deep-forked tail and a projecting mouth.

Both male and female Arctic cod are mature when about 20cm long and 3 years of age. In the northern Canadian waters, spawning is thought to occur in late autumn and winter. Off northern Russia, it is reported to occur during January and February.

Arctic cod have a short life span and the oldest individuals reach only 6 years old. The spawning stock of north-east Arctic cod catch reached a historic maximum of 1,343,000 tonnes in 1956, but had bottomed out by 1990

to 212,000 tonnes. Since 2000, the spawning stock has increased quite quickly, helped by low fishing pressure. The stock size in 2004 was 1.6 million tonnes. However, there are worries about a decreased age at first spawning, which is often an early sign of stock collapse when combined with a high level of discards and unreported catches. In spite of this decline, Northeast Arctic cod still supports a fishery worth more than US$1.2 billion in landed fish, annually. In its 2007 assessment, ICES classified the stock as having full reproductive capacity, but it's still at risk of being harvested unsustainably due to the unreported catches.

POOR COD (*Trisopterus minutes*)
The poor cod is a temperate fish belonging to the cod family (*Gadiformes*). The shape of the poor cod is very similar to pouting, but the eyes are proportionally larger, so it looks a little strange. They are a small fish and really are not worth catching, but they do look just like baby cod.
Fishing The poor cod is demersal and is understood to be more oceanic than its close relative, the bib. It is usually found in small shoals at depths of 10–300m on muddy or sandy bottoms in the eastern Atlantic and south to Gibraltar, along the Atlantic coast of Morocco, and the Faroe Islands to Portugal and the Mediterranean. They also prefer the protection of the natural sea lochs in Scotland.

The poor cod is mainly harvested for the production of fishmeal, but in some parts of southern Europe the fish is eaten. They are at present not eaten in this country, but they can be found and seen in some French markets and have often been caught in Cornwall in large numbers, where they are called blens or blinds. But who knows, in a few years' time we may be making a fish meal out of them.
Cooking Cod is a very popular food-fish, with a mild flavour that tastes quite earthy, almost like floury potatoes, and a slightly sweet anise tang. True wild cod has wonderfully firm flesh which falls apart into large white flakes once cooked, and is very moist with a silky texture. Farmed cod is more milky and has a slightly synthetic, sweet taste. The flakes are as large and dense as those of the wild cod, but they are slightly chewier and seem to have less moisture. Raw Pacific cod is opaque and creamy white and, once cooked, the flesh is white, tender-firm, lean and flaky with a mild taste. The moisture content is a little higher than that of Atlantic cod, making it less firm. As it is so lean, it cooks quickly and benefits from moist heat, so it's great deep-fried in a batter. The flesh of Greenland cod is whitish and flaky, but it's firmer and tougher than that of the Atlantic cod.

Fishermen and fish tradesmen argue that really good cod should be eaten on the day it is landed, while there are those that dispute this and like their cod a day or so older, for a better flavour and texture. As with Dover soles, you cannot eat cod straight out of the water, as that would be like eating the sole of your shoe. However, these days it's pretty much an impossibility to get cod that fresh anyway, unless, of course, you live just by the sea.

Cod is a truly versatile fish and can be poached, baked or fried and, of course, battered and deep-fried and served with tartare sauce. It also has virtually no fat at all, hence why cod is great for drying out.

CRABS

COMMON CRAB (*Cancer pagurus*)
I think as a chef I have seen the popularity of crab and crab meat increase over the years. It's not something that I

always serve, but people do love it when I put it on the menu at work. The common, or brown, crab is the heaviest crab in our waters and it's such a tasty treat.

Fishing The edible common crab is a species found in the North Sea, North Atlantic and the Mediterranean Sea. It is a robust crab with a reddish-brown colour, a characteristic 'pie crust' edge and black tips to the claws. The mature adults may weigh up to 3kg.

Reproduction takes place mostly in winter, with the females moulting first, followed about a month later by the males. During this period, soft crabs fill fishermens' pots, but are returned to the sea because of their poor quality and the regulations that protect them. It's also illegal to catch crabs of too small a size around the coast of Britain; a conservation measure brought in during the 1870s.

The main crab season commences in late March or early April and continues until late September or early October, when crabbing virtually ceases in Norfolk. Peak catches occur during May and June, but decline in July and August due to the increasing proportion of soft crabs and the poor catches associated with moulting.

There are many coastal towns and villages around Britain that once survived solely on the fishing of crabs, but many of them have now disappeared, as have a lot of the crabs. The crab-fishing place that everyone knows is Cromer. Cromer started crab fishing commercially in 1262 and nowadays crabs are still a large part of the income of the town. Historically, they were only caught in the summer months. In autumn, the fishermen brought herring to the town and in winter, cod was the main catch. This has now changed to solely bringing crab and lobster in. From March the crabs are usually found close to the shore, almost up to the low-tide mark, because they like the warmer water. The peak season lasts through to the autumn, with a lull in July and August when the crabs are breeding and shedding their shells. Cromer crabs are smaller than those from any other parts of the country, but are far sweeter and meatier and are well known for their tender flesh and high proportion of white meat to dark. No one seems quite sure what makes them different, but it may be the seabed being a combination of sand, chalk and flint, with no mud to taint the meat. The crabs in Cromer are also slower growing and moult only once a year and so are fuller in their shells. The crab fishing at Cromer has changed through the decades; there were once more than 50 boats working from the east beach, but today there are just a handful laid up by the old lifeboat slipway. The fleet now looks after just 200 crab pots, meaning that it is even more of a speciality but, encouragingly, the decline seems to have turned around.

Many crab populations are, however, over-fished and have reduced to unsustainable levels. Do not eat any undersized crabs below the legal minimum landing sizes, any egg-bearing crabs or crabs caught during their winter spawning or breeding time. Also avoid eating crab claws unless it can be proven that they have been removed from the crab during processing, otherwise the claws may have been removed from live crabs and the rest of the body discarded at sea.

Choosing crabs that have been caught in pots supports the most sustainable method of fishing. In pot fishing, the crab scents the food that's inside the pot, climbs in and drops down the hole and into the pot. A modification of this pot called the parlour pot has also come into use, where there are two rooms, one for the bait and one for the crabs. After the crab has fed and dined in the bait room, it climbs a mesh ramp thinking it is the way out, when in fact it is just about to drop into the parlour part from where there is no escape. These methods of catching the crabs are by far the most humane and the best for the environment, although some fishermen say that they are doing a level of damage to the sea bed when they are first dropped into the ocean. Pot-caught crab from the Inshore Potting Agreement Area in South Devon is a very good choice because it operates a low-impact method of fishing. It does not disturb the sea bed and inferior or damaged crabs are returned alive to heal themselves and grow. There are also strong and effective harvest controls, such as limiting fishing during certain months of the year, and the crabs are landed daily and stunned humanely. Crab fishermen in general are a very conscientious bunch and they all do seem to really care about the crabs.

The crab gets a MCS rating of 3.

Cooking A lot of people seem to think that shellfish are very fattening and contain an extremely high amount of cholesterol. In fact, crab meat is very good for you, although it must be eaten in moderate quantities, as with all foods. Crab meat contains important quantities of essential fatty acids, iron, zinc, potassium, magnesium, calcium and phosphorous, which are all important for a well-balanced nutritional diet. Crab meat is also an excellent source of protein, is very low in fat and contains few calories.

When you are at the fishmongers and are offered a crab, look out for a few things. Make sure that the crab is not carrying eggs (or berried as we call it), see if you can get them alive rather than dead and make sure that they are the right size, depending on the region (from 12–14cm). You may be offered a male cock or a female hen crab, and there is a taste difference. The cocks have more white meat, which is mainly in the claws, and slightly stronger-tasting brown meat, while the hens have more brown meat because the shell is bigger. The way to tell the female and the male apart is by its tail, which is between its legs. In the female, it will be slightly rounder and in the male, it will be more pointed and narrower. Don't buy the females between May and July when they are breeding. They will also be carrying eggs between January and March.

Some people like only the white crab meat, but the brown meat is just as tasty. The brown has a definite tang to it, like unripened tomatoes, but to counter this it has a delicious sweet taste that is extremely creamy and is great spread on buttered granary toast. Properly cooked, the white crab meat has a very sweet taste that is almost like green olives. However, if it's overcooked, the white meat will be dry and almost crumbly. Use crab meat for salads, mixed with mayonnaise, in soups or quickly fried with chilli and garlic. Personally, I think just plain boiled is best, served with home-made mayonnaise.

SPIDER CRAB (*Maia squinado*)

Spider crabs look like one of the terrors of the deep, but they are very much a favourite on the Continent and are, at last, starting to get a little more praise on our own shores. A huge migrating crab, they come from the Mediterranean but in the last few decades they have managed to turn up all around the south west and the Channel Islands, even venturing up to the North. They just suddenly appear out of the blue and in huge numbers. Hundreds can be seen on top of each other in a mating frenzy, forming a huge pile on the bottom of the sea bed.

We have over the years started to enjoy the fruits of our seas more and more, and the spider crab is one seafood that we should embrace. Without a doubt, the spider crab is the most distinctive crab in UK waters. It is the largest crab found near our shores and its orange, spiky shell renders it easily identifiable.

Fishing Spider crabs are found at a wide range of depths and inhabit some of the ocean's deepest water, while young crabs prefer shallow areas with lots of weeds and rocks for protection. The female crabs become berried (egg-bearing) from April onwards and by June all mature females are berried. The hatching period extends from July until November, with some females producing two batches of eggs in the season.

Annually 5,000 tonnes of spider crab are caught, with more than 70 per cent of those off the coast of France and just over 10 per cent off the coast of the United Kingdom. The European Union imposes a minimum landing size of 120mm for the spider crab and some individual countries have other regulations, such as a ban on landing egg-bearing females in Spain and a closed season in France and the Channel Islands. Don't buy immature crabs, those below the landing size, egg-bearing crabs or crabs caught during the spawning season of April to July.

I know from British fishermen that they used to hate landing spider crabs because they would completely mess their nets up, but now that they have realised that there is a strong market for the spider crab, they have stopped smashing them and have started to market them in a better light. Tangle nets are the main fishing method used to capture spider crabs, and they are also a common bycatch in most types of net fishing. When I have been out to sea with one of my fishermen, Chris Bean, I helped with the tangle of net that ensued once we landed a load of spider crabs and it was a nightmare. I was all fingers and thumbs and it was very difficult to get the spider crabs out from the netting. However, Chris gets a very fair price for these wonderful crabs and instead of us shipping the majority of them over to France and Spain, why not give them a go. Even pot-caught spider crabs are being made into a substantial business with thousands of tonnes caught each year, and with potting there is no bycatch of non-target species and small crabs may be returned to the sea alive.

Spider crabs are given a rating of 3 by the MCS.

Cooking When I was at the Tante Claire restaurant we used to serve spider crabs, or *araignée de mer* as they were known, and I remember picking the meat and cooking them all in huge pots. Back then they were so cheap and plentiful and Pierre's favourite thing was to get a load of these in as a punishment if you had not performed as you were supposed to have done. So when you arrived in the morning there could very well be a box of them outside, waiting to be prepared. You can boil spider crabs in a nice flavoured and herby stock and serve them with a little garlic mayonnaise or make them into a delightful crab soup with a little paprika and fennel. They are even wonderful served plain with a little green Cos salad,

some wholegrain mustard, lemon juice and a light sprinkling of olive oil.

VELVET SWIMMING CRAB (*Necora puber*)
Fishing The velvet crab is not all that popular with fishermen because, small and clever, they are very adept at nicking bait without getting caught. They also have no commercial value. This makes them a pesky nuisance, particularly in the summer months when they are most abundant and when they pinch fingers and toes looking in rock pools for hermit crabs or sea anemones.

I am afraid to say that the average velvet crab will not grace most tables in the UK, but will end up in Spain or further afield. It's another story of us having a great product and shipping it off to another country without even understanding why. It seems we are very good at blatantly giving away things that we should be trying ourselves. You are not going to find velvet crabs in the supermarket, the corner shop or even, except very rarely, in the fishmongers. If you want to embrace these little devil monsters, you might be able to get some or to bribe a fisherman to get some for you when you are down on the beach, at the seaside or near a local fishmongers just on the sea. To help the cause, you need to start demanding that the velvet devil is sold on these shores.

Cooking Velvet crabs make such a great sweet-tasting bisque that they cannot be beaten. Finish with a little crème fraîche and brandy – what could be better?

CRAYFISH (*Procambarus Clarkii*)

Crayfish, often referred to as crawfish or crawdads, are freshwater crustaceans resembling little langoustines or small lobsters, to which they are closely related. They are also just as sweet and tasty and have been regarded as a great delicacy throughout Europe since the nineteenth century.

Fishing Crayfish are mostly found in brooks and streams where there is fresh water running and where they have shelter against predators. Up until the 1980s, native British crayfish were widespread, however, there has been a drastic decline in recent years, largely due to the crayfish plague brought to this country by American signal crayfish, which were introduced into the UK as a food species in the 1970s. We were all encouraged to make way for the American crayfish and, as ever, when you introduce a new species there can be trouble. It is only now that we have realised the mistakes of this and are slowly beginning to understand that you cannot mess with Mother Nature.

The signal crayfish (*Pacifastacus leniusculus*) is indigenous to the western United States and can grow up to 15cm in length. They are bluish-brown to reddish-brown in colour with robust, large smooth claws. Signal crayfish reach maturity very quickly and produce many eggs and young. They are an aggressive and invasive species that presents a real threat to the biodiversity of rivers, streams and even lakes. Escaping from their landlocked ponds and into rivers, they dispersed and bred along watercourses very quickly and our own white-clawed crayfish did not stand a chance. Due to their migration from farming ponds, most of the signal crayfish farming initiatives collapsed in the 1990s. From a peak of 99 registered crayfish farms in 1992, there are now only 4 in England and Wales.

Other non-native crayfish species have also become established in the UK and there are 4 species, other than

TOM AIKENS

the dominant signal crayfish, now established in the UK: the red swamp crayfish, spiny checked crayfish, as well as the noble and Turkish crayfish. Most of these populations resulted from being released or escaping while being imported into the UK for human consumption.

There are now serious rules and regulations to try and reduce the spread of the signal crayfish, all of them are coming from DEFRA. In June 2005, the Environment Agency also introduced a package of byelaws that will allow them, under certain conditions, to approve the trapping of crayfish and, where appropriate, commercially exploit them. They hope that these byelaws will go some way towards protecting the remaining native crayfish populations.

Crayfish are caught alive in special crayfish pots using baits. They can also be netted or simply picked up by hand. Since crayfish are nocturnal, they are most easily caught by night, using a light to help locate them. The price that crayfish get is very good and they are an expensive shellfish to buy, but really to have to go to all the effort of those forms to allow you to trap them, you can't help wondering why we have so many poachers.

There is no rating by the MCS and it is open season, so get hunting.

Cooking Crayfish are bright red when they are cooked and the flesh inside is a pinky white. They have a delicate, slightly fibrous texture and are incredibly juicy, sweet and tender. They are very rich and filling and are great with a vermouth or brandy sauce. The tail meat is much like a sweet-tasting roast chicken. They can simply be simmered in water or an aromatic court bouillon for a few minutes, then left to cool and eaten with fingers and a pot of sweet dill sauce or mayonnaise. They are great in salads with bacon and avocado and a big bowl of prawn cocktail sauce with a little extra brandy and black pepper. And in a bisque you cannot beat them, they are just superb. The smell of these cooking with brandy, tomatoes, garlic, bay leaf and thyme is just heavenly. But if you don't want anything fancy, they are fantastic plainly boiled with a little melted butter poured over them.

CUTTLEFISH (*Sepia officinalis*)

In the popular novel *Twenty Thousand Leagues Under the Sea*, by Jules Verne, Captain Nemo and his companions engage in a fierce battle with a group of giant cuttlefish. Although he accurately describes the cuttlefish's three hearts, he describes their blood as being red instead of its actual greenish tint colour. Cuttlefish is still very underrated in this country, considering it's a cheap product and easy to cook.

Fishing Cuttlefish are found in the North Sea, Mediterranean and the Red Sea. In the western Indian Ocean there is also the pharaoh cuttlefish (*Sepia pharaonis*). The largest species is the giant cuttlefish (*Sepia apama*), which lives around southern Australia, growing to a size of up to 1.5m.

Cuttlefish have very good eyesight and their large eyes have a characteristic w-shaped pupil, so when they have their eyes almost closed, they can actually see out from both pupils. Cuttlefish have a much larger shell than the squid and a broadened and flatter body, which is suited to their habitat as a lurking predator. As well as changing colour for camouflage, different colours also show the cuttlefish's mood, especially during the mating period, and allow them to communicate with one another.

Cuttlefish live for a very short time and females do not generally reach maturity until they are 11–25cm. Each spring, cuttlefish meet to mate in the North Sea coast of Germany and the Netherlands. When the eggs hatch, each will produce a perfectly formed cuttlefish between 12 and 20mm long, able to swim, squirt ink and feed. Juveniles hatched in the early summer from the spring brood will usually participate in the autumn spawning of the following year.

Cuttlefish are caught in offshore beam trawls, inshore otter trawls and static nets, with the otter trawls particularly guilty of the overfishing of young cuttlefish. The best way to catch cuttlefish is with cuttlefish traps, because they only catch cuttlefish and are less damaging than trawl fishing. However, eggs laid in traps when the cuttlefish are caught are destroyed, so where possible, look for fisheries such as Brittany where measures have been adopted to protect the eggs.

Cuttlefish are deemed a delicacy more on the continent than they are in this country and it's a shame that we cannot take a better liking to this splendid animal. I've found that it can be quite difficult to get hold of them and you will not really find them in the local supermarket. So ask your fishmongers and even get him to prep it for you. I am sure he will be very pleasantly surprised when you place an order for cuttlefish.

Cuttlefish's MCS rating is 4. Although it has a high rating, there are no quotas for the cuttlefish and at the moment it's not seen as a pressurised stock.

Cooking The cuttlefish has a slightly sweet taste and can be incredibly tough and chewy if not cooked properly. It's even best to freeze the cuttlefish before you use it as the flesh will break down a little and become more tender. As cuttlefish is thicker than squid, it cannot be treated in the same way and is best braised, as opposed to grilled or deep-fried. If you are going to deep-fry the cuttlefish, then I would suggest choosing the smallest cuttle that you can find. And if you want to grill or barbecue it, marinate the cuttlefish beforehand in olive oil, lemon juice and a little garlic and rosemary for extra flavour. Cuttlefish can also be served raw with chilli, garlic, olive oil, ginger and a little seasoning, lime juice and zest.

DAB (*Limanda limanda*)

The dab is Britain's commonest flatfish. Similar in shape to the plaice and flounder, with both its eyes on the right-hand side of the body, they are certainly not a very handsome fish to look at and do seem rather dreary and drab, which could be the reason why they are called the dab. However, they are a beautiful fish to eat and are not just for the adventurous. With a low MCS rating, the clear message is that we need to be eating more of these fish. Some positive PR and a little marketing and branding would certainly not go amiss with this fish.

Fishing Dabs live on sandy sea beds, often close inshore, and half-bury themselves in a muddy environment, hence their sandy colour. A dab can grow up to 35cm long, reaching maturity when they are 2–3 years old and around 15cm long. They spawn from January to August off the coast of Britanny and southern England, then later in the North Sea from April to June, and in the Barents Sea from June to July. In the Baltic Sea, they spawn from April to August. Avoid eating immature fish below about 20cm and fish caught during or prior to the breeding season, from April to June.

Dabs are not at all a targeted species and are, I'm afraid, often a bycatch of a main species being caught by beam-

Glossary

trawled or bottom-trawled nets. The dab is in fact best caught by seine netting, because this method of catch causes less damage to the sea bed and the catch will be of a better quality than that taken in a demersal trawl.

The Dab is not a fish you see often, but it gets a 2 MCS rating and has no quota, so they are very much a sustainable fish to be eating. So next time you are at the fishmongers and he asks what you would like, shy away from the haddock and pollock, ask for a dab and see what kind of face the fishmonger pulls.

Cooking The texture is firm and the fillets have a good level of moistness and break into small flakes. Dab have a very pleasing buttery flavour and can be eaten steamed, pan-fried, deep-fried or just plainly grilled. As the flavour is fairly subtle, I wouldn't want to put any strong flavours with it so keep it as simple as possible. The best way to cook the dab would be baked whole with hard herbs like thyme and a little rosemary, olive oil, coarse sea salt and lemon peel. Or cook the fillets in a little brown butter with capers, parsley and lemon. Perhaps try a steamed or poached piece of dab with a white wine sauce and poached grapes, or pan-fry in butter with a parsley butter sauce.

DOGFISH

Dogfish are in fact various species of sharks, but the name 'dogfish' was adopted by fishermen who refer to schools of them chasing smaller fish as 'packs'. From the same family as skates and rays, dogfish are often sold, especially in fish and chip shops, under the much more appealing name of rock salmon.

LESSER SPOTTED DOGFISH (*Scyliorhinus canicula*)
The lesser spotted dogfish is a cat shark common and widespread all around the coasts of Britain and Ireland and found off Norway, the Mediterranean, parts of the Côte d'Ivoire to Senegal. It is also known as a small spotted cat shark, common dogfish, sandy dog or rough hound.
Fishing Essentially a small shark, the lesser spotted dogfish has a slender, shark-shaped body with a blunt head and a rounded snout, yet unlike larger sharks, its dorsal fins are small, rounded and are positioned further back on the body. It is most common in waters from 20–75m, normally over a clean sandy sea bed. Females and males mature from 54–60cm in length and at around 5 years of age. The eggs are laid two at a time and a female may lay five to seven eggs per week during the breeding season, which is from November to July.

The lesser spotted dogfish is caught nearly all year round, mainly from the beach and also from boats. Research surveys around the UK indicate that it is one of the few shark species whose abundance has been stable or increased in recent years, though in general we should avoid eating shark species as they are vulnerable to overexploitation due to the facts that they are slow-growing, late to mature and produce only a few young. These cat sharks can be a real nuisance when trying to catch more desirable species: they can deal with pollution and when they are caught and thrown back, unlike most fish who will just float on the top of the surface because of the gas in their stomachs and are picked up by seagulls, lesser spotted dogfish use their oil-filled livers as a ballast to sink them back down to the bottom.

The MCS would not promote this species as sustainable because it is unprotected and there are no stock assessments, however they do give them a rating of 3. If you do get your hands on this fish, buy the fish above the size at which the species reaches maturity and make sure that it has not been caught during the breeding or spawning seasons.

GREATER SPOTTED DOGFISH (*Scyliorhinus stellaris*)
The greater, or larger, spotted dogfish is also offered for sale as bull huss, nursehound or, most commonly, rock salmon. When dogfish were very, very cheap, you could understand why they were so popular, but now that we know they are they are a long-lived, slow-growing species that have a high age for maturity and a very unique reproductive biology, which produces just a few eggs rather than the thousands and millions of eggs that other species spawn, we must leave them alone.
Fishing Greater spotted dogfish are most common in the waters of southern Great Britain and the Channel, but can reach from the Hebrides and the Northeast Atlantic to the Mediterranean. With a fairly stocky body and large and small black, or sometimes white, spots, the greater spotted dogfish is located both inshore and offshore and is most commonly found floating around the 20–63m mark. It stays in shallow waters for protection and food until it is big enough to move to deeper waters. It matures at around 55–60cm for males and 75–80cm for females. Unlike the spur dogfish that gives birth to live young, greater spotted dogfish lay a minimum amount of eggs, designed to minimise waste. Along with their high age and long length of time to maturity, the species is particularly vulnerable to high levels of fishing mortality and overexploitation. The greater spotted dogfish is not targeted or fished commercially, but more attention is needed to look after this unique species. The North East Atlantic stock is now considered to be almost completely depleted and may be in danger of collapse. It seems to end up in a lot of nets as bycatch, due to the fact that its habitat is in all the main target areas for a variety of common species.

It is rated 5 by the MCS and it is listed on its 'fish to avoid' list, so please don't eat it.

SPINY DOGFISH (*Squalus acanthias*)
This is another British shark and one that is, again, very common in our coastal waters. There are several species to which the name *Squalus acanthias* is used, but all are readily distinguished by their two spines, which are used defensively. Also called a piked dogfish or spurdog, be careful if you capture one because it can arch its back to pierce its captor and the glands at the base of its spines release a mild poison.
Fishing This fish is found not just in waters around the UK, but in shallow waters and offshore, especially temperate,

waters all over the world, making it possibly the most abundant living shark.

Spiny dogfish form large schools of hundreds to thousands of sharks, often composed entirely of the same size or sex. The males mature at around 11 years of age, growing to 100cm in length, and the females mature at 18–21 years and are just slightly larger than males. Spiny dogfish can live at least 25–30 years, with some estimates going much higher and approaching 100 years. Mating takes place in the winter months and birth in the dogfish occurs primarily during the cold months of the year, with the mother having litters on average of 6–7.

Spiny dogfish are captured primarily in bottom trawls and with longlines and handlines, but also commonly with gill nets, seines, fish traps and other gear.

It is slow growing and produces very few young, so the stocks will be pressurised.

Like the greater spotted dogfish, the MCS give the spiny dogfish a rating of 5 so it's one to avoid.

Cooking If you do feel like having a go at one of these, I would say get someone to do all the prep for you as it's quite fiddly. It has very dense, thick and moist flesh and I was surprised at how much water came out of the very neat fillets when I first deep-fried them. I would say that they may be better in crumbs than in batter when they are being deep-fried, but try both to see and have a good tartare with it. However, at least there are no little bones to get stuck in the teeth.

EELS

EUROPEAN EELS (*Anguilla anguilla*)

One of the major influences over the food traditions of London has been the River Thames. For centuries, people converged on Eel Pie Island on the Thames for fishy fairs and a fine day out. The Thames used to be alive with eels as it ran through the capital, making jellied eels a long-time cockney favourite. However, eels are not limited to London and are in fact found in virtually all coastal and inland waters around Europe and along the Mediterranean coasts of Africa and Asia. Indeed, there is no other fish stock within the ICES area that is as widespread or involves so many fishermen as the eel fishing industry. That is, of course, if it lasts or, should I say, for as long as it lasts because the eel stock is dangerously close to collapse. Without better coordinated assessments and a local and international conservation plan, the future looks pretty bleak for the slippery eel.

Fishing The European eel is a long, thin, snake-like fish with a protruding lower jaw and small blunt teeth and it is unmistakable in fresh water. Male eels longer than half a metre are very rarely found, while females up to 1m long are common. Occasionally eels reach lengths of 1·5m and weigh up to 4kg.

Eels are catadromous, meaning that they spend their lives in freshwater rivers and return to the ocean to spawn. The eels are in fact the only European fish to leave the European coast to spawn in the sea, making an incredible 6,000km open-ocean journey to try and reach their spawning grounds. No one knows exactly where the eels spawn, but we know that the smallest larvae are found in the Sargasso Sea, just south of Bermuda, which means that the spawning grounds are nearby. Some experts believe that none of the European eel manage to reach the spawning grounds at all, and that the fishery is maintained solely by the return of adult eels from the Americas.

Eels are exploited at all stages of their life, but they are particularly sought after when they are young, meaning they do not have a chance to breed. Called glass eels or elvers, young eels returning to European and Mediterranean waters are first caught in Portugal during October, with the main catching season from January to March. No one yet knows the reasons, but beginning in the mid-1980s, the glass eels' arrival in the spring dropped drastically and is now at perhaps just 5 per cent of its average level in the 1970s. The demand for adult eels has also continued to grow and, for the first time ever, by 1997, Europe's demand for eels could not be met. However, although Europe consumes 25 million kg each year, in Japan, more than 100 million kg were consumed at a high in 1996. This means that as the European eels become less available and many concerns regarding the status of eel stocks both in the United Kingdom and in Europe grow, worldwide interest in American eels has increased dramatically to satisfy demand from Asia.

Management of the European eel is a Europe-wide issue because the fish forms a single stock that is distributed across the whole European continent. In 1998, ICES declared that the European eel stock is outside safe biological limits and the current fishery is not sustainable. Protective measures were implemented in 2007 by the European Union, requiring member states to produce Eel Management Plans. A National Eel Management Strategy has now been developed in the UK and this will represent a major step forward in the management and conservation of eels in this country.

Eels have been rated 5 by the MCS so you should not be eating wild eel at all. There is, however, one source of eel that I can recommend as an occasional treat – the farmed eels from Brown & Forrest (see page 348). Farmed eels do rely on wild juveniles for their stock, so they should really be just as an occasional treat.

CONGER EEL (*Conger conger*)

The conger eel has quite a reputation as a fearsome animal and those who have encountered a conger when it has been aroused have generally thought that, with its fearsome teeth and ferocious bite, the reputation is deserved. You don't want to be putting yourself anywhere near the jaws or teeth of a conger eel unless well protected by gloves, however they do remain docile underwater unless they are provoked, so they are more of danger to fishermen and anglers than they are to divers.

Fishing Conger eels are very common off the coast of south and west Wales, on the south and western coasts of England, Scotland and all around the Irish coast. They are found on rocky and sandy bottoms, hiding in rocky holes and crevices with usually just the head seen poking out with its huge mouth and distinctive snout with a pair of tubular nostrils. They have a smooth, powerful, snake-like body and glide through the water like a snake would on dry land. A conger eel can grow up to 2m long, and occasionally even longer – to a length of up to 3m – and weighs up to 110kg.

Conger eels spend their entire life in marine waters, staying near the coast when young and moving towards deeper waters upon reaching adulthood. They travel very long distances to spawn in the summer in the deep mid-Atlantic and the Atlantic off Portugal and in the Mediterranean between the Azores and Gibraltar. They tend to prefer deeper water and are mainly found in water more than 30m deep from the shore and 50m deep from a boat. Conger eels are usually caught with a bottom trawl and hook and line gear and are renowned for their fighting power when hooked on a rod and line.

Glossary
TOM AIKENS

The conger eel has not been rated by the MCS.

Cooking I have prepared eel lots of ways and it is one of the nicest fish to eat. It has a very delicate unfishy taste that is subtle and utterly delicious. One of the fish dishes that I put on the menu at Tom Aikens is an eel and apple soup with a little smoked eel set in an apple jelly. Eels can also be cooked just pan-fried with bacon or with chilli, garlic, spring onion, lashings of soy sauce and some fresh coriander and cucumber at the end. You can even try smoked eel in a little scrambled egg or in an omelette with chives and spring onion.

FLOUNDER (*Platichthys Flesus*)

The flounder is a beautiful fish that we very rarely see, but should be used a lot more. As well as the European flounder, there are winter flounder (*Pseuopleuronectes americanus*) and summer flounder (*Paralichthys dentatus*) found along the coasts of the USA and the olive flounder (*Paralichythys olivaceus*) found in Japan, China and Korea.

Fishing The flounder has a roughly oval shape with both eyes on the right side of its head, a small mouth and a funny pointed snout. The flounder is common to all British and Irish coasts and the western Baltic. There are important fisheries in Baltic and Danish waters and the countries with the largest catches are Denmark and the Netherlands, though it ranges from the Med to the white sea and can still be found all the way up the Thames to Teddington.

The flounder is found in both fresh and marine waters in the summer, but moves into deeper, warmer water in winter. It likes to live on muddy sea beds from the low shore to at least 50m deep.

The flounder spawns around February to May in the southern North Sea and the females may produce up to 2 million eggs at a time. As it is only a small fish, flounder are quite slow growing and males become sexually mature when they are 2–3 years old and 20–25cm and females reach maturity when they are 3–4 years old and 25–30cm. Flounder are a short-lived fish with most living for 5–7 years, but the odd one can grow to a length of 50–60cm and live up to 15 years.

There is no assessment of stocks taken by ICES in the north-east Atlantic, though there is a mixed quota for dab, lemon sole and this species in the North and Norwegian Seas. Flounder is not an important food fish and not commonly targeted commercially. It is instead taken as bycatch in trawl nets.

The flounder in the UK gets a rating of 2 by the MCS. There is no minimum landing size specified in EU waters, but in Cornwall and North Western & North Wales Sea Fisheries Districts, landing flounder below 25cm is prohibited. Avoid eating smaller fish less than 25cm during the spawning season, from February to May in the North Sea, but let's embrace this humble fish and eat a lot more of it.

Cooking With the flounder, the darker meat of the top fillet has more flavour than the paler flesh of the bottom fillet. The fish has quite a peppery taste and the texture of the fillets is soft and does not contain too much moisture, so it can be quite dry and crumbly if overcooked. I would coat the fish with flour, egg and breadcrumbs to hold the fillets together – and to keep it moist, too– then cook in foaming butter and squeeze on a little lemon juice when almost cooked with some coarse sea salt and a few scattered lemon segments. Flounder can also be cooked whole, grilled with a little butter and lemon and finished with a scattering of parsley.

GARFISH (*Belone belone*)

The long, slim garfish has been given many names, including sea needle and gore-bill. It is also known as green bone due to its weird-looking green luminous bones and mackerel-scout because garfish often arrive in coastal waters ahead of mackerel. In the Channel Islands they call it the longnose and consider this fish a local delicacy. The garfish is one of the sleekest, fastest fish in the sea with an aerodynamic body that no other fish can catch. It reaches a maximum length of around 1m and has a beak-like mouth full of very sharp teeth that can give a nasty nip. It is not like any other species in the sea, so it's very easy to tell apart from other fish. The fish looks predominately silver in the water and the bones have a bright green colour. However, this fish is a good food fish despite its somewhat scary colouration.

Fishing The garfish is a shelf oceanic fish, often found in large shoals or schooling with mackerel. They prefer warmer waters and are more prolific around the British Isles during the summer months. They are also much more common in the warmer waters of Southern Europe. Garfish, however, do seem to be in a good abundance around our coasts so there is no worry at present about the stock or its habitat.

The garfish is a surface-dwelling predator that lives close to the top of the water level. It has large scales that come off in clumps if you handle the fish and fishermen that catch them are generally covered in these tiny turquoise-coloured scales, which stick very well to anything. Garfish are not commercially caught and are mainly landed by rod and line from beaches or the end of piers.

The fish has a minimum landing size of 40cm and it's best to avoid it during the spawning period of May and June. However, it is not considered an endangered species at all and its minimum population doubling time is 1.4–4.4 years.

The garfish is not rated by the MCS and it's a species that is hardly touched and relatively unknown. Give it a whirl and you may be surprised.

Cooking Garfish is a very oily fish which can be cooked the same way as mackerel, and is moist with a similar taste. The flavour is utterly delicious, but I'm afraid to say that even though it swims in our waters, it is one fish that you are never going to see on the slab at the fishmongers. The only way that you will get to eat one of these is if you go down to the pier or beach and catch one yourself. The French love this fish. It's caught a lot on the coast of Brittany, where it's called *aiguillette* and they cook it with sorrel or sea beet. The Danes also have a good appetite for the garfish and they fry the fillets and cook them with parsley, cream and chicken stock. You can do a lot with this fish and it's very versatile. It can be fried, baked, poached, smoked, pickled or deep-fried, as the Japanese do. The Japanese eat the bones as well as the flesh, dusting the bones with a special mix of spicy flour and then deep-frying them. It's just like crackling, and it's yummy.

GURNARD

Also known as sea robins, gurnards are one of the most interesting and beautiful edible fish and they are distributed worldwide in tropical and temperate seas. The gurnard is a very fast-growing fish and, at the moment, sustainable.

Gurnards get their name from their large pectoral fins which, when swimming, open and close like a bird's wings in flight. There are the three types of gurnard as you will see below, and they are all very different in shape, size and colour.

Fishing These are not big fish, rarely exceeding 40cm in length. A fast-growing fish, they become sexually mature at a length of 18cm and mature early at an age of 3 years for the males and about 24cm and 4 years for the female. A non-targeted species taken as bycatch in trawl fisheries in inshore waters and caught by anglers, the gurnard is becoming more and more popular as it is seen as a new species of sustainable fish for the dining-room table. The MCS gives the gurnard a 2 rating, so eat more of them, but do not eat them at less than 24cm and not during spawning season, which is April to August.

Cooking The flesh on the gurnard is compact and tight, but flaky, and once cooked it has a very good flavour. You could either just pan-fry the fillets in butter or deep or shallow-fry them in breadcrumbs. You can also do so much with it on the bone and then chew and suck around the bones. Roast the gurnard whole after slashing the sides and rubbing in spices or chilli. Alternatively, make a fish stew or a bouillabaisse with saffron and capers, or even do a light fish curry with turmeric and yoghurt.

GREY GURNARD (*Eutrigla gurnardus*)
The grey gurnard is widespread all around the coasts of Britain and Ireland. There has been no assessment of stocks by ICES in the north-east Atlantic and it is a non-pressure or unprotected species, not subject to a quota restriction. A considerable quantity of grey gurnard are therefore taken in trawl fisheries in deeper offshore waters.

RED GURNARD (*Aspitrigla cuculus*)
The red gurnard appears around most of the coastline of Britain and Ireland, but it seems to be rare along the east coasts. It has a stout body, large head and eyes and its colouration is bright red. The protective bony plates on the head, which are characteristic of all gurnards, are very conspicuous in this species. The red gurnard is one of the smallest European gurnards and is mostly exploited as fish food.

TUB GURNARD (*Trigla lucerna*)
The largest of the gurnards, the tub gurnard typically grows to between 0.5–2kg. The relatively large pectoral fins make this a powerful fighter for its weight and exceptional specimens can reach 4.5kg and put up quite a scrap. The tub gurnard has brilliant blue markings on its fins like a peacock, a large head with a steep profile and conspicuous bony plates on its head.

HADDOCK (*Melanogrannus aeglefinus*)

Haddock is one of the most popular fish to eat and buy. In the North, it outsells cod at approximately three to one and they get the best and freshest haddock on the market.

Fishing
The haddock is part of the *Gadidae* family, which is the same as the cod and pollock. It is widely distributed in the North Atlantic and is found in all areas around the Scottish coasts and even as far south as the Humber Estuary. Haddock is a very popular food fish and is easily recognized by the black lateral line running along its white side.

The growth of the haddock may differ by area or by sex, but by the time they reach 4 years old, most fish are mature enough to spawn. Haddock undertake extensive migrations to their spawning grounds in the Barents Sea and Iceland and more restricted movements in the northwestern Atlantic. Their spawning runs from March until May and occurs in almost any area around the Scottish coasts to the Norwegian Deeps.

Haddock are generally caught in mixed fisheries along with cod, langoustines and whiting and are landed by bottom trawls, long lines and gill nets. The most common age of the catch is 4–6 years, weighing 1–2kg. Haddock are found close to the sea floor and often in schools, usually in depths less than 200m. In the North Sea, Norway has 23 per cent of the total allowable catch, mostly originating from bottom trawling. In addition to quota regulations, there are regulations aimed at protecting immature fish and the discarding of commercial species is not allowed. The fishery for haddock in the Northeast Arctic, where Norway and Russia account for more than 90 per cent of landings, is restricted by quotas, a minimum catching size and other measures. In early 2005, the stock was estimated at 370,000 tonnes and the spawning stock at 140,000 tonnes. The estimate of the spawning stock is above the precautionary level, but the stock could still be at risk of being harvested unsustainably.

Haddock is one of the UK's most popular fish and in some places it is endangered because of this very reason. I have been to the fish market at Peterhead in Aberdeenshire and it is full of haddock. A lot of the fishermen that are landing at Peterhead have joined up to something called the Responsible Fishermen's Scheme, and you can see the boxes of haddock in the market with the logo of the blue ship sailing on the seas. They have to

Glossary

go through various audits and health and safety measures on the quality of work that they carry out, while on the boat and while they are fishing. You can see the quality and pride that has gone into the catch and it makes all the difference to the product.

The MCS give the haddock a 3 rating.

Smoked haddock

Most of us love smoked haddock and the reason it is chosen over any other fish for smoking and drying is that the flakes are soft and break into small flakes. Smoked haddock has the wonderful aroma of smoky burnt oak and beech and two of the best are Finnan Haddie, named after the Aberdeen fishing village of Findon, and the Arbroath Smokie, which originally came from the small fishing village of Auchmithie, 3 miles northeast of Arbroath. Just make sure when you are choosing smoked haddock that it is really smoked and not dyed. The dyes are a way to give the fish a smoked look without having to go through the whole process. The real way for smoking is to place the fillets in a brine solution for a few minutes and then hang them on stainless steel racks to drain. The full racks are then placed in a brick-built chimney and smoked for 10–12 hours over oak and beech chippings.

Cooking Haddock has a great clean taste and will always be associated with fish and chip shops and being deep-fried in batter. The flesh is very flaky and most of the time when it is deep-fried it is served with its skin on. Its taste should be fresh, almost like sea air, with a lemony flavour. Although it is always seen as a fish that is served with chips, we can do more than that with it. It can be poached in milk with a bay leaf, garlic, a little thyme and parsley and served with some parsley mash. Haddock's also great in a comforting fish pie with parsley and a little mustard. If ever you get hold of smoked haddock, it can be made into fish cakes or served just with a simple poached egg and fresh spinach with a little nutmeg.

HAKE (*Merluccius merluccius*)

The hake is a fish that we don't see very much in the UK because it's never really been a popular choice among chefs or consumers. It's not the most attractive-looking fellow and it's not a species of fish that fishermen target – apart from the Spanish who love it and consume vast quantities of it. The stock of European hake, particularly the southern stock, is already severely depleted and a whole third of all hake landed finds itself in a Spanish fish stew or paella.

Fishing Hake is quite an ugly fish with its long, grey, slimy body, pointed face and vicious razor sharp teeth. They are a deep-sea member of the cod family, usually found between 70 and 370m throughout Europe and America. The adults live close to the bottom during daytime, but move off-bottom at night.

Hake is a late-maturing fish and maturity is only reached during the seventh year for most females, when they are approximately 57cm in length, and during the fifth year for males, when they are 40cm in length. Spawning is from February to July in northern waters.

European hake are mainly caught at depths of 100–150m and they are fished by bottom trawling. Pretty much every single hake that is landed will end up in Spain or be transported through Spain in one way or another.

In the 1970s, there was an international free-for-all in our waters, yielding an annual harvest well in excess of 300,000 tonnes. This caused a sharp decline in the hake stocks and the European hake is now so severely depleted that the MCS has given the poor hake a 5.

On a more positive note, the South African hake fishery has become the first hake fishery in the world to meet the MSC standard for sustainable fisheries. South African hake is by far the most valuable fish resource in South Africa and the fishery has been controlled by means of allocating quotas to companies within a conservative TAC, limitations on the number of vessels and certain closed areas that are off limits for breeding and spawning. Yearly quotas have remained stable, or increased, between 1977 and 2001 because stock levels have been healthy as a direct result of this good fisheries management.

The two main stocks for European hake are the northern and southern stocks. The northern stock harvested sustainably but the southern stock is depleted and it is hake from this stock that are rated a 5 by the MCS. Avoid eating hake from the southern stock, immature fish below about 50cm and during their breeding season from February to July.

Cooking Hake is a mild fish and has a more subtle flavour than cod. The flesh is quite soft and delicate in texture, but is moist and juicy and firms up on cooking. It is well worth trying. The taste is obviously sweet, but a little creamy as well. Hake is best left on the bone, so cut through the bone into darnes and then roast in butter with some capers, green olives and little segments of lemon added at the end with freshly chopped parsley. Alternatively, poach the hake in a court bouillon, which is an aromatic vegetable stock flavoured with carrots, fennel, celery, leeks, star anise, pink peppercorns, thyme, lemon and orange peel, dill and tarragon. The stock can be made the day before, so it's had a day to marinate and it will then be a better flavour for the fish.

HALIBUT

Halibut is a flatfish from the family of right-eye flounders, *Pleuronectidae*. The name 'halibut' comes from 'haly-butte' in Middle English, meaning the flatfish to be eaten on holy days. It is expensive to buy, but you'll still often see it on restaurant menus and it's almost always on fish counters. It is born with eyes on both sides of its head and at first swims like a round fish, but after about six months, one eye will migrate to the other side of its head, making it look more like the flounder, and it will settle close to the bottom. Halibut live in the North Pacific and North Atlantic and are a highly regarded quality fish of great renown. The Atlantic halibut (*Hippoglossus hippoglossus*) can be distinguished from most other species of flatfish by its concave tail. The Pacific halibut (*Hippoglossus stenolepis*) is a large, streamlined fish found in the northern Pacific Ocean and closely related to the Atlantic halibut, though it is very different looking with its brown, slightly speckled skin. Greenland halibut (*Reinhardtius hippoglossoides*) thrive in the cold northern waters of the Atlantic Ocean and the noticeable difference from the other halibut is the almost black colour of their skin.

Fishing The halibut is the largest of all flatfish, with an average weight of 11–14kg, and they are found at depths as shallow as a few metres to hundreds of metres. Although they spend most of their time near the bottom, halibut will move up through the sea to feed.

Halibut migrate long distances from shallow summer feeding grounds to deeper winter spawning grounds. Atlantic halibut spawn between February and May, Pacific halibut between November and January and Greenland halibut from April to July, with large mature females releasing several million eggs during the spawning season. Male halibut become sexually mature between 7 and 8 years of age and females attain sexual maturity between 8 and 12. The oldest halibut on record was 55 years old.

The halibut was not a popular food fish until the first quarter of the 19th century, but its slow rate of growth and the fact that it does not reproduce until at least aged 8, when they are approximately 76cm long, has meant that it has been unable to recover quickly from over-fishing. Fisheries usually use longline gear, but halibut are also caught along with many other bottom-dwelling fish by trawlers. Because of the distance between the harvesting areas and processing plants, Greenland halibut is frequently frozen at sea.

Atlantic halibut has been over-fished to such an extent that it is now dubbed by the IUCN to be endangered. Consequently, it is rated 5 by the MCS.

Careful international management of Pacific halibut has also been necessary because the species occupies a lot of EEZ zones and international waters of the United States, Canada, Russia, and possibly Japan. Pacific halibut stocks are, however, well managed by the IPHC (International Pacific Halibut Commission) who apply strict harvesting conditions. Longline fisheries for Pacific halibut in Alaska, Washington and Oregon were certified as environmentally friendly by the MSC in April 2006 and longline fisheries for Pacific halibut in British Columbia and Canada are currently undergoing MSC assessment. The Pacific halibut has a 3 rating.

The Greenland halibut stock levels in the areas around Iceland, Scotland, the Azores and Greenland are at an historic low and scientists advise the implementation of a recovery plan, so avoid eating halibut fished in these areas. The MCS has given the Greenland halibut a 4 rating. To minimise the impact of fishing on all halibut fish stocks, choose line-caught halibut from MSC-certified fisheries, where available.

Cooking Halibut are the meatiest of fish and it takes a lot to overcook them because they are moist and the fillets are so thick and dense. The Pacific halibut has a great juicy flavour that lasts forever in the mouth. It also has a slightly sticky texture and I feel it has a richer taste as well because it's a fairly fatty fish. Poach or pan-fry it in olive oil and a little butter. They are also great with a fresh orange butter sauce and a little caramelised endive.

JOHN DORY (*Zeus faber*)

Various explanations have been given for the origin of the name John Dory, but most are really unclear or are just tales that have been elaborated over time. 'Dory' seems to have derived from *dorée*, which is the name for it in France. However, the 'John' part is not so clear. It could be just a nickname or an allusion to the eighteenth-century actor John Quinn, who was responsible for giving the fish a good name and reputation. Others suggest that 'John' derives from the French *jaune*, or yellow.

John Dory is very odd-looking with an extendable, protrusible mouth.

Fishing John Dory are found on the coasts of southwest Africa, south-east Asia, Australia and New Zealand; the coasts of Japan and Korea; in the western Pacific, Indian Ocean, Atlantic Ocean, Mediterranean Sea and on the coasts of Europe, as well as in the south west of the UK and Scotland down to the Canary Isles, Azores and Madeira. They live near the sea bed in depths from 5–360m and are noted for their stalking abilities, which compensate for their lack of speed.

They have a lifespan of about 12 years in the wild and a length of 40–70cm, but can grow to a maximum size of 75cm and 3kg in weight. They become sexually mature at an age of 3–4 years and a length of 25–35cm. Spawning happens in June to August off the coasts of southern England, in the Bay of Biscay and the western part of the English Channel, but earlier in the Mediterranean and at the end of winter and the start of spring in the northeastern Atlantic.

John Dory is generally taken as bycatch in trawls. No assessment of stocks has been done by ICES in the morth-east Atlantic, which means it's an unprotected species and not subject to quota restrictions and there is potential for landing and marketing of mmature fish. Avoid eating immature fish less than 25–35cm long and during their breeding season from June and August. Although it's a valuable species, its habits are such that landings are sporadic and too few and far between to take any real estimates on what stocks there are.

The MCS have given the John Dory a 3 rating.

Cooking John Dory is marvellous to eat and it's a really good-quality fish that many chefs use in restaurants. The texture of the fish is very fine and it has a great fresh taste and a firm bite. It's also very simple to fillet if you are feeling brave, but just be careful of the spikes along the back spine. The Dory, once cleaned and gutted, can be baked whole in sea salt or cooked as individual fillets. The fillets can be pan-fried in olive oil with a little butter and finished with lemon juice. Try adding thyme or rosemary

Glossary

with a little garlic to the butter and serve with a simple green salad or some chargrilled Mediterranean vegetables.

LANGOUSTINE (*Nephrops norvegicus*)

Fishermen call them nephrops and prawns, chefs call them langoustines and the French call them scampi. The langoustine is the most commercially important shellfish species in the UK stock in the North Sea and west of Britain, and fishermen can earn a very good living from this shellfish. I remember when I was at Joël Robuchon in Paris I told them that we used to get all our langoustines alive, not dead as they had them. They, of course, did not believe me one little bit as they always thought that they had the best of everything when it came to food (and back then, the French pretty much did). It was not until I showed them some of the Scottish suppliers that we used in London restaurants I had worked in previously that they started to believe that maybe we did have something better than them.

Fishing Langoustines are much smaller than the common lobster, reaching a length of up to 15cm. The shell is pale pink, rose or orange-red and the claws are banded in red and white. Langoustines live in burrows in soft mud or sand and are spread throughout the Mediterranean, eastern North Atlantic, North Sea and Adriatic and are widespread around the Scottish coast. They are to be found in depths as shallow as a few metres in sheltered sea lochs, down to over 500m on the shelf edge, west of the Hebrides.

The males grow relatively quickly to around 6cm and seldom exceed 10 years old, while females grow more slowly and can reach 20 years old. Females mature at about 3 years old and reproduce each year thereafter. After mating in early summer, they spawn in September and carry eggs under their tails until they hatch in April or May. Females carrying eggs are described as being 'berried' and they very rarely come out of the burrow, where they are naturally protected from the trawlers. Males dominate the trawl catch for most of the year and are much more heavily exploited than females.

The fishery for langoustines in Scottish waters was developed from the early 1960s and they are currently one of the most valuable species landed, making about £50 million in recent years. The UK has the largest share of the world market for langoustines and around 50 per cent of the total global catch is caught in the North Sea and on the Scottish west coast.

The fishermen get a very good price for langoustines in Europe and they are a very valuable commodity, even more so than the cod; I would say almost 80–90 per cent of all the langoustine caught are going abroad.

The stocks of langoustine are mostly inside safe biological limits, except the southern stocks in the Bay of Biscay and around the Iberian Peninsula, which are exploited at alarming levels. The season is mainly from April to November. Since most of the fishing is done by trawling, langoustine are protected from trawls when in burrows, so tracking their emergence patterns is very important and the fishermen have to get it right otherwise they will be wasting their time and, most importantly, a lot of money on expensive fuel.

Trawl fisheries for langoustines are associated with large quantities of bycatch, including of protected species such as cod and juvenile fish, so to increase the sustainability of the type you eat, choose pot or creel-caught rather than trawled langoustines. The award-winning Loch Torridon creel fishery in Shieldaig has been certified as an environmentally responsible fishery by the MSC. In 1985, the 3-mile fishing limit around Britain's coasts meant that the trawlers could come near to the shore to extract fish. Their large nets not only damaged creel equipment but also caused havoc to the seabed and local marine species. Fishermen from Shieldaig campaigned successfully for a trawler-free zone and from 2001, trawling was banned in Loch Torridon. Torridon langoustines are caught mostly in creels, which are strung together in lines of over 100. The cages are dropped onto the seabed to depths of 200m and on a good day, 100kg langoustines will be caught in this way. They are shipped over the day after they are caught to Paris or Madrid, alive and at a premium. Langoustines are nowadays often sent to Europe in vivier trucks, which carry a storage system that keeps shellfish in the exact environment they are used to and in perfect condition until they arrive at their destination. These systems can keep langoustines alive and flapping for days, hence when you go to a market in Spain or France these days, they are jumping around on the fish counter.

The langoustine gets a 3 rating from MCS.

Cooking Langoustines are very popular with chefs in high-class restaurants; their flavour is amazing and so sweet and tasty you will soon be craving more of them. The langoustine does not have all that much meat because the top half is taken up by the head and claws. After blanching in boiling water, the head and the intestinal tract can be removed from the tail by twisting the centre tail fin and pulling this out. The intestinal tract is attached to this and will come straight out with it.

Langoustines can be used and cooked in many ways and every piece of the langoustine can be used to make something. They are best just simply cooked in boiling water for no more than 45–60 seconds, then left to cool, peeled and eaten cold or hot with a great garlic mayonnaise. All the shells – that's the head, tail shell and claws – can be used to make a delicious bisque. If you get very large langoustines that have big claws, you will find that they have quite a bit of meat in the shell. The langoustine tails can then be split in half on the shell and just pan-fried in olive oil with a little garlic and rosemary. This way you don't have to take them out of their shells, which can be a little tricky and time consuming.

LING (*Molva molva*)

Ling are, I am afraid to say, some of the ugliest fish in the sea and they eat pretty much anything or, should I say, are not afraid to eat anything. They are the largest member of the *Gadoid* family – the same family as cod, pollock and haddock – and they have a long slender body reminiscent of an eel with a distinctive single barbel on the chin.

Fishing Ling are demersal deepwater fish that like to stay hidden and can be found hanging out in sheltered rocks or in shipwrecks, often under the cover of seaweed. They are fairly common around the south west, the western coasts of Ireland and Scotland and the Irish Sea coasts, the eastern side of the English Channel and the east coast of England. The ling can grow to 2.2m in length, but most are between 1–1.5m and up to 35kg in weight.

Ling are a very slow-growing fish and take their time to reproduce, which makes them vulnerable to overfishing. The ling breeds between March and July and a single female can produce up to 60 million eggs at a time, although the real likelihood is that out of all those eggs, only a few hundred will survive. Length at first spawning is 60–75cm and the age at first spawning is 5–7 years. Most ling in commercial catches are less than 10 years old, but individuals of ages 19–20 years also occur.

Ling have been severely exploited for centuries over most of the areas that it chooses to swim. It is currently a bycatch in the trawl and gill net fisheries, but the major component of the landings stems from the long-line fishery, either from the long liners that target ling or from fisheries with other primary targets, such as cod or hake.

The average catch per year of ling from 1988 through to 2004 was 44000 tonnes. In 2004, the catch was 32000 tonnes, with the Norwegian catches approximately 40 per cent of the total catch. There is no overall international TAC set for ling, but the fishery is to some extent regulated by bilateral quotas and other national measures.

In 2004, ICES considered the state of the stock to be unknown, but probably varying within the large range of species. Closed areas need to be introduced to protect spawning fish and minimum catch sizes should be introduced into mixed fisheries.

I would avoid eating the ling, as it's rated as a 5 by the MCS, unless you can be assured that it comes from a sustainable source, is line- or static-net caught and not in the spawning season.

Cooking The ling has firm flesh and a thick skin. The flesh, once cooked, is very meaty with a pleasant, slightly acidic flavour, which tastes as though it is very clean. Because the flesh is compact and tight it does not fall apart when cooked and it can be cooked on or off the bone and poached, fried, baked, or literally anything. You could also cut the fish into darnes through the bone, which will help to keep the flesh moist whilst being cooked. You can use it in soups, fish stews and casseroles and it can take hearty flavours like red wine and smoked bacon or peas and bacon.

LOBSTER (*Homarus gommarus*)

The common lobster is largely nocturnal, making sightings of it very uncommon. However, when it does appear from its lair during the day, it is a magnificent sight with its dark blue armour, pale yellow markings and long, bright red antennae. Its front claws are powerful, and each is a different shape – one is heavier and used for crushing whilst the other is sharper and serves as a cutting tool. And the claws are formidable weapons in combat with foolish predators.

Fishing The European lobster is solitary, nocturnal and territorial, living in holes or crevices in the sea floor during the day and coming out to feed mainly at night. It is found around the southwest of the UK and the eastern Atlantic from northwestern Norway south to the Azores and the Atlantic coast of Morocco, north-west coast of the Black Sea and the Mediterranean, English Channel, North Sea and West Baltic.

The European lobster is slightly smaller on average than the closely related American lobster (*Homarus americanus*) with lengths of 23–50cm and weights of around 0.7kg most common. A small lobster weighing 500g can take between 4–6 years to reach this size and the cold waters that European lobsters inhabit lead to a relatively slow growth rate in comparison to warmer water lobsters. However, the cold clean water also really contributes to the sweet flavour and firm texture of the meat, resulting in these lobsters having the reputation for being the best in the world.

Females with eggs are found almost throughout the year. The eggs are laid around July and carried for 10 or 11 months before they emerge as free-swimming larvae. These larvae will go through several moults before transforming into miniature lobsters and settling down on the seabed. The smallest lobsters to be encountered in lobster pots are around 15cm long. Maturity and minimum landing sizes tend to be reached after 4–5 years and the minimum catch size for the lobster is 87mm in the British Isles.

The two methods of catching lobster are the inshore method, whereby single pots are hauled by hand, and the offshore method, where strings of creels, or woven baskets, are worked in one line. Modern lobster boats have up to 2,000 pots, which they haul day and night, covering the seabed with a blanket of traps. Lobster potting is the most selective fishing method and a lobster-pot fishery off the Yorkshire coast managed by the North Eastern Sea Fisheries Committee (NESFC) is currently undergoing assessment as an environmentally responsible fishery by the MSC. Most of the fishery is carried out with lobster pots, baited with oily fish such as scad or pieces of octopus or cuttlefish tied to lines to tempt them out of their burrows, after which they are caught by hand or with nets.

Although attempts have been made to run lobster farms, they proved to be unfeasible because of the lobsters' aggressively territorial habits. However, the National Lobster Hatchery in Padstow is a small charity that exists to try and balance the need for a sustainable and productive fishery with the needs and requirements of marine wildlife. Since they opened in 2000, they have released over 50,000 juvenile lobsters into the coastal waters of Cornwall and the Isles of Scilly. Over 25 years of extensive research they have concluded that survival rates from releases at 3 months to re-capture at 5 years could be as high as 50 per cent. Local fishermen donate egg-carrying female lobsters to the hatchery and after the eggs hatch, the lobster larvae are reared under artificial conditions until they grow into juvenile lobsters, at which point they are released to suitable habitats. The hatchery raised and released 8,399 lobsters last year, which is amazing.

Lobsters are a high-value species and many traditional lobster grounds are depleted and stocks below a quarter of their potential level. Avoid eating lobsters that are below the legal minimum landing size, or egg-bearing or larger lobsters, which are mainly females which contribute to the breeding stock.

The lobster has an MCS rating of 4 because, even though there are breeding and spawning programmes in place, they have a slow growth and long gestation period.

Cooking The lobster is the ultimate shellfish to eat and one of the most prized by chefs. The sweet-tasting meat is salty and lemony with a hint of seaweed, a squeaky texture and bite. I would say that for such a beautiful shellfish it's best to keep it as simple as possible. The trick is not to overcomplicate such a great creature and definitely not to overcook the beast because it can end up becoming tough, fibrous and chewy. If you are squeamish about having to kill the lobster, then place it in the freezer for 2 hours and it will slowly fall asleep. Once it does, insert a very sharp knife into its head. The taste of the lobster is very pure and clean and it does not need hidden flavours or extra ingredients to make it special. When cooked, lobster can be served cold with mayonnaise or a garlic aioli or it can be cooked in a aromatic court bouillion and eaten hot out of the pot with a great glass of Vouvray or Sauvignon Blanc. One of the best ways, I think, of cooking lobster is eating it split and roasted over a real wooden fire, barbecue-style. Use lobster crackers to extract the tasty claw and knuckle meat.

MACKEREL (*Scomber scombrus*)

The mackerel is a marvellous fish to eat and it is incredibly beautiful in and out of the water, its sleek, streamlined shape fast swimming like a mini torpedo, the striking silvery-blue skin marbled with streaks of dark and light blues.

The mackerel is a species of the *Scombrid* family, which contains many of the most important and familiar food fishes, including mackerels, tunas and bonitos. They are found worldwide in tropical and warm temperate seas and mackerel is a common fish in the North Atlantic. The Atlantic mackerel is by far the commonest of the 10 species of the family that have been caught in British waters and it is found in huge shoals, migrating towards the coast to feed on small fish and prawns during the summer. During the winter, they retreat to deeper water and go into a state of near-hibernation, fasting and waiting for the spring.

Fishing Total catches of mackerel have been relatively stable since 1969 with official statistics accounting for on average about 665,000 tonnes annually. Since 2001, mackerel has also been regulated by internationally agreed TACs that apply to the entire distribution area of the stock. In addition to the TAC, a number of management measures are in place to protect the North Sea component of the stock that is considered depleted, and to protect the juvenile mackerel (maturity is attained at an age of 2–3 years of age).

The South West Handline Fishermen's Association was originally set-up to represent the many mackerel handline boats fishing in the south west of England and in 2000, the association was one of the first to receive accreditation from the Marine Stewardship Council (MSC). Mackerel can in fact be fished for almost 12 months of the year. In the spring, a fleet of 20–25 mostly single-handed boats fish from Newlyn, Mousehole and the surrounding coves of Penberth and Lamorna. These boats tend to fish at dawn and dusk using lines of 25 or 30 hooks baited only with brightly coloured feathers or plastic tubing. During the summer, the fishery moves onto St Ives on the north Cornish coast where a fleet of up to 40 boats from St Ives, Hayle, Sennen and Portreath handline for mackerel until the autumn. From October to January, a fleet of fast, modern vessels handline for mackerel from Looe with 2 or 3 crew per boat. These boats often have to travel up to 50 miles a day to search for fish.

The fishery at Hastings has been in existence for more than a thousand years and there were fishermen here before William the Conqueror was a twinkle in his father's eye. The methods they use have also remained largely unchanged over time. Since the 12th century, they have used beach-launched boats and Hastings now has the largest beach-launched fleet in Europe. This means that the fishermen fish to the rhythm of the tides, catching on a daily basis. They are also constrained by the weather, being unable to fish in anything above a force 5. This means that out of 365 days a year, they only fish on average 200 days, helping the sustainability of the stocks.

Mackerel has a MCS rating of 3.

Cooking Mackerel is an oily fish, rich in Omega-3, that needs to be eaten very fresh and spoils quite quickly because of its oil content. The flesh has a pinky-brown tinge and, like the sardine and herring, it is best served with something piquant or acidic to counterbalance the oils in the fish. Because of the high level of oil, it can also take strong flavours. Mackerel is very adaptable to different ways of cooking and can be baked, grilled, barbecued and even eaten raw or marinated. The best cooking method for me is actually eaten raw, but slightly marinated with lemon juice, olive oil, diced avocado and some fresh herbs. Or you can fillet the fish, dice it up and then add a little soy sauce, sesame oil and a lime zest. Or just serve it plain, grilled with a little rosemary olive oil and lemon and served with either pickled beetroot or a nice acidic potato salad with spring onions and grain mustard.

MONKFISH (*Lophius piscatorius*)

The monkfish is a fearsome creature and an amazing sight to see coming over the side of a boat as they are landed, their mouths wide open as they gasp for air and big enough to fit a man's head. In the 60s and 70s, monkfish was mainly used as cat food and was a bycatch to many other fish species. It was not until the early 80s that chefs started to really use monkfish and see its full potential. And, of course, as we got to really like the fish, it started to get into trouble. By the early 90s, stocks were already becoming depleted, especially off the coast of Spain.

Fishing The monkfish is a very distinctive fish. Its wide mouth curves inward to a sharp row of pointed teeth, while its squashed-looking head and body taper to a short, thickset tail. Brown or greeny brown with reddish or dark brown mottles, it can change colour to camouflage itself against the seabed, where it spends most of its life. Found on both sides of the Atlantic, the Mediterranean and the Black Sea, monkfish also live all around the coastline of the UK. They occur in a very wide range of depths, although larger, mature fish are now scarce in shallow waters.

Monkfish have a long spawning season but unlike, say, cod or haddock, each female probably produces only one batch of eggs per season. Female monkfish also only begin to reach maturity around the age of seven and the majority do not spawn until they are even older. Females are therefore likely to be caught long before they spawn. The majority of catches, especially the trawled catches, comprise immature or young fish (females mature at 70cm, males at 50cm) and the south-western stock is the only stock in the north-east Atlantic assessed by the ICES as having full reproductive capacity, meaning the stock is in a healthy state and above the minimum level recommended.

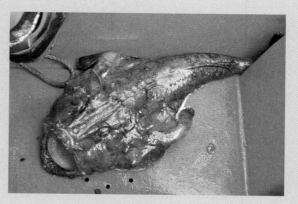

Monkfish are caught commercially with bottom trawls, gill nets and bottom longlines. The use of gill nets with larger meshes is a more selective method of fishing for this species than trawling, and therefore more sustainable. There are currently no size restrictions on landings, no distinction between different species and no measures to protect spawning stock. However, recent restrictions on the fishing and TACs for other deepwater species have resulted in less monkfish being caught in deeper waters from the northern stock.

Monkfish has a rating of 4 from the MCS. This makes it a fish that should really be avoided, although handline-caught monkfish are okay. The stock levels in the south west of the UK are now beginning to get into a healthier state than they have been for years, so you can eat them if they have been line or net caught. Make sure the monkfish is above 70cm and do not fish for or eat them during the breeding season of spring to early summer.

Cooking You rarely see the head of a monkfish on a counter, probably because it looks so scary it would put customers off. This is a fish that is a very easy to prepare, with one central spine and two thick fillets either side – you can cook it on or off the bone. Monkfish tail is covered in a thick, skin-like membrane, which protects the ivory-white, delicate flesh underneath. Once you have trimmed all the brown skin and membrane (if left on it will discolour and go an unpleasant grey when cooked) you will be left with a beautiful white tail. The gelatinous bones make really great fish stock.

A very meaty fish, monkfish is great roasted, baked, fried, barbecued and even poached (the classic dish of poached monkfish with saffron and capers is exquisite). Try roasting it on the bone, cut into darnes (see page 298) to keep the fish moist. Just colour in a little frying pan over a high heat, add some butter, thyme and a few capers and place in the oven for 15–20 minutes on a medium heat. Because of its meaty texture and flavour, monkfish is also great cooked with red wine (or served with it). One of the most popular ways of cooking monkfish in the 80s was wrapped in Parma ham and roasted and I remember doing this dish many times at college and in my early years as a chef. The main reason for the Parma ham was that you could put this fish up against meat, but it also helped to keep the fillet nice and round whilst cooking. Monkfish is quite hard to overcook because it's such a solid piece of fish. Because of this, and the fact that it's so juicy, I would say it's best to rest it on a wire rack for 5 minutes before tucking in.

MULLET

RED MULLET (*Mullus surmuletus*)
The red mullet is a wondrous animal to look at and its redness cannot really be matched in terms of beauty by any other fish. In the kitchen, they are even called *rougets* because of this pink or reddish colour.

The red mulllet belongs to the *Mullidae* family and has an elongated body, blunt, steep nose and two long barbels on the chin, which are sensory organs that detect food on the sea bed and give the red mullet its alternative name of 'goatfish'.

Fishing You will find mullet throughout the world in tropical and warm temperate seas, especially in the Mediterranean. Due either to global warming or a slight increase in the water temperature, the mullet now ventures into waters as far north as Britain and Ireland in the summer.

Red mullet reach a minimum size of 11cm and a maximum of 40cm and grow quickly, maturing young at 2 years and about 22cm in length. This makes them a good sustainable choice if you avoid eating immature mullet. The season to avoid is from May to July when they are spawning.

The young juveniles are surface feeders until they migrate down to sandy, muddy or rocky sea floors and swim to depths of up to 400m. They are caught mainly with gill nets, trammel nets, bottom trawls and by hand-line sports anglers.

Red mullet is subject to high fishing pressure in Mediterranean fisheries because it is extremely popular in this part of the world. They are also often taken as bycatch and in mixed trawl fisheries.

If you ever get the choice between net-caught or line-caught mullet, always choose the line as you can see the clear difference just by the brighter red colour, which indicates the fish is healthier.

The red mullet is rated as a 3 by the MCS.

Cooking There is very little fat on a red mullet and plenty of iodine, iron and phosphorus for brainpower, so it is a very good fish for your health. It has a great oily and lemony taste and its savoury, roasted flavour is very difficult to beat. The skin adds another taste element, but it has to be crispy and golden brown to give a taste a little reminiscent of roast chicken. Red mullet is also a really moist fish, but it must not be overcooked otherwise it will be dry and crumbly. The French sometimes refer to the strong-tasting red mullet as 'the woodcock of the sea' because, like woodcock, they can be eaten whole, with their innards intact, after being grilled. However, personally I would not recommend cooking them this way.

For chefs, the red mullet is a great fish, but it's not a fish that is really used all that much at home because it's fiddly to cook with all the pin bones. The mullet can be cooked either whole on the bone or filleted. If cooking the red mullet whole, I would gut the fish first and then give it a little wash after the scales have been removed. Chop a little garlic, thyme and rosemary and mix these together. Smear the mullet in a little olive oil and then rub over the herbs and garlic, season and place on a tray and into the oven. Alternatively, remove the fillets off the bone and take out all the little pin bones. Pan-fry them very quickly in a hot non-stick pan with a little olive oil until the skin is crispy and golden brown, then add a squeeze of lemon. It's a typical Mediterranean fish and therefore is great served with Mediterranean-style vegetables and salads. Try with a simple fennel salad with lemon juice, olive oil and a few chopped black olives.

Glossary

GREY MULLET (Family *Mugilidae*)

The grey mullet is part of the large *Mugilidae* family, which comprises some 80 species worldwide with three inhabiting our coastal waters: the thick lipped *Chelon labrosus*, the thin-lipped *Liza ramada* and lastly the golden grey mullet, *Liza aurata*. They are a poor relation to the beautiful red mullet, but they are a great substitute in terms of value.

Fishing Grey mullet are all very similar looking and are almost flat on top with a blunt nose, small mouth and soft extending lips. Mullet have found an ecological niche by mostly eating mud and their phenomenally long digestive tracts allow them to digest the goodness of all the microscopic creatures that live there. They also feed on the green algae that grow on rocks and in the surface film that forms on the water on calm days, which is when you may see them and puzzle at their silly behaviour as they seem to gulp at the air.

Grey mullet swim to the eastern Atlantic and from Norway to Morocco, including the Mediterranean, the Black Sea and even some tropical waters. In British waters they are very common in estuaries and can grow to about 75cm and 4.5kg, but they are slow growers and a 3kg mullet is likely to be at least 15 years old.

They spawn in the Channel and in Irish waters in July to August, earlier in the southern part of the distribution area. Grey mullet become sexually mature at a length of 30–35cm and at an age of 3–4 years. Avoid eating fish below the 35cm size at which it matures and during its summer spawning season. Most mullet are caught by rod and line as it is not at all commercially fished. You can buy then from fishmongers, but not supermarkets.

They are rated by the MCS as 3, so they are a good sustainable fish to eat.

Cooking As with red mullet, grey mullet has iodine, iron and phosphorus for brainpower, so make sure your kids eat more of it and you will also be doing something great for the publicity and marketing of this less well-known fish. The grey mullet has an earthy taste and flavour as a result of feeding and hoovering up mud on the sea bed and this does affect the flavour somewhat. The flesh is also fibrous and has a very low level of moisture because the grey mullet are such a lean fish with not much fat on them. So they can be a little chewy sometimes and are perhaps best suited for pan-frying just in olive oil, with a little butter added towards the end. I would also suggest that the grey mullet can take some heavy flavourings, so try some fresh herbs like coriander and mint in a marinade with some chilli or garlic and even ginger. Once it has marinated, pan-fry the fish on the skin side and once you have got a nice crispy skin, turn the fish over and cook for a further few minutes. Dash on a little soy sauce and then add some of the marinade back to the pan to cook. Add a sprinkle of sesame oil and that's it – a great dish from the grey mullet. Grey mullet can also be baked whole in salt in the oven with some soft herbs like dill and parsley, and some orange and lemon peel mixed in.

MUSSELS (Mytilus edulis)

Mussels have been an important source of food in Europe for 300,000 to 400,000 years, but almost all the mussels that we eat today are cultured. There is a legend that mussels were first farmed on *bouchots* (poles) in France in 1235 by a shipwrecked Irishman, though I think this is a little bit much to believe (maybe just a few too many ales were drunk the day that story was told!).

Mussels are one of the most popular of all shellfish, particularly in Belgium where they are served with chips (and beer!) and are known as *mosselen met friet*, with the same dish in France called *moules frites*. In Ireland and in the west of Scotland, they are popular boiled and seasoned with vinegar.

Fishing Mussels are bivalve molluscs and 13 species are found around our shores as well as others throughout the Mediterranean, North Atlantic, North Sea and Baltic coasts. Their size and shape vary widely. The length is usually 50–100mm, but some species are unlikely to reach more than 30mm, while others can exceed 150mm. The minimum landing size required for sale in the UK is about 55mm. Everyone is familiar with the dark blue or blackish shells, but some varieties are paler with dark brown, purple or blue markings. Mussels become sexually mature when they are a year old and can live for 10–15 years or more. The female mussels spawn from May to October.

Mussels have been farmed for hundreds of years and by the 19th century the use of post-grown mussels had spread around France, with farmed mussels starting in the Netherlands from about 1860. Today they are widely cultivated and stocks are generally considered underexploited from both natural and cultivated beds. Fisheries are located in sheltered estuaries and bays, such as the Wash and Morecambe Bay, and mussels are grown by several methods. Rope-hanging culture is one of the most widespread methods used in Spain, Ireland, Scotland and New Zealand and at the restaurant, we use rope-hung Isle of Shuna mussels, which are cultivated in the warm plankton-rich streams surrounding the Scottish west coast and the Shetland Islands. There they grow the mussels on long lines and they were the first to sell mussels boxed and iced. The mussels are cultivated in a sustainable manner, making as little impact as possible on the surrounding areas. Mussels on the west coast are mainly harvested between July and early the following year, while the Shetland harvesting season tends to occur later due to the colder waters of the region. Because of this, the Isle of Shuna has almost year round continuity of mussel production. The mussels are also a lot more plump than other mussels and they taste really good.

The *bouchot* technique so common in France involves planting and placing poles, known as *bouchots*, into the sea bed. The ropes on which the mussels grow are then tied in a spiral method on the pilings and mesh netting is attached to prevent the mussels from falling away. This method of farming needs an extended tidal zone.

Mussels are filter feeders, requiring large quantities of water to pass through their system just to get adequate food to survive. This means that any pollutant will concentrate in their flesh and if eaten by us, can have dire results and even cause serious illnesses, such as paralytic shellfish poisoning. Poisoning of wild mussels can be due to a bloom of algae or red tides and mussels are usually safe if they have been professionally farmed.

The mussel has a 2 rating from the MCS.

Cooking Mussels should always be sold alive. Check when you are buying that they are closed because being open is the first clue that they might not be all that fresh. If they are open when you get them home, press them shut lightly and they should re-close. If they don't, throw them away. Another way of checking to see if they are okay is by putting them in a large bowl of cold water. The ones that float to the surface are no good and should not be eaten. Once cooked, do not eat any mussels that are shut. Before cooking them, I always leave mussels in water for a few hours so they start to clean themselves as there is nothing worse than eating gritty mussels. Once they've soaked, just give them a light brushing with a nail brush. You might see part of what's called the mussel beard poking out of the shell. If so, give this a little tug to remove as it's unpleasant to eat.

Mussels contain many vitamins and minerals and are wonderfully nutritious and rich in protein, minerals and Omega-3 fatty acids, yet low in fat and cholesterol. The pale, creamy-yellow soft part of the mussel has a similar rich taste to cooked egg yolks, while the outer part has a slight smoky bacon flavour. The green-lipped mussel has a more lip-like skin inside, which hangs off the central creamy part of the mussel and has the flavour of squid, but again is really sweet tasting.

Mussels are of course best eaten cooked in their shells, such as for *moules marinière* with its copious amounts of garlic, white wine and parsley. The smell of this cooking in any kitchen is glorious and the mussels have an incredibly sweet taste, especially if you add a little butter to the sauce to enrich it. Mussels are also great in stews with other fish, added to a fish pie or baked.

NORTH SEA HERRING (*Clupea harengus harengus*)

The herring is a beautiful fish to look at with its green and silver skin really making it stand out from other fish. Streamlined for swimming, if you turned an Atlantic herring sideways, it's so thin you could probably slide it under your closet door. This compressed body and silvery scales serve as camouflage in the open waters of the ocean, scattering light and helping to conceal herrings from predators attacking from the deep. Silvery scales, however, are of no help during attacks from above. Even in murky water, the flash of silver alerts fishermen to the herring's presence.

Herrings belong to the same family of *clupeids* as sprats and pilchards and form one of the most important commercial fisheries in the world. Over the centuries, herring fisheries have been exploited by a series of countries on the northwest side of Europe, particularly since the tradition of curing herring with salt in barrels was mastered and herring could travel. Today, the general picture is of dwindling stocks being pursued by fewer boats than ever before, but with more and more sophisticated equipment. However, an increase in restrictions has been important in attempts to restore the stocks to something like their former self. Herring remains a very important food product for much of Northern Europe, especially the Scandinavian countries and Holland.

Fishing Herring can grow to 43cm, although size can vary amongst races (different distinct breeding stocks). Important stocks or species in the Atlantic are the winter-spawning Norwegian and Icelandic herrings, the autumn-spawning Icelandic and North Sea herrings and the Baltic herrings. Herring are sexually mature at 3–9 years and at least one population in UK waters spawns in any one month of the year. Most herring landed now are around 25cm and the season is from May to December.

By the 1960s and 70s, North Sea herring had been almost fished out by fishermen who had got extremely rich from this little fish. Bottom trawling by the British and Dutch had allowed fishermen to specifically target concentrated spots of spawning herring and when Britain joined the Common Market in 1973, the North Sea came under the management of the Common Market. This was a bad idea as no agreement was made on how to maintain the fishery; I guess because they were all as greedy as each other. By 1977, the stock of herring had collapsed and the fisheries began to close. After another decline in the mid-1990s (mainly due to a high bycatch of juveniles in the industrial fishery), the implementation of a recovery plan for herring in European waters, including a system of Total Allowable Catches and quotas, began to be successful.

Today, Eastern European factory ships, known as Klondykers, have moved in, initially fishing on licenses bought from the European community and more recently on contract to a variety of British fish processors and distributors. They are a vital part of Britain's fishing industry, processing more than half of Scotland's annual mackerel and herring catch for export to the Continent and Far East. The vessels sail into the North Sea and Atlantic waters each winter and summer at the start of the mackerel and herring seasons. At the height of the season, there are more than 100 vessels anchored off Shetland and the west coast. Local fishermen do well out of the arrangement because the Klondykers can process their catch far more cheaply and efficiently than land-based factories can. However, very few of the ships meet European health and safety requirements or pay their workers anything approaching European levels of wages, which is why they are so cheap. It is also why Shetland Islanders, who do not directly benefit from their presence, are viewing the Klondyker phenomenon with increasing concern.

The Thames herring fishery at Blackwater in Essex has become the first fishery to be certified for the second time for meeting MSC sustainable requirements. The Thames herring (*Clupea harengus*) is smaller than the North Sea herring and is distinguished by having one less vertebra. The stock is fished between October and March by both drift nets and mid-water trawls and trawl fishing for herring is prohibited from a designated area within which only gill netting is allowed. Thames herrings are sold at Sainsburys, Tesco and Waitrose, however prices do not reflect the costs of fishing and the fishery at the moment is barely viable. Fishing by gill net from small, inshore boats is a totally different proposition to the industrial fishing of North Sea herring, but the market, and hence prices, is dominated by the latter. The hope is that the certification against the MSC standard will help to differentiate Thames herring from North Sea herring and so enable fishermen to obtain a fair price for their product.

As with all oily fish, herring are fast growing and mature quickly, so the rejuvenation of the stocks makes them sustainable. In May 2006, the North Sea and the east English Channel autumn-spawning stock were certified as reaching sustainable levels by the MSC, while ICES continues to assess other stocks as being healthy and harvested sustainably. The MCS rate the herring as a 3.

Cooking The herring is a very oily fish and, as we all know, eating fish with high fish oils is very good for us. Herrings are sold fresh: whole or filleted, gutted or ungutted, and have almost the same taste as the anchovy – slightly salty and oily, but also peppery with an almost livery, seaside taste. The herring does have a strong aroma, unique to oily fish, when being cooked, which some of us love and some of us loathe (apart from cats, of course). One of the nicest fish to eat when it's very fresh, just keep it simple because a fish like the herring does not need any fussing over at all. It is best simply pan-fried with a little olive oil on the skin until its nice and crispy and finished with some fresh black pepper and a little lemon juice. The oiliness of the fish needs something acidic, lemony or piquant, so serve with it some escabeche, pickled beetroot, tomato salsa or simply on toast with homemade chutney. It's also great

Glossary

just lightly pickled, brined or cured in a little olive oil, lemon juice or even soy sauce. It is such a versatile fish to use and one that can stand up to strong flavours.

In Scandinavia and Holland, the herring is popular in the form of roll mops, which are herring fillets rolled up with pickled onions and vinegar. Some come with sweet dill, juniper or sherry, etc. For the very simplest of offerings, kippers are a delight, but choose wisely as you can get some from say, Loch Fyne, that are sublime or there are those that look like they have been dyed a nasty yellow smoky colour and taste revolting. Smoked herrings, such as bloaters, are from my part of the world: Norfolk and Suffolk. Bloaters are smoked with the guts in, have a slight tang to them and are definitely an acquired taste. They can be eaten raw or grilled and even made into a paté. Pickled and smoked herrings with bacon and horseradish are also yummy.

OYSTERS

The oyster has a lot of history but it has also been used and abused more than any other shellfish on the planet. Eaten by the most famous of kings, queens and emperors from ancient and mythical lands to the present day, oysters are one of the most revered and expensive of all shellfish, but it is remarkable that we have any left at all. Once as common as sliced white bread, sadly we have over-fished them and ruined a lot of the natural oyster beds that once were around the whole of the UK. However, despite over-fishing and the destruction of their environment, they have lasted the test of time.

NATIVE OYSTER (Ostrea eduis)
To say that people have been eating oysters for a long time is an understatement: they have been an important food source in Europe from as far back as Roman times. The native oyster was once the main food for a lot of poor people in coastal villages and as soon as the transport system started taking shape and the industrial era kicked in, oysters were transported to main towns from the coasts allowing even more to be eaten. By 1864, about 700 million oysters were eaten in London alone. This boom lasted for about 20 years, but by then, overfishing and pollution reduced the wild stocks to their present low levels.
Fishing Native oysters, also known as the flat or common oyster, are bivalve molluscs, meaning they have two hinged shells and they are round with rough, flaky shells. They live on the seabed in relatively shallow water and, while some may live for as long as 15 years, their usual lifespan is thought to be around six years.

Native oysters grow in shallow coastal waters and estuaries around the British Isles, the North Sea, the Mediterranean and the Black Sea. They prefer muddy sea beds, but they need something hard like shells or stones for the larvae to settle on. The main UK stocks are now located in the rivers and flats bordering the Thames Estuary, the Solent, River Fal, in sea lochs on the west coast of Scotland and in Ireland.

Within the UK, the town of Whitstable in Kent is particularly special for oyster farming and the oyster beds have been used since Roman times. There is evidence that the Romans consumed huge quantities of oysters during their occupation of Britain and though oysters have been grown in Colchester in Essex since soon after the last Ice Age and well before the Romans invaded Britain, it was the Romans who were the first to start commercially rearing them and the town is still well known for its great oyster beds.

The native oyster has a remarkable sex life! They may start life as males, but are able to change sex many times throughout their lives. This is an evolutionary adaptation to help native oysters maximise their reproductive potential. If conditions are good the oysters will start to breed in the summer of their third year, a process triggered by the maximum temperature that the water reaches in the summer. A single female oyster can produce up to 100 million eggs annually, which develop inside the female's shell for a while, until they hatch into minute swimming larvae.

Oysters are traditionally only harvested when there is an 'r' in the month; ie, from September to April. An oyster with eggs is not considered edible, which is why oysters should not be eaten in summer. Certainly they are less meaty and more likely to die and to go bad in hot weather. They cannot be sold by law during the months of May, June, July and August when they are spawning and this ban on eating oysters in summer allows them to breed and so produce a new crop of baby oysters. These measures are certainly necessary because by the late 1870s, over-fishing and disease had had a devastating effect on British oyster beds. The industry went into a sharp decline and today production in most areas is still very low. The UK catch was 40 million in 1920, falling to just 3 million in the 1960s. A survey in 1957 of Scotland's Firth of Forth, which at peak production produced 30 million oysters per year, reported that native oysters were not only commercially extinct there, but were biologically extinct, since not a single living oyster was found.

The native oyster has a 4 rating from the MCS.

PACIFIC OYSTER (Crassostrea angulata)
Pacific oysters are teardrop shaped and their shells are smooth, deeply ribbed and often frilled at the edges. Pacific oysters are available all year round and if you've ever eaten oysters in a restaurant or seen an oyster farm, you've most likely encountered the non-native Pacific oyster, also known as the Portuguese oyster (they are the same species). Pacific oysters are currently the preferred aquaculture species in many areas because they grow faster than native oysters.
Fishing Pacific oysters are a relative newcomer to Northern European coastal waters and have thrived over the past 30 years. They grow at more than twice the rate of the native oyster, reaching a marketable size in less than 2 years, and are more resilient than their counterparts to both the conditions and diseases that affect the natives.

It was the Portuguese oyster that was initially introduced to fisheries around the South coast and Essex coastline in the early 1900s. These oysters proved to be reasonably successful, but it wasn't until the disease Bonemia virtually wiped out the UK native oyster industry that these oysters came into their own. This time the same species of oyster from Japan and south-east Asia proved to be the better quality and a more commercially viable oyster.

Pacific oysters have a fantastic flavour and are very plump compared to other oysters from around the British Isles. As these oysters originate from the warmer waters of the Pacific Ocean, they cannot naturally spawn in the cold waters surrounding the UK. This means that the oysters are putting on condition throughout the year, other than when it's very cold, hence the 'r in the month' rule does not apply to Pacific oysters and they can be eaten all year round.

The Pacific oyster has a 1 rating from the MCS.

Cooking Oysters were once the main staple diet of everyone in the coastal areas where they flourished and they were cooked in a variety of ways: fried in an omelette, cooked in breadcrumbs or poached in a stew with meat. People even ate the oysters with fish and chips out of a paper bag. Whether you prefer the native or pacific oyster is your own taste, but they are both equally delicious – just keep them simple. Some people feel squeamish at the thought of eating raw oysters, but at some point you must try them as there is really nothing better than a beautiful, clean-tasting oyster with a turn of freshly milled pepper and a squeeze of lemon. Freshly shucked out the shell with a dash of Tabasco is a favourite or serve them with a red wine shallot vinegar. They are also great simply poached in a red wine sauce or added to a soup with other shellfish. If you love the taste of oysters and are feeling a little pluckish, see if you can stomach the Guinness World Record for the most oysters eaten in 3 minutes. The record to beat is a staggering 187 set by a Norwegian!

PATAGONIAN TOOTHFISH OR CHILEAN SEA BASS (*Dissostichus eleginoides*)

The story of the Patagonian toothfish is of a fish that was once very unpopular and unloved. That was until someone decided to change its name to Chilean sea bass and made, basically, a ton of money. At that moment, I don't think they could truly have realized the consequences of what happened over the next three decades, but this incredible bit of marketing and a new brand name almost wiped out the entire stock of a fish.

More than 30 years ago, Chilean dictator Augusto Pinochet, in a frenzy of deregulation, threw open his country's territorial waters to foreign factory fishing. This decimated the local supplies of cod and hake and sent Chilean fishermen into deeper and more dangerous waters. Soon, from depths that exceeded 1500m, they began hauling up the Patagonian toothfish, an enormous, hideous creature whose ugly exterior hid a body that was almost totally white flesh. However delicious this fish was, to be a success story it needed a twist and a new name because nobody would ever have taken a bite out of something called the Patagonian toothfish. In 1977, the product known as Chilean sea bass was born and its popularity exploded around the world throughout the 1990s. Chefs, in particular, could not get enough of this fish and by the end of the decade, Chilean sea bass was the most popular fish in the world.

Fishing The toothfish comes from the southern ocean around the Antarctica, which is one of the most hostile places on earth. It has some of the worst weather conditions for fishermen to fish in but the rewards, as with tuna, can be huge. The Patagonian toothfish is one of the two largest species in the Antarctic. It lives on the bottom of the ocean and is a predatory species that can grow up to 2m in length, weigh 9 to 10kg and live for as long as 50 years.

Antarctic fish are especially vulnerable to over-fishing due to the fact that most species are slow-growing and late-maturing with a low reproductive capacity. Along with tuna, the Patagonian toothfish is one of the world's most endangered and some researchers have predicted a total collapse of the fishery within 2–5 years.

One of the other main threats to the toothfish is from illegal fishing. The fish has been called the white gold of the Southern Ocean and by 2001, it was estimated that 50 per cent of toothfish traded internationally was caught illegally. In fact, illegally caught fish may be up to 5 times the legal catch limit. Illegal toothfish catches are unloaded at so-called 'pirate ports' in countries such as Namibia and Mauritius. The fish are then sold on the black market with a single sashimi-grade specimen fetching as much as £500 and a single trip making anything from £100,000 to £250,000 profit. It is fairly difficult to patrol the waters around a fish that lives in almost arctic conditions and so for fishermen willing to take risks, the chances of actually getting caught are very low. These illegal fisheries are also a huge threat to seabird populations, particularly albatross. Of the 21 species of albatross, 19 are threatened with extinction, largely because of illegal longlining.

All 24 member nations of CCAMLR (Convention for the Conservation of Antarctic Marine Living Resources) have agreed that they will not deal in Patagonian toothfish caught by any boats listed on the commission's blacklist. They have a catch scheme designed to track the landings of toothfish caught in the Convention Area and systems to identify the origin of toothfish entering the markets of all the parties to the scheme and to help determine whether toothfish taken in the Convention Area are caught in a manner consistent with their conservation measures.

The fishery around South Georgia, with a TAC of about 3000 tonnes per year taken by approximately 10 vessels, was certified as an environmentally responsible fishery by the MCS in March 2004. MCS-certified toothfish have a MCS rating of 3, so avoid eating this species from all other fisheries. I hope with all the damage that has been done since the late 70s, we can now start to see more of a positive change. This is a fish that has gone through a huge amount, but at least now there are measures in place to try and stop the pirates and keep the toothfish around for a little longer than another decade.

Cooking Chilean sea bass is sold largely to the USA and Japan and mainly into fine dining restaurants. The properties of toothfish are quite unique. The skin is black and the flesh is white with no pin bones. When filleted, it is just a solid piece of white, flaky flesh that is slightly sweet tasting. The flesh also contains a high level of Omega-3 fatty acids.

PLAICE (*Pleuronectes platessa*)

Plaice is one of the UK's most popular flatfish species and in 2006, the UK caught more than 17,000 tonnes, which was worth about £38 million at retail. The smell and thought of plaice has always made my mouth water, particularly the aroma of it just slowly cooking in butter.

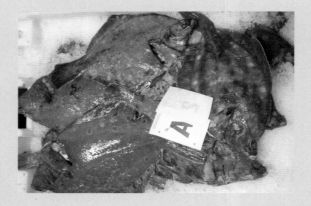

Glossary

Fishing The plaice is a demersal flatfish that swims close to the sea bed. It is oval in shape and is a right-eyed fish. The upper side is basically brown with numerous orange or red spots. They change their colour to suit the bottom of the sea for camouflage, but the orange spots sometimes give them away. The underside of the plaice is white, as with other 'flatties', and they have very strong teeth for crushing through shells.

The plaice is one of the smaller flatfish found around the British coast and though small fish are still very common around our shores, larger specimens are becoming increasingly rare. Plaice are a relatively slow-growing fish, which is why they are a pressurised stock in a lot of places, although they may live for up to 20 years when not subjected to intense fishing pressure. The males require between 2–6 years to reach sexual maturity, whilst the females require 3–7 years. The usual size limit is about 50–60cm, but exceptional specimens can reach 90cm. Plaice mostly spawn between end of December to April with each female producing up to half a million eggs. The largest of the spawning grounds is in the Flemish blight, between the Thames Estuary and the Dutch and Belgian coasts, and most of the plaice from the Northern Sea spawn here.

The plaice is a very common fish or should I say, 'was' a very common fish, as most stocks are now overfished. In a lot of the waters around the UK and the North Sea, I am afraid the plaice is currently not at very healthy stock levels. Plaice is caught by demersal towed gears, otter trawls and anchor seines. There is a recovery plan in place and the European Commission is trying to reduce the fishing mortality rate by 10 per cent each year until the correct target levels are reached. Historically, the main English ports were Lowestoft and Grimsby, but with the decline of the English beam trawl fleet, plaice is mainly landed into Grimsby and Hartlepool and abroad.

However, stocks in the Irish Sea are currently within safe biological limits and harvested sustainably and the Faroe and Iceland stocks appear to be stable. A 'plaice box' was also established in 1989, which is a closed conservation area for plaice in the North Sea close to Scandinavia and running down all the way to France and large parts of the Wadden Sea.

The MCS gives the plaice a 4 rating. To minimise the impact of fishing on stocks that are under pressure, choose plaice above the 30cm size at which it matures and avoid eating them in the spring when they are breeding. Pick either line-caught from the Irish Sea or Hastings, otter trawl caught or even static nets.

Cooking You have most likely eaten plaice that has been grilled or pan-fried and it's a beautiful fresh fish to eat. You can serve plaice whole, on the bone and grilled or pan-fried off the bone. Plaice can also be breaded, fried and served with a little lemon or tartar sauce. It has a very clean taste that's a little lemony and is flaky and delicate at the same time.

ALASKAN POLLOCK (*Theragra chalcogramma*) and POLLACK (*Pollachius pollachius*)

Although these two fish are related – both are members of the *Gadidae* family (the cod family) – and are often referred to as the same species, the Cornish pollack and the Alaskan pollock are in fact from different geni; the *Pollachius* and the *Theragra*.

Fishing The pollack is distributed throughout the northeast Atlantic, all around European waters and around the coast of Britain, particularly in the West and western Ireland. It spawns between January and April, can reach a length of 120-130cm and an age of more than 8 years. Alaskan pollock is distributed throughout the colder waters of the north Pacific. Like its cousin, Alaskan pollock generally spawns in late winter and early spring. The fish can live for at least 15 years and are relatively fast growing during the first few years of life, with maturity occuring at around 4 years of age. Like all the other members of the cod family, both live on or near the bottom and are found from very shallow waters to depths as great as 200m.

Cornish pollack is becoming popular and the boats handlining for pollack work from the many small coves and harbours dotted around the coasts of Cornwall and Devon. The best choice to make, in terms of selectivity and sustainability, is line-caught pollack. You can get line-caught and tagged pollock from Cornish waters at www.linecaught.org.uk. All of the pollack tagged here come from members of the website and they are caught using a sustainable handline technique, with the fish immediately placed into slush ice to ensure premium quality. Tagged pollack gives you complete hook to plate traceability for a sustainable premium species. The MCS give the pollack a rating of 3. Avoid eating immature fish below 50cm and during its breeding season from January to April. Pollack are available all year round, but the best time for the line-caught pollock is from May to October.

The Alaskan pollock fishery in the Bering Sea is the largest single-species food fish fishery in the world and Alaskan pollock is the largest food fish resource in the world. Alaskan Pollock is certified as sustainable and meets the Marine Stewardship Council (MSC) environmental standard for well managed fisheries. The MCS give this fish a 2 rating for sustainability, but look for the MSC label.

Cooking The only difference between the Alaskan pollock and Cornish pollack is that the Alaskan, being in slightly colder waters, is a little fattier than the Cornish, so it has a more pronounced oily taste.

Pollock lends itself particularly well to fish pie because of its flaky flesh, either on its own or in a mix with other white fish species. They are both relatively thick-skinned like cod and have pretty much the same large flakes once they are cooked. The skins, though, have a slightly bitter taste, but not in an unpleasant way. These fish can be treated in exactly the same way as cod and can either be pan-fried, deep-fried in batter, poached or grilled. My favourite way is deep-fried in a batter. You can leave the skin on when deep-frying and just serve with some home-made tartare sauce. They also work well pan-fried in a brown butter with capers, garlic and parsley, or you could use them straight out of the water, have it as sushi or carpaccio with just olive oil, a little lemon juice and a few fresh herbs.

POUTING (*Trisopterus luscus*)

Now, no laughing please. Yes, I know that a lot of you will not have heard of this fish or even thought about using it. Fishermen don't like it, fishmongers hardly stock it and chefs very rarely cook with it, but we should all demand this fish and get its popularity rising because, believe it or not, the pout bib or pout whiting is a member of the *Gadidae* family, so it's related to cod. This is rather tough luck for the poor pouting and a bit like Samson and Goliath, but this underused and undervalued species

TOM AIKENS

is just as good as other species of fish we have in our waters and is relatively cheap as well.

A distinctive fish with a relatively deep body, the pouting has a much bronzer colour than other members of the cod family and it is a very handsome fish when viewed in its natural environment.

Fishing The pouting is widespread all around the coasts of Britain and Ireland, throughout northern Europe and extending to southern Spain. Found in shallow water, often within a few metres of the shoreline, it is very common in water down to 70m and often found in and around ship or boat wrecks and rocky areas.

Pouting spawn in the spring and huge shoals of fish, numbering several thousand, are found during spawning before the fish once again disperse into smaller groups. Sexual maturity happens at the end of their first year, making them very quick breeders, which is why we should be using more of them. They are a relatively short-lived species, living for only 6–8 years, but the fish are able to spawn several times and this, coupled with their small size (adults are between 20–30cm long) explains their abundance.

The main problem with unfashionable or unheard of species is that consumer information is not necessarily readily available. This needs to change and it's down not only to chefs and restaurants, but supermarkets and retailers and, to an extent, even the press, food agencies and NGOs to do this. We can go on about species of fish that are on the red or endangered list, but the public must then be given alternatives to look for and a chance to buy fish that is available. This means a whole new approach to public awareness, if things are going to change.

The pouting gets a 2 rating from the MCS so, again, eat more of these. When buying, choose mature and over 20cm, locally caught fish and avoid eating fish caught during their spawning season of March to April.

Cooking The pouting has a very thin skin, a clean buttery taste and the flesh is white and almost semi-translucent. It has delicious large flakes when it's cooked and is a very juicy piece of fish. Because this fish does not have an overriding flavour, it can take quite bold tastes. It is great in fish cakes and even in a curried fish stew, in fish soups and, of course, just deep-fried in a batter and served with tartare sauce – after all, it is the brother of cod.

PRAWNS AND SHRIMPS

Once upon a time, a prawn was a very special treat, but as its popularity soared in the 80s and the classic prawn cocktail and prawn sandwich became as ubiquitous as Duran Duran, eating prawns became about as exciting as the plastic-wrapped prawn sandwich itself. The humble prawn is now so mass produced that it has become one of the cheapest seafoods in the United Kingdom. We import about 80,000 tonnes a year from all around the world, while our own fleet catches 3,000 tonnes. The prawns found in most of our sandwiches are fished by trawlers or grown in tropical farms and I am afraid to say that both these fishing methods are increasingly bad for the environment.

Fishing In 2000, world prawn production reached 4.2 million tonnes, of which around 3 million tonnes came from wild-caught sources and the rest farmed. Chinese prawn fisheries caught over 1 million tonnes, with India and then Indonesia the second and third largest producers.

Prawns are generally fished by trawling, which is very damaging to the seabed. Prawn fishing also accounts for a third of the world's total bycatch, despite producing less than 2 per cent of the world's seafood. The high bycatch rates are partly explained by prawn fishing's demersal trawling, with large numbers of fish and other marine life congregating on or just above the seabed where prawns are found.

The ecological limits to wild prawn exploitation may in fact have already been reached and many large-scale prawn fisheries, particularly in tropical and subtropical areas, have seen reductions in their prawn 'catch per unit effort' (CPUE). This is most likely due to growth overfishing, where too many prawns are caught in their juvenile stages. Demand continues to grow, but with prawn stocks declining and the costs of fishing rising, many prawn fishermen are struggling to compete against cheap farmed prawns of a higher quality. Sadly, the result is that they fish harder and longer to get a good catch to make a living, putting an already damaged marine ecosystem under further stress and pressure.

Despite all this, wild-caught prawns remain the largest contributor to world prawn production and the total global output increases every year. For many countries, it is a temptingly high-value export.

Prawns have been farmed for centuries in Asia using traditional low-density methods such as ponds and rice paddies, but the origins of industrial prawn farming can be traced back to 1930s Japan. Today, over fifty countries have prawn farms, with most farming taking place along the coastal, mangrove-forested areas of underdeveloped tropical nations. Realising that there is huge money to be made, farmers have been caught up in a new gold rush with very poor communities destroying thousands of acres of mangrove forests, flooding the areas and then filling them up with prawns. Up to 50 per cent of mangrove swamps have disappeared worldwide and the loss has been linked to even bigger ecological disasters. Mangroves protect low coastlines and act as a natural barrier against the sea. It is thus possible that the 2005 tsunami could have been at least hindered if mangrove swamps had been left intact. Mangroves are also among the most productive ecosystems on the planet and support a great variety of marine life. When the mangroves are destroyed, local fisherman find that their catches of other fish collapse. In Bangladesh, there are close to 400,000 prawn farmers along the southwestern coastal belt and its prawn exports are the country's second-largest foreign exchange earner after clothes, but in this area, many fisherman are reporting an 80 per cent decline in catches since the creation of dykes for prawn farming. Salination and chemical pollution of drinking water and agricultural land are also a regular result of prawn farming. In Sri Lanka, 74 per cent of fishermen in prawn farming areas no longer have ready access to drinking water because the farms pump out wastewater into the canals, rivers and nearby seawater.

Regulations and conservation requirements are the responsibility of each individual nation that operates a prawn fishery and many countries do not sufficiently enforce any conservation measures. There are, of course, many areas of good practice and some UK supermarkets are starting to make a stand. Marks & Spencer, for instance, has created its own clear code of practice on farmed prawns to ensure both higher quality and to help prawn farmers understand how they can become better practitioners of prawn farming. However, the European Commission has had to ban the import of all prawns from China because of fears over use of the antibiotics employed to speed up growth and raise the quantity of prawns grown, and all prawns from Thailand, Indonesia and Burma must still be checked before they are allowed into Europe.

NORTHERN OR DEEPWATER PRAWN (*Pandalus borealis*)
This Atlantic deepwater prawn was one of the first prawns that we imported and, most likely, the first time you ever ate a prawn cocktail, this is where the prawn came from. A large coldwater species, as the name implies it occurs mainly in deeper waters off the British coast, Norway and in the Barents and Bering Seas and further afield in the cold waters of the northern oceans, North Atlantic, North Pacific and Arctic oceans. Most of the prawns are caught using otter trawls and they are trawled in huge amounts, then precooked, packed and frozen in their shells, which protects the meat from getting freezer burn and bashed.

The deepwater or northern prawn is rated by the MCS as 3 and these prawns are the ones to eat if you want to be environmentally friendly as they are the least ecologically damaging. Buy prawns from an MSC-certified fishery and from one that is using sorting grids to reduce the amount of bycatch (in the US, Canada and Norway this is now compulsory).

Freshwater prawns have not been rated by the MCS. **Cooking** Northern or deepwater prawns are best served with slices of fresh lemon and some home-made brown bread with unsalted butter.

BLACK TIGER OR GIANT TIGER PRAWN (*Penaeus monodon*)
Instantly recognisable by the dark stripes on its shell, hence the name, the warmwater black tiger prawn supplies about 80 per cent of the world's wild-caught prawn. Favoured because of their fast rate of growth, high commercial value and large size, over 900,000 tonnes are consumed annually, two-thirds of it coming from farming, mainly in south-east Asia. Many of the tiger prawns coming from tropical parts are an unbelievable size and these can go for crazy prices. I have seen some that are almost 15cm long going for £40 per kg, which will equate to approximately 6 prawns. Caught year round, with peak supplies from February through May, most are captured by bottom trawling methods, which have a severe impact on the marine habitat and take high levels of bycatch, including significant numbers of endangered and threatened sea turtles. Whilst technological innovations such as the Turtle-Excluder Device (TED) have reduced bycatch in recent years, not all countries that have prawn fisheries require or enforce the use of TEDs.

However, the majority of large prawns on the shelves in supermarkets are farmed and I would urge you to stay clear of farmed varieties – they are the prawn equivalent of a battery chicken. Fattened fast and sold quickly for large amounts of money, these prawns may look very nice on a platter covered in garlic and chilli, but warmwater species are in a fair amount of danger.

The MCS lists warmwater tiger prawns as one of its 20 species of fish to avoid. This is because of both the high levels of bycatch of other species and the severe threat to turtles when they are caught in the wild and the extensive habitat destruction associated with farmed production. If you do buy these prawns, look out for certified organic tiger prawns from Ecuador or Madagascan tiger prawns. Madagascar is working towards making all its prawn fisheries sustainable and is a better choice than other countries.

FRESHWATER FARMED PRAWNS
The genus *Macrobrachium* includes about 200 species, almost all of them living in freshwater for at least part of their life cycle and native to all continents except for Europe. The water prawn, also called the giant river or Malaysian prawn, is the favoured species for farming and they have been farmed using traditional methods in south-east Asia for a very long time. The technologies used in freshwater prawn farming are basically the same as in marine prawn farming, but due to the aggressive nature of the water prawn and the hierarchy between the males, stocking densities are kept much lower. The ecological impact is therefore less severe, with less concentrated waste products and a lesser danger of the ponds becoming breeding places for diseases. The growout ponds also do not salinate agricultural land as do those of inland marine prawn farms and do not endanger the mangroves, which is better news all around and make them more amenable to small-scale family businesses. The global annual production of freshwater prawns in 2005 was about 310,000 tonnes, of which China produced some 210,000 tonnes.

BROWN SHRIMP (*Crangon crangon*)
We all think of the brown shrimp as something typically English and they are of course, served as a paste in a sandwich with a cup of afternoon tea or as potted shrimp. In hotels like the Ritz, Dorchester and the Hilton, you will never see potted shrimp far from the menu. The distinction between shrimp and prawns can be very confusing. In some countries, the penaeid species are referred to as 'prawns' and smaller carideans as 'shrimp'. In other parts of the world, such as some areas of the USA, this differentiation is the other way around.
Fishing The brown shrimp is the most common shrimp species and is a long, thin animal, mottled brown in colour, abundant and well camouflaged in sandy areas. The brown shrimp lives all around the UK coastline but the best habitats are in the muddy and silty waters of estuaries like Morecambe Bay, the Severn and the Wash, the Solway Firth and the Bristol Channel. Fixed net fishermen in the Severn Estuary are continuing a shrimp fishing tradition that was recorded in the Doomsday book.

Brown shrimp are caught using various designs of beam and otter trawl and there has been a considerable amount of recent research on the effects of beam trawling on seabeds. While there is no limit on the volume of brown shrimp that can be landed, the way it is caught does have an impact on other marine life: it's estimated that more than 1,000 million plaice, whiting, cod and sole are discarded by the North Sea brown shrimp fishery every year. To address some of the impact of shrimp fishing, a group of industry representatives and environmentalists have teamed up to look at ways to improve its methods, which should be enough to get certification by the MSC. One way to reduce bycatch is by preventing the trawl nets dragging along the seabed, which is known as bottom trawling. And the first priority identified during a meeting with the MSC was to reduce the catch of baby shrimp that are too small to eat. The best shrimp to buy are those that have been caught by offshore trawl fisheries that use something called a veil, which is a bycatch reduction device attached to the nets. Alternatively, look for shrimps that have been caught by the traditional method of tractor shrimp catching in Lancashire and in North Norfolk. These are sold through local fishmongers along the coast and the great thing is that they are protected in the pot so they will freeze very well.

The next time that you are in an area of the brown shrimp, as most beaches are, just get yourself a little shrimping net with your kids and get down to the beach, wade through the sea on the shore and away you go.

Brown shrimp are best to eat and catch between September and November. They are rated 3 by the MCS but try to look for shrimp that have been caught using the veil nets.

Cooking Cook shrimps in sea water or just simmer a litre of water with salt and cook them for no more than 2–3 minutes at a simmer. Leave to cool in a tray, remove the heads and tail and eat them as they are or have a go at making your own potted shrimp using my recipe on page xx. The potted shrimp will last at least a week if the shrimps are fresh.

RED SNAPPER *(Lutjanus erythropterus)*

The red snapper is a beautiful and stunning fish to look at, although its amazing red colour may be offputting to some because it just does not look right being so brightly coloured.

Sadly, I have a feeling that not a lot of you will be able to get hold of a red snapper, but seeing as it is one of the many fish that we import into this country, I have included it in the book. A reef fish, it is found off the Atlantic and Pacific coasts of the Americas and the Gulf of Mexico, the Indo West Pacific, the Gulf of Oman to south-east Asia, Japan and Australia. There are numerous snapper species, such as the mangrove snapper, mutton snapper, lane snapper and dog snapper, and all of them are gregarious, friendly, social fish who form large schools around wrecks and reefs. The red snapper is very much a prized food fish.
Fishing The red snapper commonly inhabits waters from 10–6om, but can be caught as deep as 100m or more. Reef fish, they stay relatively close to the bottom and inhabit rocky bottoms, ledges, ridges and artificial reefs, including offshore oil rigs and shipwrecks. The juveniles range from about 2.5cm in length and have a fast initial growth rate, maturing at 4 years old, although they can live for more than 30 years.

Commercially, they are caught on multi-hook gear with electric reels. Gill netting has now been banned in the Gulf of Mexico, from where most of the commercial harvest comes. Stock levels of red snapper caught off the northwestern Australian coast are currently healthy. The fishery is tightly managed through the use of transferable effort allocations and most of the management area is closed to trawling. The trawl fishery has a moderate bycatch and habitat effects, but this is mitigated through the use of large-scale closed areas. The MCS gives the snapper a 2 rating, which means eat more of them.
Cooking The snapper has thick, fatty outer skin whose taste, when cooked, almost resembles that of roast chicken. The flesh is very juicy with a clear fat line running along the length of the fish, so that it has milder white flesh and meatier and slightly metallic-tasting darker meat. Ideally, the snapper should be pan-fried in a hot pan. Brush a little olive oil on the skin side and fry until the fish is almost cooked through and the skin amazingly crispy, then flip the fish over and finish it off on the flesh side for a minute or two, squeezing over some lemon. Or you can bake the snapper whole in the oven. Remove the head and cut off all the outer fins, leaving the tail remaining. Rub in a little olive oil, sprinkle over coarse sea salt and black pepper and place onto a wire rack in a roasting tray. Under the wire rack, place some aromatic herbs, garlic, white wine, lemon peel and then cover in foil and then bake in the oven for approximately 25 minutes a kg at 170°C/Gas 3. This will steam and bake the fish at the same time and give it an incredible flavour.

SAITHE (COLEY) *(Pollachius virens)*

Saithe is very similar to pollack and is a member of the cod family. Also called coley or coalfish, there are more than 140 names on record that have been used in the UK for this species, more than for any other British commercial fish. These include local names like sillack, sillock, greylord, piltock and black Jacks.

Saithe is plentiful and is caught and landed in large quantities by British fishing vessels. However, it has not traditionally been highly prized as a food fish and used to be made mainly into cat food. The flesh is darker and less attractive in appearance than that of related species like cod, even though when cooked it is considered by many to be superior in flavour. It is indeed a great sustainable fish that has seen its popularity rise over recent years.
Fishing An active, gregarious and friendly fish, saithe usually enter coastal waters in spring and return to deeper water in the winter. The mature fish is found from Norway and Iceland in the north to Biscay in the south and all around the UK. It has a powerful body and is an excellent swimmer, found at all depths down to 300m and most commonly in shoals chasing fry, herring and crustacean animals.

The majority of adult fish caught are from 60–90cm long and fish weighing up to 7kg are quite common. Growth is rapid and maturity is reached between 5 and 10 years of age in the European population. Breeding and spawning occur from January to April.

In the main north-western Atlantic fishery, 80 per cent of catches are taken from October to December when the fish form large schools. Like most fish, they vary in abundance throughout the year, but can be caught all year round as part of a mixed fishery. Saithe are caught with purse seines and Danish seines, trawls and longlines. They are mainly targeted by French, German and Norwegian otter-trawlers, but some UK vessels also participate in the fishery.

Because the saithe has traditionally been regarded as an inferior fish, its price at the ports has remained low and, consequently, there has been little incentive for fishermen, traders and restaurants to handle this species with the same care that is given to more valuable species. For this reason alone, quality is often poorer than it need be and the market for saithe remains depressed. Better quality and more imaginative use could make saithe a more important food fish.

The most sustainable saithe stock is from the north-east Arctic, the Barents and Norwegian seas. The saithe stock in the North Sea, the west of Scotland and Rockall is also currently healthy and is harvested sustainably as well. Choose line-caught fish where possible and do not eat saithe below 50–60cm or when they are breeding between January and March.

The saithe gets a 2 rating from the MCS, so eat lots more of this marvellous fish.
Cooking The very dark, grey-black colour of the skin of the saithe is not that attractive and the flesh, even when the fish has been handled very carefully, is not as white as that of cod and has a slightly greyish appearance. When the skin is removed from a fillet, a wide band of brownish-red flesh is exposed, giving that side of the fillet a discoloured and sometimes bloody appearance. However, it has the same firm and meaty but tender texture and large flakes as cod once cooked. It is a great alternative to cod and should be looked upon at being the new pollock. Saithe has a kind of buttery flavour and is best pan-fried, poached or deep-fried in a batter.

Glossary

ATLANTIC SALMON (*Salmon salar*)

The Atlantic salmon is an incredibly beautiful and unbelievable species of fish, yet from over-fishing the wild stocks, farming, and through pollution we have done incredible damage to it and have helped turn this once king of fish into a shadow of its glory days. The salmon's very complex life cycle and breeding does not make it easy to sustain. Despite this, it is made of very stern stuff and there are not many things that the salmon can't combat or beat. The journey that it must take to spawn and how it conquers and navigates the roughest waters and steepest waterfalls back to where it once came is a magical story that can seem truly unbelievable.

Yet taking the fish from its river habitats, estuaries and seas have left it nowhere to hide or swim, and we have now paid the price with very limited stock levels which are now less than a quarter of what they once were before the real push for salmon farming began.

Fishing Salmon spawn in the tiniest rivers right up to at the beginning of the tributaries. The River Tay is the longest river where wild salmon spawn and in 1999, the catch here was 7,230 fish – over 10 per cent of the Scottish total. Salmon hatch from their eggs in the springtime and stay in freshwater for between one and four years. They soon realise that they cannot live on the river's tiny aquatic insects so the salmon smolts (young salmon) leave the rivers and head thousands of miles across the sea to colder sub-Arctic waters where there are rich feeding grounds. The changes on this long journey are huge: the smolts swap the fresh, sweet-tasting clear water for the salty, acid-like water of the sea. The water change attacks their eyes, gills and tissues they become disorientated and very weak. The death rate is huge and out of approximately 5,000 eggs, only 50 or so will make the complete journey to the sea and travel the hundreds of miles to the feedings grounds. While at sea salmon feed heavily on shrimps, krill and various species of small fish. All of these are very high in protein and they will give the salmon the real spurt they need to change from a 20cm weakling to a 30kg machine. After spending 1–4 years at sea, the salmon swim back to the river in which they were born to breed. After the salmon finds a mate and the female lays her eggs, only a mere 5 per cent will return to the sea to make the journey back to their feeding grounds. The rest will die, mainly from sheer exhaustion, and the cycle continues.

The price that wild salmon fetches is huge; anything upwards of £30 a kg. During the 1960s, the salmon's feeding grounds were discovered in the northern waters of the Atlantic off the Faroe Islands and around Greenland. Devastating over-fishing then took place using modern fishing techniques and by 1981, over 1,000 tonnes of fish were caught off the Faroe Islands alone. Stocks of wild Atlantic salmon are now severely depleted from overfishing and other factors such as pollution, environmental changes, aquaculture, freshwater habitat deterioration and impediments to migration routes. In 2005, ICES advised that there should be reductions in exploitation for as many stocks as possible to allow the species to reach conservation limits.

However, it is all getting a little better as, bit by bit, we are beginning to behave as we should by treating the waterways with respect, halting the pollution and curtailing excessive hunting. There are specific conservation groups like the North Atlantic Conservation Organisation and certain groups are being paid not to fish, giving the salmon that little extra chance and help it needs to survive.

But could the farming of salmon be the final nail in the coffin for this fish? Many years ago, people thought that farmed salmon would be very beneficial to the survival of salmon and that it would take the pressure off the true wild species, but that was before so many farmed fish escaped. All farmed fish are inoculated against diseases and fungal infections through the feed they are given in the farms, but the wild ones are not. The increased levels of sea lice, fungal infections and disease brought by escapees have killed thousands of wild salmon. The pollution that occurs in the netted farms and sea lochs is also a huge problem: rotting leftover feed, fish excrement and all the fish chemicals that are fed to the fish cause a lot of damage to the ecosystem and to the sea bed. The escapees have also mated with the wild stocks and we have now weaker, diluted species and stocks of fish. Wild salmon have been around for tens of thousands of years since the end of the ice age and in the space of 30 years, we have managed to seriously damage their habitat and livelihood.

The MCS rating for wild Atlantic salmon is 5. We all have to make the choice about the salmon we eat and choose to buy. It's not easy and it never will be. The choice between truly wild and farmed is huge and you cannot beat the taste of a truly wild species, but should we really be eating something that is still very fragile? With farmed salmon, the question is whether it is right that we farm fish. My own view of the farmed salmon is that I am afraid it is necessary. We have used and abused the stocks we once had of true wild salmon and now we are left with a distant cousin. We must encourage the farmed variety of salmon because, as of today, there is simply not enough salmon to go around. Yes, the taste, the colour and texture are all very different, but go for organic salmon or Loch Duart salmon (see page 348 to find out about the wonderful work that the Loch Duart salmon farm are doing) where at all possible and I'd urge you strongly to refrain from buying the sad piece of salmon that you see in a polystyrene tray covered in a single sheet of clingfilm. I cannot bear to see this on the shelves as I find it very disheartening to see that we have turned the most beautiful fish into a flabby, watery second-rate citizen.

Cooking The salmon is suited to many ways of cooking, from poaching, baking, grilling, pan frying and barbecuing to steaming. The easiest way of cooking salmon once you have your portions of fish cut, is to place them on a baking tray and season them well with coarse sea salt and fresh black pepper, sprinkle in a little olive oil and then bake in the oven. This way you have no smoke and no hassle and if you are not confident about cooking salmon, then this is the way for you. Another way of cooking salmon is by

TOM AIKENS

simply pan-frying the fish on the floured skin-side down in a non-stick pan in a little olive oil on a low to medium heat. Once you can see that the flesh is cooking and the skin is crisping up, which will be after about 5–7 minutes, then you can turn it over and cook for a further 3 minutes. Lastly, to poach salmon just take a little fish stock, place it into a shallow pan and add some fresh dill and parsley, a few slices of lemon, black peppercorns and a couple of bay leaves. Bring this to a simmer and turn the heat right down, then add the seasoned salmon and cook for 3– 5 minutes, then turn the salmon over and do the same again. Eat instantly with some minted new potatoes with butter and black pepper. If you are going to eat the salmon cold, then cook the salmon a few minutes less on each side and leave to cool in the stock. Once cool, tuck in with some fresh mayonnaise.

SARDINE (*Sardina pilchardus*)

Sardines, or pilchards, are members of the herring family and have a green back, yellow sides and a silver belly. There is this notion that the sardine and the pilchard are two different species, but they are not. When they are young (about 15cm) they are sardines, while adult sardines (about 16cm) are pilchards.

Fishing The sardine is a pelagic schooling fish. They are very much nomadic wanderers and stay together in a tight shoal of fish, swimming at around 40m below the surface by day and 25m by night. They range from the Mediterranean to the southern coasts of England and Ireland and sometimes further north in warm weather. Elsewhere, other species congregate in cool, plankton-rich waters, with major stocks found off Japan, in the eastern Pacific, south-west Africa, Australia and New Zealand. Sardines spawn in spring and summer in open sea and females produce 50–60,000 eggs.

Cornish sardines were once salted and either pressed or pickled, then exported in large numbers, especially to the Catholic countries of Italy, France and Spain where they were much in demand during Lent. However, from the mid-1880s, the coming of the railway made it possible to send fresh fish to inland towns and cities and possibly this led to the gradual decline in sales of cured fish. By the early 1920s, the drop in sales was considerable. Processing on a small scale has continued in Newlyn up to the present day but, with improved refrigeration and fast travel, it is the fresh sardine that has gained in popularity and continues to be in demand.

My friend Nick Howell renamed the unfashionable

pilchard 'Cornish sardines' and has been producing canned and vacuum-packed products and selling them to Waitrose and Marks & Spencer ever since. In 1997, Cornish fleets brought in 7 tonnes of pilchard. Last year, it was more than 800 tonnes. Nick has introduced some new products liked canned sardines, smoked and in flavoured oils like tomato, lemon and basil. I have tried them all and they are really delicious.

The MCS give the sardine a 3 rating. There are still very good stock levels of the sardine in the Southwest and the best choice to make in terms of selectivity is to choose pilchards sold as Cornish sardines, which are caught in coastal waters off Cornwall using traditional drift or ring nets.

Cooking The season for sardines is from November to April and if you buy sardines, you'll find the flesh is pink in colour and they have a fine, soft texture. With a high fat content, sardines have a stronger and heavier flavour than white fish species and, as with the rest of the oily fish, they are rich in Omega-3 fatty acids, which makes them very good brain food. The sardine is a very oily fish, but most of the oil is held in the skin, which means it largely disappears in the first few mouthfuls, leaving a dry texture. The taste can be slightly metallic because of the oil and there is also almost an aubergine flavour. The sardine needs some strong flavours to counterbalance the oily taste and they can either be grilled or pan-fried. If you are going to pan-fry the fish, then sprinkle the fillets with a little olive oil, rosemary and garlic, plenty of black pepper and a little sea salt. They can also be floured if you wish, then cooked for just for a few minutes on each side so they remain pink, otherwise they will be dry and crumbly. If you are going to grill them, make sure the grill is at the hottest setting then place under the grill and spoon over the juices as it's cooking, cooking for just 2–3 minutes each side. Serve with a spring onion and grain mustard potato salad or a pickled beetroot salad with a few wild rocket leaves. Alternatively, the simplest way to serve them is just on toast with a little shallot chutney. The sardine has very tiny bones that you will be able to eat once the fish has been cooked.

SCALLOPS

KING SCALLOPS (*Pecten maximus*)

Scallops, also known as king scallops or coquille St Jacques, are found in most areas around Scotland and its islands. The king scallop is a bivalve mollusc, but it differs from the many other bivalve molluscs in that the two halves of its shell are not identical in shape. The lower half is curved like a bowl, whilst the top half is flat, like a lid.

Fishing The scallop cannot close and seal its shell completely and will only survive in the deeper depths of the sea. Scallops, believe it or not, have about 60 primitive tiny bright eyes, which under a microscope look like a row of illuminated blue lights and are able to detect motion and light and dark. Although they are capable of moving reasonable distances, scallops only seem to move when disturbed or to escape predators. They can move forwards backwards, make turns, and even right themselves up the correct way.

The growth rate of the scallops is affected by several factors; including salinity, temperature, competition from other scallops, water depth and food supply. In favourable conditions, they can reach the minimum legal landing size of 10cm in three years, but if the conditions for growth are exceptionally poor, even a 10-year-old scallop may fail to

Glossary
TOM AIKENS

reach this size. The shell of the scallop can measure up to 15–20cm across and I have had some scallops so large that once they have been taken from the shell, they will take up almost the entire middle of my palm.

They reach sexual maturity after several years, though they may not reach a commercially harvestable size until 6–8 years of age, Scallops usually spawn for the first time in the autumn of their second year. Adult scallops in Scottish waters spawn in the spring with a later spawning in the autumn. The scallops are hermaphroditic, which means they are capable of switching sexes and they will produce in excess of 100 million eggs.

The fishery for scallops in Scottish waters started in the early 1930s and is now the second most valuable shellfish species landed in Scotland, bringing in up to £25–30 million a year and landing approximately 30,000 tonnes per year. Most scallops are caught by 10–30m vessels towing specialised scallop dredges from each side of the boat, which are dragged along the bottom of the sea bed scooping up anything and everything that gets in the way. There is such a difference between the hand-dived variety and those dredged that once you have tried the dived, you will not be tempted back, even though the dredged scallops are half the price. The soaking of scallops immediately after they have been cut from the shell encourages the muscle to absorb and temporarily retain water. The effect of this process, apart from increasing the weight of the meat, is to 'improve' its appearance. These changes are, however, short-lived since they always adversely affect the cooking properties of the scallop, when the absorbed water is quickly released. This is why, when you ever try and pan-fry or griddle a dredged scallop, they release water, which gives you a half-caramelised scallop and all the liquid comes out, along with half the flavour.

Scallops have a rating from the MCS of 2 and a MLS is 10cm across the shell. Avoid them from May to August when they are spawning.

Cooking Scallops are not the cheapest of shellfish to buy, but they are very popular with chefs. A small scallop will cost anything from 60p to a £1 and the huge hand-dived scallops that I use mainly in the restaurant are from £1.50 to £2.50 and are utterly delicious. The scallop is one of the most delicious shellfish and has to be treated simply as its flavour is very subtle. It has a very sweet taste that is great with many flavours. The scallop is best pan-fried in a very hot pan in olive oil for literally minutes and finished with a little butter to give them a golden colour all over. They must be cooked within minutes because once they are overcooked, they will lose that lovely sweet juicy taste and become watery overcooked pieces of rubber. The best way to cook plumped-up, dredged scallops is to dry them thoroughly and leave them in the fridge on a cloth on a tray or plate so the air gets around them and dries them out to an extent. The hand-dived are the best scallops that you can get and these will always cook nicely and caramelise beautifully with a delicate texture. These can be eaten with a tomato salsa, pork belly or pickled beetroot. Anything with a piquant flavour will go very well with scallops and in stews or with spices they are utterly delicious.

QUEEN SCALLOP (*Aequipecten opercularis*)

The tiny queen scallops are no bigger than the size of your thumbnail, but once they are taken out of the shell, they have an even sweeter taste than the king scallop.
Fishing Both sides of the shell are convex and the outline is rounded with ribs and projections, which looks like little ears, on each shell. The queen can grow up to 9cm in diameter and the shell is variable in colour, but often light-pink to brown, orange or yellow and often with bands, zigzags, rays or spots of darker or lighter shades.

The queen scallop is found between tidemarks to depths of 100m, on sand or gravel and often in high densities with lots of them together. Individual shells mature at about 40–50mm and 18 months to 2 years old. The spawning occurs in spring and autumn and they commonly swim at a 60m depth.
Cooking Queen scallops have an almost vanilla flavour with a nutty aftertaste and I would say are slightly richer in taste then kings. They are great in risottos like pumpkin or plain herb, or they can be cooked in the shell with lemon, garlic and parsley, either over an open fire or on a grill on the beach. Just baked in the oven is also very tasty indeed. I used to source a lot of these when I was the chef at Pied à Terre; they were very popular and we used to go through an awful lot of them. I am sure that you will enjoy them as much as I did.

SEA BASS (*Dicentrarchus labrax*)

The sea bass belongs to a family of spiny-finned fish called *Moronidae*. It is a relatively common fish in the sea around England and Wales, Ireland and the southern North Sea coasts. It is also found in the east Atlantic from Norway to Morocco, the Canaries and Senegal, the Mediterranean, Black Sea and the Baltic Sea. Sea bass are fast, predatory fish that look almost torpedo-like and have very sharp teeth for eating their prey. From the 1990s, sea bass became much more popular because of new sushi restaurants opening up and the fact that they became seen as a high-quality fish for restaurants. As their popularity has grown, the knock-on effect has been that fishermen know they can get a premium price and therefore are hunting them much more.
Fishing Adult bass live both offshore and inshore, sometimes entering freshwater during summer, but generally keeping to deeper, warmer offshore waters during winter. They breed from March to mid-June in deep water, mostly in the western English Channel. Once the bass eggs hatch, they find their way back to estuaries around the coast, sometimes hundreds of miles away from their spawning grounds. These estuaries become the nursery areas where the bass spend most of their time until they reach 4–7 years old and adopt the migratory movements of adults.

A long-lived species, sea bass may live to 25 and achieve a length of up to 100cm with a weight of 12kg. Nowadays, though, fish exceeding 55cm and 2kg are becoming rare. Males are sexually mature at 36–38cm and the minimum landing size at the moment is 36cm, though many would like to increase this to the 40cm mark. Females are sexually mature at 42–45cm and 6 years old.

Sea bass have come under increasing pressure from fishing because they now attract a higher price than any other native British fish. Fishermen have found the bass's spawning grounds and stocks are falling. Today, even bass anglers have noted a drop in the amount of bass and the size has also decreased. Certainly, I was getting larger line-caught bass five years ago than I am today.

Sea bass are taken by gill nets, pair trawling and pelagic midwater trawlers. The northern limit of the British commercial bass fishery is on the Yorkshire coast, where trawl-caught fish are increasingly landed into Scarborough and Whitby. From Norfolk southwards, bass are often caught as part of a mixed fishery in drift nets, fixed nets and trawls as well as on longlines and by rod and line. Pair trawling is the most damaging way of catching sea bass and I have to say that French pair trawling must be held largely responsible for squandering sea bass stock levels, with fishermen having to catch a huge amount of fish to pay high costs. Until the mid-eighties, bass were also caught in fairly large numbers by inshore fisherman using fixed nets, but as stocks declined, the use of netting in estuaries was banned to protect the crucial nursery areas. Fishing for bass from any vessel is now prohibited in 34 areas for all or part of the year around the UK, including Chichester Harbour, Langstone Harbour and Portsmouth.

Bass that spawn in the Channel and the Bay of Biscay. Until the mid-1980s bass were very prone to being caught in fairly large numbers by small groups of inshore fisherman using fixed nets, which are also used to catch sea trout and salmon, All the stocks of these fish declined and then the use of netting in estuaries was banned. These are the crucial nursery areas where the bass where spending most of their lives, but now most of the young fish are being returned to the sea for being too small.

Line-caught bass from Cornwall and Devon is generally available from May to January, with the height of the season being October to December. Line-caught sea bass is very popular in restaurants and can go for very high prices. The fact that more and more bass are being marketed in this way is far better for the industry and it would be great if this were the only way they was sold and marketed. In the south west, a lot of the handline-caught fish are tagged and this is a great way of marketing the fish. Have a look at the South West Handline Fishermen's Association (see www.linecaught.org.uk) and you can trace the fish you've bought all the way back to the fishermen and the boat from which it came.

Recently, bass has become the focus in the UK of a conservation effort by recreational anglers. The anglers that catch bass have many arguments and discussions about it but, in a way, if all the bass caught by the sports anglers were released, this would help hugely. In the Republic of Ireland there are strict laws regarding bass. As well as all commercial fishing for the species being banned, there are also restrictions in place for anglers, including a closed season from May 15 to June 15, minimum sizes of 400mm and a bag limit of two fish per angler in a 24-hour period.

Sea bass is also now widely farmed in the Mediterranean in cages out at sea. From a conservation point of view, this has single-handedly saved the wild bass population, but there are still the same concerns of farming these fish as there are for salmon (see page 331).

The sea bass's MCS rating is 3. Make sure you're choosing line-caught seabass.

Cooking Sea bass is very popular in the restaurant trade and is deemed an extremely high-quality fish. It has a wonderful texture and its flesh is full of flavour. If you can imagine the taste of sea air in your mouth, that would be sea bass – very clean, but with intense flavour. However, the taste of sea bass can vary hugely depending on what time of year they are caught and the taste of farmed bass is also slightly different. Farmed bass is not as sharp or as clean as wild and I would say that the oily taste is increased as well. Most of the farmed bass is about 500g in weight so the fillets will always be one portion size. In one way this is a nice portion to serve, but you will never get that really moist taste you get from a great wild piece of bass. Sea bass can be cooked in a multitude of ways, from grilling, poaching and baking to marinating and eating raw, sashimi-style. The flesh is meaty, slightly oily and flakes very easily. It is also one of the juiciest fish to eat if cooked to perfection. When cooking bass, always make sure that the fish is almost cooked all the way through on the skin side, and then turn over to finish the cooking. This will give the best chance of a crisp skin.

SEA BREAM

BLACK BREAM (*Spondylisoma cantharus*)

Bream is a beautiful, really underutilised fish and one of the many largely forgotten, but truly great, species that swim in our seas and close to our shores. Fished in the South West, Cornwall, Devon, the Northwest and parts of Wales, I must say that when you look at a bream, it doesn't really seem like it belongs to these waters of ours at all, but should be swimming happily in the Mediterranean instead.

Black bream, also known as 'old wife', is the most common of the six species of bream found in British coastal waters. Black bream are grey, not black, and a little stripy too and I have used them now and again because they are so adaptable. It's a fairly easy fish to prep as well, but the real problem with it is the huge dorsal fin along its back. I have on numerous occasions stabbed myself in the finger and then been in real pain trying to get one of the sharp little fins out.

Fishing Being principally a warm water fish, the British Isles is right on the outermost fringe of the black bream's range and they are much more abundant towards the Mediterranean. As a migratory fish, the black bream are summertime visitors, moving in schools along the English Channel and arriving by mid-April to the Sussex region. The majority of fish are therefore caught between July and November. Their spawning season is between April and May and if you avoid eating them then, this will give them a chance to spawn and reproduce.

An hermaphrodite, the black bream is a female first, becoming a male at a length of over 20cm. The Sea Fisheries Committees of Cornwall and North Western and North Wales no longer allow their districts to land sea bream below 23 cm and I would therefore choose fish from Cornwall, the Northwest of England or North Wales.

Also, always choose line-caught fish where available or fish taken in fixed nets where measures to deter marine mammals have been adopted.

Do also be careful of where you are ordering or buying it from as there is a little confusion sometimes between the wild and farmed species. The farmed bream is gilthead bream, which is a different fish altogether, but it's sometimes passed off as sea bream just so that the person selling it will make a little more pence for their pound. So when you are asking about the bream, ask if the fish is farmed or wild. If it's farmed, then it's not black bream.

The MCS rate for this fish is at 2 for sustainability, so eat more of it.

Cooking This lovely fish has a simple taste and I would therefore suggest, as ever, to keep it simple. It is great eaten raw or marinated with olive oil, lemon juice, fine lemon zest, perhaps some chopped dill, sea salt and black pepper and then cooked. It can be baked whole, wrapped in foil with some white wine, seasoning, soft herbs and maybe a little lemon peel. I also like to bake it in a salt crust, the salt flavoured with dill, anise, garlic, lemon and orange peel. You can even barbecue the whole fish over a naked flame. Bream makes great 'portion-size' fillets as well, which can be pan-fried or grilled. Heat up a pan with some olive oil and fry the fish, skin-side down ,until the skin is going crispy around the edges and is golden brown.

Flip it over and cook for another minute, finishing with a little lemon.

GILTHEAD BREAM (*Sparus auratus*)

Generally considered the best tasting of the breams, in France the gilthead bream is known as *dourade* (*dourada* in Portugal) due to the golden band between the fish's eyes.

Fishing Found in the Mediterranean and the eastern coastal regions of the North Atlantic Ocean, eastern Atlantic, British Isles, Strait of Gibraltar to Cape Verde and around the Canary Islands, gilthead bream migrate north from the Bay of Biscay and the temperate coastal waters of Spain and Portugal for something of a summer holiday, lasting from April through to the back end of October. First indications that the bream have arrived in the UK are found off the far west coast of Cornwall and then, within a few days, they will be found way up on the shallow reefs of Dorset, the Isle of Wight, Hampshire and Sussex.

The species is hermaphrodite and the majority are first males, then become females. Spawning occurs from October to December and they reach maturity at 1–2 years (20–30cm) for males and 2–3 years (33–40 cm) for females.

The bream are found in sea grass beds, sandy bottoms as well as in the surf zone, commonly to depths of about 30m up to 150m. They are caught on line gear, with trammel nets, bottom trawls, beach seines and traps and are fished most intensively from February to October.

Gilthead bream are also farmed in open sea pens and in Greece fish farming has emerged as a fast-growing industry, now accounting for around 50 per cent of the European Union's production of sea bass and sea bream. When buying farmed fish, look out for organically farmed sea bream, which are farmed with lower stocking densities and fed more sustainable feeds. Also, ask your fish supplier if they have a buying policy to ensure they only source fish from farms with high environmental and welfare standards. These fish are okay to eat.

The MCS rate the gilthead bream as a 4.

Cooking Despite its amazing colour, a lot of people do not like to eat the skin of the gilthead bream because it's fairly tough and has a strong taste. If you're pan-frying the fish, it's best to cook the skin almost all the way through on one side, then flip it over to finish it off. The skin has to be pretty crispy to be palatable. The fillets can be bought as portion sizes or you can go for a bigger bream where the fillets are going to be slightly juicier. The flesh is richer in taste than bass and although farmed bream is not as good as wild, it is still a clean-tasting fish that is very adaptable to all types of cooking. The cooking methods for the gilthead bream are very similar to those of black bream and the fish can be poached, fried, baked whole or served as sushi or sashimi. One of the best ways I think to cook it is baked whole in the oven with aromatic herbs, thyme, dill, parsley and some great olive oil, lemon juice and zest, seasoned well with coarse sea salt and black pepper. If you bake it with no foil, keep the oven lower or the herbs will burn. If you do cover it in foil, turn the oven slightly higher and the bream will steam in its own juices.

RED SEA BREAM (*Pagellus bogaraveo*)

The red sea bream is again from the *Sparidae* family. The Greeks call it 'the fish with a golden head' and you will find red sea bream not just in our waters, but in the eastern Atlantic, Norway, the Straits of Gibraltar to Mauritania, Madeira, the Canary Islands and the western Mediterranean. They tend to be a shoal fish, although the size of the shoals decreases as they become more independent when they get older.

Fishing Red sea bream have a summer inshore migration and breed in the late summer and autumn in the south west, but even earlier in southern regions. Like other bream, they are hermaphrodites, which means they are male during their first sexual maturity and become female at 20–30cm length and between 2 and 7 years of age. They grow very slowly to a maximum size of 70cm and a weight of 4kg. Because they are hermaphroditic and slow growing, red sea bream have a low resilience to exploitation and the stock levels at the moment are fully exploited to severely depleted.

The MCS suggests that we should not be eating them and they have been given a 5 score.

Cooking Red sea bream are not used all that much in restaurants and I certainly do not use them. I suggest that you use black bream instead.

SEA TROUT (*Salmo trutta*)

The sea trout looks nothing at all like the river-based brown trout, which is smaller and a true bronze rather than a silvery colour, yet they are in fact from exactly the same egg and start out in the same way. The only difference between them is that one decides to head out to the ocean and the other one will not move a mile from the area in which it was born. The eggs are laid all together by the mother on the river bed and it is only a year or two after birth then the differences start to appear. There are various factors affecting the different directions taken – the fish's environment, the amount of food that is readily available and its genetics all affect the make up of the trout.

The sea trout is a lovely fish and I often use Irish sea trout in the restaurant. It's very similar to salmon and I look at them as almost distant cousins.

Fishing Just like wild salmon, the sea trout goes through the excruciatingly painful process of moving from the fresh water where they are born to sea water, exchanging the sweet-tasting clear water for salty sea water. Eventually the sea trout grows salt glands and the gills start to be able to cope with the salty water, which makes the trout very strong. However, unlike the wild salmon, the sea trout doesn't travel vast distances between its feeding and breeding grounds, which means that it can go back and forth up the river much more often and may breed anything from 3–12 times, which is largely why they are not in such danger as the wild salmon.

Although the sea trout don't have the absolute stress and danger that wild salmon put themselves through and are far more adaptable to change, over the last few years we have seen a huge decrease in the numbers of sea trout. One of the main reasons for the decline is, as with wild salmon, the amount of farmed salmon escapees not far from the estuaries to which the sea trout swim. The wild trout have to swim through these waters risking infection from sea lice which leaves them weak and covered in sores. Thousands lose their lives because of this cross contamination, which is harming the stability and future of the species.

The southern hemisphere population, especially in Argentina, Chile and New Zealand, has grown very large and the size of them has grown significantly too, up to the heaviest recorded at 15kg. The main reason for this is the quality of food they are eating and the fact that they aren't having to run the gauntlet of interaction with farmed salmon as they do in Britain.

We are now farming a lot of sea trout, but when we do get the wild species, it can be a bit of a disappointment to have to go back to the farmed product. However, it's something that we will have to continue to get used to as farmed fish has become the best alternative to the wild species. Over the next few years and decades, it will be very interesting to see how far we go in making farmed fish not only sustainable, but gain a real understanding of the effects on taste, texture and quality of this farming.

The MCS rating for sea trout is 3.

Cooking Sea trout is best eaten in its truly wild state and I hope that you all at some stage will get to taste the real difference between the wild and farmed fish. It is adaptable to many ways of cooking and preparation. To eat as a whole poached piece of fish, gut and scale the trout and give it a good wash, then poach in an aromatic vegetable stock with herbs and lemon. Fillets can be marinated, baked or pan-fried in a little olive oil and eaten hot or cold with a really nice lemony herb mayonnaise. One of the easiest ways of cooking this fish is by cutting a nice skinless steak, weighing about 120g, then butterflying the piece, opening it out so the thickness is reduced by half and fanning it out. Take a sheet of baking parchment and smear on a little olive oil and some coarse sea salt and fresh pepper. Sprinkle a few fresh herbs like chervil, dill and tarragon on to the paper, then add the butterflied fish fillets. Season with salt and pepper and a little squeeze of lemon juice and place into the oven at 180°C/Gas 4 on a baking tray. Cook for just 3–4 minutes so it's still rare, then enjoy.

SKATES AND RAYS

Skates and rays are flat cartilaginous fishes related to sharks and dogfish. They are kite-shaped with 2 wings, which are the only part of the fish that is obviously edible. There are over 500 species of them worldwide, of which about 12–15 are found in our coastal waters. One of the most frequently asked questions about skates and rays, especially those found in UK waters, is what is the difference between them? The answer is simply that in the UK, species with long snouts are usually known as skates, while those with shorter snouts are called rays.

Skates and rays are among the most vulnerable of all marine species to overfishing due to their slow growth, high age at maturity and low reproductive rates. The 'once common' common skate is now known to be extinct in the Irish Sea and has not been recorded in surveys of the southern North Sea since 1991. It is widely recognised that improved management measures are required to ensure sustainable fisheries for skates and rays in European waters.

Fishing Skates and rays are long-lived large predators that live in deep water down to 300m and even as deep as 600m. The skate is a slow-growing fish and takes at least 5–10 years to reach sexual maturity. Unlike most other fish that spawn and have external fertilisation, skates copulate and have internal fertilisation, spawning in the spring and summer. They lay eggs on the sea floor and produce relatively few eggs, at about 40–150 a year, making them particularly vulnerable to over-fishing. Rays give birth to 'litters' of live young that hatch as miniature adults.

Skates and rays are landed as bycatch in demersal trawl fisheries for white fish. For many years, anglers have operated a voluntary ban on taking common skate and commercial fishermen have been urged to return any skate they catch. They are also taken in targeted long line and tangle net fisheries by a few inshore vessels. Landings peaked in the 1950s and 60s, but have declined

substantially since then. There has been a change in the species composition and distribution, with the stocks of larger-bodied species, such as the common skate and thornback ray declining considerably. However, the abundance and range of some smaller-bodied, faster-growing species, such as the cuckoo, starry and spotted rays, has remained relatively stable. The management of skate and ray fisheries are, in the MCS's opinion, totally inadequate because no distinction is made between any of the species. They are usually landed and reported in mixed categories such as 'skates and rays', which makes assessment and management impossible. There is also no Minimum Landing Size (MLS) and wings are often removed at sea and the remainder of the body discarded or landed separately, as bait for example.

Rays and skates are rated 5 by the MCS, which has recommended consumers avoid eating all species except the mature cuckoo, spotted and starry rays, which get a 3 for sustainability. Make sure you eat them above the size at which they mature: 54cm for male spotted rays and 57 cm for females; 54–59 cm for cuckoo rays; 40cm for starry rays.

Cooking Skate or ray wings are, I feel, a real delicacy because of their soft, delicate texture and taste. The fish needs to be eaten very fresh and certainly not more than a day after you've bought it. Skates and rays can have this terrible smell of ammonia from the urea they use as a defence against the salinity of the seawater and once they start to turn, this gives the most unpleasant taste and smell.

Ray wings should be bought skinned. If they have the skin on them, ask the fishmonger or supermarket to remove them as they are a pain to do. They should be cut into a nice neat and tidy triangle shape, with a little of the bone remaining at the thick end of the wing, then tapered down to a neat thin trimmed end.

Skates and rays are very popular with chefs and restaurants because of the amount of things that you can make and cook with them. The flesh is delicious, moist and sweet-tasting and peels away from the bone in delicate little strands. They can be poached, grilled, pan-fried or deep-fried. If you are pan-frying them in butter, just lightly flour and season them first, then place in a hot pan with a little oil and butter until they turn almost golden brown. Add the ray wing on the thick side first and cook slowly for 5–7 minutes, then turn over and finish cooking. Add some sage or capers at the end and a good dose of chopped parsley and fresh lemon. The alternative is to take them off the bone and deep-fry them in a batter and serve with chips. They were once very much a favourite in fish and chip shops cooked this way,

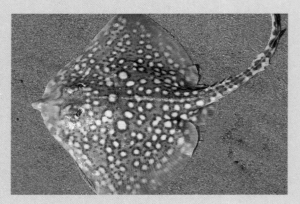

Glossary

but this was before the stock of ray and skate started to rapidly decline. They are very gelatinous once they are cooked, and you will notice this even more if you just plain poach the wings.

SPOTTED RAY (*Raja montagui*)
This species of ray is found mainly from the Mediterranean to the Shetland isles. The spotted ray has a flattened, diamond-shaped body with broad wings and a long tail. The spotted ray is similar in size and shape to the thornback ray, however the other has characteristic large spines scattered over its back. Its stock status is uncertain.

CUCKOO RAY (*Raja naevus*)
One of the easiest rays to identify, this fish has a large black with yellow marbling spot on each wing. They are found all around the UK, Ireland and the Mediterranean to Morocco and Senegal. Their stock status is uncertain.

STARRY RAY (*Raja radiata*)
This ray, growing up to nearly a metre in length, is found from the Mediterranean to Iceland and is the most common ray in British waters. Males and females mature at a length of about 40 cm (between 4 and 5 years old) and the species has a maximum recorded age of 16 years.

THORNBACK RAY (*Raja clavata*)
The thornback ray remains one of the most abundant rays in the north-east Atlantic and is an important commercial species. Skate are commonly claimed to have been caught from the south east, but most of these fish are actually the much smaller and tastier thornback ray, which is often sold by fishmongers as skate. Like all rays it has a flattened body with broad wings and a long, thorny tail. The thornback ray is usually found on mud, sand or gravel sea beds at depths between 10–60m. The distribution area and abundance of this species has strongly decreased over the past century. The North Sea stock is considered depleted and it would have warranted assessment by IUCN as threatened if catch rates in other areas were not more stable. Instead, the thornback ray is listed on the IUCN 'Red List', although it is assessed as being at lower risk than the common skate. Measures designed for the benefit of thornback ray would likely have comparable benefits to other skate species of a similar or larger size.

COMMON SKATE (*Raja batis*)
Now a relatively rare fish around the shores of Wales, as well as other parts of Britain, the common skate is the largest skate in European waters and can weigh up to 110kg with an overall length of nearly 3m, and they are long-lived animals. The males are covered with spines that can inflict a serious wound to anyone grabbing the edges of the wings. Skate make poor eating compared to thornback rays and most of the commercial fishery that once existed for skate was for the animal feed market, a sad fate for such a tremendous fish. The common skate is currently assessed by the IUCN as Critically Endangered in NW European shelf seas and is also the subject of a European Biodiversity Action Plan.

WHITE SKATE (*Raja alba*)
These skates have a long pointed snout and are black and grey with indistinct whitish spots. The underside of adults is white with a greyish band. It's often caught on the same grounds as the common skate and it is not unknown for it to be wrongly identified as a common skate.

SOLES

The soles are flatfishes with various families, but generally speaking, they are the members of the family *Soleidae*. However, outside Europe, the name 'sole' is also applied to various other similar flatfish, especially other members of the sole suborder, *Soleoidei*, as well as members of the flounder family. The common, or Dover, sole is the most esteemed and widely available. The name 'sole' comes from its resemblance to a sandal, the Latin *solea*, and the Greeks considered it would form a sandal fit for an ocean nymph.

DOVER SOLE (*Solea solea*)
The Dover, or common, sole and often simply called 'sole', is the most highly regarded and sought-after of all the soles. The name 'Dover' comes from the fact that this was where most soles were landed in the 19th century to be easily transported up to Billingsgate market.

The Dover sole is a remarkable species and it has been the most popular flat ish for almost 2 whole centuries. Many great chefs, including Auguste Escoffier and Louis Saulinier, have cooked the Dover sole in hundreds of ways. In fact I think just between them, there are over 500 different recipes for this one fish. All the most expensive and luxurious ingredients have been used; from truffles and foie gras to cèpes, lobsters, creamy sauces, champagne-flavoured sauces and muscat grapes. I would imagine it all tasted very nice, except that you could not in fact taste anything of the fish at all.

Fishing Dover sole is usually found on sandy and muddy seabeds down to 300m and also near and in estuarine places. The Dover sole is a right-eyed flatfish that can they grow up to 70cm in length, but is more commonly between 30–40cm.

The maximum reported age is 26 years and Dover soles reach maturity at 3–5 years, when they are 25–30cm in length. They spawn from January to April and the main spawning and nursery grounds for sole are in and around the estuaries on the English and continental coast, with the main fishery for the sole lying between Kent and the Dutch coast.

Dover sole is mainly caught by Dutch beam trawlers in a mixed fishery with plaice in the southern North Sea. There is also a directed gill net fishery around the Danish coast. In the English fishery, the high value of sole makes it one of the most important species targeted by inshore vessels using trawls and fixed nets. The main fishery is from March to October and sole is also taken as a target and bycatch species by offshore beam and otter trawlers and gill netters. The main ports of landing in England are Ramsgate, West Mersea, Felixstowe and an MSC fishery in Hastings.

North Sea Dover stock is classified as healthy and harvested sustainably, Stocks in the areas of Skaggerak and Kattegat, the Eastern Channel and Celtic Sea are also healthy, but the level of fishing pressure is too high or unknown. Stocks in the Western Channel and Biscay are below the minimum level recommended by ICES and harvested unsustainably, so avoid eating these. The state of the stock in southwest Ireland is unknown and catches the lowest on record, so, again, avoid eating these. Dover sole from the Hastings fleet and trammel net fishery in the Eastern Channel is certified as an environmentally responsible fishery by the MSC.

The MCS gives the Dover a 4 rating but that depends entirely on where that you are getting the sole from. Don't eat or buy immature sole less than 28cm or fish caught during the breeding season from April to June.

Cooking Soles cannot be eaten spanking fresh as this is like putting a piece of rubber in your mouth. They are better after a few days at least, after the rigamortis has subsided. However, I don't think that you will have a problem of them being too fresh because the Dover that we get are generally at least 5–6 days old. The Dover sole is very adaptable and can be baked, grilled, poached, pan-fried or steamed. Ask your fishmonger to skin the sole for you and then you can either have it grilled whole and served with a parsley butter or have it as fillets and poach them in a very simple white wine sauce with some tarragon and grapes in it.

LEMON SOLE (*Microstomus kitt*)

The lemon sole is often overlooked because we all go for its more commonly known brother or sister, the Dover sole. The lemon sole will never get the respect of the other flatfish and they will never get the market value that they do. It's largely a bycatch species and is rarely targeted outright as a fish to catch.

The lemon sole is a right-eyed flatfish, similar in shape to the dab but with a smoother and more slimy skin and a fleshier body. Lemons have an oval body and are more rounded than Dover sole. The head and mouth are very small, hence the name *Microstomus*, which is Latin for 'small mouth'.

Fishing Lemon sole can reach a maximum length of 70cm, however most are between 20–30cm. They are a widely distributed flatfish in northern European waters, all around the coasts of Britain and Ireland, the Northeast Atlantic and Bay of Biscay to the White Sea and off Iceland. They are bottom-dwelling fish that live mainly in rocky or stony areas. Spawning occurs during April to August and the young reach maturity at 3–4 years for the males and 4–6 years for the females.

Lemon sole is a moderately important food fish, caught mainly in trawl nets and seine nets, with the most common fishing technique being demersal bottom trawling. The fishery for lemon sole is largely unregulated and it is often also taken as a bycatch in trawl fisheries. The only stocks in the Norwegian and North seas are subject to mixed quota restrictions.

The lemon sole gets a rating of 3 from the MCS, so choose fish landed in Cornwall, where a recommend minimum landing size of 25cm and above is enforced, and don't buy during its breeding period of April to August.

Cooking The fish has a less meaty flavour and bite than the Dover sole and has a pleasant texture that is very moist and flaky. Get your fishmonger to prepare the fish for you if you want it skinned or just left whole. Cook the lemon sole exactly the way you do Dover sole, either poaching, pan-frying, grilling or whole.

MEGRIM SOLE
(*Lepidorhombus whiffiagonis/Pleuronectes megastoma*)

The megrim is a left-eyed flatfish that has a slightly larger head than is usual in flatfish and a narrower body. Flatfish are all very closely related and the megrim and the witch, in particular, are hard to tell apart to the untrained eye. The megrim has been caught for generations in the south west, but you very rarely see them at the fishmongers because they are mainly exported, with almost 75 per cent of the total landings going to Spain, France and Italy. There is no market for them in this country because, again, there's been a lack of education combined with us being a little bit fussy. The fact that fishermen do not get any valuable income for this flatfish means there is just no point trying to sell the fish here. However, this does mean that if you do want to eat megrim (or witch) they will be a quarter of the price of Dover sole.

Fishing Megrim is a deepwater fish found in European waters from 100–700m below sea level. Megrim range from 180g–1kg and can attain a length of about 60cm, although they are more usually 35–45cm with a maximum age of about 14–15 years. For both sexes, half of all individuals mature at about 20cm and 2½ years old. The fish spawn between January and April in deep water.

Megrim used to be taken mainly as bycatch in trawl fisheries, however, now it's a very important commercial species in its own right. Most of the UK landings of megrim are made by beam trawlers and Irish megrim landings are mostly made by multipurpose vessels. Otter trawlers account for the majority of Spanish landings and the remainder are taken in a mixed gill net fishery for anglerfish, hake and megrim. Megrim is abundant all year round, although less so during March and April when it is breeding.

The MCS gives megrim a rating of 3. Choose fish otter-trawled from waters west of Ireland and the western Channel where stock is classified as healthy. Avoid eating immature fish less than 25cm and during their spawning season from January to April.

Cooking Megrim is a loose-textured sole with a sweet, clean flavour and is superior in my view to witch, which are also prolific in southwesterly waters. It is a lovely fish and is popular in France where it's called *cardine*, though most of it goes to Spain, where it's called *gallos*. It's cheaper than lemon and Dover sole, though the fish is not as meaty as either of these and the fillets are much more delicate, soft and flaky than other soles. The taste is different as well. The Dover has a slightly meaty, chicken flavour, while the megrim has more of a lemony sea flavour with a good moisture content. The best way for this sole to be cooked is on the bone, with the fish skinned first on both sides and then pan-fried in butter with a little garlic and rosemary, cooked until golden brown and finished with a little lemon juice. Or if you like, you can slightly flour the fish then pan-fry it and you will get a slightly crisp skin. The other alternative is to breadcrumb the fillets in a flour and egg wash and breadcrumbs, then pan-fry in foaming butter or even do it with a parley and garlic butter.

WITCH (*Glyptocephalus cynoglossus*)

The witch, or gray sole as it is named in the United States, is a right-eyed flatfish with a very small head. The witch is a very funny thing because although it is pretty much the same as megrim, it does not have the same reputation. The fish has been primarily exported to Europe and was not thought of as saleable in the UK because its name put off consumers. Witch is now hitting British shelves under its new name, the Torbay sole, and just as calling the megrim a Cornish sole did wonders for marketing and sales, hopefully this will do the same.

Fishing The witch stays in moderately deep water at temperatures of between 2–6°C on both sides of the North Atlantic. In European waters it is found from Norway and Iceland south to the west coast of France and the southwest of the UK.

Spawning between May and September, its growth is rather slow and sexual maturity is attained at 3–4 years. The witch may live for 14 years and to a length of about 62cm, but seldom grow more than 35–40cm.

The most common fishing technique is demersal bottom trawling. The fish are mainly taken by beam trawlers, though a better way to get them is to otter trawl, as it has less impact than the beamers. When the witch is living on the bottom, it seems to be even more stationary than other flounders because it is caught year round with no evidence that it moves in- or offshore with the change of the seasons.

Glossary

TOM AIKENS

The witch is caught by UK fishermen off the southwest coast and landed at Newlyn in Cornwall, but one of the main reasons that you have not see this fish anywhere near restaurants, fish counters or fishmongers until recently is that the Spanish and Italians have been taking pretty much everything that the fishermen were catching. However, it is now on sale at Marks & Spencer and, with the new name, I am sure it will have a greater appeal to the public. With current concerns over stock depletion, the advantage of Torbay sole is that it's a sustainable species as well as a great tasting fish and it's very cheap compared to the Dover sole.

The current stock of this fish is in better shape than the Dover, so you will be helping out the stock of that fish too if you try the witch. I urge you all to try it.

It's rated a 3 by the MCS, the same as the megrim and I'd also suggest cooking it in the same way.

SPRAT (*Sprattus sprattus*)

Watching sprats in the water is like seeing a mass of silver darts in a very tight, compact group. The reason for this formation is for protection from the predatory gulls that attack from above and pick and poke at the fish. It's like the sea is literally alive as they try to eat as much as they can until their bellies are going to pop.

The Baltic sprat, *Sprattus sprattus balticus,* is a herring-like marine fish from the family *Clupeidae*. We very rarely get to see these little fish fresh because they are hunted by everyone from sardines, sharks and rays to sea lions, seagulls, cod, pollock and herring. If you are small, tasty and nutritious, you are going to get eaten.

Fishing Sprats can be found in the north-east Atlantic, eastern central Atlantic and the Mediterranean and Black seas. They are quick at maturing and reproducing, so the next year's youngsters easily replace them. They sometimes enter estuaries, especially as juveniles, and they have strong migration patterns between winter feeding and summer spawning grounds. Some spawn almost throughout the whole year, but it is mainly in the spring and summer, so avoid eating them between January and July and in the North Sea from March to August.

They are often caught by seine or trawl nets.

Small sprats are sold to canneries and are known as 'brislings', but most are used in the production of fishmeal and as fish food, with far less put aside for human consumption.

They do not have a quota or a rating from the MCS and are fine to eat.

Cooking Sprats are an oily fish and are high in Omega-3, which is vital to cell structure and functioning, particularly in the brain. They also are an important source of the vitamins A and D. Sprats are very easy to cook, but they have to be eaten super fresh. They can be grilled, deep-fried in flour, pan-fried with a little garlic and thyme or even cooked and spread on toast with some chutney. You can eat them whole – head, bones and all. Or just nibble around the middle bone and head. Either way, they are scrummy.

SQUID (*Loligo forbesi*)

Squid occur all over the world and are part of a group called cephalopods, which are complicated beings. They are a very short-lived species and because of this, they cram a lot into their short lives and have many ways of protecting themselves against their enemies. They eject black ink to warn off predators and some communicate or camouflage themselves by changing colours or illuminating their organs to distract enemies or attract prey. Squid have an enormous amount of power and agility, jetting among the other cephalopods with such ease and moving backwards through the water like a rocket.

Fishing There are squid of various sizes, from the 30cm *Loligo vulgaris* up to the giant squid, whose size we only can guess (estimates as large as 20m have been put forward). *Loligo forbesi* occurs in the north-east Atlantic and around Britain, swimming into the open sea of the Mediterranean where it's replaced by its cousin, *Loligo vulgaris*, which is very similar and can be treated in the same way. A squid's eyes are strikingly large and in comparison to the size of their body, squid have the largest eyes in the animal kingdom. Cephalopod means 'head-footed' and for the squid this refers to the way the 8 arms and 2 tentacles come directly out from the head.

Loligo is an annual species, which means it has a 1-year life cycle with a single breeding season and it grows to maturity and dies within 12 months of being spawned. The squid and other cephalopods are unique because of this ability to grow and mature in such a short period of time and yet still have fairly complicated resources to feed efficiently and effectively. The *Loligo forbesi* spawn in parts of the Channel in the summer months and once they have spawned, they should hatch at the beginning of February.

Squid have been exploited as a fishery resource around the British Isles for at least 100 years and are commonly found throughout the Northeast Atlantic, but because of their fast-growing cycle and short life, they are a sustainable species of fish. The fisheries in UK waters are mostly in Scottish waters and tend to be small and non-targeted groups. The squid is not part of any established fishery in Scottish water and at the moment they are generally being taken as bycatch in trawl fisheries for nephrops and white fish species, with the main methods of capture being trawling and jigging.

Squid landed in the UK is mainly for the export market and only a small amount is sold here. The British Seafish Industry Authority (Seafish) is doing a lot of tests with squids to try and really understand how sustainable they are. Seafish say that the squid populations are abundant and they have carried out research to investigate the best catching methods to use and understand more about the sustainability issue with squid.

The squid has a 3 MCS rating. The minimum landing size is 15cm and avoid the spawning season from December through to May.

Cooking Squid can be prepared in countless ways: in many Mediterranean countries squid rings are often served deep-fried; the Spanish serve it in its ink in the dish *calamares en su tinta* or as part of a seafood paella with mussels and prawns, while Croatians grill it and stuff it with cheese. Squid ink risotto is a dish thought to have originated in Venice – it is famous for its delicate taste and unusual black colour. In China, squid is found either floating in seafood soups or with chilli and rice and in Japan it is used in sashimi and sushi. My preferred ways of serving squid are either just sautéed quickly in a little olive oil, garlic, cayenne pepper, paprika, rosemary, coarse sea salt and pepper, then finished with lemon juice or deep-fried with an aioli.

SWORDFISH (*Xiphias gladius*)

Full-grown swordfish are so fast, so powerful and so well armed that, with the exception of humans, large sharks, sperm and killer whales and short fin mako shark, they have very few predators as adults. The 'sword' in swordfish is not used to spear any of the fish that it catches, but instead to slash at its prey in order to injure it and make it an easier catch. The sword is also used defensively for protection from its few natural predators.

The swordfish is found in tropical, temperate, and sometimes cold oceans worldwide, including the Atlantic, Pacific and Indian oceans. Swordfish are a very elongated, predatory fish, its streamlined physique cutting through the water with great ease and agility. Apart from the sword, the head is short, the lower jaw is pointed and the mouth so wide that it gapes far back of the very large eyes, which are then set close to the base of the sword. The swordfish are not schooling fish at all and are born loners, swimming alone or in very loose groups.

Fishing The male swordfish matures first at a smaller size and at 3–4 years, which is younger than the females at 4–6 years and a length of 150–170cm. Swordfish caught by commercial fisheries in the Pacific are generally the largest swordfish caught, measuring an average of 120–190cm. Atlantic swordfish reach about 320kg in weight and in the Mediterranean the typical weight is less than 230kg.

In the Atlantic, spawning takes place in spring in the southern Sargasso Sea, in spring and summer in the Pacific and June to August in the Mediterranean, when swordfish will form huge schools, with the best-known spawning grounds found in the Mediterranean Sea off the southern part of the Italian Peninsula and Sicily.

Swordfish are normally found in shallower waters and bask on the surface of the sea. This means that traditionally fishing for swordfish was by harpoon until the global expansion of longline fishing came along. Almost half the worldwide catch of swordfish occurs in the Pacific and the north-western Pacific, while in 1995 the Atlantic swordfish industry caught 36,645 tonnes, or 41 per cent, of the world's total catch of swordfish and the Mediterranean catch accounted for 9 per cent. Fisheries in the Atlantic primarily rely on longlines, though bycatch remains a significant problem.

Demand for swordfish in North America and Europe remains high, which has put tremendous pressure on swordfish stocks. Most stocks are unmanaged and over-fished, with large catches of immature swordfish.

In the USA in 1998, a campaign called 'Give Swordfish a Break' was very successful with 750 prominent American chefs agreeing to remove North Atlantic swordfish from their menus. This led eventually to President Clinton calling for a ban on the sale and import of swordfish, with the federal government placing 13,2670 square miles of the Atlantic Ocean off-limits to fishing. The North Atlantic swordfish stock is in the process of being rebuilt and it is still very vulnerable. However, protective measures have been introduced to protect juvenile swordfish, which has helped swordfish stocks replenish. Overfishing is also occurring in the Indian Ocean and all these stocks are considered of high conservation concern.

The swordfish has a rating of 5 from the MCS, so please don't eat it.

TUNA

Tuna is hugely popular and is currently THE fish to eat for the health conscious and fashionable, but maybe not the worldly conscious. Humans have been catching tuna for many thousands of years, but industrial fisheries for these large ocean predators – a result of increasing demand for tuna in canneries – did not start until the 1940s and 1950s. The total world catch of the major commercial species of tunas – albacore, bigeye, bluefin, skipjack, and yellowfin – has increased continuously and tenfold during the last 50 years from 0.4 to over 4 million tonnes. Today, many stocks of the major commercial tuna species are fully or over-exploited. Skipjack is by far the main tuna species caught, followed by yellowfin, bigeye, albacore and the two bluefin species. There are, however, approximately 40 species of fish occurring in the Atlantic, Indian and Pacific oceans and in the Mediterranean Sea.

The main commercial tuna fishing nations are Japan, Taiwan and Spain. About 2 million tonnes of tuna were caught worldwide in 2004, with 530,000 tonnes of tuna going to Japanese markets in 2005, according to the fisheries agency. Japan, which consumes more than half the world's catch of the at-risk Atlantic bluefin tuna, has admitted overfishing, but blamed poor communication between its fishermen and has denied all accusations of fishing illegally. Japan's huge appetite for tuna has taken the most sought-after stocks of tuna to the brink of commercial extinction unless the fisheries agree on much more rigid quotas.

There has been general agreement by governments that something significant needs to be done. Proposals have included requiring the fishermen to produce certificates of origin for their tuna catches and for fish to be monitored from when they are caught until they reach the market. After the EU reached its 2007 quota of tuna,

the European Commission banned the fishing of endangered bluefin tuna in the eastern Atlantic and Mediterranean for the rest of the year to curb over-fishing and dwindling stocks of fish.

Fishing Tuna are excellent swimmers and their bodies are designed for high performance at both sustained swimming and bursts of high speed. They must swim constantly and, in fact, their survival depends on it because they obtain their oxygen supply from water flowing over their gills. They will suffocate if they stop swimming. Capable of travelling vast distances through the open oceans for migration, the distances tuna travel exceed those of any other fish and the reason it can do this at such a pace is that tuna are warm-blooded, which allows them to roam from the Arctic to the tropics.

A long time ago, tuna were caught in a very simple but brutal method where they were just rounded up in a huge network of nets laid down by fishermen, encircled and trapped and then bludgeoned and speared to death. Today, the vastly increased killing power of new tracking devices, boats and fishing technology has led to a network of international companies making huge profits from the trade. Basically, tuna are hunted in every conceivable ocean which they inhabit.

Tuna for Japan is usually caught by longline, but purse-seine fishermen also catch tuna, which has a disastrous amount of bycatch. If fishermen are netting a catch of 40 tonnes of tuna, the bycatch can be as much as a third or a quarter of the total catch, which will go back over the side, dead or dying. Longline fishing ensures the best handling of the fish and comprises baited hooks on lines that are about 80 miles long (if you saw the film *The Perfect Storm* with George Clooney, that's what they were dropping off over the back of the boat). French and Spanish purse seiners are kitted out with the finest fish spotting and catching equipment and spotter planes, which makes it impossible not to be able to find the fish. A better way of catching tuna is by using pole and line from bait boats, like they do in the Indian Ocean. Bait boats try to create a feeding frenzy by throwing chopped up buckets of fish bait into the water around the boat. The tuna are then hauled up into the boat one by one and this way there is relatively little bycatch. If you do buy tuna, always see if you can get it fished by this method.

Today, many stocks of the major commercial tuna species are fully or over-exploited. According to the latest assessments carried out by the International Commission for the Conservation of Atlantic Tunas (ICCAT), the organisation responsible for managing tuna fishing in the Atlantic Ocean, virtually all Atlantic tuna stocks are heavily exploited, some unsustainably so, and catches are, in many cases, in decline.

Canned tuna
Spain and the UK are the main consumers of canned tuna in the EU and all the UK's tuna is imported. Per person consumption in both countries is 4kg, which in the case of the UK is a very important part of the total seafood consumption of the country, which is estimated at 20kg.

Sashimi
Tuna for sushi or sashimi comes mainly from the longline fleets of Japan or Taiwan. Generally, the larger fish such as blue fins are preferred. Tuna for the sashimi market is graded on aesthetic characteristics, such as the bright/clear appearance of the skin and eyes, undamaged abdominal walls and on the high fat content of the fish. The higher the fat content, the lighter the colour and the more valued the sashimi will be. The best sashimi comes from toro, the peripheral layer of lighter-coloured tuna meat with a fat content of around 25 per cent.

BLUEFIN TUNA
The bluefin tuna is one of the most beautiful fish on the planet. It is an unbelievable creature that can swim as fast as 80km per hour and accelerates faster than a Porsche. Of all the principle tuna species, bluefin have suffered the most from the ravages of overexploitation for two main reasons: their slow reproductive rate and their exceptionally high value in the sashimi market, where a single fish can be worth up to $100,000. Creating effective fishing policies for bluefin tuna is difficult since they're highly mobile and swim through the territorial waters of many different nations.

The MCS give all species of bluefin tuna a 5 rating, so please don't eat it.

NORTHERN, ATLANTIC OR GIANT BLUEFIN TUNA (*Thunnus thynnus*)
No more magnificent fish swims the world's oceans than the Atlantic, northern or giant bluefin tuna, yet it is now a species that is seriously under threat. The story of the giant bluefin tuna begins with unfathomable abundance, as they surged in their millions through the Straits of Gibraltar each spring, fanning out across the Mediterranean to spawn. Over decades, fishermen devised a method of extending their nets from the shore to intercept the fish and funnel them into chambers where they were slaughtered. The biggest trouble for Atlantic bluefin began in the mid-1990s when stocks of southern bluefin tuna were fished to between 6 and 12 per cent of their original numbers. The bluefin is the slowest growing tuna species, which makes it more vulnerable to over-fishing.

Fishing The bluefin tuna swims from the surface to a depth of 200m and will come near to the shores seasonally. It can grow to 4m in length, weigh 680kg (which is bigger than a horse) and live for 30 years. The giant bluefin tuna is a species native to both the western and eastern Atlantic ocean as well as to the Mediterranean and Black seas.

Spawning in the Gulf of Mexico happens from April to June and in the Mediterranean from June to August.

Purse seine nets are currently responsible for 60 to 80 per cent of the bluefin tuna catch in the Mediterranean and over the past few decades, a high-tech armada of boats, often guided by spotter planes, have pursued giant bluefin from one end of the Mediterranean to the other, annually netting tens of thousands of the fish, many of them illegally.

In fact, the magnificent bluefin tuna is the only fish in the Mediterranean that is subject to a quota system. The countries that surround the Mediterranean Sea have finally given in to warnings from scientists about the parlous state of bluefin and agreed a recovery plan. Quotas were lowered and the fishing season curtailed, while mechanisms were also established to track the fish from the sea to the plate and to try and curb illegal, unreported and unregulated (IUU) fishing, which according to the International Commission for the Conservation of Atlantic Tuna (ICCAT) scientists, has been as much as 50 per cent each year to the amount extracted legally from the seas. However, environmental groups believe that even the modest restrictions that have been passed are being undermined.

In the last decade, the drive to provide the Japanese market with sashimi-grade bluefin tuna has led to the capture of small tunas for fattening in sea cages. The number of tuna farms has increased exponentially since they first appeared in 1996 to over 60 today, with a potential farming capacity of 55,000 tonnes of tuna, which compared to the yearly TAC of 28,500 in 2008, is going to encourage huge over-fishing. Strangely, the farms in the

Mediterranean are also eligible for EU subsidies for aquaculture development even though they are not really aquaculture, as the tuna are caught from the wild. This also explains why most bluefin tuna in the Mediterranean are now caught using purse seines, because this is the only fishing method that allows capture of live tuna that can be moved. In 2004, around 22,500 tonnes of Atlantic bluefin tuna were transferred to tuna farms, representing nearly two-thirds of the entire annual quota for the Mediterranean and eastern Atlantic.

Tuna farming is actually going to damage the industry even more, as it will lead to an increase in supply and therefore a drop in the price of the fish. And unless techniques can be developed for domesticating bluefin tuna so that they reproduce in captivity, current fattening operations will remain dependent on wild populations, thereby perpetuating the sustainability problem.

THE SOUTHERN BLUEFIN TUNA (*Thunnus maccoyii*)
Southern bluefin is considered the ultimate delicacy of the tuna family in Japan. For bluefin sashimi, the Japanese are willing to pay extremely high prices due to its size, colour, high fat content and texture and taste. One of the world's most expensive fish, the high price is caused by the fact that it is very hard to get hold of this species.
Fishing Found in the open southern hemisphere waters of all the world's oceans, the southern bluefin tuna is a large, streamlined fast swimming fish. Reaching a weight of over 200kg and measuring more than 2m in length, it is one of the largest bony fish that swims in the sea. It can live for up to 40 years, but reaches an average age of 12.

There is uncertainty about the size and age when they become sexually mature, and their only known breeding area is in the Indian Ocean, south east of Java and Indonesia. Mature females produce several million or more eggs in a single spawning period and breeding takes place from September to April. The juveniles migrate south down the west coast of Australia. During the summer months from December to April, they tend to congregate near the surface in the coastal waters off the southern coast of Australia and spend their winters in deeper, temperate oceanic waters.

Since the 1950s, when industrial fishing started, the total population of southern bluefin tuna has been decimated and it has declined hugely by about 92 per cent. Most fishing is pole and line, surface trolling and long-line fishing. This terrible situation has triggered actions by several environmental groups such as WWF and Green Peace, and Japan, Australia and New Zealand have imposed restrictions on the catching of this species.

The southern bluefin tuna is classified as Critically Endangered on the IUCN red list of threatened species and is the most overexploited tuna species.

PACIFIC BLUEFIN TUNA (*Thunnus orientalis*)
The biggest and fastest fish in the Pacific, evolution has streamlined the Pacific bluefin tuna's body to reduce water resistance and conserve energy for trans-Pacific migrations.
Fishing This tuna spawns in the western Pacific between Okinawa and the Philippines and probably in the Sea of Japan. Maturing slowly, they can live for up to 30 years, reach up to 3m in length and can weigh up to 555kg. Pacific bluefin tuna are over-fished throughout the world. They're hooked on longlines or illegally netted everywhere they swim and many young bluefins are captured before they even reproduce.

ALBACORE TUNA (*Thunnus alalunga*)
Due to its white-coloured meat, albacore tuna is called 'the chicken of the sea' and it is very popular in the USA. The meat has a somewhat dry texture and even tastes like chicken. Albacore is a very valuable food, as is most tuna, and is economically significant because it's this tuna that is canned the most.
Fishing Albacore is one of the larger species of tuna and is found in tropical and temperate seas and the Mediterranean. It's length is up to140cm and it weighs up to 60kg. Albacore is a highly migratory species and is always on the move seeking the best feeding and spawning grounds.

In the Pacific Ocean, the maturity of the albacore may be reached at about 90cm in length for the females and 97cm in length for the males, whilst in the Atlantic Ocean, it is reached at about 94cm for both sexes. In the warm waters of the Pacific Ocean, peak spawning time is from March through to July.

Albacore is fished by pole and line, longline, trolling, and some pure seining.

Although the South Atlantic albacore stock is thought to be relatively healthy, the North Atlantic stock of albacore is considered overfished, with the spawning stock 30 per cent below the estimated sustainable level. In the Mediterranean, the opinions seem non-conclusive. In the Northern Pacific they are fully exploited and in the Southern Pacific they have reached their critical level. It is very hard to predict if the albacore can support any further growth. The MCS rating is 4.

BIGEYE TUNA (*Thunnus obesus*)
Bigeye tuna look a lot like yellowfin tuna and it is hard sometimes to distinguish between the two. Bigeye swim at a far greater depth than the skipjack and yellowfin and so have more fat to insulate them from the cold water. This makes them especially attractive for the Japanese sashimi market. The meat turns light grey and somewhat darkish after cooking or grilling, so the colour makes it less fit for canning. The colour and taste of this big fish is almost near to that of beef and in quality, it is second only to the blue fin.
Fishing The bigeye is a deepwater swimmer and is found in the open waters of all tropical and warm oceans, but not the Mediterranean Sea. Bigeye tuna are deep-bodied, streamlined fish with large heads and eyes. Its length is between 60–250cm and the body colour is dark metallic blue on the back with a grey-white belly and a brilliant blue band running along each flank.

Bigeye mature much slower than other tuna and at 100–130cm in length in the eastern Pacific and the Indian Ocean and about 130cm in the central Pacific Ocean. At the age of maturity, which will be about 4–5 years old, they spawn and may produce as many as 10 million eggs per spawning season.

Catches of bigeye peaked in 1994, but have since then plummeted by almost 50 per cent. The large quantities of illegal catches for many years have meant that scientific assessments of the once abundant stock are very uncertain. An analysis conducted in 2004 indicated that the bigeye stock had declined significantly due to large catches being made since the mid-1990s. In the Eastern Pacific, up to 60 per cent of the bigeye tuna catch are now very small, juvenile fish, which means it has had insufficient time to breed and replenish its stocks. A new report from TRAFFIC, the wildlife monitoring network, and the WWF warns that bodies set up to protect stocks are failing to meet legal obligations, are way too slow to respond to scientific advice and have failed to halt overfishing.

Glossary

TOM AIKENS

The bigeye is on the endangered list and is facing a high risk of extinction. The MCS rating is 5.

SKIPJACK (*Katsuwonus pelamis*)

Skipjack is the most popular tuna for eating. Of the major commercial species, skipjack reach sexual maturity earliest and produce the greatest number of eggs, which has meant that this species has been able to withstand substantial fishing pressure and has been described as 'the rat of the sea' due to its rapid reproductive rate. The meat of the skipjack has a somewhat darker colour and can even be slightly pinkish. The small size of the fish gives small loins and chunks, making it excellent for canned tuna chunks.

Fishing The skipjack tuna swims from the surface to 200m. The maximum length is about 108cm with a maximum weight of 34.5kg, though a more common size is 80cm and 8–10kg in weight. The skipjack is highly migratory and can be found all over the world within tropical waters. Large schools of skipjack sometimes mix with small yellowfin, but dolphins do not swim with the small skipjack, which almost makes it a guaranteed dolphin-safe species.

Skipjack tuna spawn all year-round in warm equatorial waters, while further away from the equator, the spawning season is limited to the warmer months. They will reach sexual maturity at a length of 40cm, but most fish appear to mature at a larger size.

Skipjack tuna is mainly caught by purse seine, gill net and bait boats using pole and line. Total annual catches averaged 507,000 tonnes over the period 2002–2006 and are increasing. The populations of skipjack tuna in the Atlantic Ocean have appeared to be declining in recent years, while populations in the Pacific Ocean appear to be stable.

The characteristics of Atlantic skipjack tuna stocks and fisheries make it extremely difficult to conduct stock assessments, ICCAT has not conducted a stock assessment for Atlantic skipjack tuna since 1999 and there are no definitive conclusions available on the status of the stocks.

At this moment, the skipjack tuna is not listed as threatened or endangered in the World Conservation Union (IUCN) Redlist and is considered to be in no immediate threat. Skipjack tuna has a 3 rating from the MCS but try and buy skipjack from the Pacific where it is being fished at sustainable levels.

YELLOWFIN TUNA (*Thunnus albacares*)

The yellowfin is also known as ahi tuna after the Hawaiian word for 'fire'. This is due to the smoke from the Hawaiians' fishing ropes rubbing violently on the gunwales of their wooden canoes while pulling the fish in. Yellowfin is the second most popular tuna species in terms of volume caught, and they are becoming a popular replacement for bluefin tuna because of the yellowfin's low conservation threat level and the severe depletion of the number of bluefin tuna. The large size of the yellowfin makes it good for canning, and once cooked the meat tends to have a very light yellow/brown colour. The structure of the meat is quite firm, and the taste is mild. If the fish gets larger then 10–15kg, the meat tends to become slightly darker and somewhat dryer.

Fishing Yellowfin are easy to recognise by the sickle-shape of their bright yellow anal and second dorsal fins. They are the second largest tuna species and grows up to 239cm in length and 200kg in weight. They are found in the open waters of tropical and subtropical seas worldwide and swim in the top 100m of sea.

The yellowfin juveniles grow very quickly, weighing approximately 3.4kg at 18 months and reach maturity by the time they are 120cm in length and at an age of approximately 2–3 years. The reproduction of yellowfin tuna occurs all the year round, but is more frequent during the summer months in each hemisphere.

Yellowfin cover enormous distances around the globe and all of the stocks intermingle. It is a big fish which can swim at a very high speed, which is one of the reasons why in some areas dolphins and larger, full-grown yellowfin swim together for protection from other predators. Through extensive measures from the tuna industry and good monitoring programs, the volume of bycatch from dolphins has become a lot less now in relation to times before.

Commercial fisheries catch yellowfin tuna with purse seines and also longlines. Catches increased threefold between 1991 and 2002, but there has been a steady decline in overall catches in the Atlantic since 2001. According to the most recent ICCAT assessment, the stock of yellowfin has been very heavily fished and is now getting to the point of being overexploited. The yellowfin is exploited to its maximum in the Eastern Pacific ocean and also in the Western Pacific. The general concerns on yellowfin are that due to increased catches of baby yellowfin stocks are likely to suffer in the long term. Despite this problem, the yellowfin tuna is currently listed as having a low risk and is of least concern in the red list of the World Conservation Union (IUCN).

The MCS rating is 3 so you can eat it, providing you check where it's from.

ATLANTIC BONITO (*Sarda sarda or sarda spp.*)

Bonito is part of the huge tuna family and is one of the smallest fish in the family. Bonito meat has a firm texture and darkish colour. The smaller young bonito have a lighter colour, like a skipjack, and have quite a high fat content.

Fishing The Atlantic bonito swims in the top 200m of the ocean and is also found in shallow coastal waters. The average size is around 50cm in length and approx 2kg in weight and the minimum length of maturity is about 39.5cm in males and 40.5 cm in females.

In most parts of the Mediterranean Sea, the spawning occurs between May and July, while in the eastern Atlantic, it's from December to June. In the north-western Atlantic, bonitos spawn between June and July. This species is mostly fished in coastal waters by small local boats and is caught by purse seine, pole and line and static nets. It is also caught as a bycatch, so it can be quite hard to determine what the stock is.

Catching volumes in the Black sea and Mediterranean have been decreasing since the last decade and the size of the fish have become a lot smaller as the supply is irregular and quite limited. The catches in the Gulf of Thailand, along the Burmese Coast and in the South China Sea supply the canned tuna industry. It's a far cheaper substitute for skipjack tuna and so is mainly used for canning as opposed to being sold fresh.

TURBOT (*Psetta maxima*)

Turbot are the largest of the flatfish family and are amazing predators who grow to be amazingly powerful fish. They tend to wait buried in the sand until something comes along – either a dead fish or a very unlucky fish.

Fishing A large, rounded flatfish with a broad body, the turbot is about 50–80cm in length, but can occasionally reach up to 1m. The turbot lays on its right side with the left side uppermost and its eyes are on the upper left side. It has a variable colour, which changes to match its background and blend in with the sea bed. It is usually a dull sandy-brown to grey, with minute brown, blackish or greenish specks scattered over the body. The turbot is found on sandy or gravel bottoms around the coasts of Britain and Ireland, but are most common in the south, from about 20m to a depth of 80m.

The turbot reaches sexual maturity at about five years, when they are approximately 30–40cm long. They are a slow-growing fish and can live for up to 40 years. Spawning usually takes place between February and April in the Mediterranean and between May and July in the Atlantic. The females can each produce a staggering amount of eggs – as many as 10 million.

The turbot is fished by beam trawling, which is not the most environmentally sound way of catching fish. The trawling is doing a huge amount of damage to the sea floor and I would not have any turbot from the North Sea at all. The best way of catching the turbot is either handline or static net.

Turbot farming is becoming more and more popular. It started in the 1970s in Scotland and was then introduced to France and later to Spain. Spain, with its highly suitable oceanographic conditions, is now the major producer worldwide, but turbot is also currently farmed in Denmark, Germany, Iceland, Ireland, Italy, Norway, Wales and Portugal. Turbot has also been introduced to other regions, notably Chile in the late 1980s and, more recently, China.

Turbot is rated 4 by the MCS, so you need to be careful about where you source it. Avoid turbot from the North Sea and fish below the minimum landing size, which is 30cm. There should be no eating or catching during the spawning season of April to August.

Cooking Turbot will always be a favourite of chefs because of the quality of the flesh and the sublime fresh, clear taste. The turbot has traditionally been used for banquets in France as well as London and the great Escoffier regularly cooked turbot for royalty. It. A very large turbot can have slightly tough and sometimes stringy flesh, so middle-sized turbot, roughly 2–3kg, are the best size for cooking and conservation. When cooking good fresh turbot, elaborate flavourings or accompaniments are completely unnecessary. The turbot can be cooked in a multitude of ways and steaming, poaching, shallow-frying, baking and grilling are all suitable methods for cooking a turbot. The fins and bones should be used to make a fish stock, as they are the best for making a really flavoursome stock. To grill or pan-fry the fish, take a hot pan and add in a little olive oil, then once the pan is hot, place in the turbot fillet, skin-side down, and cook for 3–4 minutes over

a medium heat, adding a little fresh rosemary and thyme and then some butter. This will start to foam and colour the fish, so cook for another 1–2 minutes, then turn the fish and spoon over the cooking oil and butter. Cook this for a further 2–3 minutes, squeeze on a little lemon and serve. If you are baking the turbot whole, then you can remove the head and cut all the fins off around the body. Place into a large enough baking tray for the fish to fit, then add some butter on top, coarse sea salt, some dill and white wine and maybe a few pieces of lemon peel and bake in the oven for roughly 20 minutes a kg at 180°C/Gas 4. Or you can simply poach the seasoned fillets in a little fish stock with some parsley, lemon and white wine.

WHELKS

There are 16 species of whelks recorded in British waters, with the common whelk fished commercially in some parts of the country using baited pots. In the past, many people used to eat whelks at little shellfish stores along the piers on their summer holidays, cold and with some pepper and vinegar. This tradition has now largely died out and it was not until the 1980s that the industry started to boom again when the Koreans and Japanese found something else to eat that most countries don't even want to consider.

Fishing Whelks have a solid yellowish-brown shell with vertical wavy folds. A whelk moves like a land snail by gliding along on its wide, flat foot, powered by muscular waves that flow backwards along its sole. This species is a familiar part of the marine life in the United Kingdom and is also found in France, Norway, Iceland, some Arctic islands and the coast of North America, as far south as New Jersey. Living in crevices and burrowing into the seabed, this large shellfish can grow up to 110 x 68mm big, with big ones found in deeper waters. They live to about 15 years, can grow up to 10cm and become sexually mature between 5 and 7 years old. Whelks lay their eggs between November and January and these hatch in the spring. Each capsule contains hundreds of eggs, but only a few of these are fertilised and it's normal for the first lavae to hatch and to eat the other ones.

Whelks are very unpopular with fishermen because they eat oysters and scallops, drilling through the shells until they can scrape out the juicy flesh. Whelks have traditionally been fished for food in several countries around the North Sea, either by baited pots or by special trawl nets. Compared to other options, the whelk fishery is considered to be a relatively cheap fishery to get involved in. Whelks are often fished for with homemade pots that are constructed using plastic five-gallon containers, which cost about a sixth of the price of a crab pot. The whelk fishery in Northern Ireland has been going for many years and whelk stocks are considered to be in good shape, based on the consistent landings made by the vessels participating in this fishery.

In Europe, the French consume the most whelks, but the main markets for whelks are the Far East, mainly South Korea where they are considered a delicacy. Products on the market include packets of dried and spiced whelks and whole whelks marinated and preserved. Koreans love their whelks steamed, boiled, cooked with vegetables or sliced and washed down with beer. The influence of the Far East market has a significant effect on the fishery in the UK. After a boom, in the 1990s Britain's whelk industry faced a crisis because of the collapse of the South Korean economy. Northeast

Glossary

fishermen, hurt by European restrictions on white fish catches, had been making a profitable living selling the whelk, but the inability of Korean importers to pay their bills really damaged the industry. Whelk fishermen, who were once dropping 17–20,000 whelk pots a year did not even do half of that in the 90s and the price per tonne, which was about £300, then dropped by half compared to the boom times of the 80s.

There is no present assessment of stocks by ICES. The minimum landing size for whelks in EU waters is 45mm and they are rated a 3 by the MCS. Do not eat immature whelks and not during their breeding season between autumn and winter.

Cooking If you do fancy eating a whelk, then let's make an effort and make them taste a bit more special than just being served cold with pepper and malt vinegar. Wash them really well and then place into a pan of cold water, bring to a slow simmer and cook for approximately 10 minutes. Add to this a little wine, bay leaf, thyme, garlic, parsley, fennel and dill seeds, black peppercorns and, of course, a little white wine vinegar. If they are larger than normal, then cook for a few more minutes. Once they are cooked, you can eat them straight out of the shell or pick them all out, not forgetting to remove the little black foot or trap door. Alternatively, keep them in the chilled liquid to take on more flavour, then just make a nice simple parsley and white wine sauce and slowly reheat these and eat instantly. Keep them away from any passing Koreans!

WHITEBAIT

Uncooked whitebait can resemble slimy little translucent worms, but these small fish, which used to appear in large shoals in the estuary of the Thames during the summer months, have been held in great esteem as a delicacy for the table for hundreds of years. In Britain, they are a tradition dating back to medieval times, when they became a central feature of City of London banquets. Even today, you see them in pubs in London, deep-fried in flour and eaten whole, head, bones, tails and all, and served with a garlic mayonnaise or tartare sauce.

Fishing Whitebait are young baby fish. In Europe, the term applies to the young fry of herrings and sprats in varying proportions, though undoubtedly these mixed with probably quite a few other species, such as sardines, plaice and mackerel, as well. Whitebait are very tender and the entire fish is eaten, including the head, fins and gut. Typically, each whitebait is only 2.5–5cm in length and about 3mm across.

By the 1890s, the whitebait that had been so popular in London and was being caught all the way up to Greenwich had almost disappeared, while the shoals of whitebait that swam through Tower Bridge to the docks of Greenwich had vanished for good. It was not just over-fishing that led to their demise, but the pollution of the river: the industrial scene in London eventually led to all the waste from the factories and tanneries going into the Thames. Today, whitebait is still caught in reasonable quantities at the mouth of the Thames Estuary at Southend and it commands high prices, to the extent that it is the most costly fish on the market if available. It can normally only be purchased fresh, in small quantities, although some is frozen to extend the sale period. Thse are most likely from another country, trying to identify the fish is impossible and I would imagine there would be a few endangered species in there. There is no MCS rating for whitebait as it's not a particular species and if you think about it, it's

a ludicrous idea to consider eating the baby fry of so many fish before they have a chance to breed.

WHITING (*Merlanguis merlangus*)

In the past whiting has been loved by cats more than it has by us as it's thought to have quite a bland flavour, but you can easily make a delicious meal from whiting, you just need a little creativity. Whether you put it in a crispy beer batter, spice it up with some paprika or bake it in whole with spices and ginger you can pack flavour into its soft white flesh. Buy whiting filleted and pinboned by your fishmonger; the rest is down to you and me.

Fishing Whiting are widely distributed around the Scottish coasts and throughout the North Sea. They are also found in the English Channel but as they seem not to like warm water, they tend to be found in deeper, cooler water in the south. They are also found inshore and are a very common shore catch by rod and line in many parts of the British Isles during the Winter months.

Whiting grow very quickly in the first year, after which the growth rate becomes much slower. There are very large differences between the growth rates of individual fish and a 30cm fish can be as young as 1 or as old as 6, however at 2–3 years old, most whiting are mature enough to spawn. By the time they reach 4 years old, a single female fish can produce more than 400,000 eggs. The recommended size for them to be eaten are no smaller than 30cm and do not have them in the spawning season, which is between March and April. Whiting are a relatively slow-growing species because of a mainly crustacean diet, which is not as rich as that of other members of the cod family.

The majority of whiting landings are from the mixed demersal fishery in the northern North Sea. They are landed by Scottish trawlers and seiners targeting langoustine and by beam trawlers targeting flatfish. The total catch of whiting in the North Sea in 2007 was 23,800 tonnes, with discards from the bycatch estimated at 12,300 tonnes.

The whiting has been given a rating of 4 by the MCS, which means you need to be careful about where you are sourcing it. There are areas that are being fished sustainably and where the stocks are healthy, like the Southwest and the Channel, but up North there is too much that is hauled up as bycatch and for this reason, we should try to avoid sourcing it from here.

Cooking The whiting has a sharp and savoury taste, but is also quite creamy and the texture is soft, flaky and slightly crumbly. This is a great fish for putting in a fish pie, breaded or in a batter and deep-fried or simply pan-fried with brown butter and lemon segments. In a stew with tomatoes, garlic and a little thyme would also be fantastic. I would always serve with the skin on because it has a delicate flesh and it will stay together better.

BLUE WHITING (*Micromesistius poutassou*)

Very few people have heard of the blue whiting and it's normally its cousin, the common whiting, that we see in fish and chip shops and at the fishmongers. But this member of the cod family is approximately 50 times more numerous than the common North Sea cod and is the largest remaining source of edible white fish in the world. However, who knows whether we will ever see this fish on the slab of your fishmonger or sold at your local supermarket.

Fishing Blue whiting is widespread in the northeast Atlantic and off the continental shelf and is most often caught at 200–600m. It is a rather small fish and its flesh is intrinsically not as white as that of cod or haddock. Spawning occurs between February and May and the fish becomes sexually mature between 2 and 4 years of age and at a length of 20cm or more.

Once mature, blue whiting migrate annually to their spawning areas. The most important fishing areas are the spawning grounds west of the British Isles, where the fishery takes place before, during and after the spawning.

Blue whiting is a fish that fishermen will turn to when they are not catching something where the stock has run low or the quota has been met. The price for whiting is not that high and it's mostly used for biofuel, fish fertiliser and for feeding farmed fish.

The blue whiting has not been graded by the MCS.

WINKLES (Littorina littorea)

Winkles are still very much a favourite today, though not as much as they were in the Victorian times when thousands of tonnes of them were eaten. In those days, they were deemed food for the poor and not the well-to-do, but in reality it was not like that at all and gentlemen would very sheepishly consume just as much as their poorer conterparts.

The winkle man would arrive in the morning with his handcart and, in a matter of no time and after a couple of shouts, he would soon have a long queue. He was a noisy man, pushing his fishy smelling barrow along the road shouting 'shrimps and wink-er-alls' and bringing housewives out with their bowls or basins to buy the fishy delicacies to eat with crusty bread for tea. Even in the 1950s, Sunday tea was always seafood with bread and butter or margarine. Winkles were also sold outside London pubs by vendors who, in the absence of scales, used a pint glass as a measure.

Fishing Periwinkles eaten in Britain and Ireland are commonly referred to as winkles. In the north east of England they are known as 'willicks' and the most widespread species is the Grey or Silver Top. With a conical-shaped shell, a pointed top and spiral ridges, they crawl using a muscular, fleshy foot, which is lubricated by a film of mucus. Winkles are found on rocky coasts, but in sheltered conditions they can be on sandy or muddy places such as estuaries and mud flats.

Winkles are expected to live from 5–10 years of age and they reproduce annually. A female may have between 10,000 and 100,000 eggs and matures between 2–3 years of age.

Winkles are Scotland's sixth-largest shellfish business after scallops, crabs and lobsters, with 90 tonnes a week being picked. Most of the winkles go for export to the continent, but they are also consumed locally. Winkles are never farmed; generally they are collected or gathered by hand, which is a selective method of harvesting that causes less habitat disturbance.

Winkles are now being heavily overexploited because travellers and holidaymakers routinely pick winkles during the summer. This interferes with the winkle breeding patterns because they are harvesting them when they are too small. However, since winkles are so plentiful nationwide, they will probably re-establish themselves after a few years and they do not have legal protection. They are given a 3 rating by the MCS. The minimum landing sizes for winkles vary among regions, but selecting larger, mature winkles over 2cm allows for

them to have spawned. Choose winkles harvested by hand-gathering methods in areas that are well managed.

Cooking Winkles are often found in huge *plats de fruits de mer* in on the coastal regions of the French coast, particularly in the northern parts. The French treat them like the land snail, *escargot*. Winkles have a nutty flavour and a salty taste and they are very nice cooked with lots of parsley and garlic, a splash of wine and a few bay leaves. The way to pick them out is with a pin, minding the shell-like disc that is attached to the front of the winkle. I would recommend that you do not eat this scab as it's part of the winkle's foot and does taste like it as well – a fishy toenail. We use to cook with these snails a lot when I was at the *Tante Claire*, putting them into a *garbue de turbot*, which was essentially a fish stew with a very light saffron stock flavoured with a little orange, lemon, duck fat, duck confit, the winkles and the roast turbot on top. It was a great classic dish that was very popular, but on the downside, picking the snails took rather a long time.

WRASSE (Family Labridae)

The two wrasse species that I have included in this book are the two most commonly found in the UK. The cuckoo wrasse (*labrus mixtus*) and ballan wrasse (*labrus bergylta*) are some of the most colourful fish that occur in the seas around Britain and Ireland and would seem better suited to the warmer climates of the Caribbean or the Great Barrier Reef. With a slender body and head, they reach a maximum length of 35cm and are hermaphrodite, with the female able to change into a male. The true males are quite rare.

Fishing Generally not a large fish, the cuckoo won't get bigger than 500g, while the ballan is between 2–3kg. Females mature at around 2 years and 16cm in length and males at around 6–9 years and 24cm in length.

The males work very hard to please the females. Breeding during May and into July, the males build the perfect nest for the female to lay her eggs. If it's not spot on or just as she wishes, she won't lay her eggs and will instead give him the big heave ho and find some other male, or should I say female. Poor, confused fish, the male creates the nest by cleaning rocks or pebbles into a little shallow. Gathering up seaweed, he will then use his mucus a bit like super glue to bind it together, making almost a bird's nest underwater. At spawning time, the females lay about 1,000 eggs in the nest and then it is the male that looks after them, and what a lot he has to do. He uses his tail to fan the eggs, which keeps them clean and increases the oxygen around them, and he will also stay with the eggs until they hatch and go off into the big wide world of the ocean.

I would not try and eat them because, although they are not rated by the MCS, they are slow growing, which makes them vulnerable. Stock levels are unclear.

Glossary

BIBLIOGRAPHY

Clover, Charles, *The End of the Line* (Ebury Press, 2004)

Davidson, Alan, *Mediterranean Seafood* (Penguin, 1972)

Davidson, Alan, *North Atlantic Seafood* (Prospect Books, 2003)

Dipper, Frances, *British Sea Fishes* (Underwater World Publications, 1987)

Foote Arnold, Augusta, *The Sea-beach at Ebb Tide: A Guide to the Study of the Seaweeds, and the Lower Animal Life Found Between Tide Marks* (Dover Publications, 1901)

Gibson, Robin N., *Flatfishes: Biology and Exploitation* (Blackwell Science, 2005)

Kurlansky, Mark, *Cod: A Biography of the Fish That Changed the World* (Jonathan Cape, 1997)

Marine Conservation Society, *Good Fish Guide* (Marine Conservation Society, 2002)

National Geographic, 'Saving the Sea's Bounty' (April 2007)

Naylor, Paul, *Great British Marine Animals* (Sound Diving Publications, 2nd edn., 2005)

Piscator (William Hughes), *Fish: How to choose and How to dress* (Longman, Brown, Green and Longmans, 1843)

Roberts, Callum, *The Unnatural History of the Sea* (Gaia Books Ltd, 2007)

Starkey, David J., *England's Sea Fisheries: The Commercial Sea Fisheries of England and Wales Since 1300* (Chatham Publishing, 2003)

Warner, William W., *Distant Water: The Fate of the North Atlantic Fisherman* (Penguin, 1977)

Watts, Elizabeth, *Fish: and How to cook it* (Frederick Warne & Co., 1866)

Wood, Chris, *Seasearch Observer's Guide to Marine Life of Britain and Ireland* (Marine Conservation Society, 2007)

WEBSITES

Atlantic Herrings
www.gma.org/herring/biology/what/default.asp
Provides detailed information on the Atlantic herring.

British Marine Life Study Society
www.glaucus.org.uk
Provides information on the marine life of Britain's seas.

Captain Dave's Fishing and Boating Pages
www.cptdave.com/species.html
Provides a variety of marine, saltwater fishing and boating information.

First Nature
www.first-nature.com
Provides articles and pictures of a range of wildlife.

Fishbase
www.fishbase.org
Provides information on different species of fish and their environments.

Fisheries.co.uk
www.fisheries.co.uk
Provides information on angling throughout Britain.

Fisheries Research Services (FRS)
www.marlab.ac.uk
Provides expert scientific and technical advice to the Government on marine and freshwater fisheries, aquaculture and the protection of the aquatic environment.

Fishing in Norway
www.fiskeri.no/english/Haddock.htm
Provides details of haddock fishing in Norway.

Fishlink
www.fishlink.info/fishlink/
Provides information on aquaculture and fisheries.

Fishonline
www.fishonline.org
Provides information to help you identify fish from well managed sources and/or caught using methods that minimise damage to marine wildlife and habitats.

Food and Agriculture Organisation of the United Nations
www.fao.org/fishery
Fisheries and aquaculture department of the Food and Agriculture Organisation of the UN.

Illegal Fishing.info
www.illegal-fishing.info
Provides background information on the key issues in the debate around illegal, unreported and unregulated fishing.

Information Centre of the Icelandic Ministry of Fisheries
www.fisheries/is/stocks/haddock.htm
Information on haddock, plus other species of fish.

The Living World of Molluscs
www.weichtiere.at/english/cephalopoda/index.html
Provides information on different species of molluscs.

The Marine Fauna Gallery of Norway
www.seawater.no/fauna/
Provides information on and images of a range of marine life.

The Marine Life Information Network for Britain and Ireland (MarLIN)
www.marlin.ac.uk/species/Lophiuspiscatorius.htm
Provides information on marine environmental management, protection and education.

Marine Lobsters of the World
http://ip30.eti.uva.nl/bis/lobsters.php?selected=beschrijving&menuentry=sorten&id=89
Provides information of different species of lobsters.

Marinet
www.marinet.org.uk
A voluntary network which campaigns to protect the marine environment of the UK's coastline.

Northwest Atlantic Fisheries Organisation
www.nafo.int/about/frames/history.html
An inter-governmental fisheries science and management body.

PZNOW
www.pznow.co.uk
Guide on Penzance and its wildlife.

Sea-Ex
www.sea-ex.com/fishphotos
Provides images and information on Australian fish and seafood.

Seaweb
www.seaweb.org/resources/writings/writings/diversity.php
A communications based non-profit organisation that aims to advance ocean conservation.

UK Marine SACs Project
www.ukmarinesac.org.uk
Information from the UK Marine SACs project completed in 2001.

Victorian London
www.victorianlondon.org/markets/billingsgate.htm
Provides information about Billingsgate fish market.

www.fishing.co.uk
www.fishing.co.uk
Source of numerous angling articles.

Young's
www.youngsseafood.co.uk/web/fish_species_info.asp
Comprehensive guide to different species of fish.

Aberdeen Sea Products Ltd

Unit 2, Toulmin Street, London, SE1 1PP
020 7407 0247 www.aberdeenseaproducts.co.uk
Wholesale fishmongers specialising in raw fish for sushi restaurants and very good-quality fresh, smoked and frozen fish and shellfish at a reasonable price. They have daily supplies of the freshest fish from fish markets around the country and abroad, which can be filleted and prepared to an exact size and specification.

Atari-ya Fish

595 High Road, North Finchley, London, N12 0DY
020 8446 6669 www.atariya.co.uk/en/index.html
Staff will slice your purchases for sushi and sashimi on your request without extra charge.

Billingsgate Fish Market

Trafalgar Way, Poplar, London, E14 5ST
020 7987 1118 www.cityoflondon.gov.uk/billingsgate/
Billingsgate is served by almost every port in the United Kingdom, from Aberdeen to Penzance; the fish are transported by road directly from the coast and arrive at the market in the early hours of the morning.

British Cured Pilchards Ltd

Tolcarne, Newlyn, Cornwall, TR18 5QH 01736 332 112
www.pilchardworks.co.uk
Suppliers of a range of canned pilchards, including smoked Cornish sardine fillets in sunflower oil and sardine fillets.

Brown and Forest

Bowdens Farm, Hambridge, Somerset, TA10 0BP
01458 250 875 www.smokedeel.co.uk
A small family run smokery, started 22 years ago in Somerset, producing the finest smoked eel and salmon as well as a whole range of delicious smoked food that includes smoked chicken, duck, lamb and trout.

Channel Fisheries Ltd

13 Penpethy Road, Brixham, Devon, TQ5 8NN 01803 858 126
One of the UK's leading coastal suppliers of quality fresh fish and seafood. They source all the fish daily from day boat fleets at Brixham, Plymouth and Looe, with speciality products sourced from Scotland, Brittany and Rungis market in Paris.

The Chelsea Fishmonger

10 Cale Street, Chelsea, London, SW3 3QU
020 7589 9432 www.chelseafish.co.uk
Passionate fishmongers who stock a range of produce from Manx kippers to wild sea bass line-caught off the Sussex coast the night before.

Colchester Oyster Fisheries

Pyefleet Quay, Mersea Island, Colchester, Essex, CO5 8UN
01206 384 141 www.colchesteroysterfishery.com
One of the UK's leading suppliers of fresh shellfish, specialising in quality live shellfish.

Cove Shellfish Ltd

12 Didcot Road, Poole, Dorset, BH17 0GD 01202 660 667
Shellfish and wet fish wholesalers in Poole; a very good fish supplier, which I have used countless times and one of the first fishmongers I used when I came to London.

Cuan Oysters

Sketrick Island, Killinchy, Newtownards, Co. Down,
N. Ireland 028 9754 1461 www.cuanysters.com
Specialises in direct sales of high-quality oysters.

Direct Seafoods

Unit 4, 57 Sandgate Street, London, SE15 1LE
0844 884 1176 www.directseafoods.co.uk
Suppliers of fresh fish and seafood sourced locally and internationally with depots situated around the country. They work with accredited fish bodies like the MSC, The Sea Fish Industry Authority and Friends of the Sea.

Falmouth Bay Oysters Ltd

The Docks, Falmouth, Cornwall, TR11 4NR
01326 316 600 www.falmouthoysters.co.uk
Oysters are fished using traditional sailing boats unique to Falmouth, which create no pollution or impact on the environment.

The Fresh and Freeze Company Ltd

Unit 6a Guildford Road Industrial Estate, Hayle,
Cornwall, TR27 4QZ 01736 756 689
Supplier of Cornish sardines and pilchards dedicated to environmentally friendly fishing methods that do no damage to the seabed, or seals, birds or crustaceans. Any surplus catch not pre-ordered by customers for fresh same-day or frozen next-day sale is released unharmed.

H. Forman & Son

Stour Road, Fish Island, London, E3 2NT
020 8525 2399 www.formans.co.uk
Suppliers of smoked salmon, caviar and other smoked and fresh fish products.

Hastings Fisherman Enterprises Ltd

Office 5, Fishmarket, Rock-a-Nore Road, Hastings,
East Sussex, TN34 3DA 01424 717 869
All the fish caught are from ten-metre in-shore boats, so you can be guaranteed exactly where the fish was caught, from whom and when. Hastings also has MSC-accredited Dover soles.

Isle of Shuna

Walls, Shetland, ZE2 9PF
01595 809 348 www.isleofshuna.co.uk
One of the largest independent producers of rope-grown Scottish mussels. The mussels are cultivated in a sustainable manner in the waters surrounding the Scottish West Coast and the Shetland Isles.

J. H. Turner and Co

The Coombe, Newlyn, Penzance, Cornwall, TR18 5HS
01736 363 726 www.jhturner.co.uk
A small diverse company, which deals in all species of fresh fish landed in Newlyn. The species diversification in Newlyn is enormous with over 50 marketable species of fish available during the course of each year.

Jefferson's Seafoods

Unit 1, Buller Quay, East Looe, Cornwall, PL13 1DX
01503 263 808 www.jeffersons-seafoods.co.uk
Suppliers of a variety of fresh fish and hand-made products ready to cook. Fish is sourced from local 'dayboats' and the catch can be delivered to your door within 48 hours of being landed.

Keltic Seafare (Scotland) Ltd.

Unit 6, Strathpeffer Road Ind. Est., Dingwall, Rossshire,
IV15 9SP, Scotland 01349 864 087 www.kelticseafare.com
Specialists in the supply and delivery of live scallops, hand--dived off the West Coast of Scotland. They also supply creel caught langoustine and wild mushrooms, which can be delivered to all parts of the UK and abroad.

Loch Duart Ltd (Direct)

Badcall Salmon House, Scourie, Lairg, Sutherland,
IV27 4TH, Scotland 01674 660 161 www.lochduart.com
Suppliers of salmon who apply a sustainable and environmentally responsible approach that gives priority to the health and welfare of the fish and long-term protection of the environment.

M and J Seafood

Head Office, The Gate House, Gatehouse Way, Aylesbury,
Bucks, HP19 8DB 01296 333 800 www.mjseafoods.com
Suppliers with local branches and a range of fresh, frozen and chilled seafood products offering a local service to over 13,000 chefs around the UK. They are supplying increasing numbers of sustainably caught fish.

Marks & Spencer

www.marksandspencer.com
Marks & Spencer is doing more and more in the development

Suppliers

TOM AIKENS

of sustainable fish in the retail sector; they are becoming more committed to sustainable fish sourcing with all the fish they use in fresh and processed food and they are the only retailer to employ a marine scientist. Marks & Spencer also maintains a 'Banned Species List' of seafood species it considers unsustainable, as well as extending its range to relieve pressure on more traditional species. Witch and dab were introduced in 2005 as an alternative to flatfish such as plaice, and Cornish pollack and farmed tilapia were launched in summer 2006 as an alternative to traditional species such as cod and haddock. Marks & Spencer only sources wild species once they have reached maturity and spawning.

Matthew Stevens & Sons
Back Road East, St Ives, Cornwall, TR26 3AR
01736 799 392 www.mstevensandson.co.uk
Traditional fishmongers supplying quality fresh fish and shellfish which are delivered direct to customers throughout the UK.

Red Snapper Seafoods
Gladden Place, Skelmersdale, Lancashire, WN8 9SX
01695 550 934 www.redsnapperseafoods.co.uk
Suppliers of fresh or frozen fish and seafood delivered the next working day.

Seafayre Cuisine
Unit E, St Erth Industrial Estate, Hayle, Cornwall, TR27 6LP
01736 755 961 www.seafayrecuisine.co.uk
Wholesale fish merchants with a reputation as one of the leading suppliers of freshly prepared and portioned seafood in Cornwall.

Southbank Fresh Fish & Frozen Foods
Unit 26, Kent Park Industrial Estate, London, SE15 1LR
020 7639 6000
One of the more well known fish suppliers in London, used by a whole host of busy restaurants and hotels, they are always delivering the best that you could ask for or need.

Waitrose
www.waitrose.com
For a fish to be termed 'sustainable' in Waitrose, it must meet the following criteria:
1. Be a species that is not regarded as threatened or endangered.
2. Be caught from a well managed fishery with scientifically based quotas.
3. Be caught using the most responsible fishing methods.
4. Be fully traceable from catch to consumer.
Suppliers of Waitrose fish must demonstrate a high level of traceability that eliminates the risk of illegally caught fishing entering the supply chain. Waitrose regards this as an essential step in preventing what is a very damaging criminal activity that undermines conservation and causes serious economic issues. Fisheries used in Waitrose must be able to demonstrate sustainable management of the stock through effective quotas based on scientific advice and stock assessments.

OTHER USEFUL CONTACTS

Bahamas Reef Environment Educational Foundation (BREEF)
Caves Village, West Bay St., P.O. Box N 7776, Nassau, Bahamas +242 327 9000 www.breef.org
BREEF was founded in 1993 by Sir Nicholas Nuttall, an amazing man who had a huge concern for the state of The Bahamas' marine environment. Almost single handedly, Sir Nicholas turned the organisation into a leader in educating Bahamian's about the marine resources. BREEF's aim is to support the implementation of a network of marine reserves, to protect fish spawning aggregations and to ensure a continued supply of fish and conch for the Bahamians. They organise marine conservation teacher training workshops, fisheries workshops, working with teachers and local schools to increase public education and awareness of what really goes on in the sea and fisheries for sustainable management. They also work with other Bahamain conservation organisations to further increase the great work that is being done. Sir Nicholas had learnt three classic lessons. First, that our interest in conservation stems from the wish to conserve our life support system, particularly our food supply. Second, that by studying our fellow creatures who have also survived three billion years of evolution we can find all the answers we need to keep *homo sapiens* going for its natural span as a species. Lastly the best thing we can each do for conservation is to obey the spirit of our laws. BREEF is funded entirely by donations and foundation grants, it's an amazing conservation group that is doing an incredible amount for the preservation of marine life.

Billingsgate Seafood Training School
Office: 30 Billingsgate Market, Trafalgar Way, London, E14 5ST
020 7517 3548 www.seafoodtraining.org
A charitable company promoting the awareness of fish to young people and offering professional courses aimed at increasing the knowledge of those already working in the industry in areas such as fishmongering, supermarkets, restaurants and hotels. The school also offers the general public practical seafood preparation and cookery courses.

Environmental Justice Foundation (EJF)
5 St Peter's Street, London N1 8JD
0207 359 0440 www.ejfoundation.org
EJF is a charitable organisation that campaigns internationally on many issues including pirate fishing, shrimp farming, pesticides and wildlife.

Fisheries.co.uk
www.fisheries.co.uk
Provides information on angling throughout Britain.

Food and Agriculture Organisation of the United Nations
www.fao.org/fishery
Fisheries and aquaculture department of the Food and Agriculture Organisation of the UN.

International Council for the Exploration of the Sea
H. C. Andersens Boulevard 44-46, DK-1553, Copenhagen V, Denmark + 45 3338 6700 www.ices.dk
ICES is the organisation that coordinates and promotes marine research in the North Atlantic. (For more information, see page 14.)

The Marine Conservation Society
Unit 3, Wolf Business Park, Alton Road
Ross-on-Wye, Herefordshire HR9 5NB
01989 566 017 www.mcsuk.org; www.fishonline.org
A UK charity that campaigns for cleaner seas and beaches, sustainable fisheries and protection for all marine life. MCS has developed resources to help the public ascertain the sustainability of the fish they are buying, including the fishonline website. (For more information, see page 14.)

The Marine Stewardship Council
3rd floor, Mountbarrow House, 6–20 Elizabeth Street, London SW1W 9RB 020 7811 3300 www.msc.org
An independent organisation that promotes responsible fishing practices by finding a solution to the problem of overfishing and promote environmentally responsible stewardship. The MSC rewards environmentally responsible fisheries management and practices with a distinctive blue-tick label for fish.

WWF
Panda House, Weyside Park, Godalming, Surrey, GU7 1XR
01483 426 444 www.wwf.org.uk
A charitable conservation organisation which works to ensure a healthy future for our planet. They are very involved in campaigning for a large number of marine issues.

Index

TOM AIKENS

ACKNOWLEDGEMENTS

This book has taken me what has seemed forever to write; there have been endless nights and long weekends, with my face either stuck in a book or in front of the computer. My very patient wife Amber, who has had to endure many nights of me finishing at 2am, has been so supportive of me writing this book and it has taken her to her wits' end and back. I could not have done it without her and her huge support, patience and love.

The book you have read is a slimmed-down version of what I originally wrote as that was almost three books' worth: it may be something for another time.

I have been very lucky to have come into contact with so many people across the whole spectrum of the fishing industry, from fishermen and fisheries officers to wholesalers, conservationists and NGOs. All of them have been very helpful in giving me their knowledge as well as their passion.

My journey with fish and the book began a couple of years ago and it was largely due to my late father-in-law, Sir Nicholas Nuttall, who founded BREEF. His passion and knowledge about the preservation and conservation of fish was inspiring.

One of the first books that I read on the fishing industry was the Cornish Fishing and Seafood Book, which is a great read. It explains a lot about the fishing industry and the fishing port in Newlyn. The reason that I first went to Newlyn was that it is still very much a working fishing port, not one that has to rely on tourism. It is still integral to the fishing industry and brings in approximately £20 million a year which is a huge chunk of revenue for the British fishing industry. There are a few people in Newlyn that I would like to thank: my friend Spike Searle who is totally crazy about fishing and seems to have all the right answers to a lot of things – he has been so helpful and always willing to chat about anything fishy with amazing passion, knowledge and understanding; Nick Howell, who has been brilliant in all his introductions to various fishing folk; Laurence Hartwell, who is one of the best photographers in the south west; Nathan de Rozarieux, who is Project Director of Seafood Cornwall; Tom Hooper from Finding Sanctuary; Eddy Derriman who was the fisheries officer for the south west; Caroline Bennet whose real passions and understanding of the fishing industry have made some very positive changes; Peter Grosvenor from Jeffersons Seafood has a brilliant understanding of what chefs require in quality and provenance. I also would like to thank Nick Joy and Andy Bing from Loch Duart who were key to my understanding of farmed salmon, as I had serious doubts about any farming of fish, but these guys and their company are the most passionate people in their field and they changed my whole outlook on what farming fish can really be about if it's done with the right ethics.

Thanks to all the fishermen that I have been using for all the restaurants: Chris Bean, Quentin Knights, Dave Pascoe, Dave Stevens, Stefan Glinski, Richard Edgeley (Dick Ede), Drew Davies, Paul Joy, Frank Powle, Chris Wightman, Steven Wightman. I am indebted to them all for the great fish they provide me with and for the way that they fish.

Charles Clover, who is the environmental journalist for the Daily Telegraph and author of The End of The Line, has been immensely helpful, providing me with facts and figures on the fishing industry as well as unbridled passion and commitment as has Rose Prince with her fabulous introductions and guidance.

This has been a process of learning and fact-finding – it's not one that's always easy to understand as there are so many people involved and everyone has their own version of the wills and ways of the fishing industry and beliefs about how it should be run. Everyone is trying to make a difference, and although many of the fishermen may disagree with the NGOs on what they communicate, they do offer an important service to the industry with information and by championing the fishing communities that practice sustainable fishing. There are many individuals and NGOs that I have been involved with whom I would like to thank: Andrew Mallinson from M&S has an incredible knowledge of fisheries in the UK and worldwide – it's been a real eye opener to see how such a big brand like M&S are raising the game in sustainability; Stephen Potter from Hastings Fisheries Management; Mike Berthet from M&J Seafood, whose passion for sustainable fish sourcing is second to none; David Mcandless, a Chief Fisheries Officer in the northeastern sea fisheries; Dominic Boothroyd from the National Lobster Hatchery in Padstow, who is working very hard to protect and promote the humble lobster; Mick Bacon and Hazel Curtis from Seafish; Martin Glenn who is the CEO at Birdseye is really shaking things up there and has been instrumental in the company becoming more sustainable. Libby Woodhatch from Seafood Scotland is incredibly knowledgeable and works tirelessly in support of the Scottish fishing industry. Melanie Siggs, Emily Howgate and Julia Roberson from Seafood Choices have been very helpful in giving me information about their stand on the industry and sustainability. From the Marine Stewardship Council, I would like to thank the CEO Rupert Howes, who has made huge changes and steps in the organisation, and Laura Stewart who has given me a lot of her valuable time and information. Dawn Purchase, Caroline Roberts and Melissa Moore from the Marine Conservation Society have also given me so much information. WWF, EJF and DEFRA have been very supportive of what I have been working on. And finally, thanks go to Duncan Copeland, who has been tireless in his fight for the cause about IUU fishing in Western Africa, and I hope with more support that this whole illegal mess is taken seriously.

The Publishers would like to thank Alex and Emma at Smith & Gilmour for their fabulous design and for being such a joy to work with; John Lawrence-Jones and Cristian Barnett for their beautiful pictures; Bridget Fish for her expertise and patience; and Annie Lee, Kay Halsey and Gráinne Fox for their invaluable help.